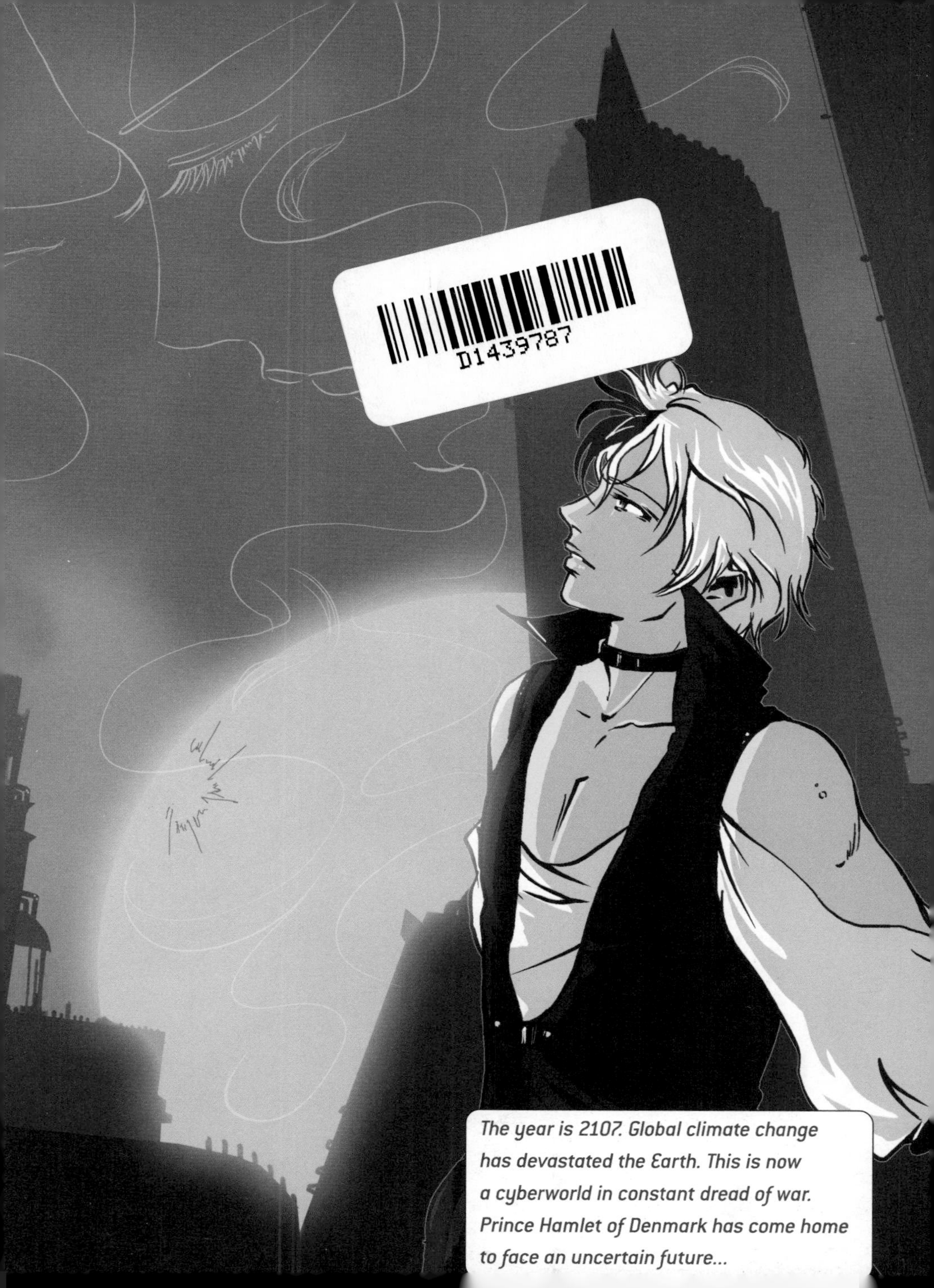
The year is 2107. Global climate change has devastated the Earth. This is now a cyberworld in constant dread of war. Prince Hamlet of Denmark has come home to face an uncertain future...

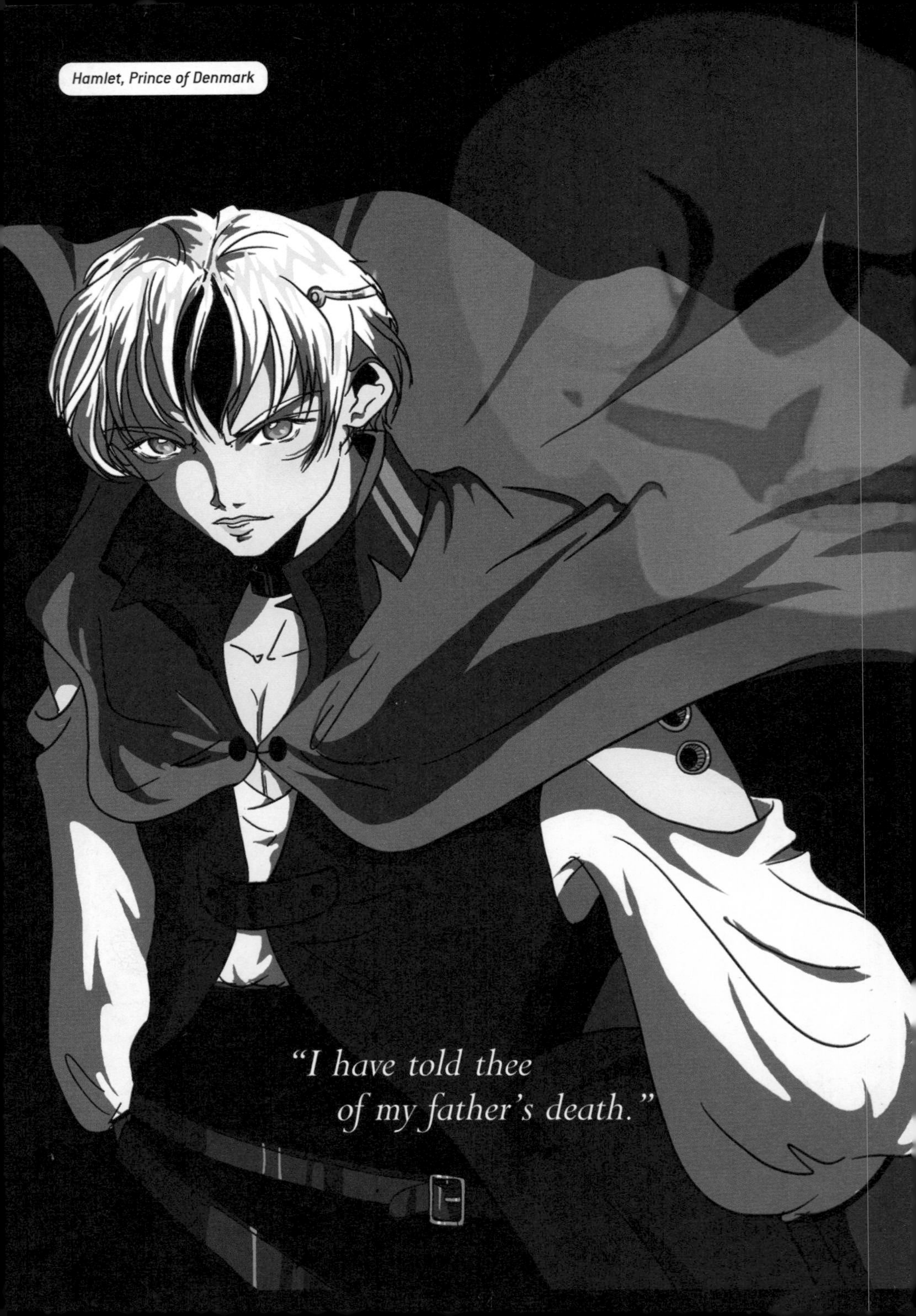
Hamlet, Prince of Denmark
"I have told thee of my father's death."

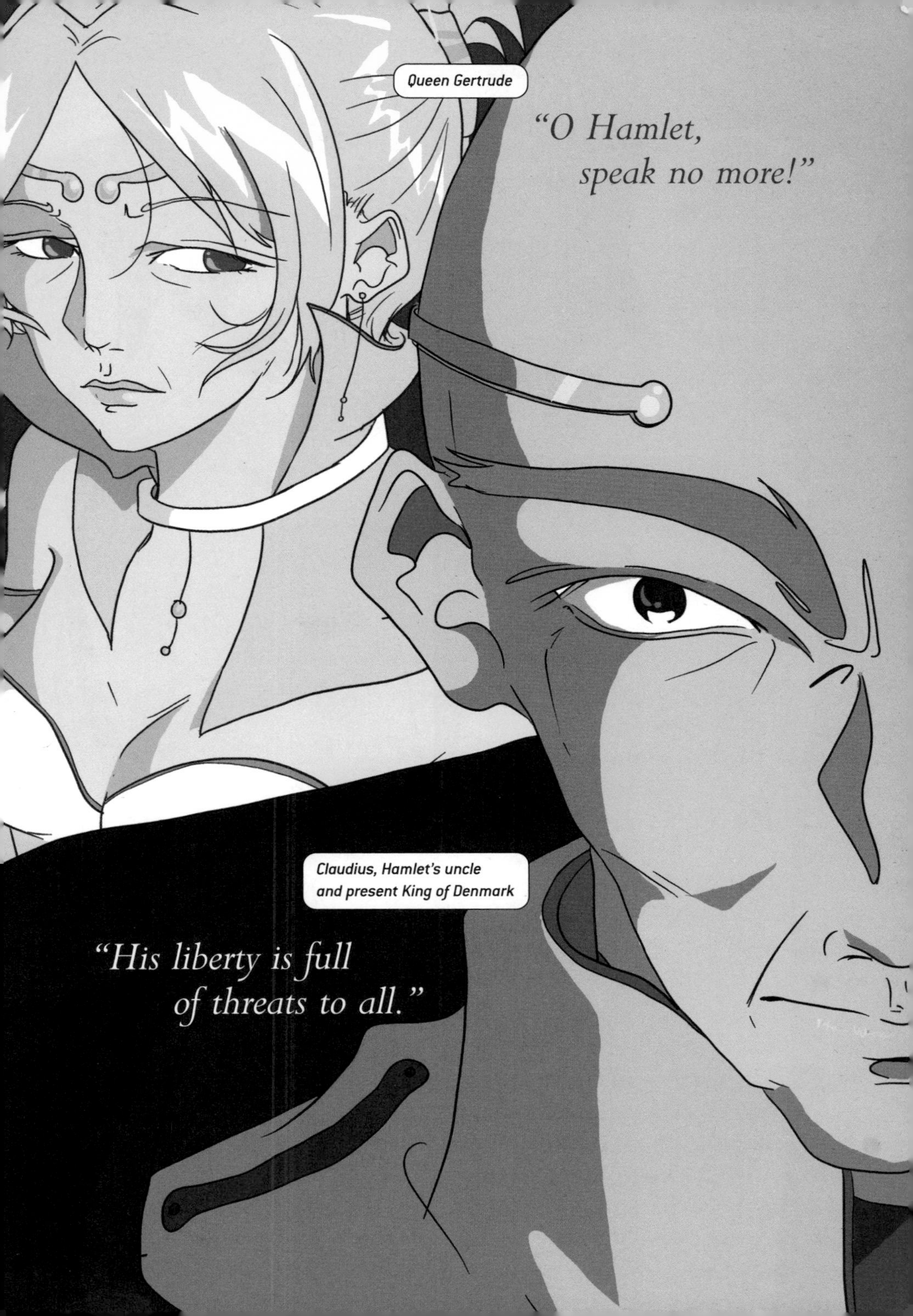
Queen Gertrude
"O Hamlet, speak no more!"
Claudius, Hamlet's uncle and present King of Denmark
"His liberty is full of threats to all."

loyalty betrayal

Rosencrantz *Guildenstern*

Hamlet's so-called friends

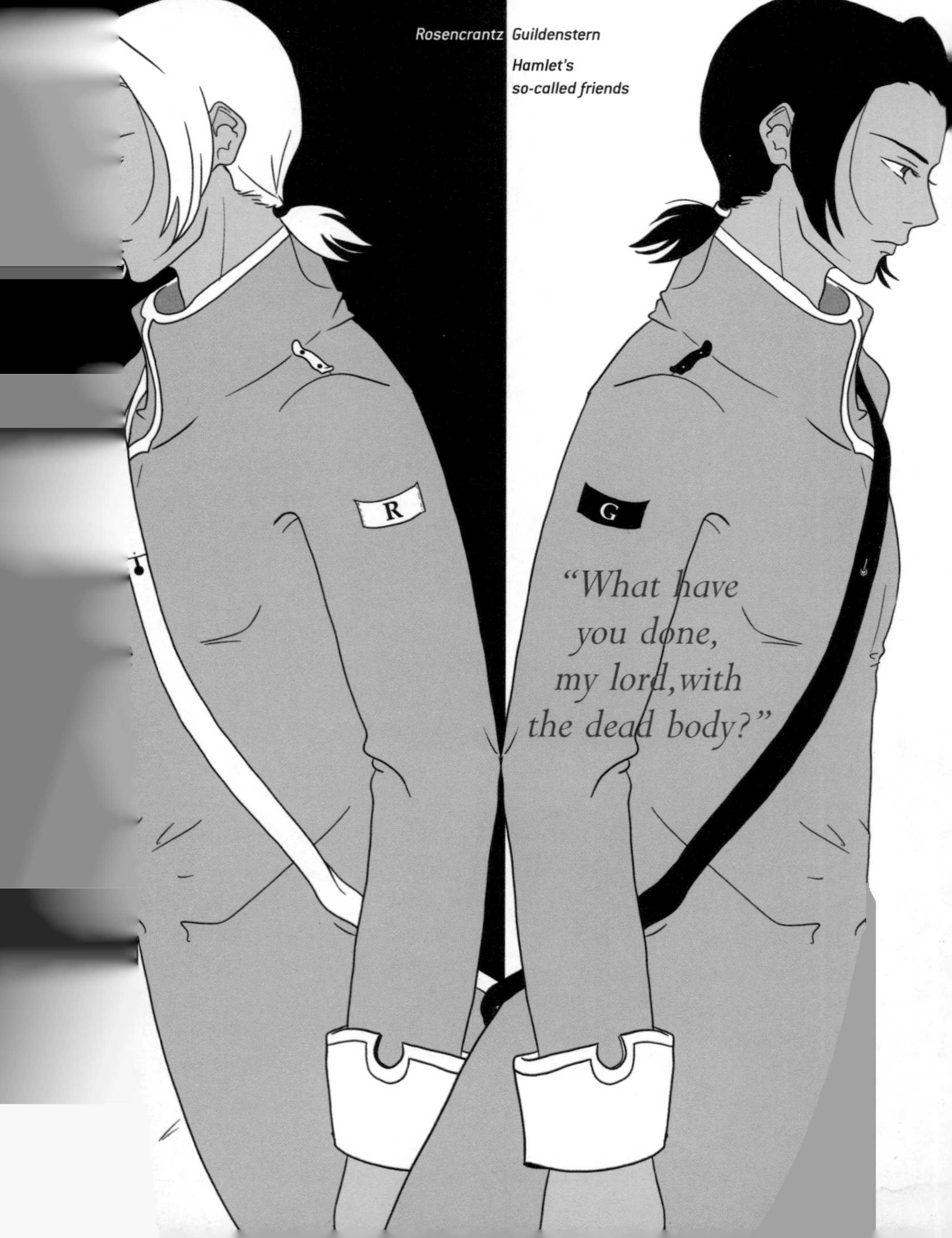
R
G
"What have you done, my lord, with the dead body?"

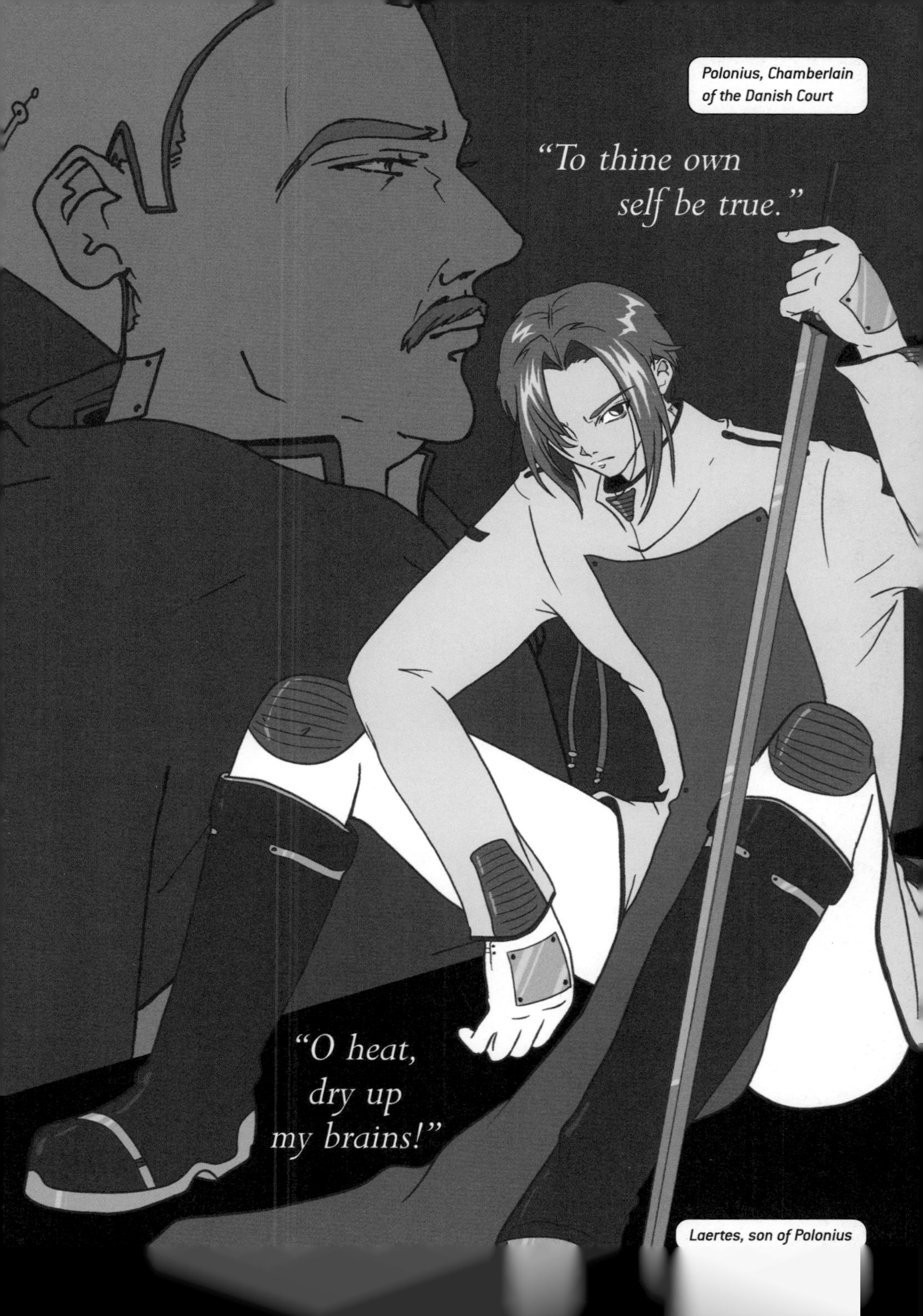
Polonius, Chamberlain of the Danish Court
"To thine own self be true."
"O heat, dry up my brains!"
Laertes, son of Polonius

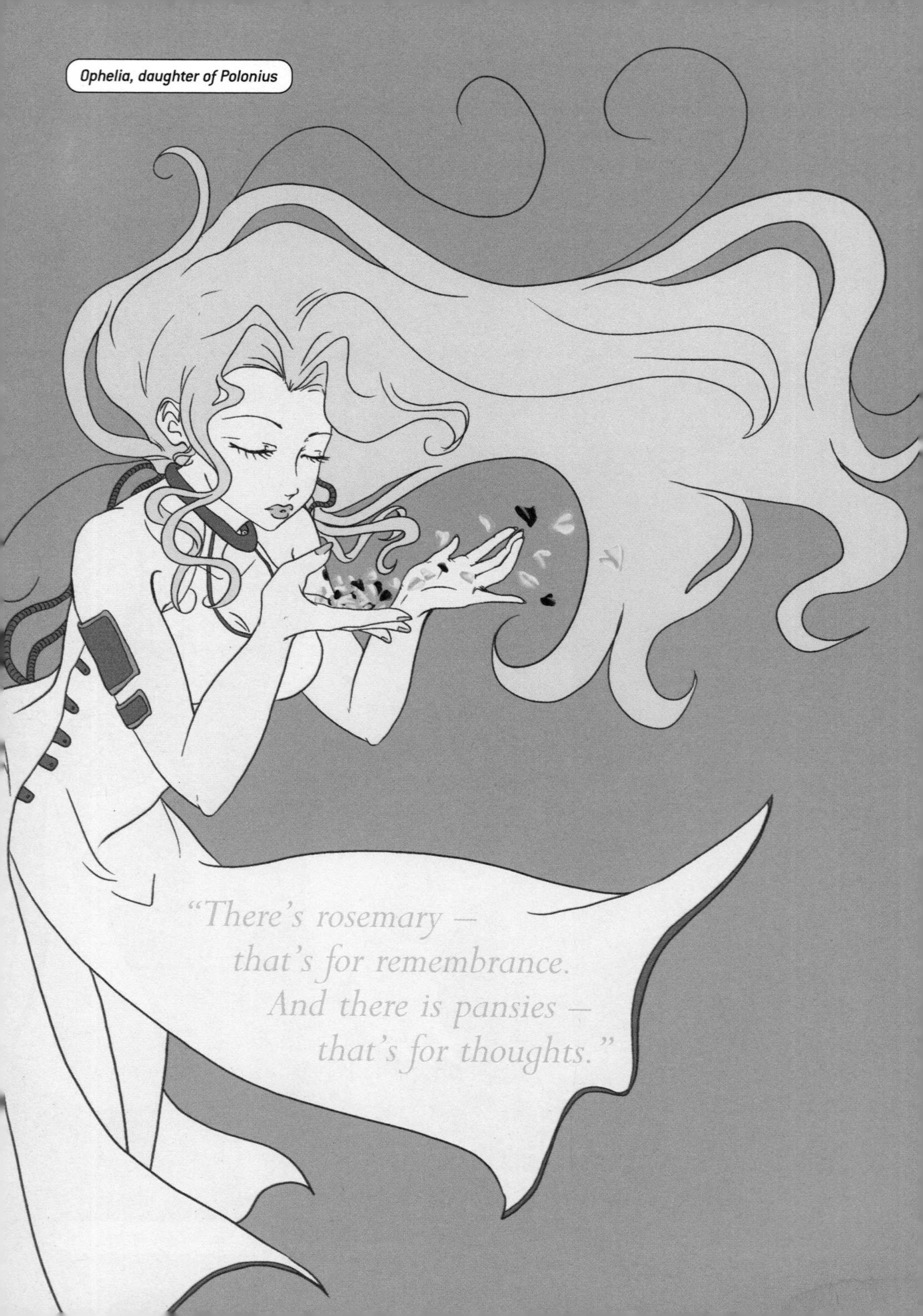
Ophelia, daughter of Polonius
"There's rosemary –
that's for remembrance.
And there is pansies –
that's for thoughts."

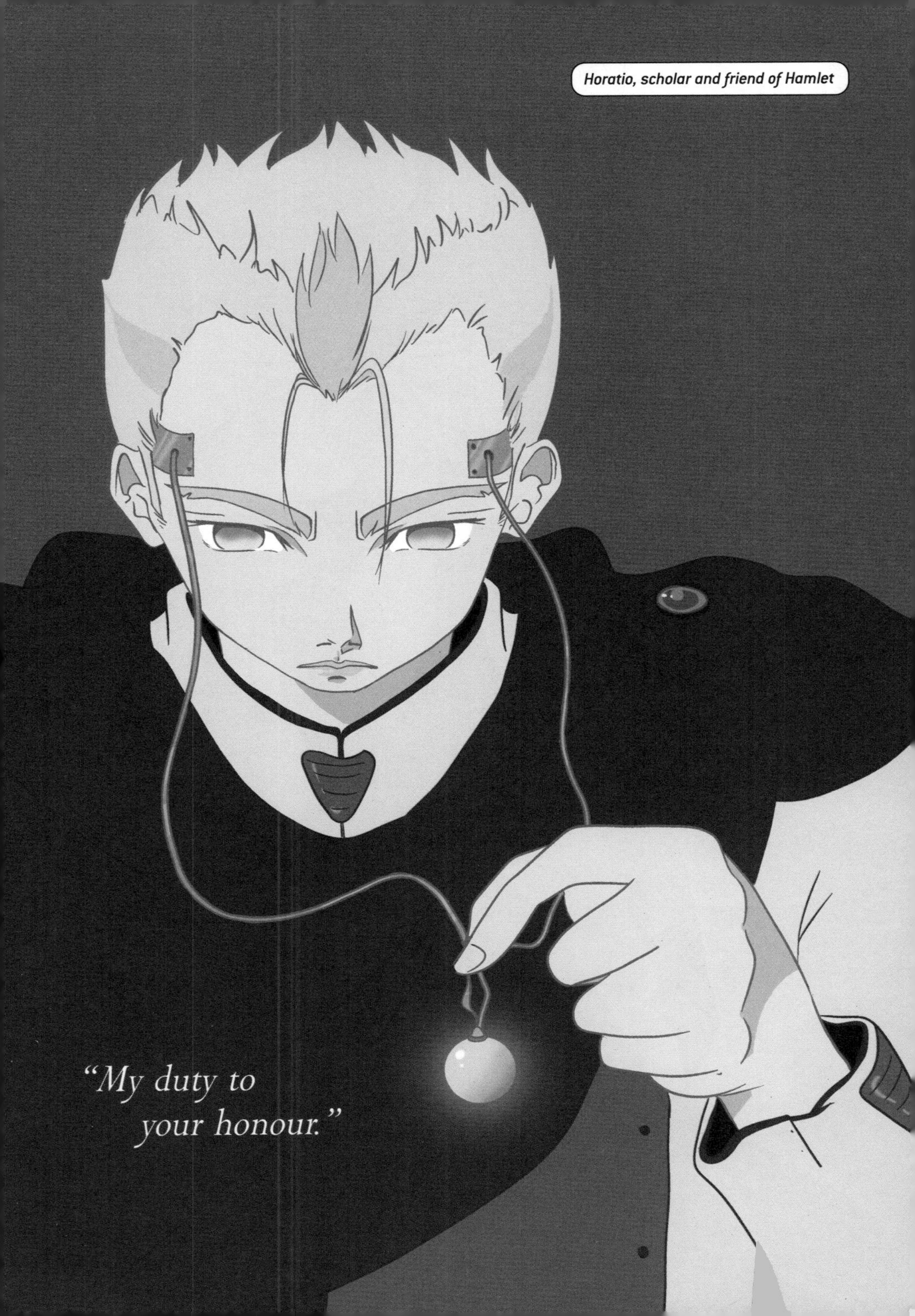
Horatio, scholar and friend of Hamlet
"My duty to your honour."

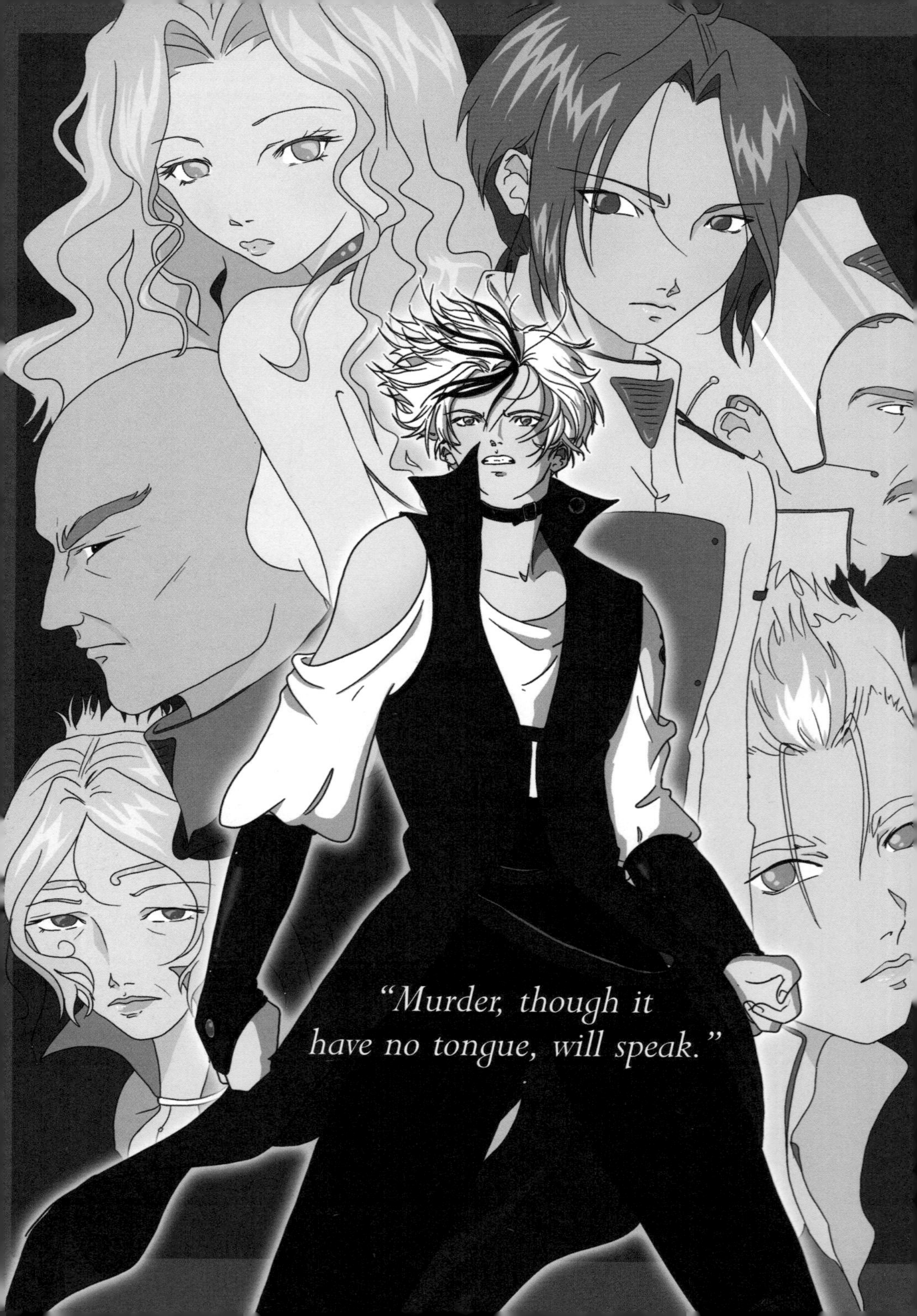
"Murder, though it have no tongue, will speak."

The Tragedy of

HAMLET
Prince of Denmark

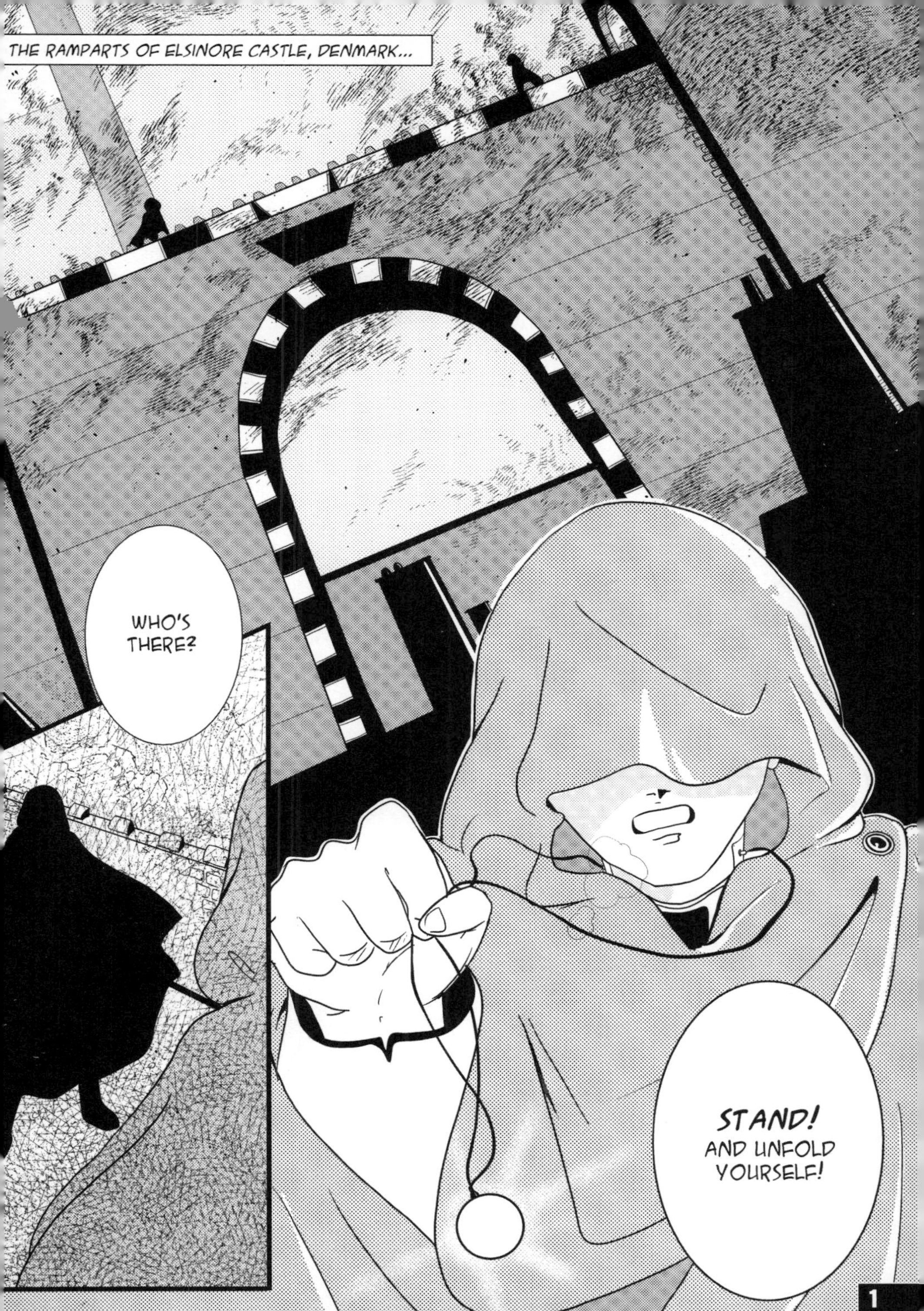
THE RAMPARTS OF ELSINORE CASTLE, DENMARK...
WHO'S THERE?
STAND! AND UNFOLD YOURSELF!

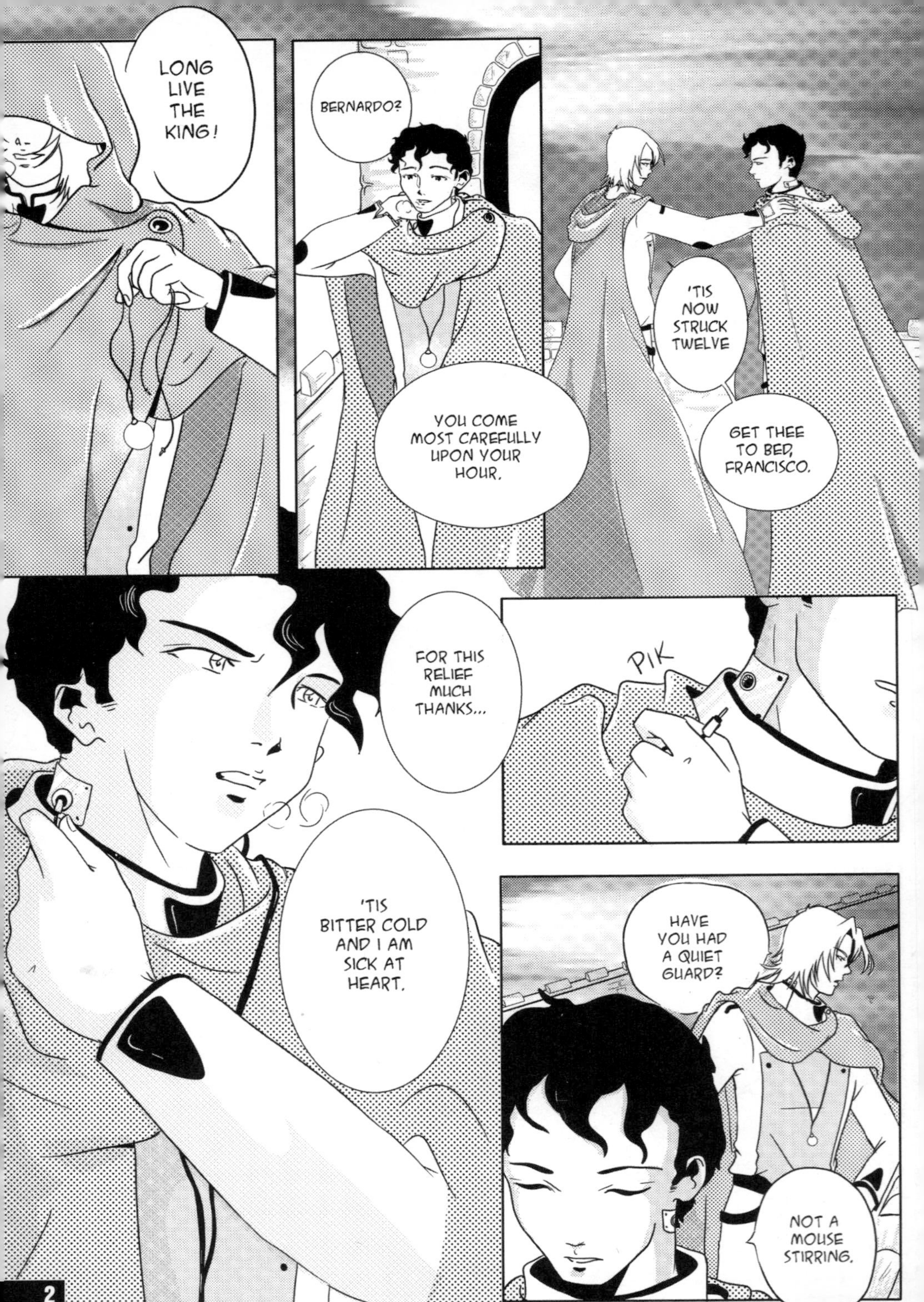
A–
LONG LIVE THE KING!
BERNARDO?
YOU COME MOST CAREFULLY UPON YOUR HOUR.
'TIS NOW STRUCK TWELVE
GET THEE TO BED, FRANCISCO.
FOR THIS RELIEF MUCH THANKS...
'TIS BITTER COLD AND I AM SICK AT HEART.
PIK
HAVE YOU HAD A QUIET GUARD?
NOT A MOUSE STIRRING.

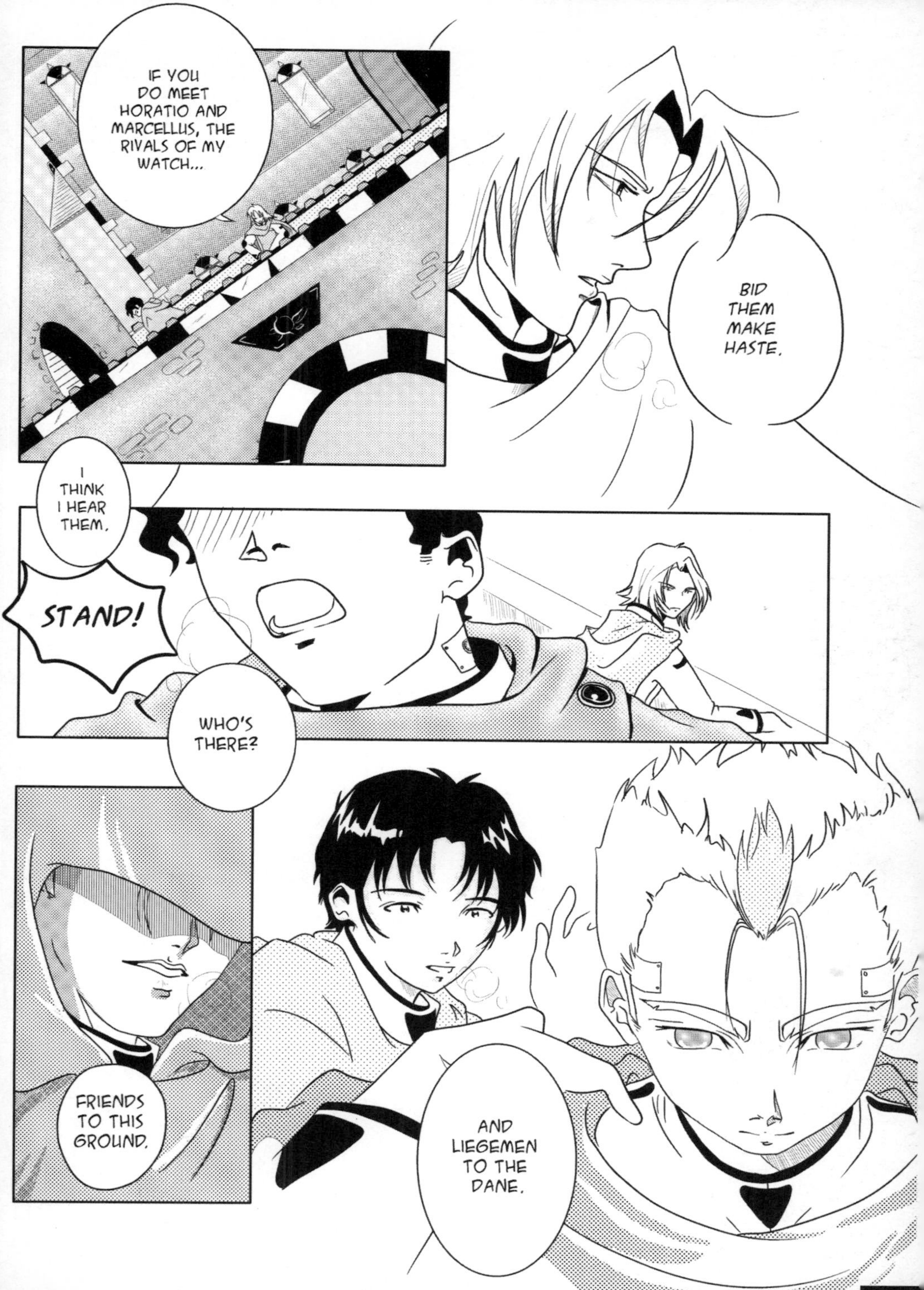
IF YOU DO MEET HORATIO AND MARCELLUS, THE RIVALS OF MY WATCH...
BID THEM MAKE HASTE.
I THINK I HEAR THEM.
STAND!
WHO'S THERE?
FRIENDS TO THIS GROUND.
AND LIEGEMEN TO THE DANE.

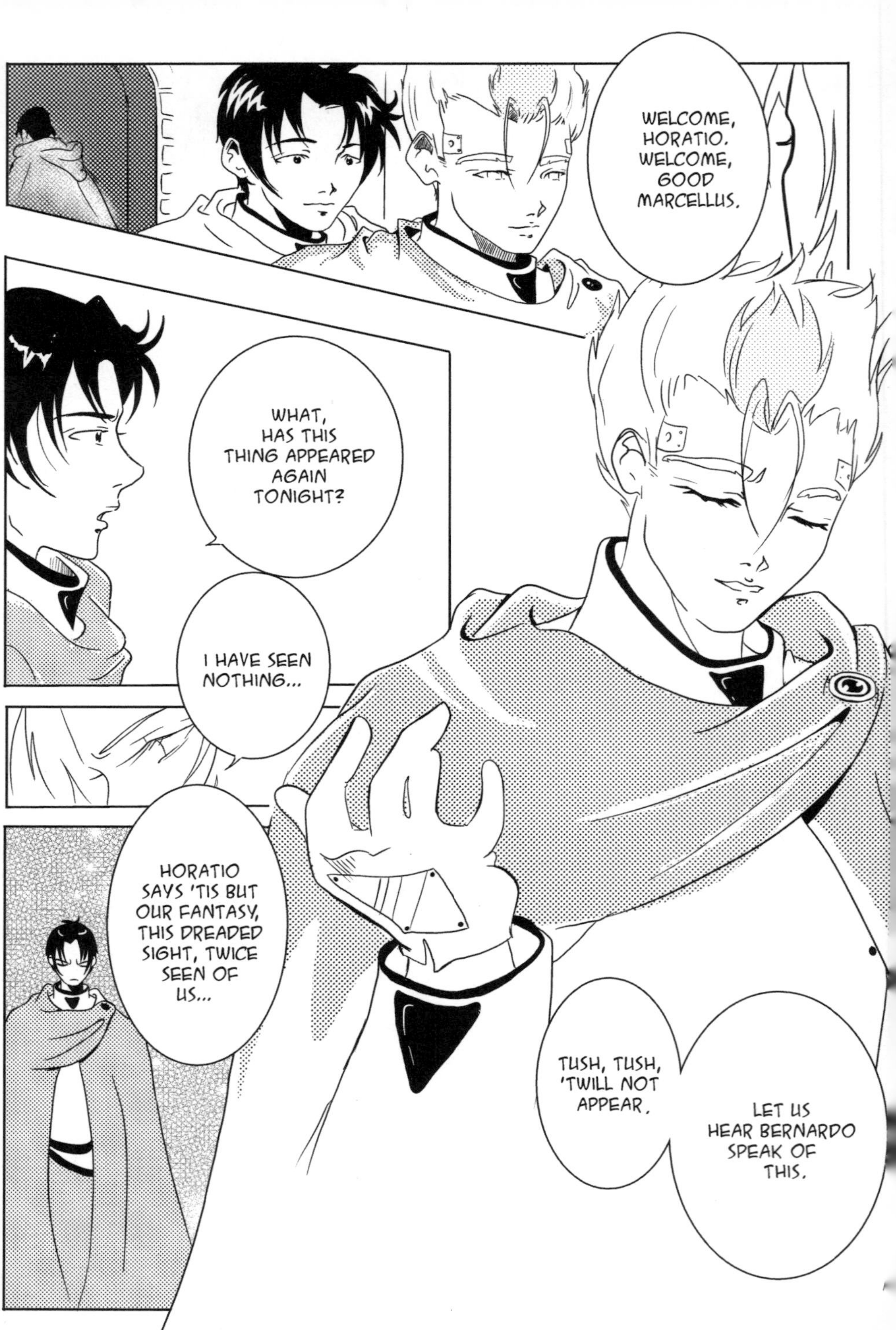
WELCOME, HORATIO. WELCOME, GOOD MARCELLUS.
WHAT, HAS THIS THING APPEARED AGAIN TONIGHT?
I HAVE SEEN NOTHING...
HORATIO SAYS 'TIS BUT OUR FANTASY, THIS DREADED SIGHT, TWICE SEEN OF US...
TUSH, TUSH, 'TWILL NOT APPEAR.
LET US HEAR BERNARDO SPEAK OF THIS.

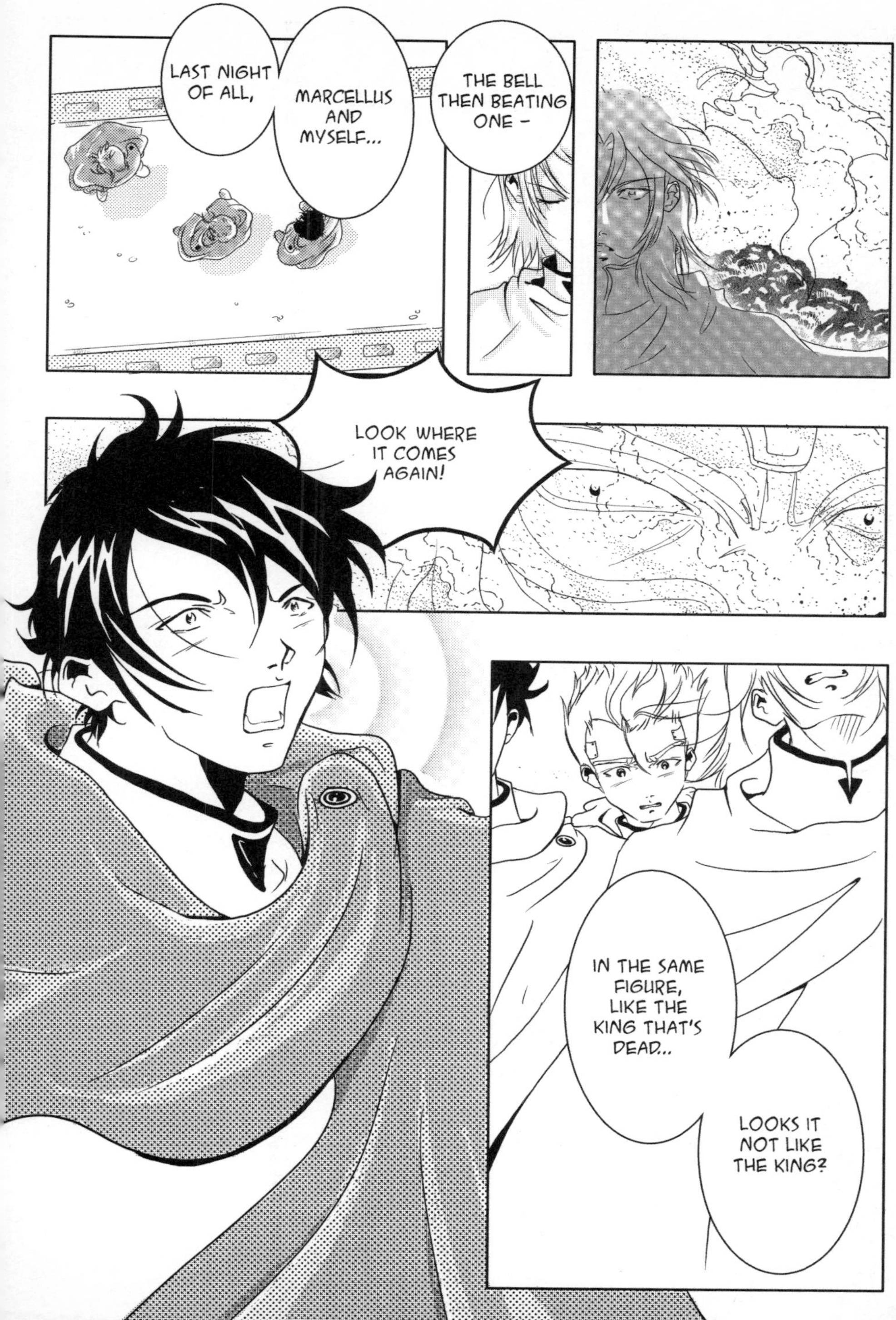
LAST NIGHT OF ALL,
MARCELLUS AND MYSELF...
THE BELL THEN BEATING ONE -
LOOK WHERE IT COMES AGAIN!
IN THE SAME FIGURE, LIKE THE KING THAT'S DEAD...
LOOKS IT NOT LIKE THE KING?

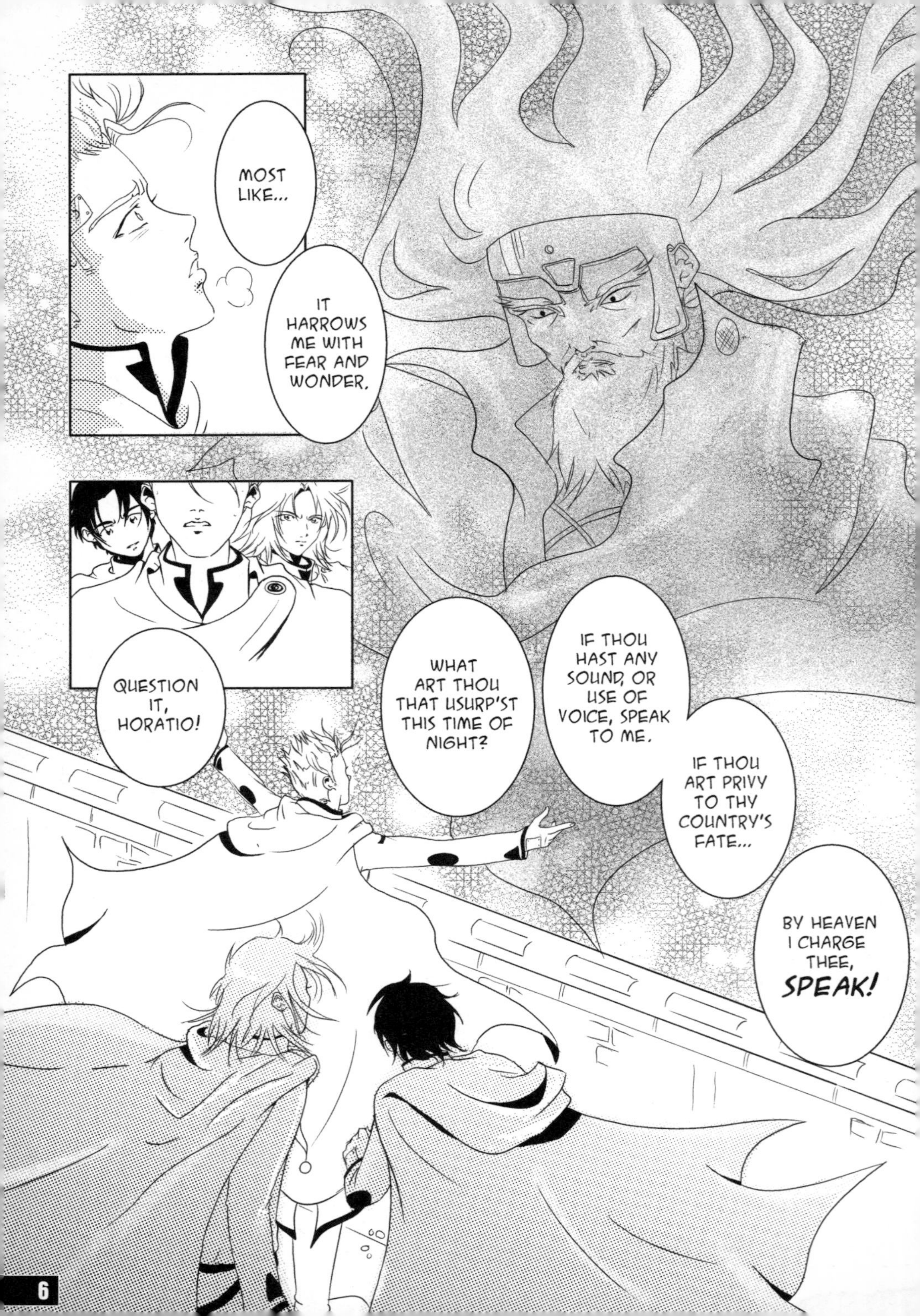
MOST LIKE...
IT HARROWS ME WITH FEAR AND WONDER.
QUESTION IT, HORATIO!
WHAT ART THOU THAT USURP'ST THIS TIME OF NIGHT?
IF THOU HAST ANY SOUND, OR USE OF VOICE, SPEAK TO ME.
IF THOU ART PRIVY TO THY COUNTRY'S FATE...
BY HEAVEN I CHARGE THEE, SPEAK!

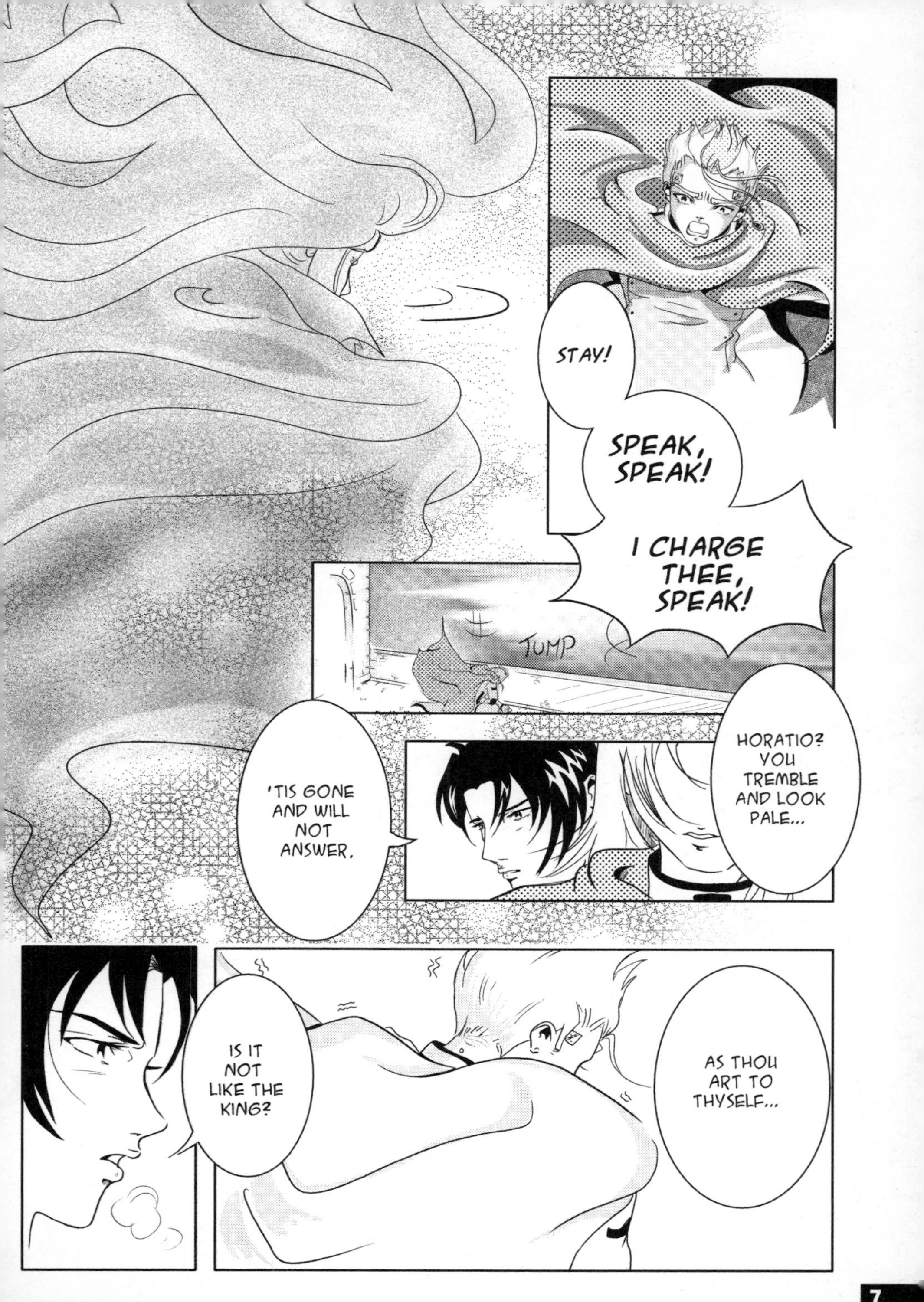
STAY!
SPEAK, SPEAK!
I CHARGE THEE, SPEAK!
JUMP
HORATIO? YOU TREMBLE AND LOOK PALE...
'TIS GONE AND WILL NOT ANSWER.
AS THOU ART TO THYSELF...
IS IT NOT LIKE THE KING?

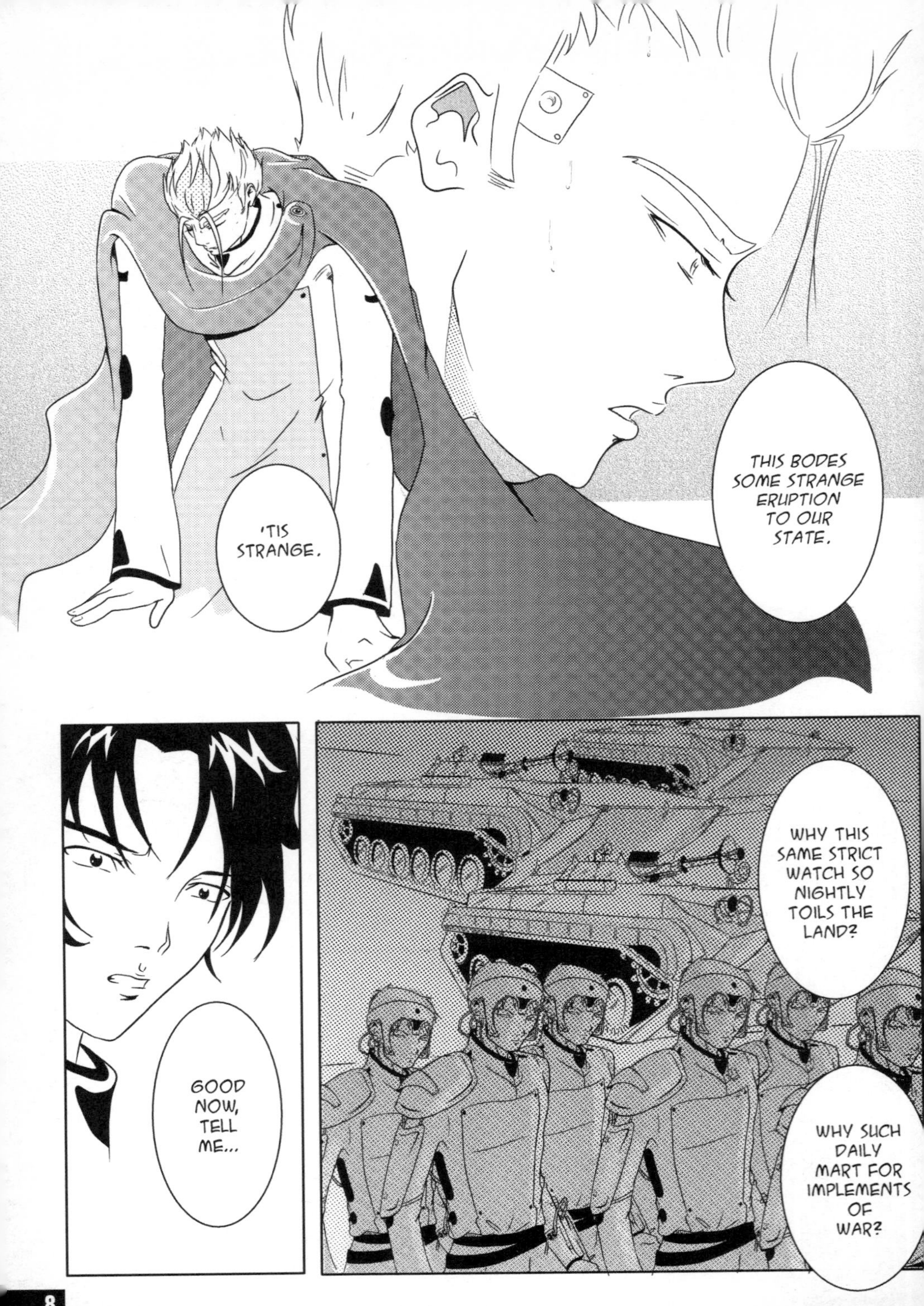
'TIS STRANGE.
THIS BODES SOME STRANGE ERUPTION TO OUR STATE.
GOOD NOW, TELL ME...
WHY THIS SAME STRICT WATCH SO NIGHTLY TOILS THE LAND?
WHY SUCH DAILY MART FOR IMPLEMENTS OF WAR?

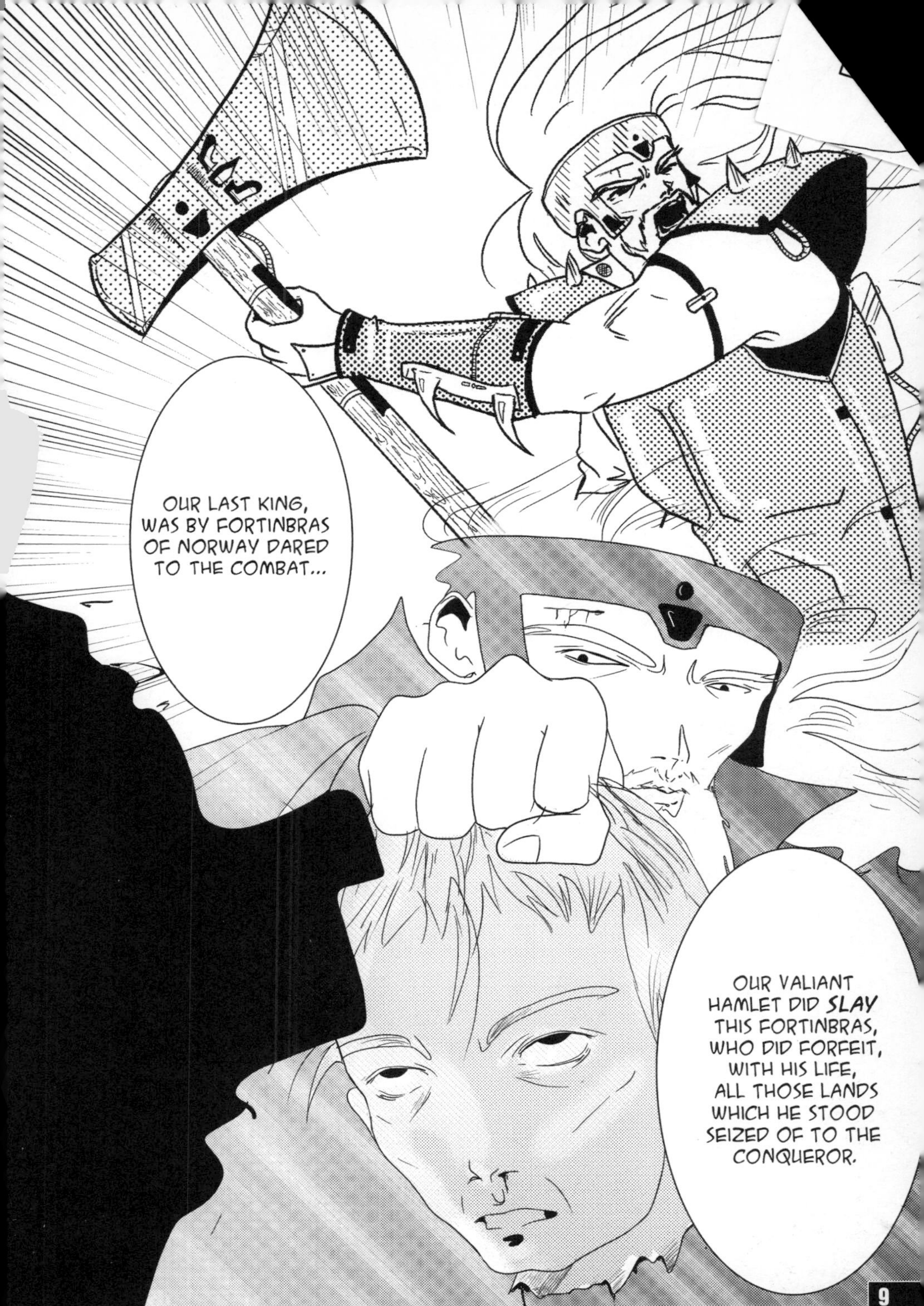
OUR LAST KING, WAS BY FORTINBRAS OF NORWAY DARED TO THE COMBAT...
OUR VALIANT HAMLET DID SLAY THIS FORTINBRAS, WHO DID FORFEIT, WITH HIS LIFE, ALL THOSE LANDS WHICH HE STOOD SEIZED OF TO THE CONQUEROR.

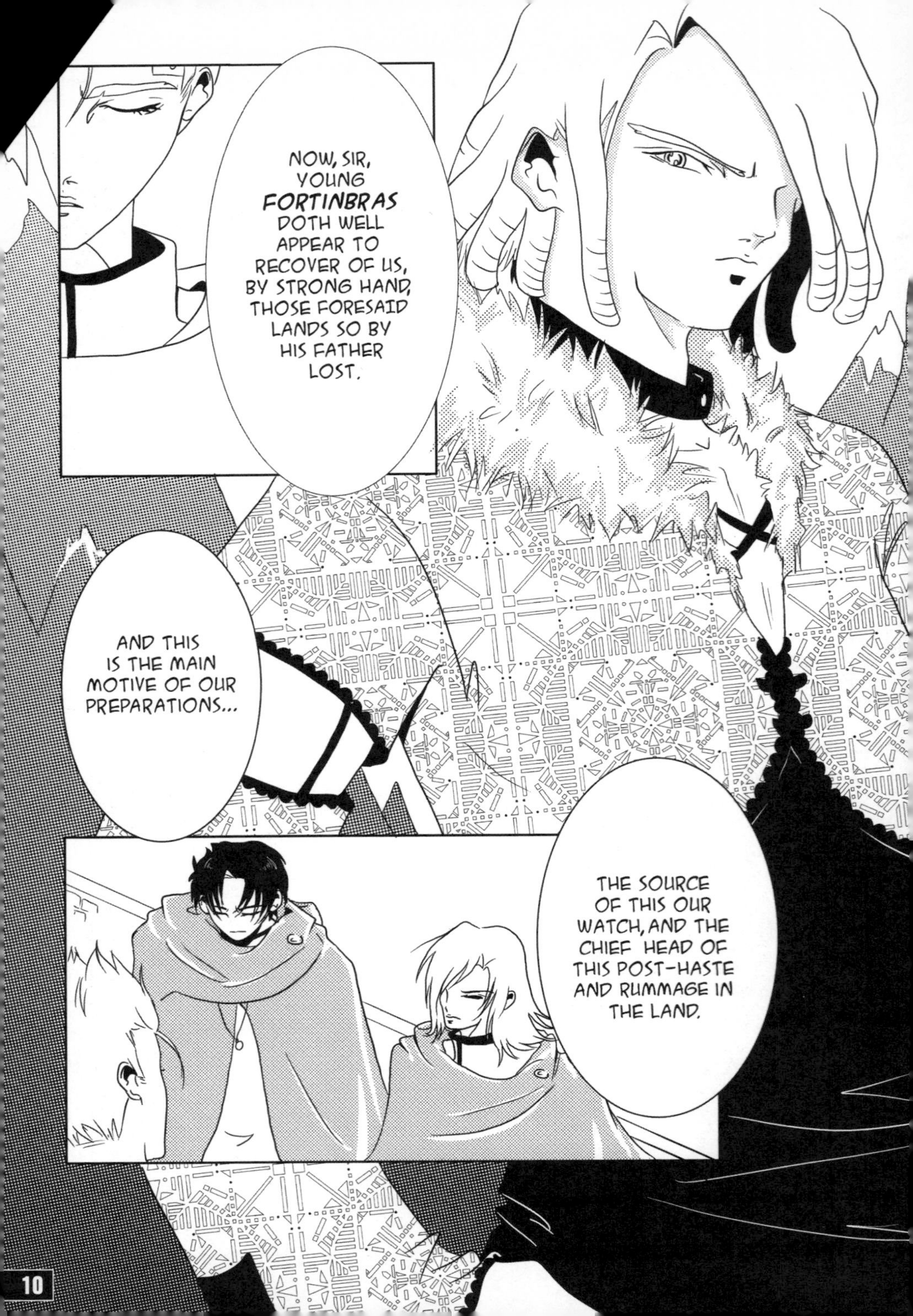
NOW, SIR, YOUNG FORTINBRAS DOTH WELL APPEAR TO RECOVER OF US, BY STRONG HAND, THOSE FORESAID LANDS SO BY HIS FATHER LOST.
AND THIS IS THE MAIN MOTIVE OF OUR PREPARATIONS...
THE SOURCE OF THIS OUR WATCH, AND THE CHIEF HEAD OF THIS POST-HASTE AND RUMMAGE IN THE LAND.

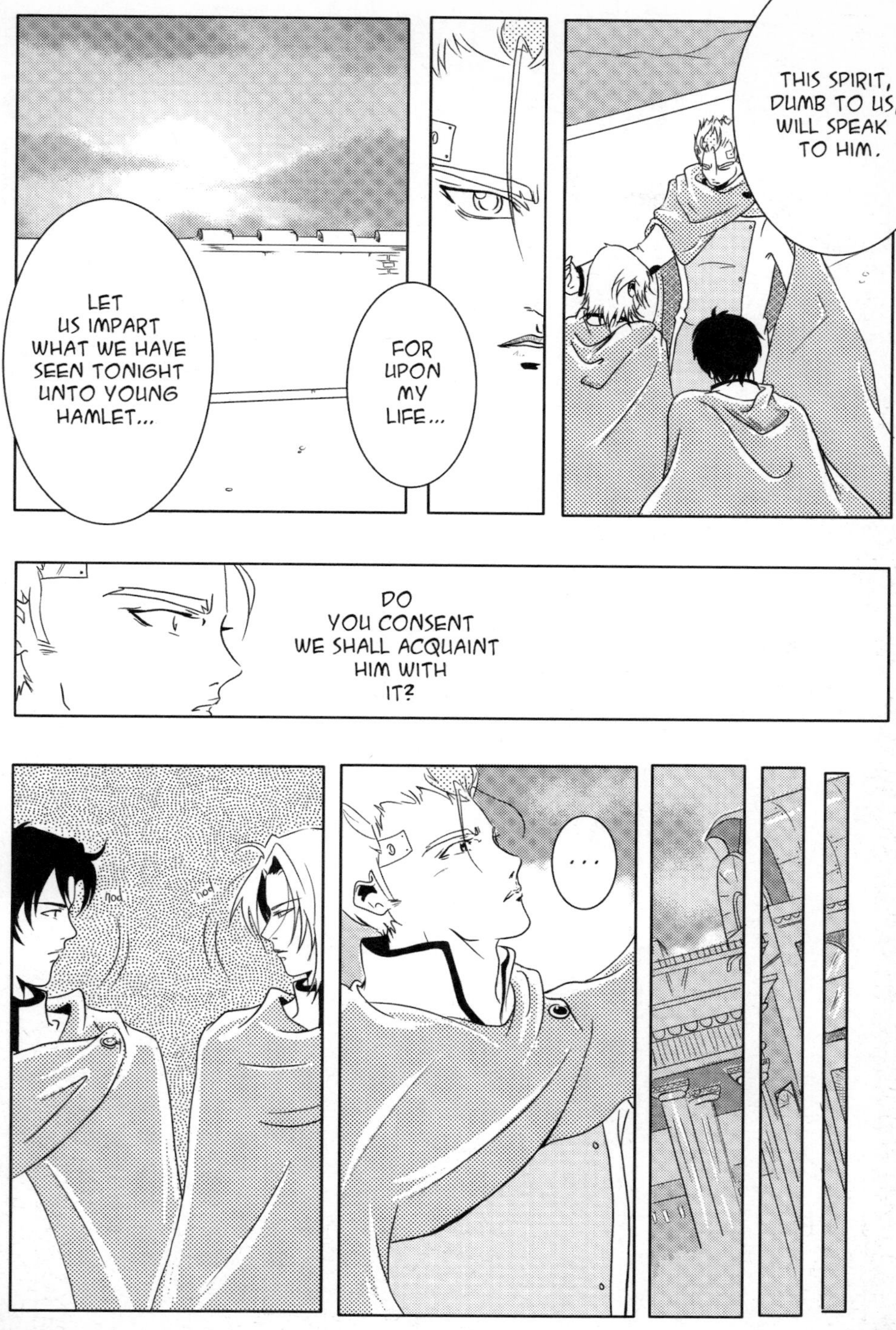
LET US IMPART WHAT WE HAVE SEEN TONIGHT UNTO YOUNG HAMLET...
FOR UPON MY LIFE...
THIS SPIRIT, DUMB TO US, WILL SPEAK TO HIM.
DO YOU CONSENT WE SHALL ACQUAINT HIM WITH IT?
nod
nod
...

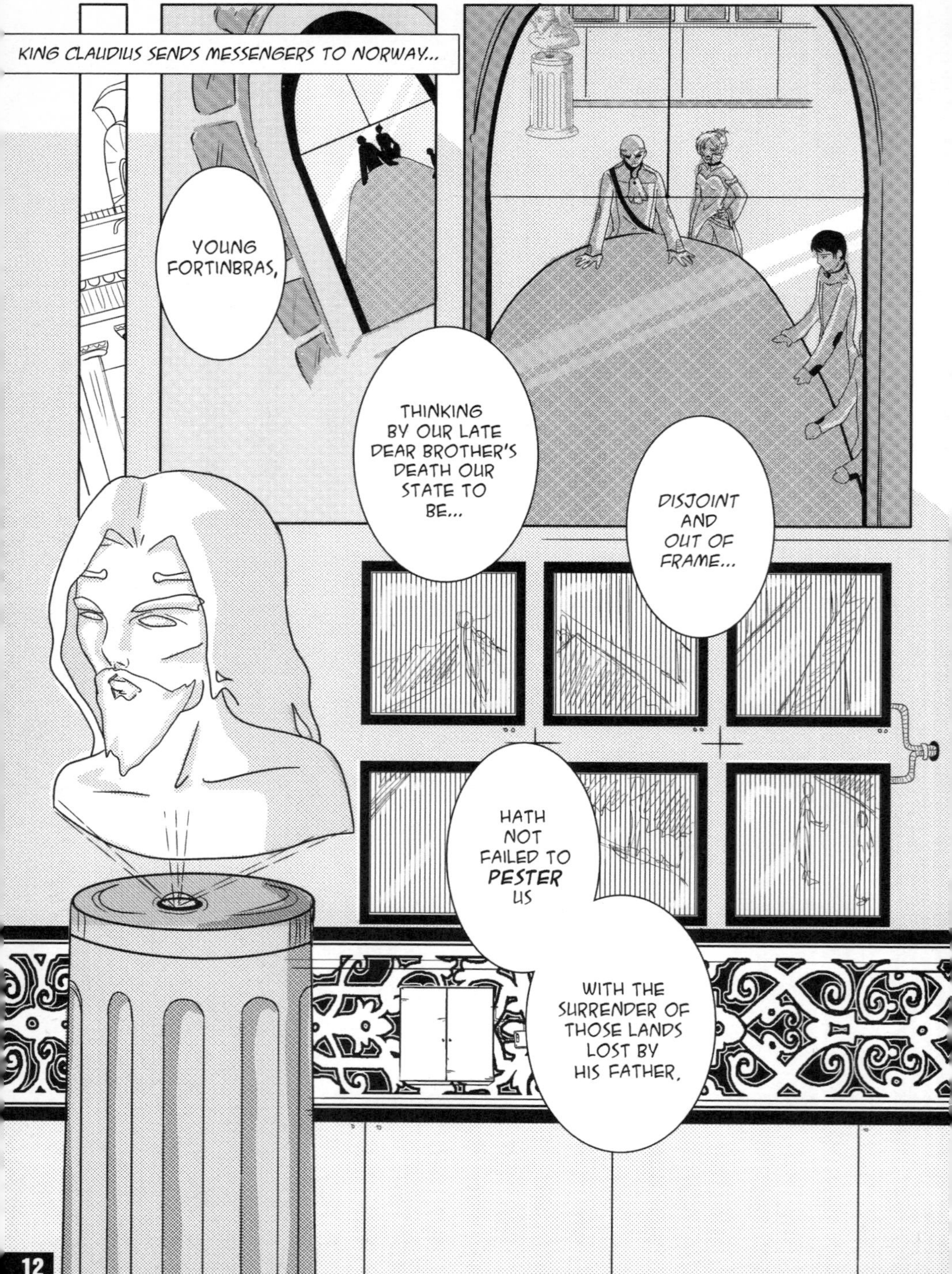
KING CLAUDIUS SENDS MESSENGERS TO NORWAY...
YOUNG FORTINBRAS,
THINKING BY OUR LATE DEAR BROTHER'S DEATH OUR STATE TO BE...
DISJOINT AND OUT OF FRAME...
HATH NOT FAILED TO **PESTER** US
WITH THE SURRENDER OF THOSE LANDS LOST BY HIS FATHER,

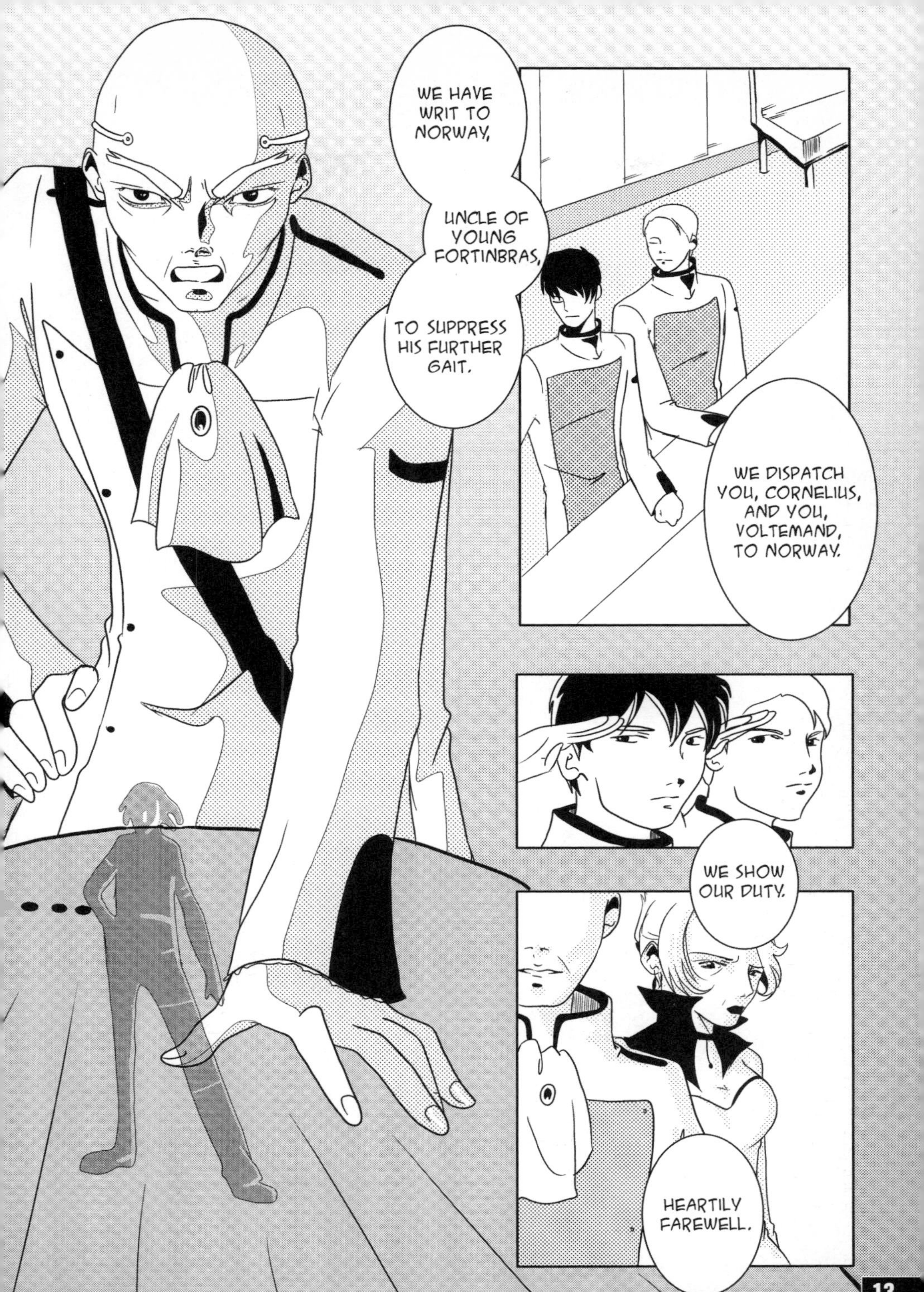
WE HAVE WRIT TO NORWAY,
UNCLE OF YOUNG FORTINBRAS,
TO SUPPRESS HIS FURTHER GAIT.
WE DISPATCH YOU, CORNELIUS, AND YOU, VOLTEMAND, TO NORWAY.
WE SHOW OUR DUTY.
HEARTILY FAREWELL.

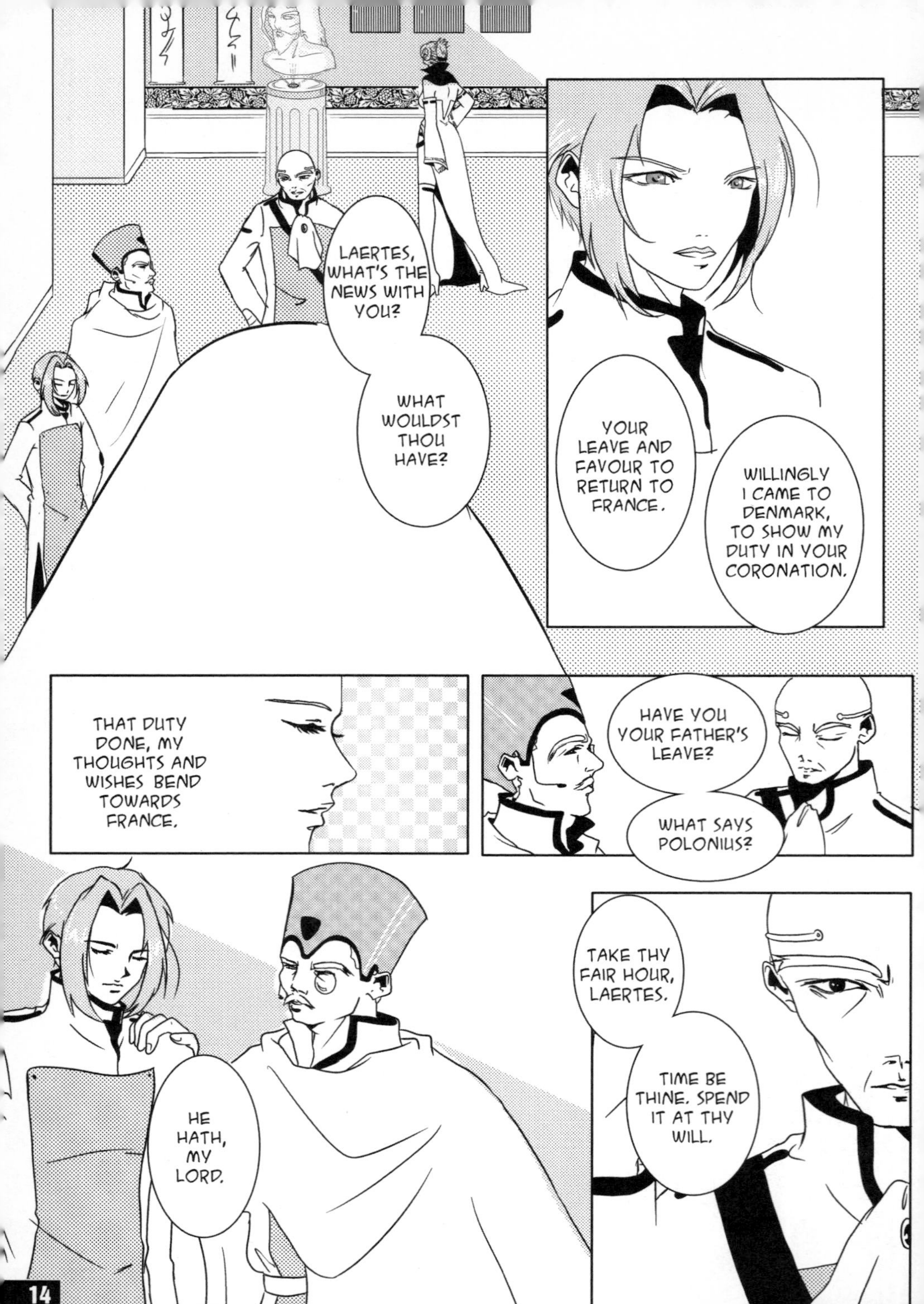
LAERTES, WHAT'S THE NEWS WITH YOU?
WHAT WOULDST THOU HAVE?
YOUR LEAVE AND FAVOUR TO RETURN TO FRANCE.
WILLINGLY I CAME TO DENMARK, TO SHOW MY DUTY IN YOUR CORONATION.
THAT DUTY DONE, MY THOUGHTS AND WISHES BEND TOWARDS FRANCE.
HAVE YOU YOUR FATHER'S LEAVE?
WHAT SAYS POLONIUS?
HE HATH, MY LORD.
TAKE THY FAIR HOUR, LAERTES.
TIME BE THINE. SPEND IT AT THY WILL.

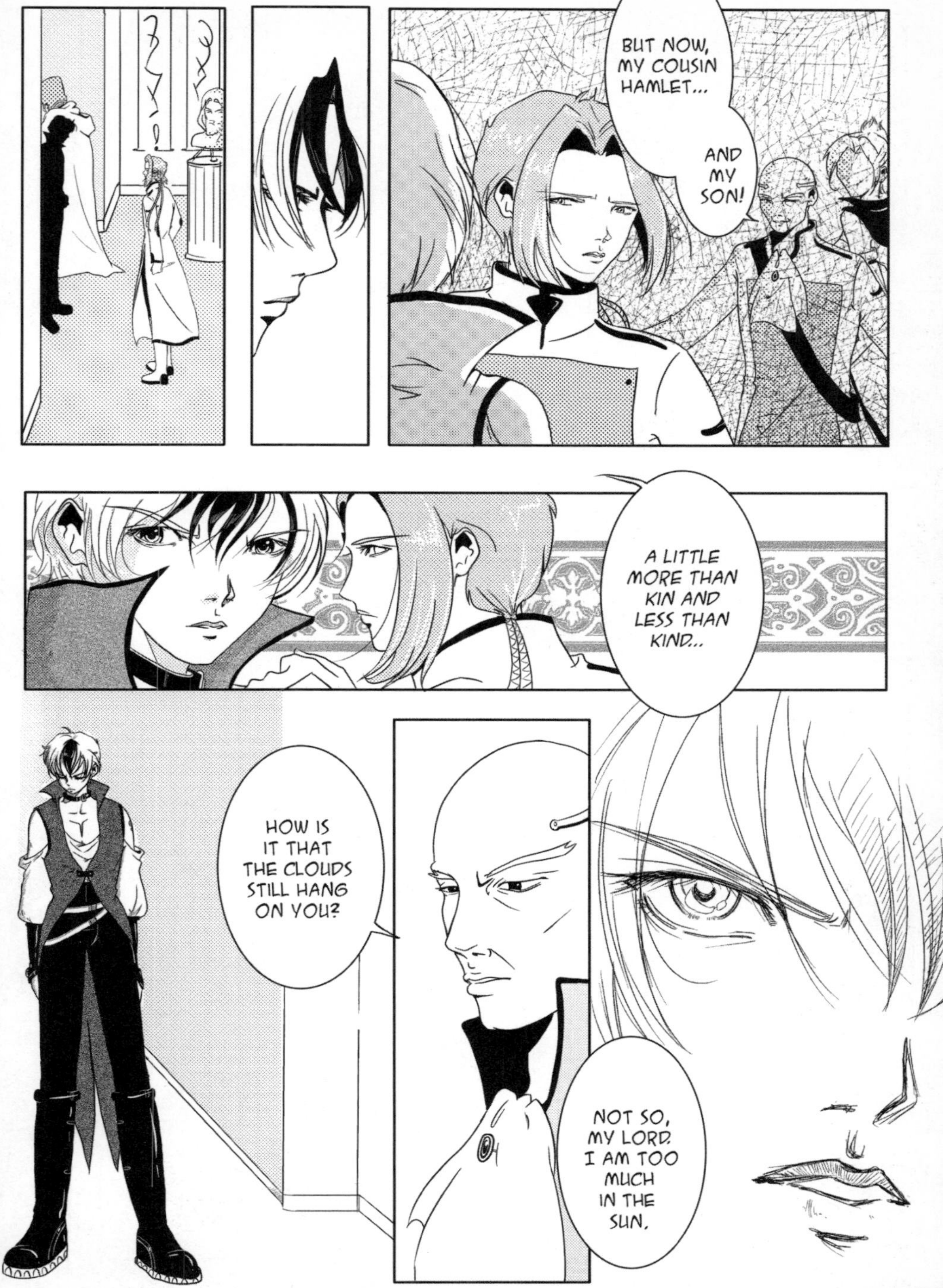

BUT NOW, MY COUSIN HAMLET...
AND MY SON!
A LITTLE MORE THAN KIN AND LESS THAN KIND...
HOW IS IT THAT THE CLOUDS STILL HANG ON YOU?
NOT SO, MY LORD. I AM TOO MUCH IN THE SUN.

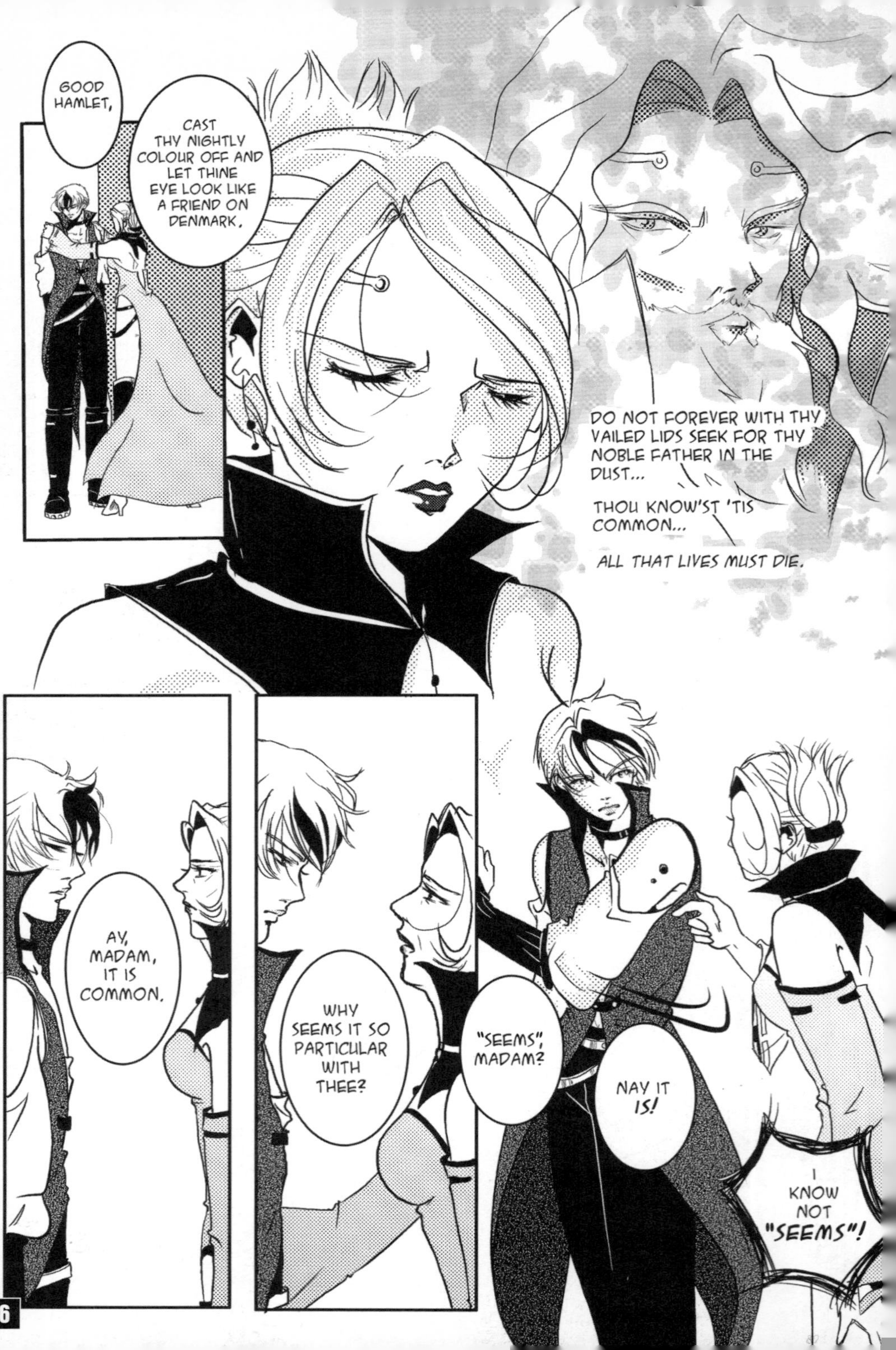
GOOD HAMLET,
CAST THY NIGHTLY COLOUR OFF AND LET THINE EYE LOOK LIKE A FRIEND ON DENMARK.
DO NOT FOREVER WITH THY VAILED LIDS SEEK FOR THY NOBLE FATHER IN THE DUST...
THOU KNOW'ST 'TIS COMMON...
ALL THAT LIVES MUST DIE.
AY, MADAM, IT IS COMMON.
WHY SEEMS IT SO PARTICULAR WITH THEE?
"SEEMS", MADAM?
NAY IT IS!
I KNOW NOT "SEEMS"!

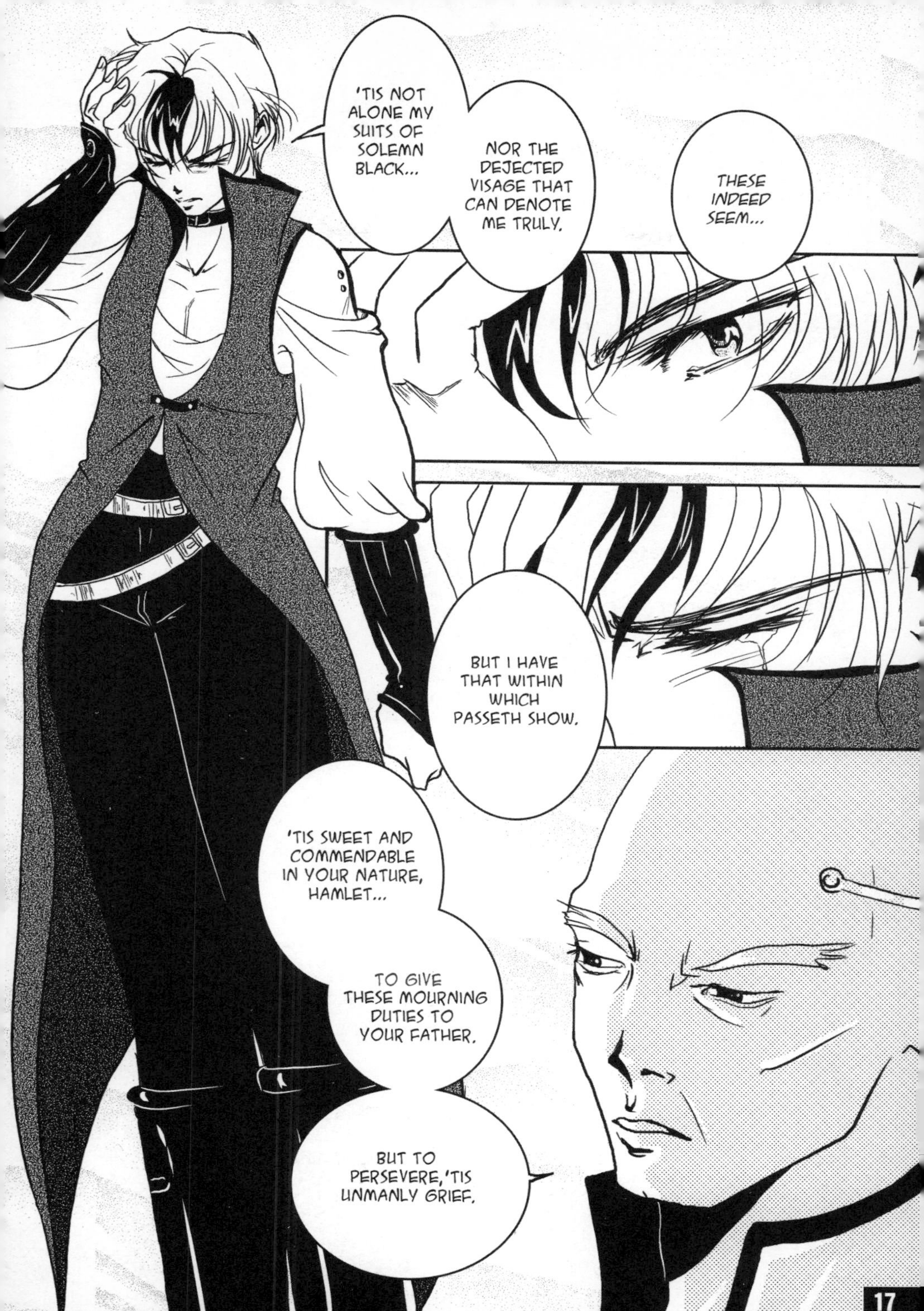
'TIS NOT ALONE MY SUITS OF SOLEMN BLACK...
NOR THE DEJECTED VISAGE THAT CAN DENOTE ME TRULY.
THESE INDEED SEEM...
BUT I HAVE THAT WITHIN WHICH PASSETH SHOW.
'TIS SWEET AND COMMENDABLE IN YOUR NATURE, HAMLET...
TO GIVE THESE MOURNING DUTIES TO YOUR FATHER.
BUT TO PERSEVERE, 'TIS UNMANLY GRIEF.

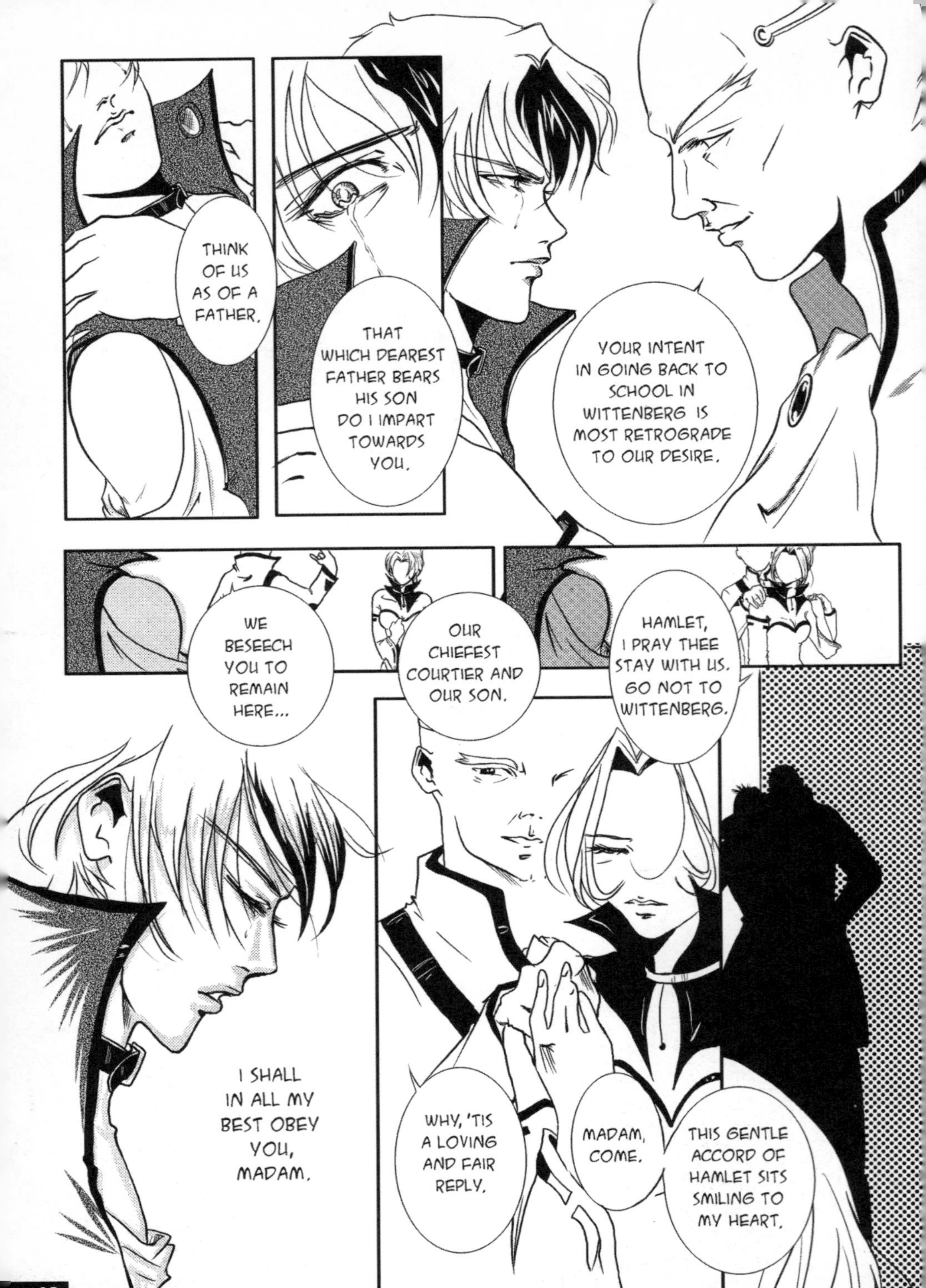
THINK OF US AS OF A FATHER.
THAT WHICH DEAREST FATHER BEARS HIS SON DO I IMPART TOWARDS YOU.
YOUR INTENT IN GOING BACK TO SCHOOL IN WITTENBERG IS MOST RETROGRADE TO OUR DESIRE.
WE BESEECH YOU TO REMAIN HERE...
OUR CHIEFEST COURTIER AND OUR SON.
HAMLET, I PRAY THEE STAY WITH US. GO NOT TO WITTENBERG.
I SHALL IN ALL MY BEST OBEY YOU, MADAM.
WHY, 'TIS A LOVING AND FAIR REPLY.
MADAM, COME.
THIS GENTLE ACCORD OF HAMLET SITS SMILING TO MY HEART.

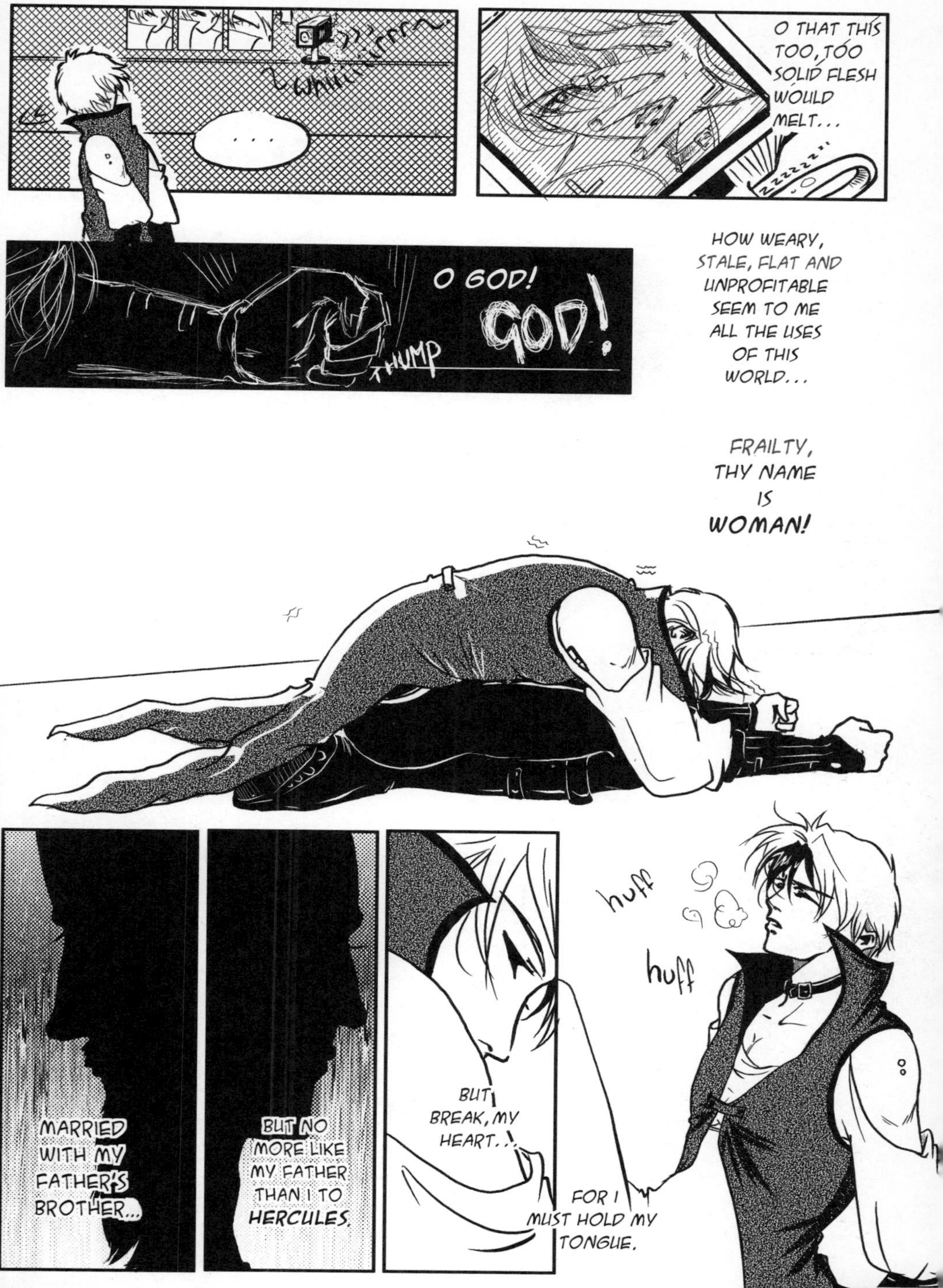

whiirrrr~
...
O THAT THIS TOO, TOO SOLID FLESH WOULD MELT...
zzzzzz
O GOD!
GOD!
THUMP
HOW WEARY, STALE, FLAT AND UNPROFITABLE SEEM TO ME ALL THE USES OF THIS WORLD...
FRAILTY, THY NAME IS WOMAN!
MARRIED WITH MY FATHER'S BROTHER...
BUT NO MORE LIKE MY FATHER THAN I TO HERCULES.
BUT BREAK, MY HEART...
FOR I MUST HOLD MY TONGUE.
huff
huff

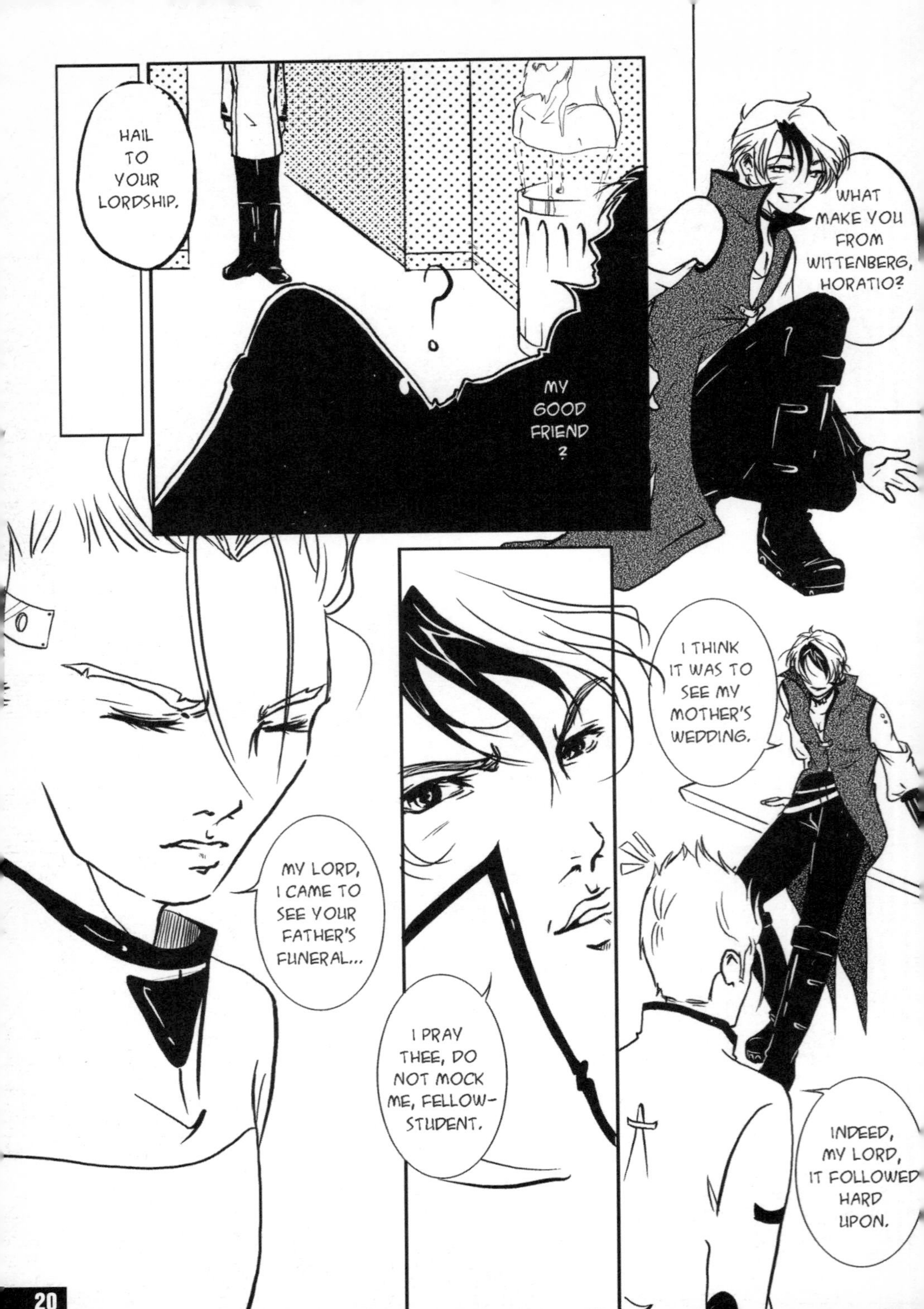
HAIL TO YOUR LORDSHIP.
?
MY GOOD FRIEND?
WHAT MAKE YOU FROM WITTENBERG, HORATIO?
MY LORD, I CAME TO SEE YOUR FATHER'S FUNERAL...
I PRAY THEE, DO NOT MOCK ME, FELLOW-STUDENT.
I THINK IT WAS TO SEE MY MOTHER'S WEDDING.
INDEED, MY LORD, IT FOLLOWED HARD UPON.

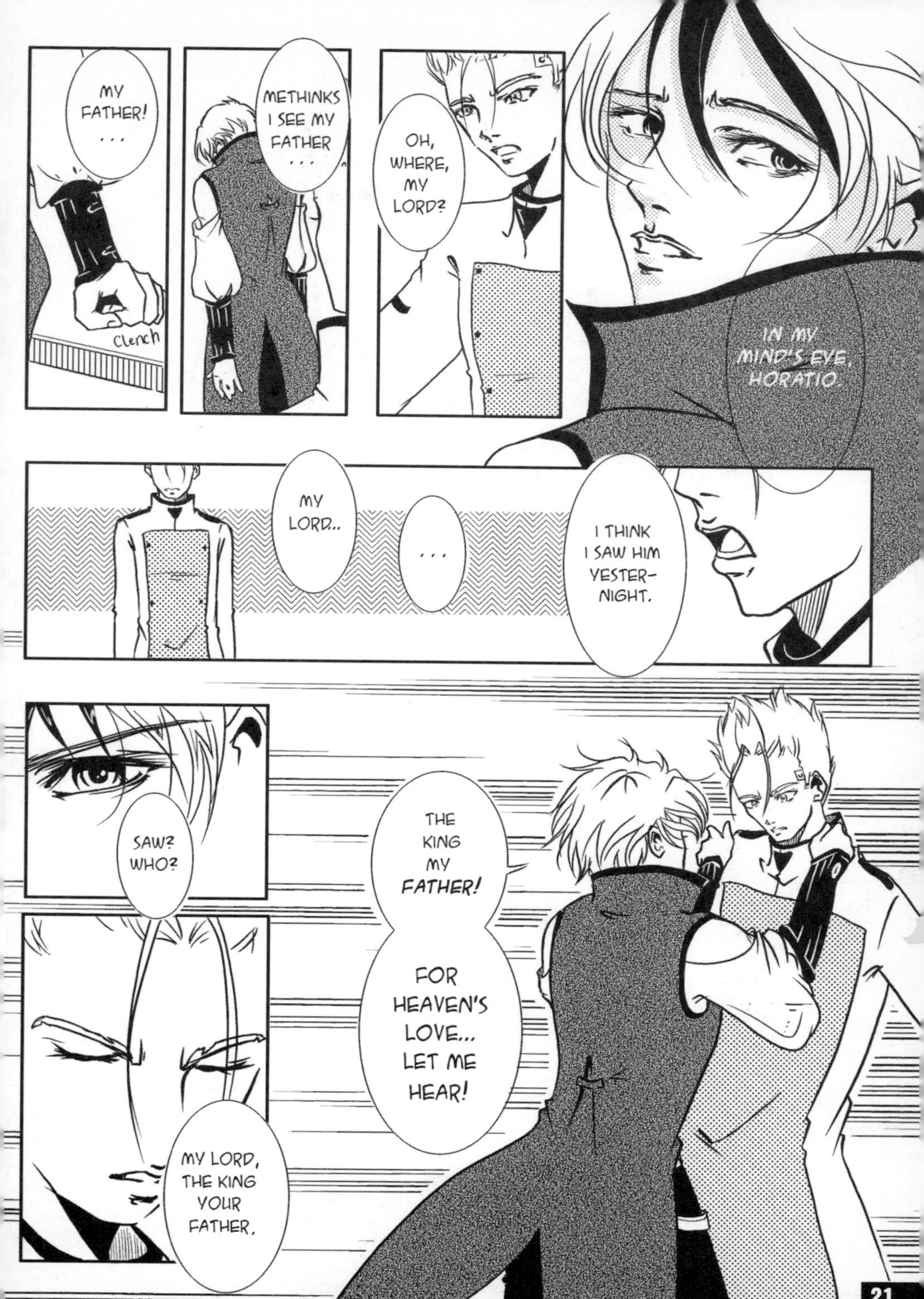

MY FATHER! ...
Clench
METHINKS I SEE MY FATHER ...
OH, WHERE, MY LORD?
IN MY MIND'S EYE, HORATIO.
MY LORD...
...
I THINK I SAW HIM YESTER-NIGHT.
SAW? WHO?
MY LORD, THE KING YOUR FATHER.
THE KING MY FATHER!
FOR HEAVEN'S LOVE... LET ME HEAR!

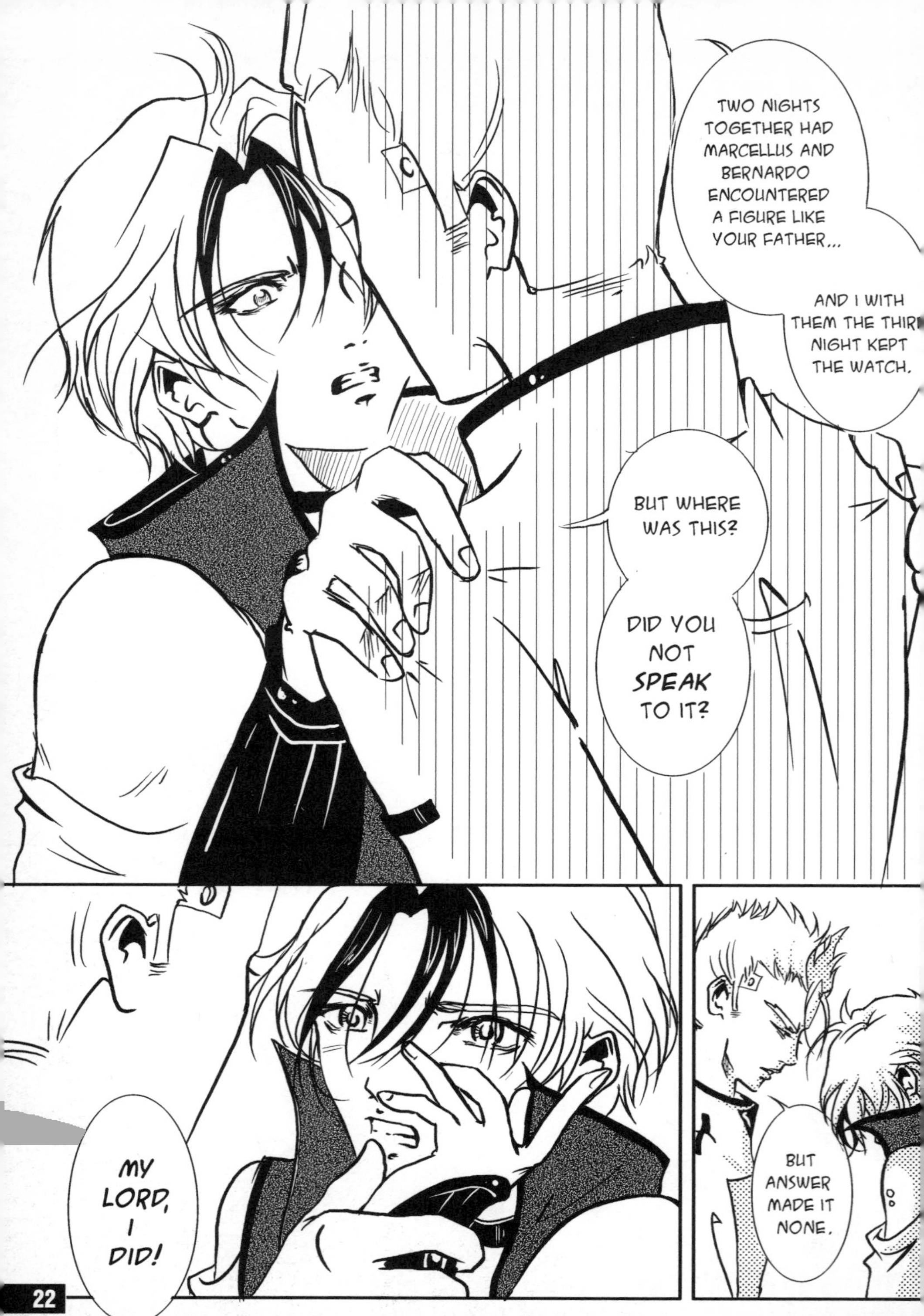
TWO NIGHTS TOGETHER HAD MARCELLUS AND BERNARDO ENCOUNTERED A FIGURE LIKE YOUR FATHER...
AND I WITH THEM THE THIRD NIGHT KEPT THE WATCH.
BUT WHERE WAS THIS?
DID YOU NOT SPEAK TO IT?
BUT ANSWER MADE IT NONE.
MY LORD, I DID!

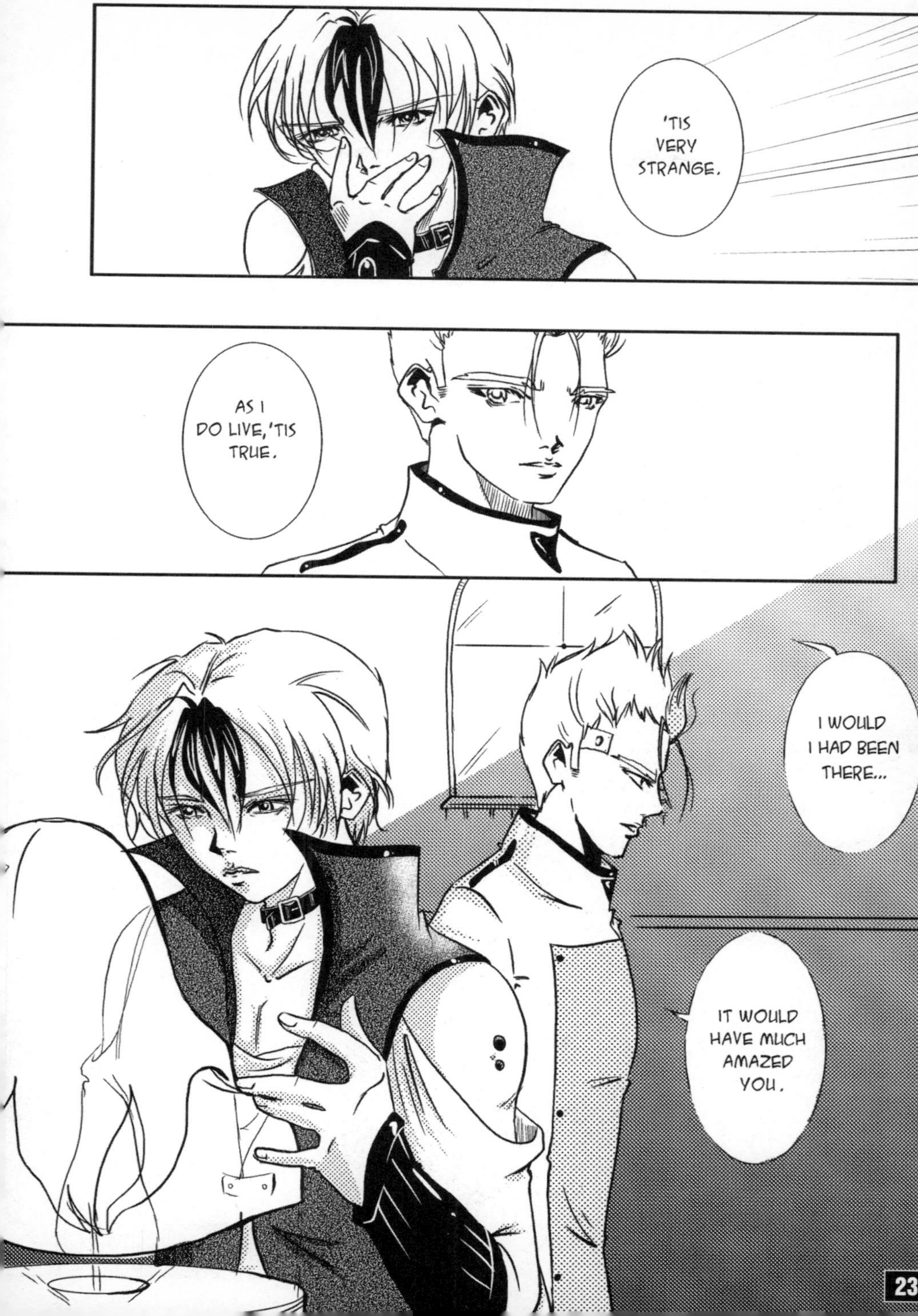
'TIS VERY STRANGE.
AS I DO LIVE, 'TIS TRUE.
I WOULD I HAD BEEN THERE...
IT WOULD HAVE MUCH AMAZED YOU.

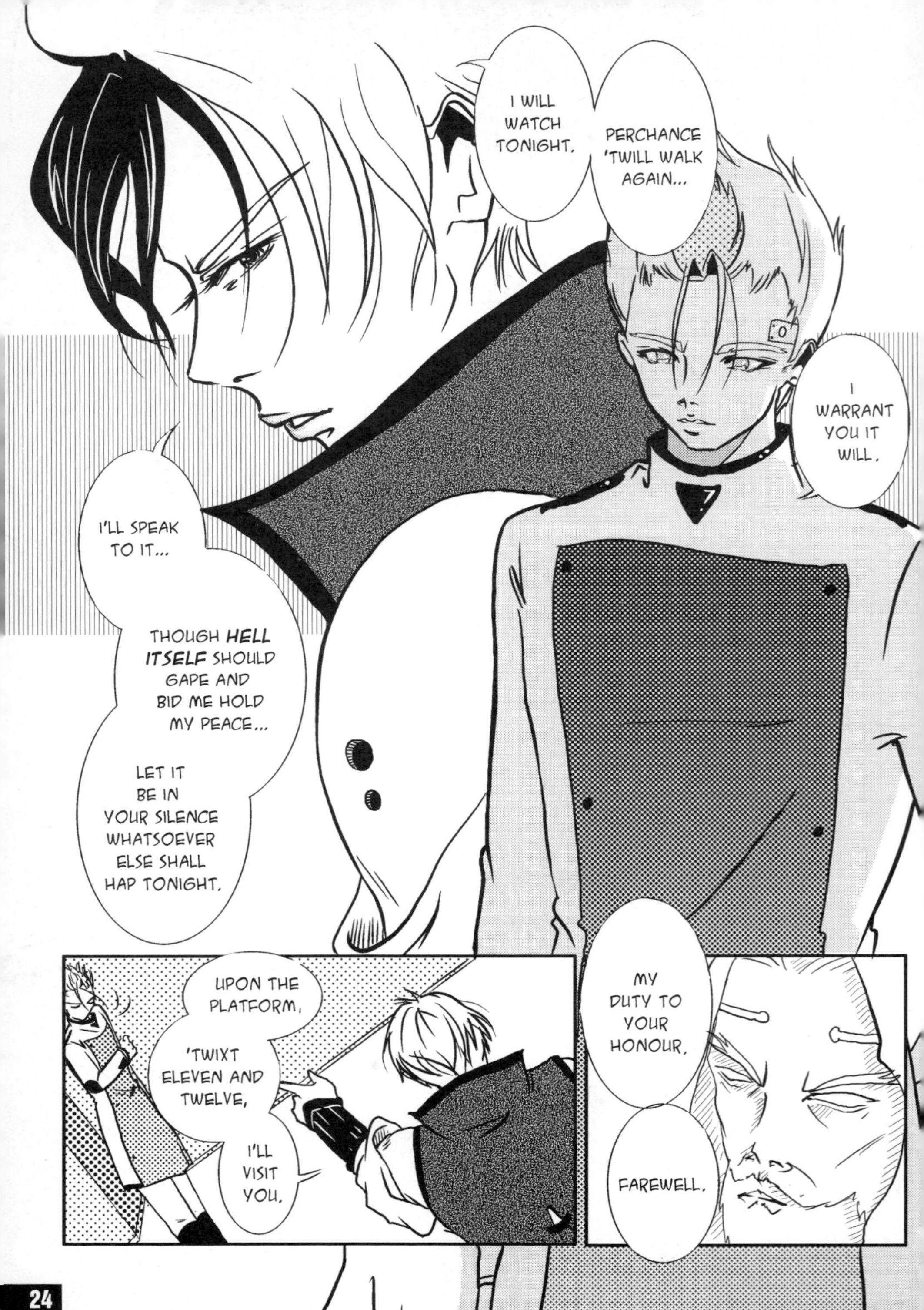

I WILL WATCH TONIGHT.
PERCHANCE 'TWILL WALK AGAIN...
I WARRANT YOU IT WILL.
I'LL SPEAK TO IT...
THOUGH **HELL ITSELF** SHOULD GAPE AND BID ME HOLD MY PEACE...
LET IT BE IN YOUR SILENCE WHATSOEVER ELSE SHALL HAP TONIGHT.
UPON THE PLATFORM,
'TWIXT ELEVEN AND TWELVE,
I'LL VISIT YOU.
MY DUTY TO YOUR HONOUR.
FAREWELL.

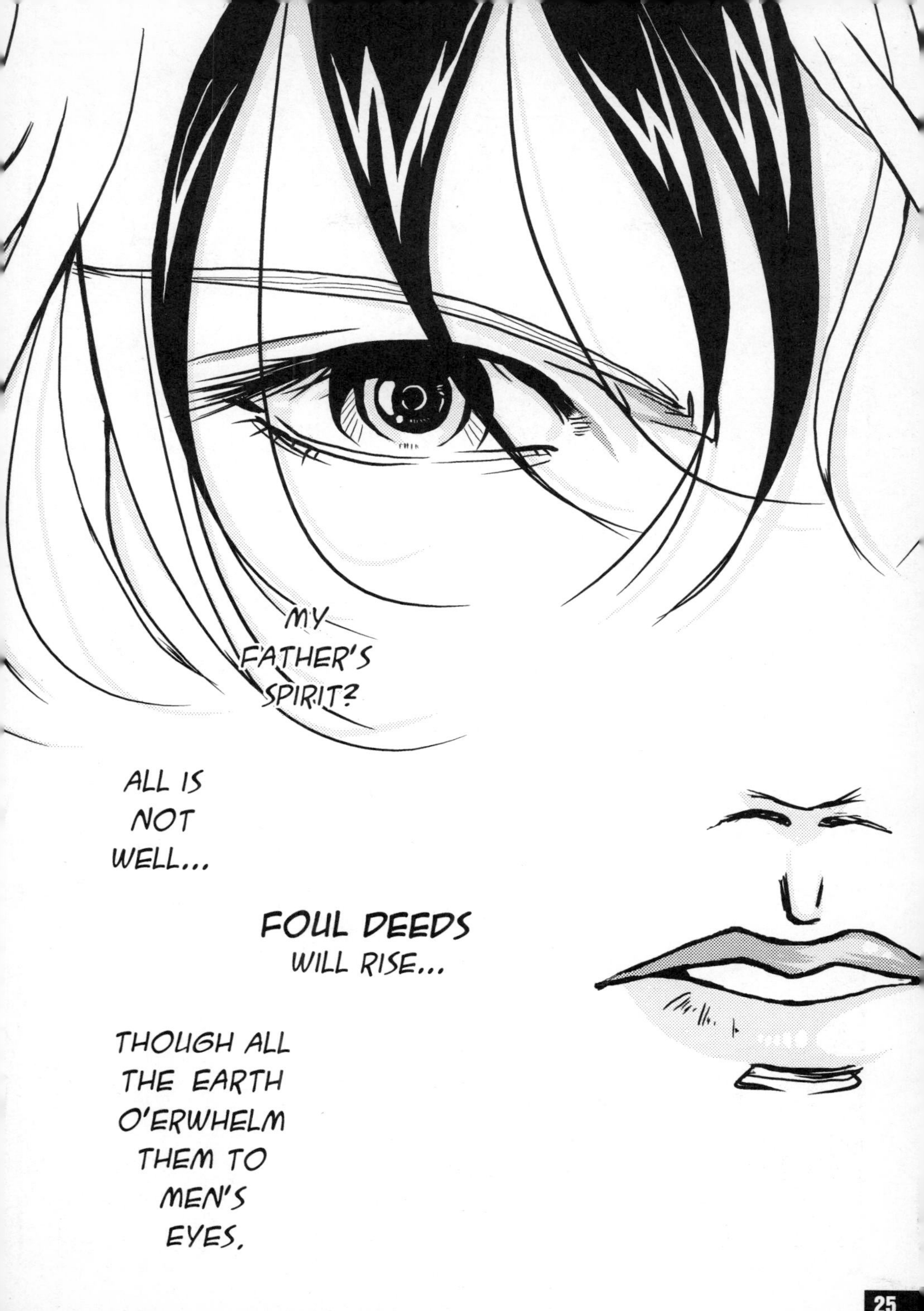
MY FATHER'S SPIRIT?
ALL IS NOT WELL...
FOUL DEEDS WILL RISE...
THOUGH ALL THE EARTH O'ERWHELM THEM TO MEN'S EYES.

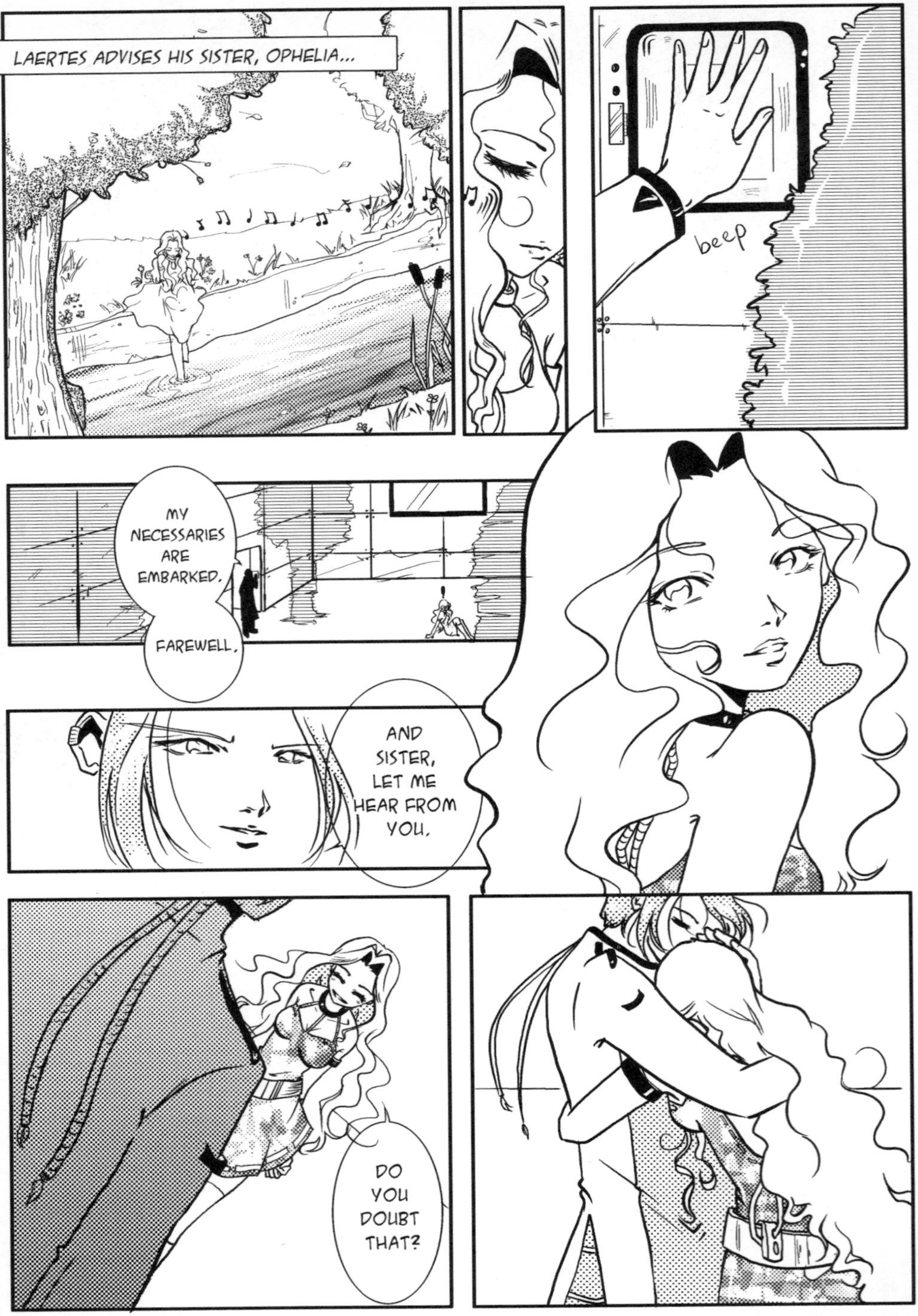
LAERTES ADVISES HIS SISTER, OPHELIA...
beep
MY NECESSARIES ARE EMBARKED.
FAREWELL.
AND SISTER, LET ME HEAR FROM YOU.
DO YOU DOUBT THAT?

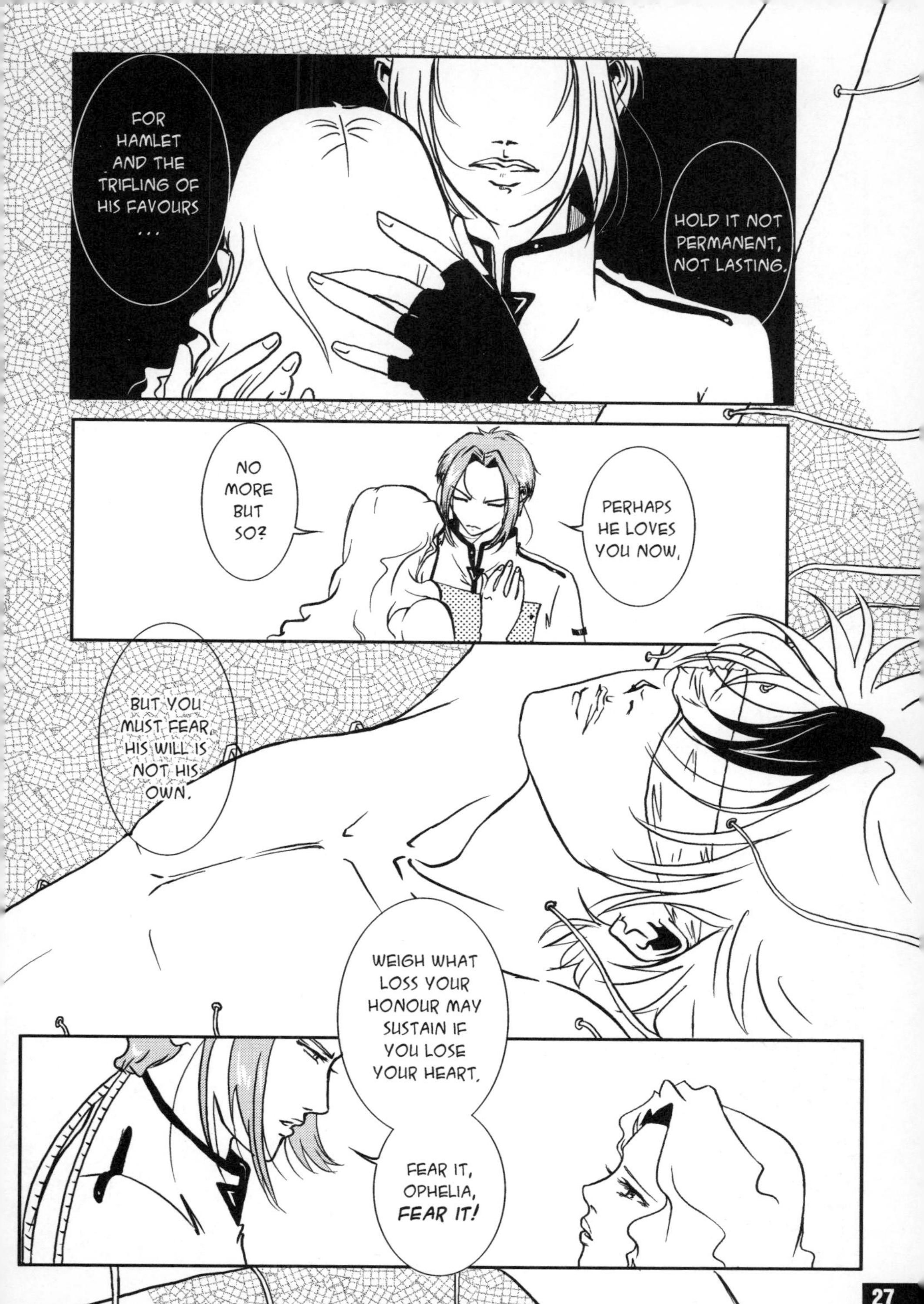
FOR HAMLET AND THE TRIFLING OF HIS FAVOURS . . .
HOLD IT NOT PERMANENT, NOT LASTING.
NO MORE BUT SO?
PERHAPS HE LOVES YOU NOW,
BUT YOU MUST FEAR, HIS WILL IS NOT HIS OWN.
WEIGH WHAT LOSS YOUR HONOUR MAY SUSTAIN IF YOU LOSE YOUR HEART.
FEAR IT, OPHELIA, **FEAR IT!**

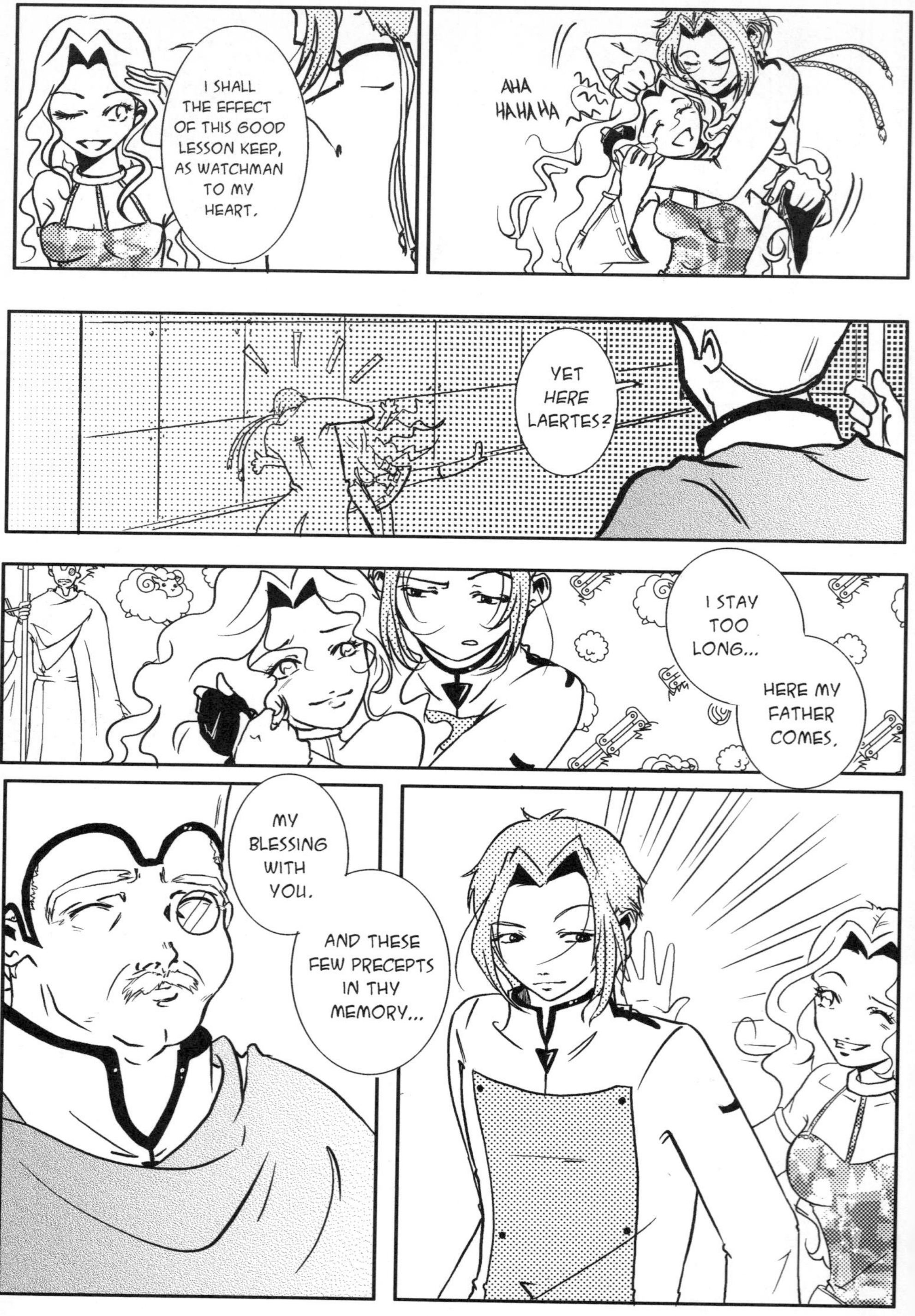
I SHALL THE EFFECT OF THIS GOOD LESSON KEEP, AS WATCHMAN TO MY HEART.
AHA HAHAHA
YET HERE LAERTES?
I STAY TOO LONG...
HERE MY FATHER COMES.
MY BLESSING WITH YOU.
AND THESE FEW PRECEPTS IN THY MEMORY...

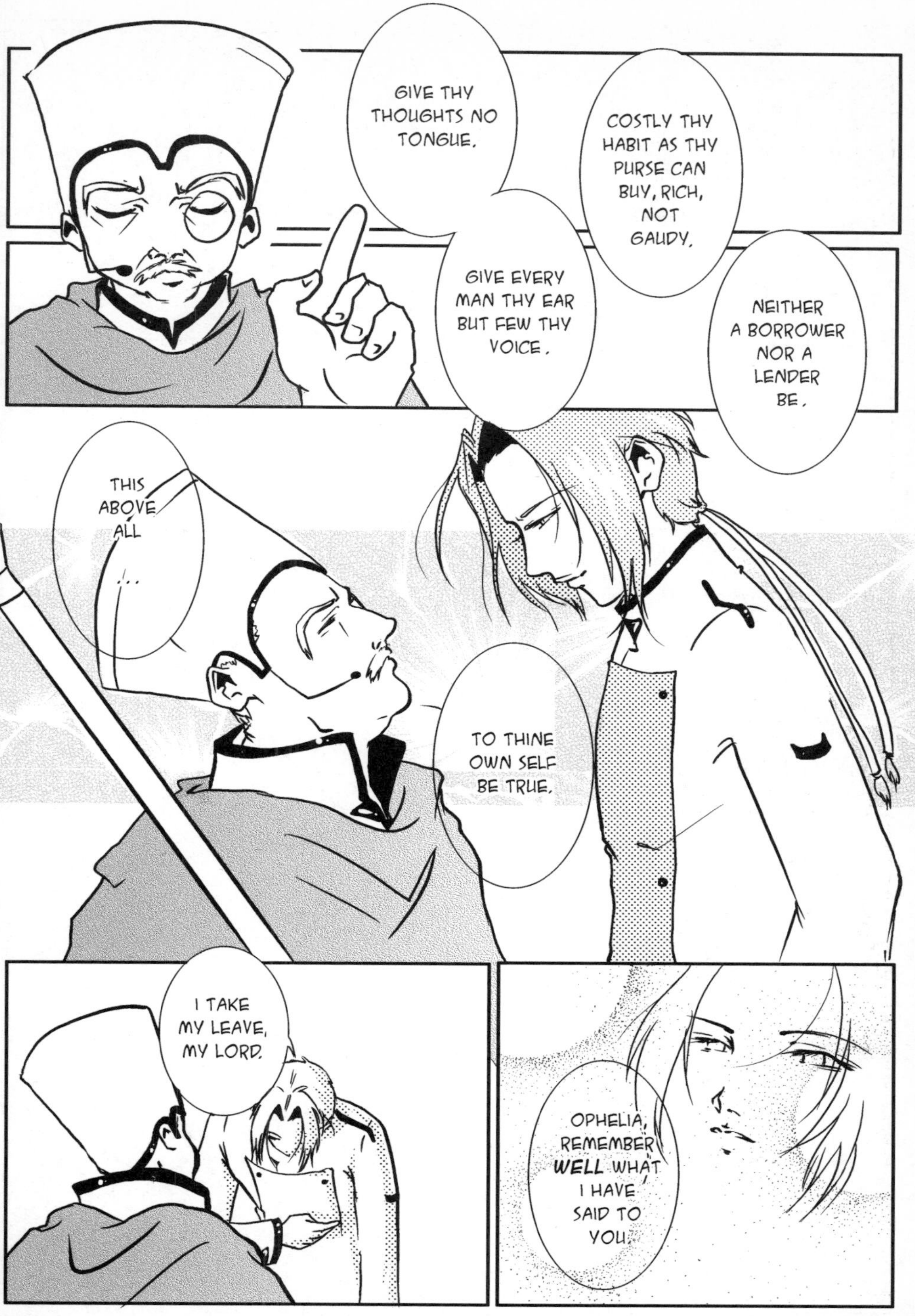
GIVE THY THOUGHTS NO TONGUE.
COSTLY THY HABIT AS THY PURSE CAN BUY, RICH, NOT GAUDY.
GIVE EVERY MAN THY EAR BUT FEW THY VOICE.
NEITHER A BORROWER NOR A LENDER BE.
THIS ABOVE ALL ...
TO THINE OWN SELF BE TRUE.
I TAKE MY LEAVE, MY LORD.
OPHELIA, REMEMBER WELL WHAT I HAVE SAID TO YOU.

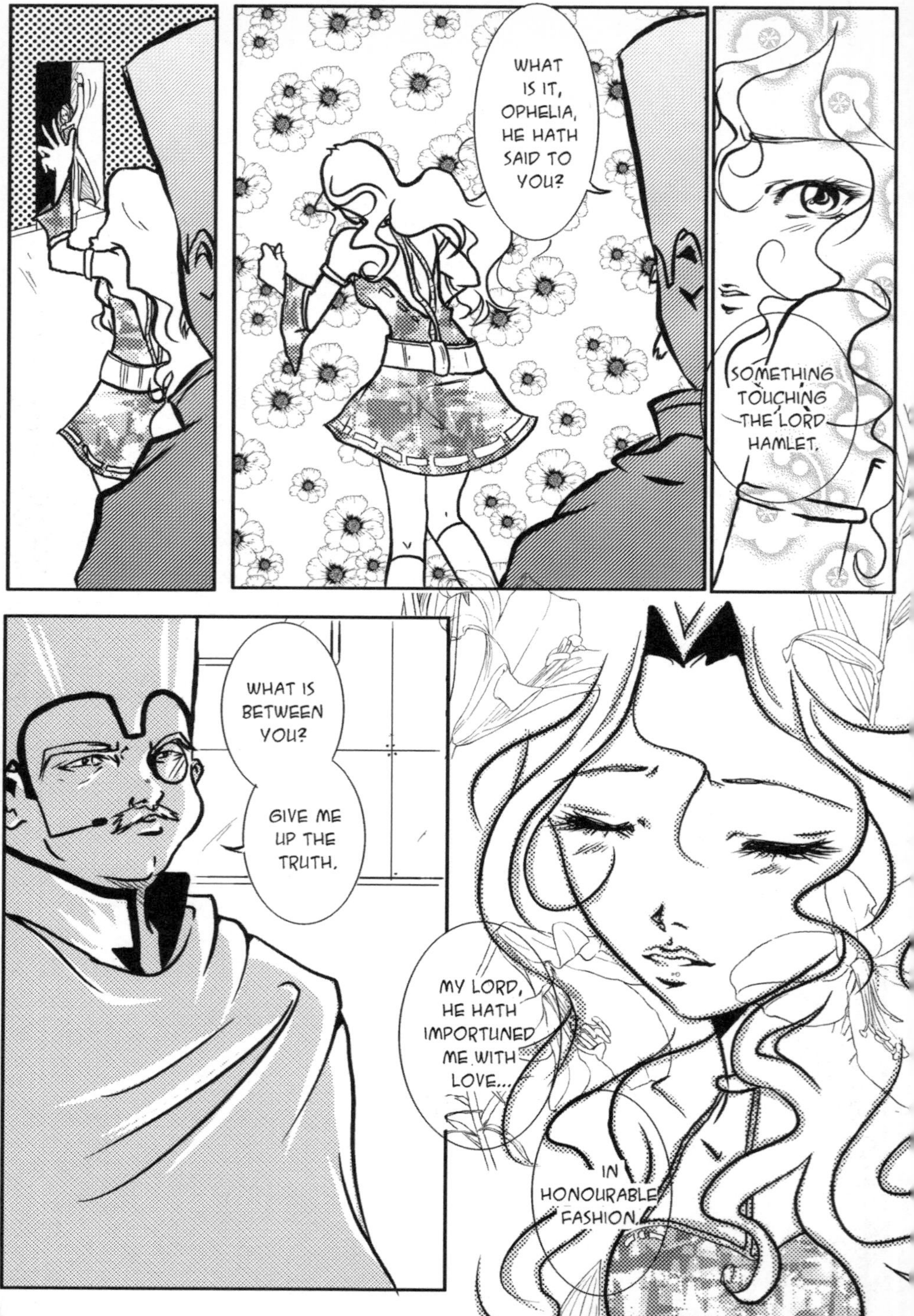
WHAT IS IT, OPHELIA, HE HATH SAID TO YOU?
SOMETHING TOUCHING THE LORD HAMLET.
WHAT IS BETWEEN YOU?
GIVE ME UP THE TRUTH.
MY LORD, HE HATH IMPORTUNED ME WITH LOVE...
IN HONOURABLE FASHION.

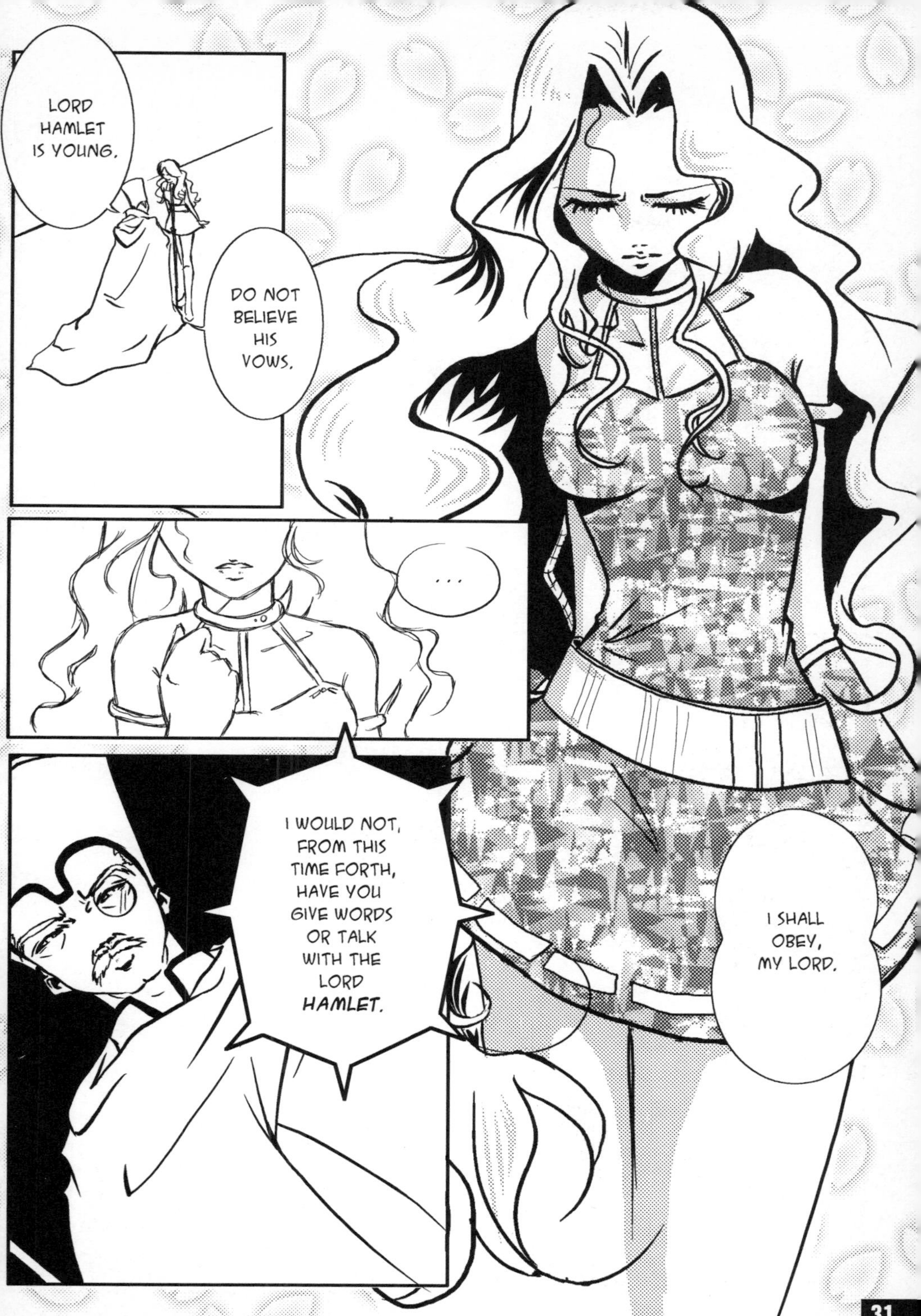
LORD HAMLET IS YOUNG.
DO NOT BELIEVE HIS VOWS.
...
I WOULD NOT, FROM THIS TIME FORTH, HAVE YOU GIVE WORDS OR TALK WITH THE LORD HAMLET.
I SHALL OBEY, MY LORD.

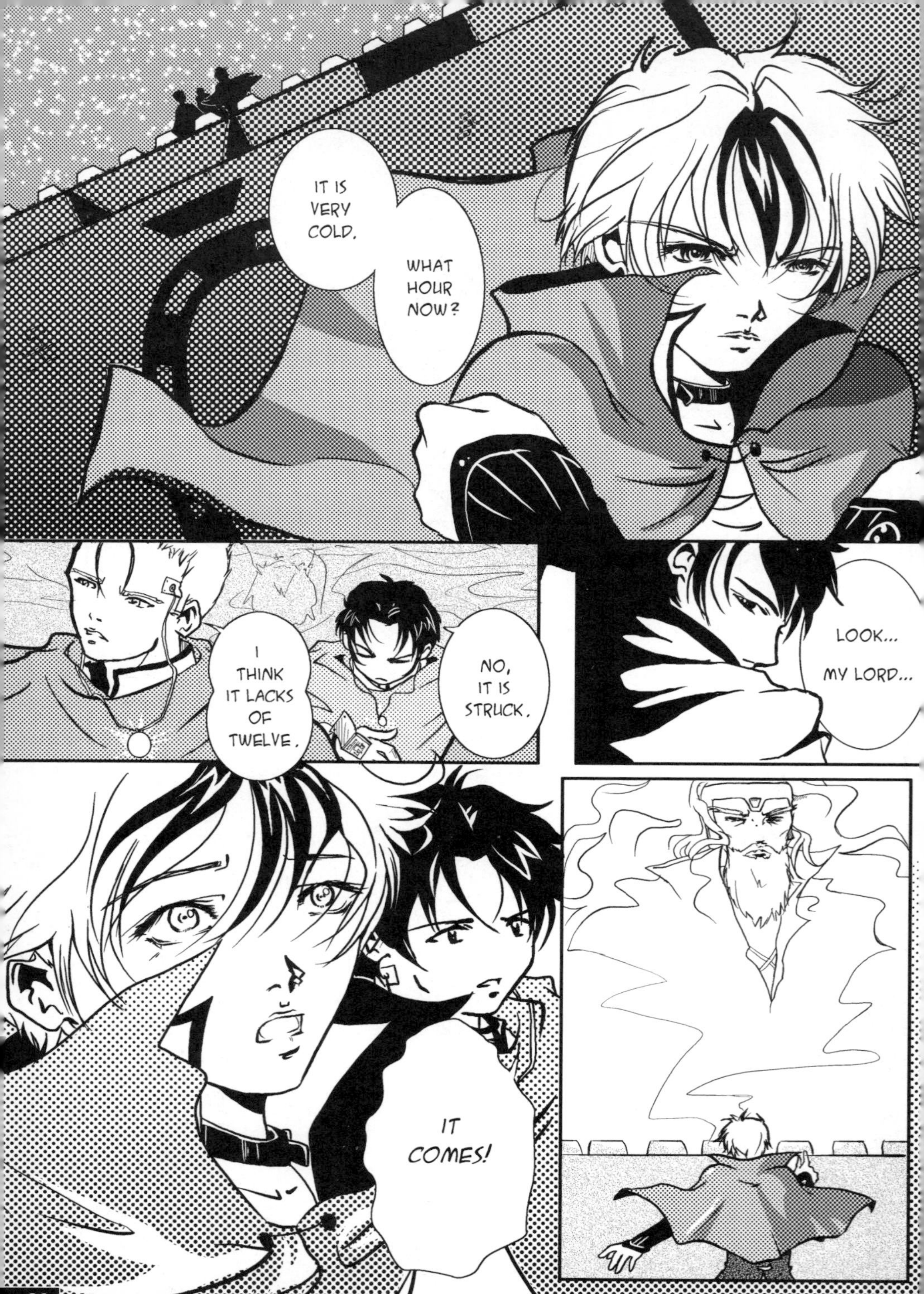
IT IS VERY COLD.
WHAT HOUR NOW?
I THINK IT LACKS OF TWELVE.
NO, IT IS STRUCK.
LOOK... MY LORD...
IT COMES!

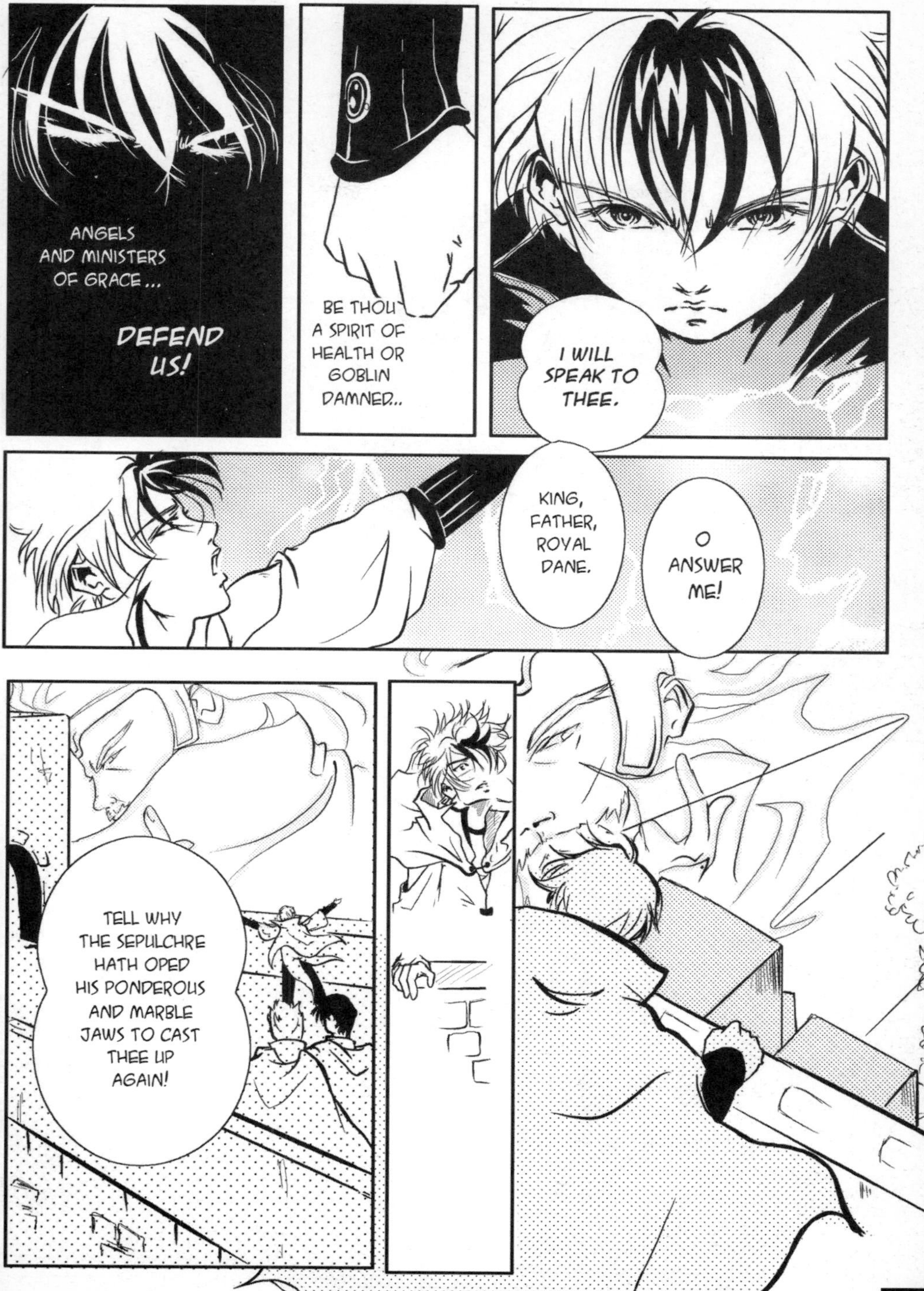
ANGELS AND MINISTERS OF GRACE...
DEFEND US!
BE THOU A SPIRIT OF HEALTH OR GOBLIN DAMNED..
I WILL SPEAK TO THEE.
KING, FATHER, ROYAL DANE.
O ANSWER ME!
TELL WHY THE SEPULCHRE HATH OPED HIS PONDEROUS AND MARBLE JAWS TO CAST THEE UP AGAIN!

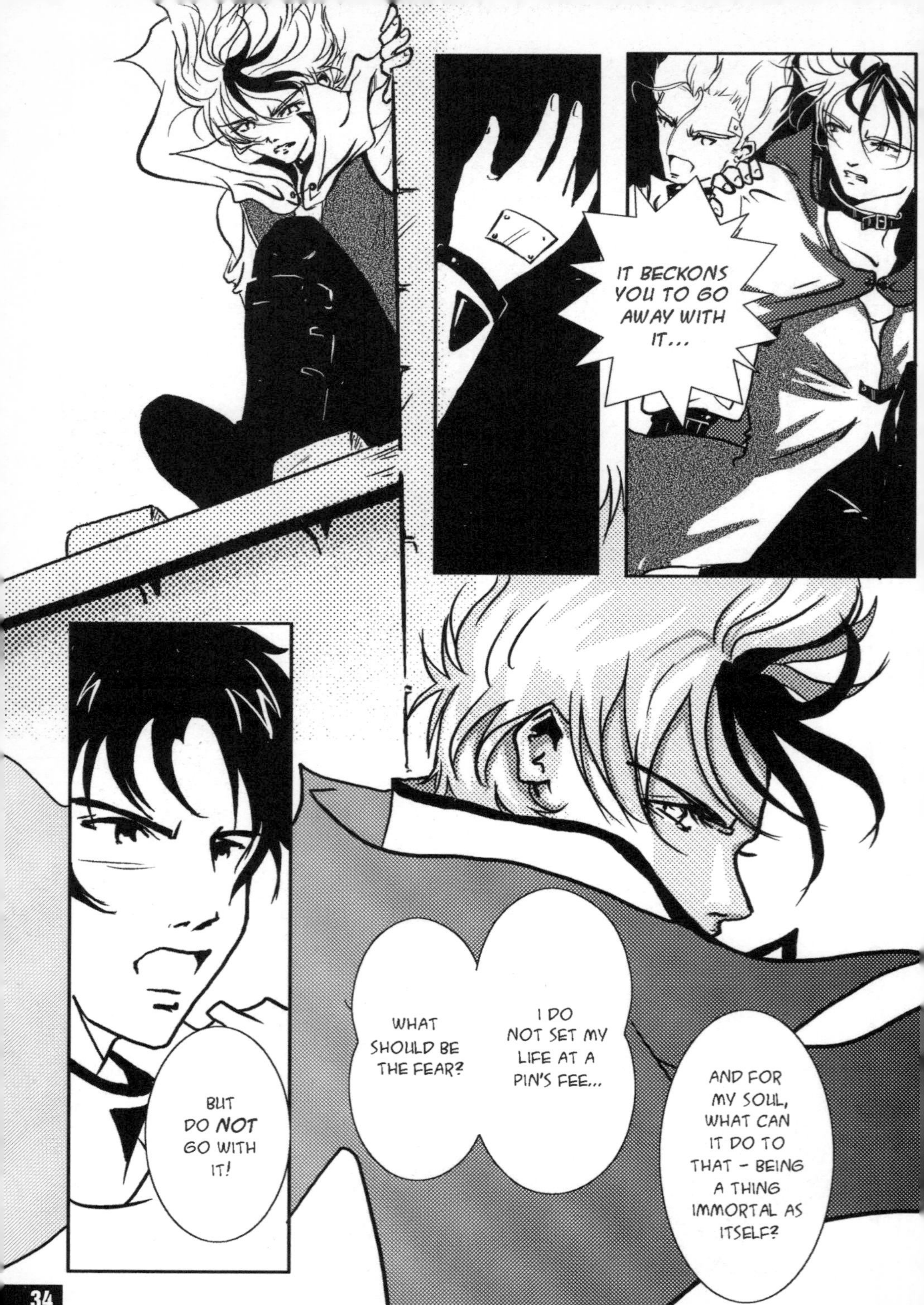
IT BECKONS YOU TO GO AWAY WITH IT...
BUT DO NOT GO WITH IT!
WHAT SHOULD BE THE FEAR?
I DO NOT SET MY LIFE AT A PIN'S FEE...
AND FOR MY SOUL, WHAT CAN IT DO TO THAT - BEING A THING IMMORTAL AS ITSELF?

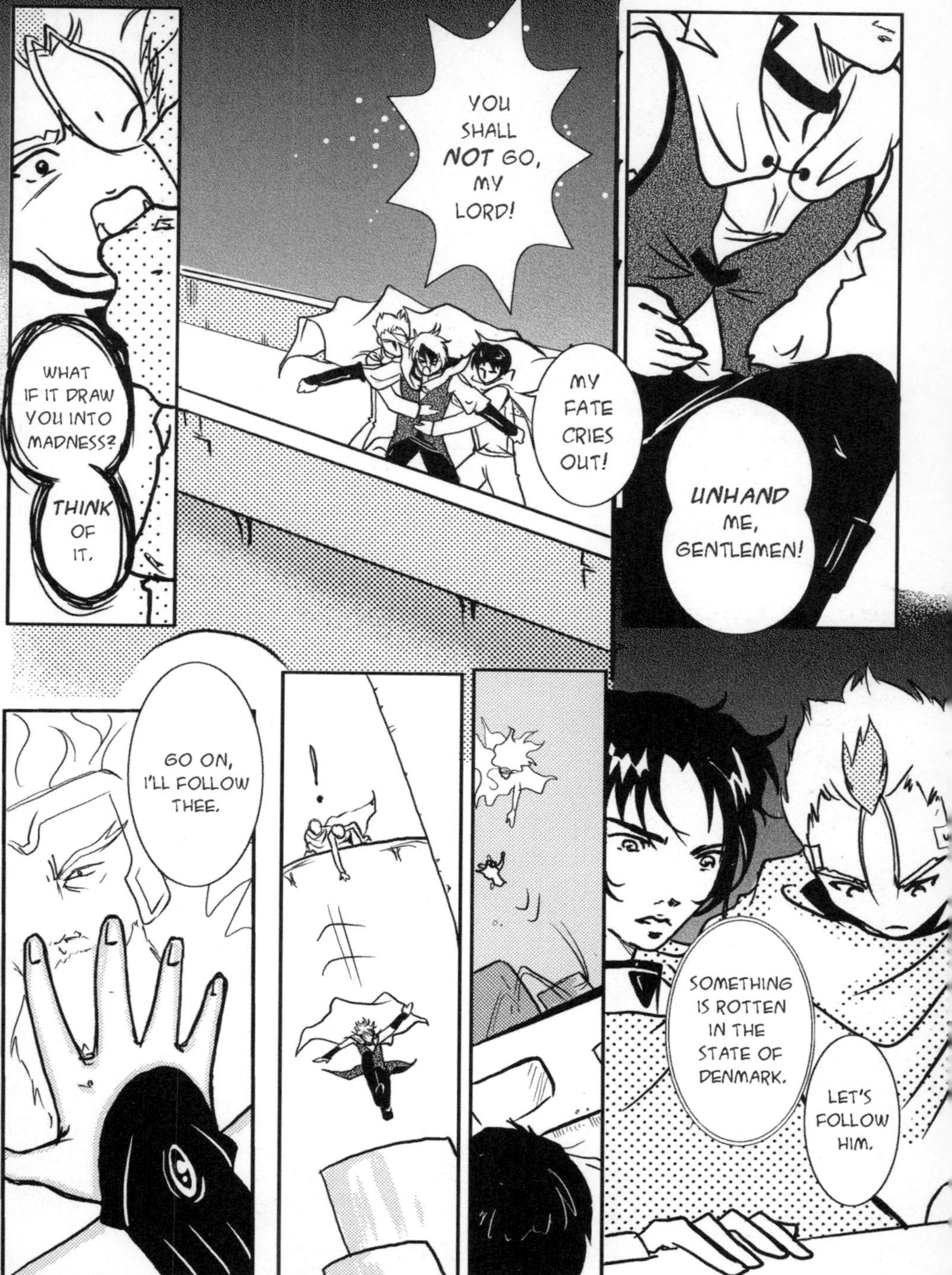
YOU SHALL NOT GO, MY LORD!
WHAT IF IT DRAW YOU INTO MADNESS?
THINK OF IT.
MY FATE CRIES OUT!
UNHAND ME, GENTLEMEN!
GO ON, I'LL FOLLOW THEE.
!
SOMETHING IS ROTTEN IN THE STATE OF DENMARK.
LET'S FOLLOW HIM.

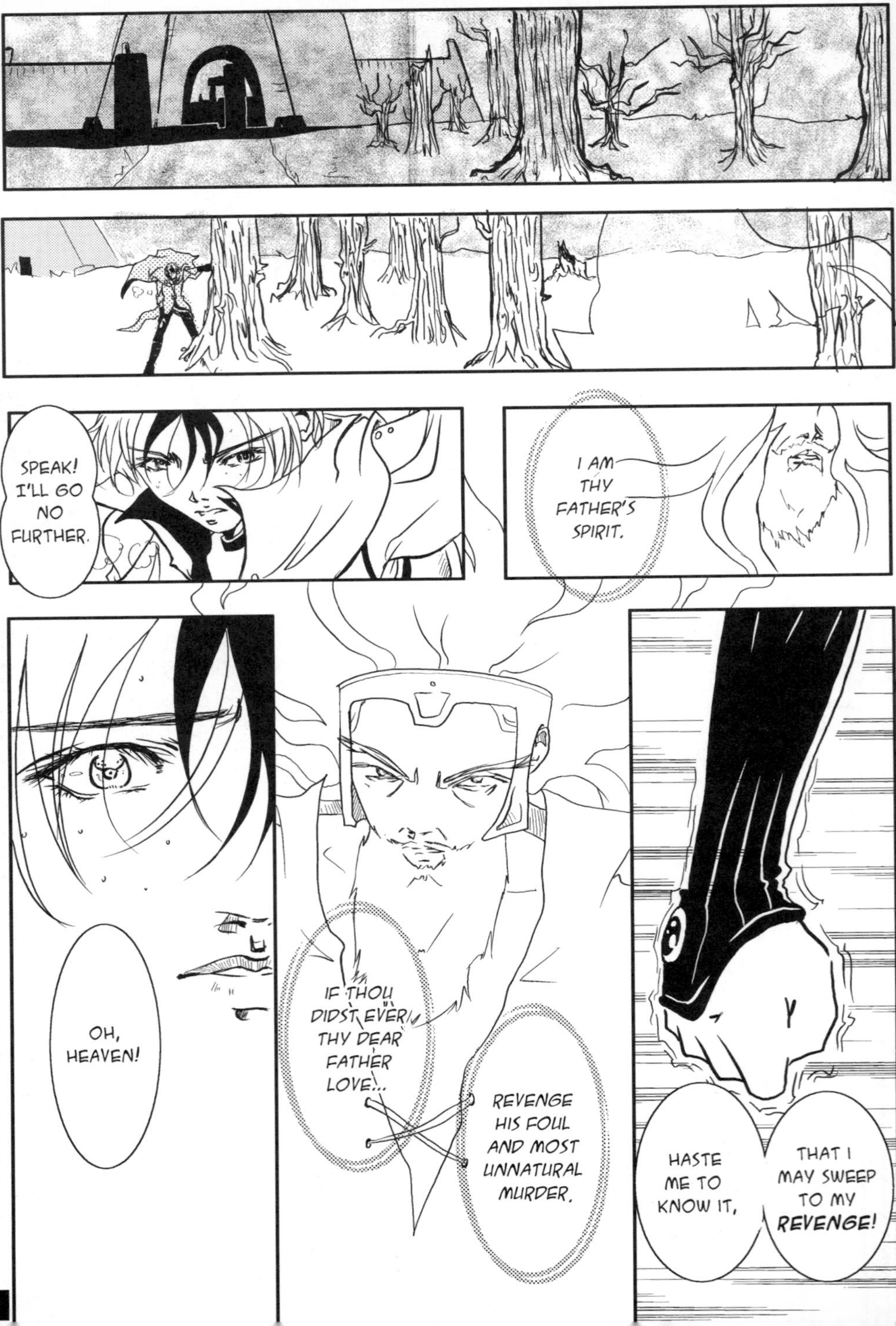
SPEAK! I'LL GO NO FURTHER.
I AM THY FATHER'S SPIRIT.
OH, HEAVEN!
IF THOU DIDST EVER THY DEAR FATHER LOVE...
REVENGE HIS FOUL AND MOST UNNATURAL MURDER.
HASTE ME TO KNOW IT,
THAT I MAY SWEEP TO MY REVENGE!

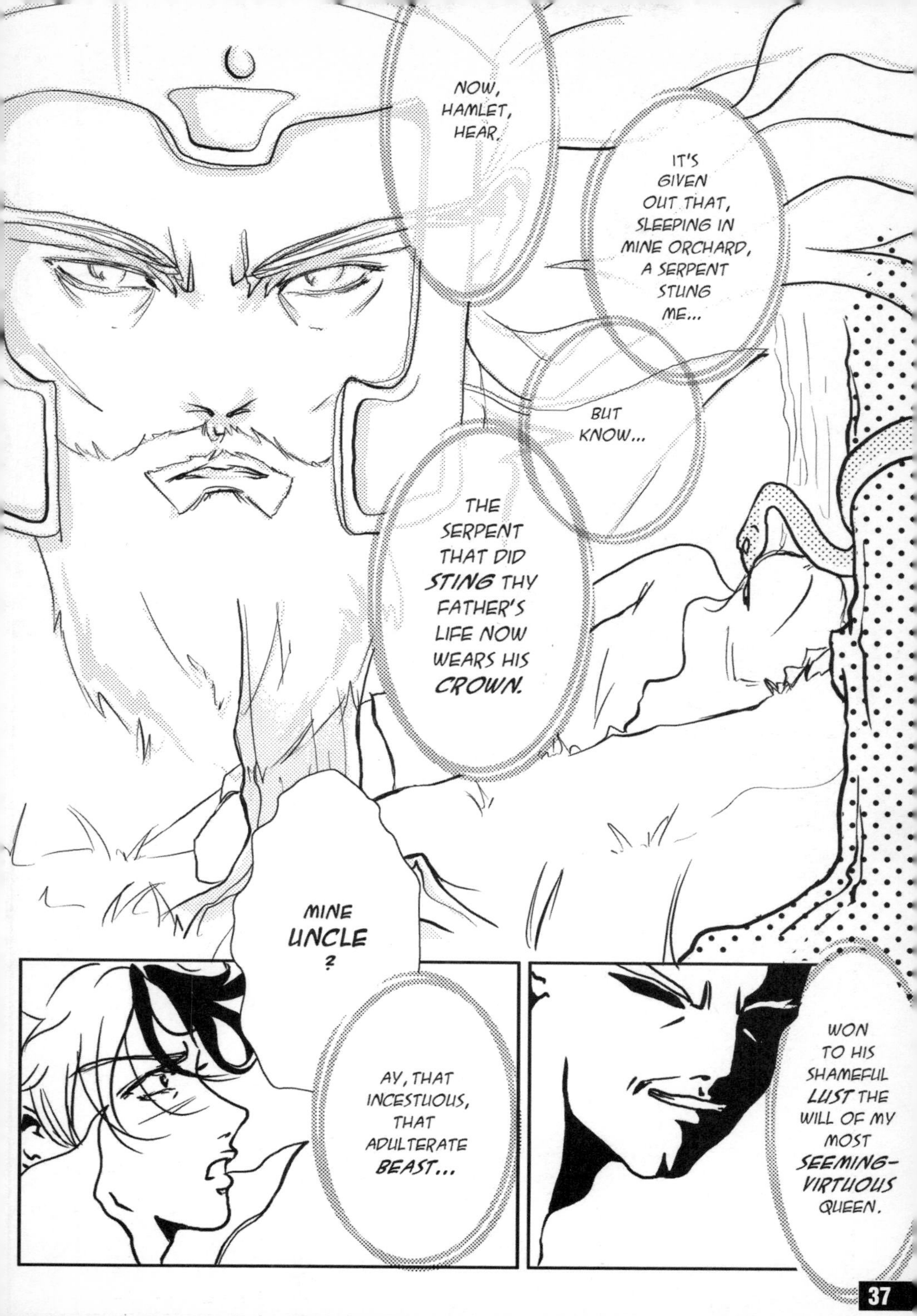
NOW, HAMLET, HEAR.
IT'S GIVEN OUT THAT, SLEEPING IN MINE ORCHARD, A SERPENT STUNG ME...
BUT KNOW...
THE SERPENT THAT DID STING THY FATHER'S LIFE NOW WEARS HIS CROWN.
MINE UNCLE?
AY, THAT INCESTUOUS, THAT ADULTERATE BEAST...
WON TO HIS SHAMEFUL LUST THE WILL OF MY MOST SEEMING-VIRTUOUS QUEEN.

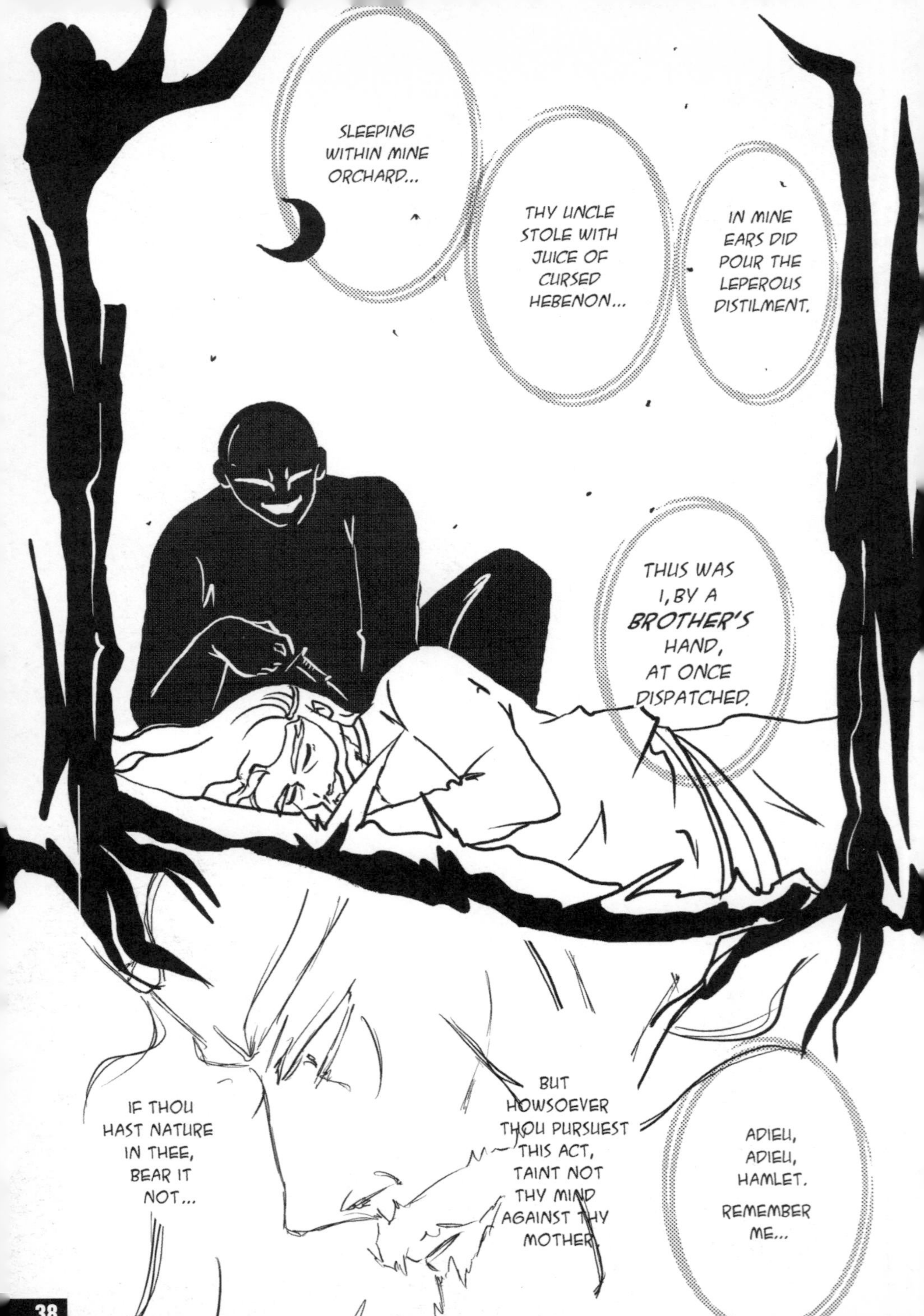
SLEEPING WITHIN MINE ORCHARD...
THY UNCLE STOLE WITH JUICE OF CURSED HEBENON...
IN MINE EARS DID POUR THE LEPEROUS DISTILMENT.
THUS WAS I, BY A BROTHER'S HAND, AT ONCE DISPATCHED.
IF THOU HAST NATURE IN THEE, BEAR IT NOT...
BUT HOWSOEVER THOU PURSUEST THIS ACT, TAINT NOT THY MIND AGAINST THY MOTHER.
ADIEU, ADIEU, HAMLET.
REMEMBER ME...

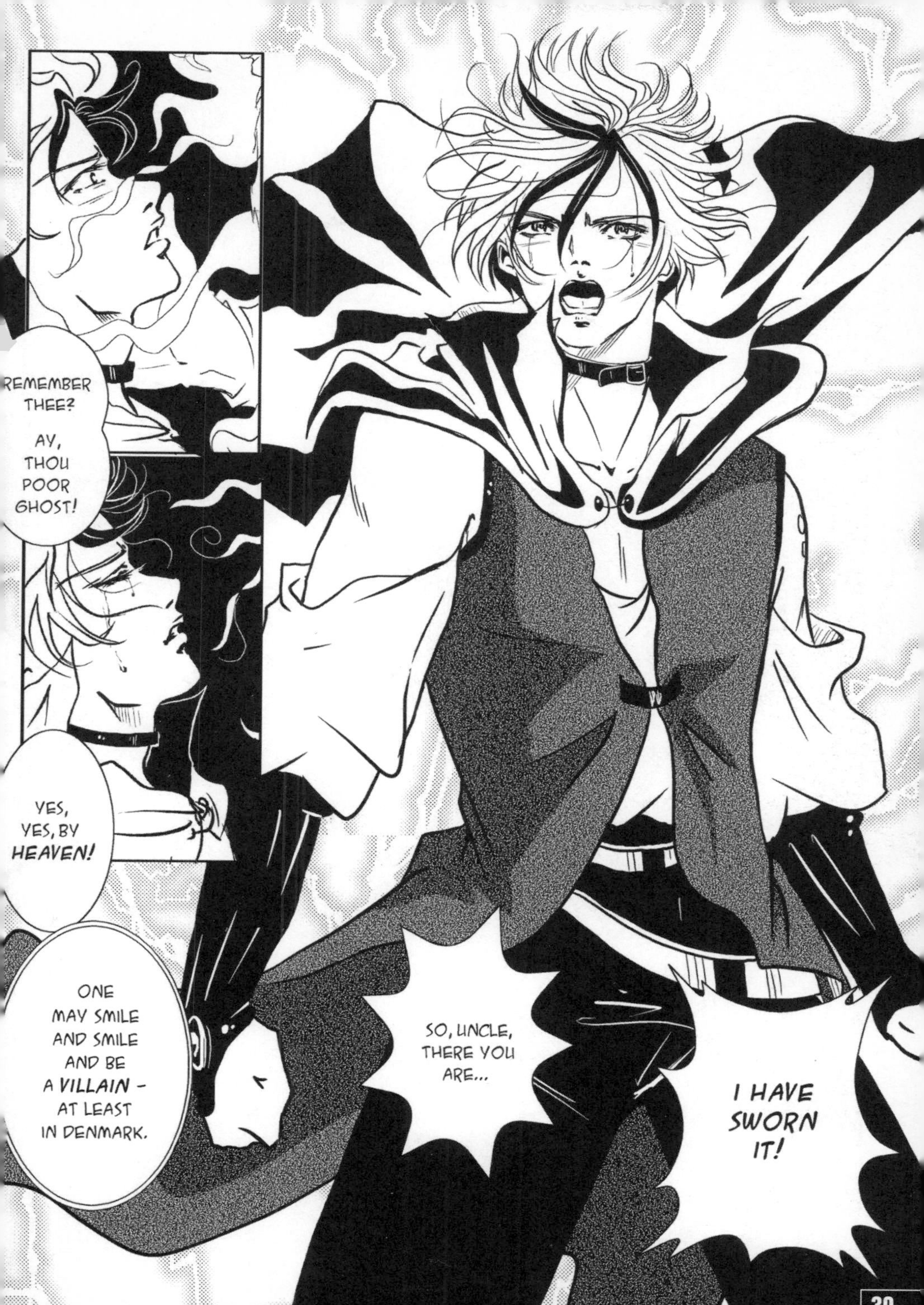
REMEMBER THEE?
AY, THOU POOR GHOST!
YES, YES, BY HEAVEN!
ONE MAY SMILE AND SMILE AND BE A VILLAIN - AT LEAST IN DENMARK.
SO, UNCLE, THERE YOU ARE...
I HAVE SWORN IT!

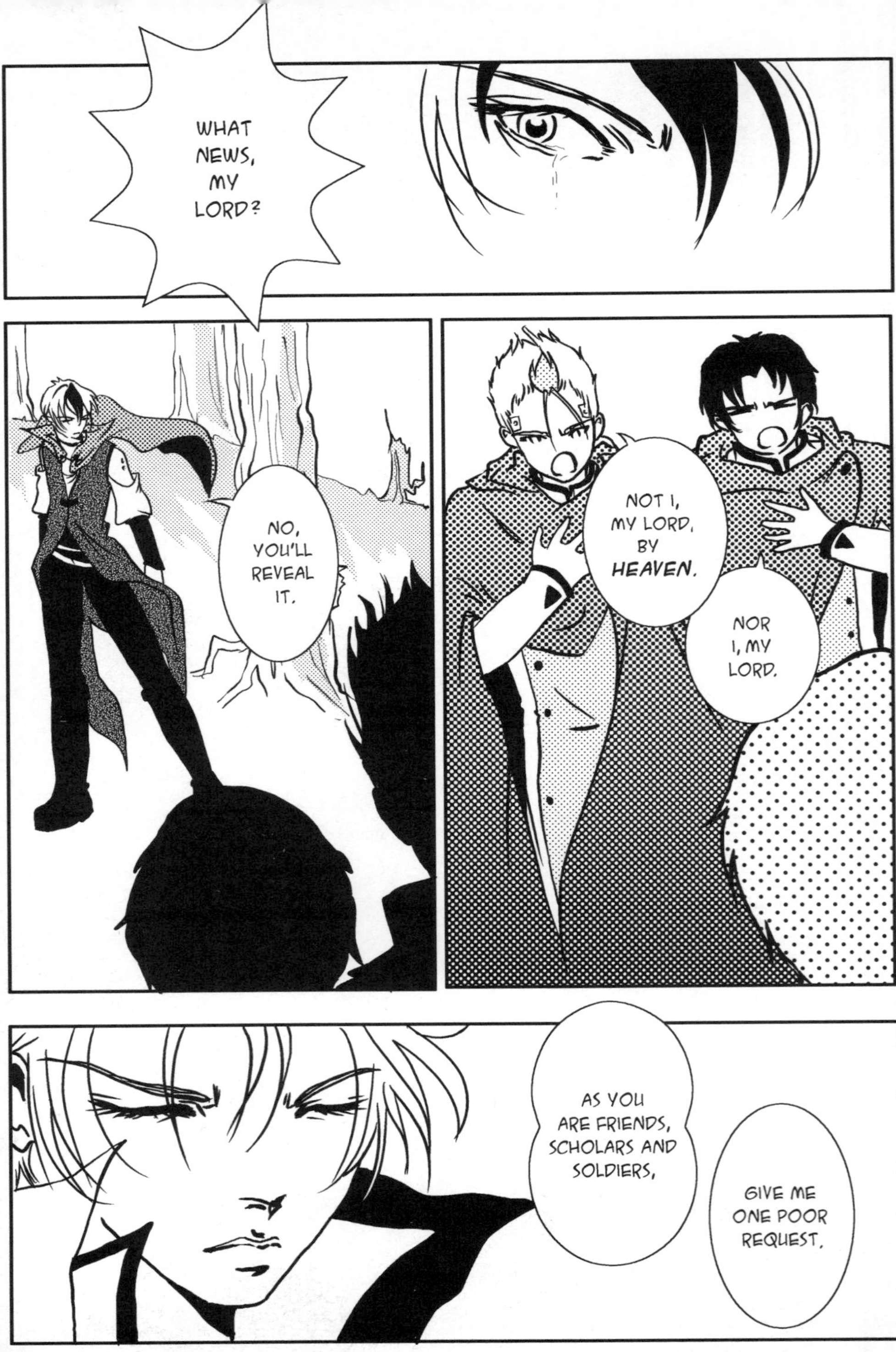
WHAT NEWS, MY LORD?
NO, YOU'LL REVEAL IT.
NOT I, MY LORD, BY HEAVEN.
NOR I, MY LORD.
AS YOU ARE FRIENDS, SCHOLARS AND SOLDIERS,
GIVE ME ONE POOR REQUEST.

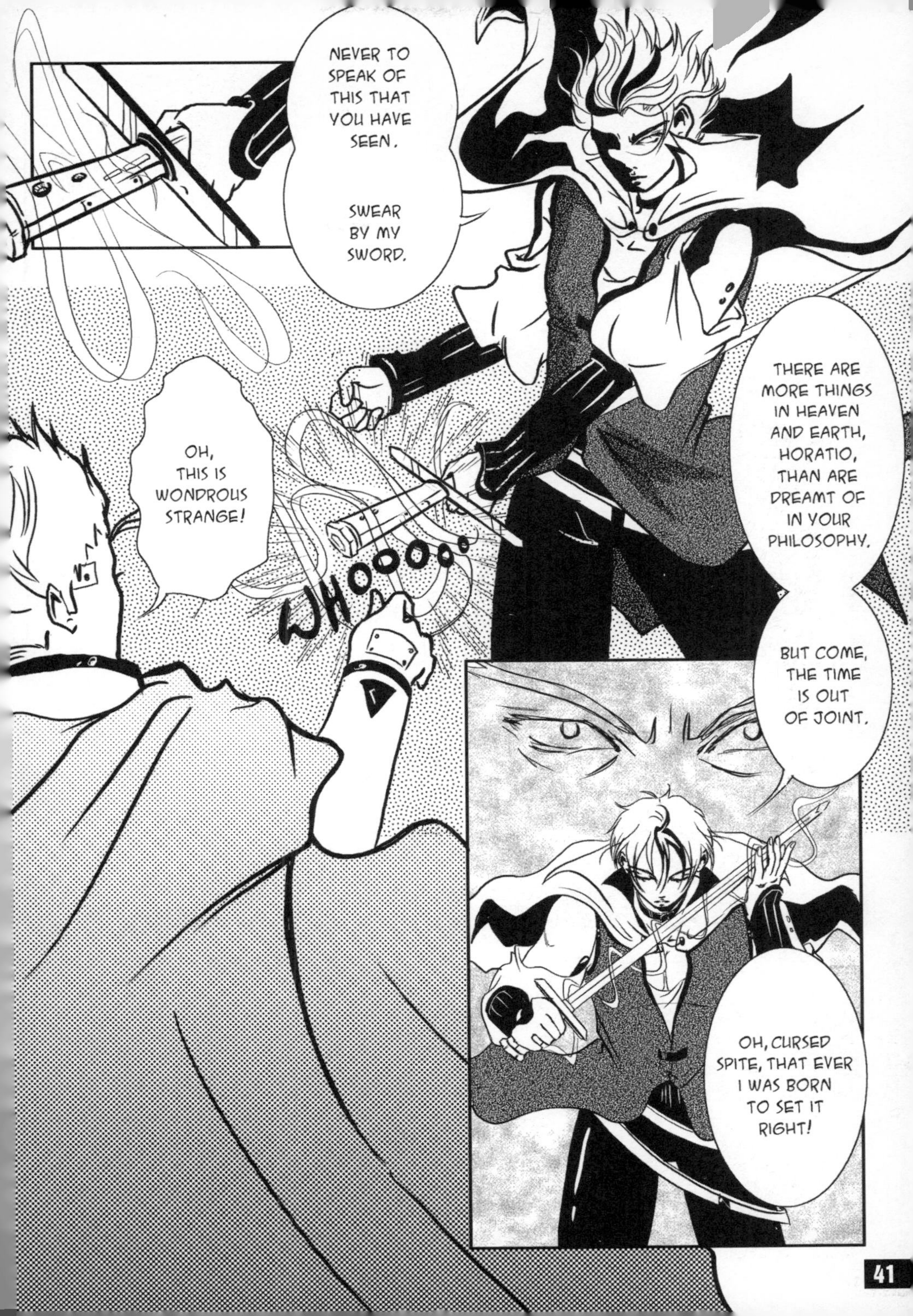
NEVER TO SPEAK OF THIS THAT YOU HAVE SEEN.
SWEAR BY MY SWORD.
THERE ARE MORE THINGS IN HEAVEN AND EARTH, HORATIO, THAN ARE DREAMT OF IN YOUR PHILOSOPHY.
OH, THIS IS WONDROUS STRANGE!
WHOOOOO
BUT COME, THE TIME IS OUT OF JOINT.
OH, CURSED SPITE, THAT EVER I WAS BORN TO SET IT RIGHT!

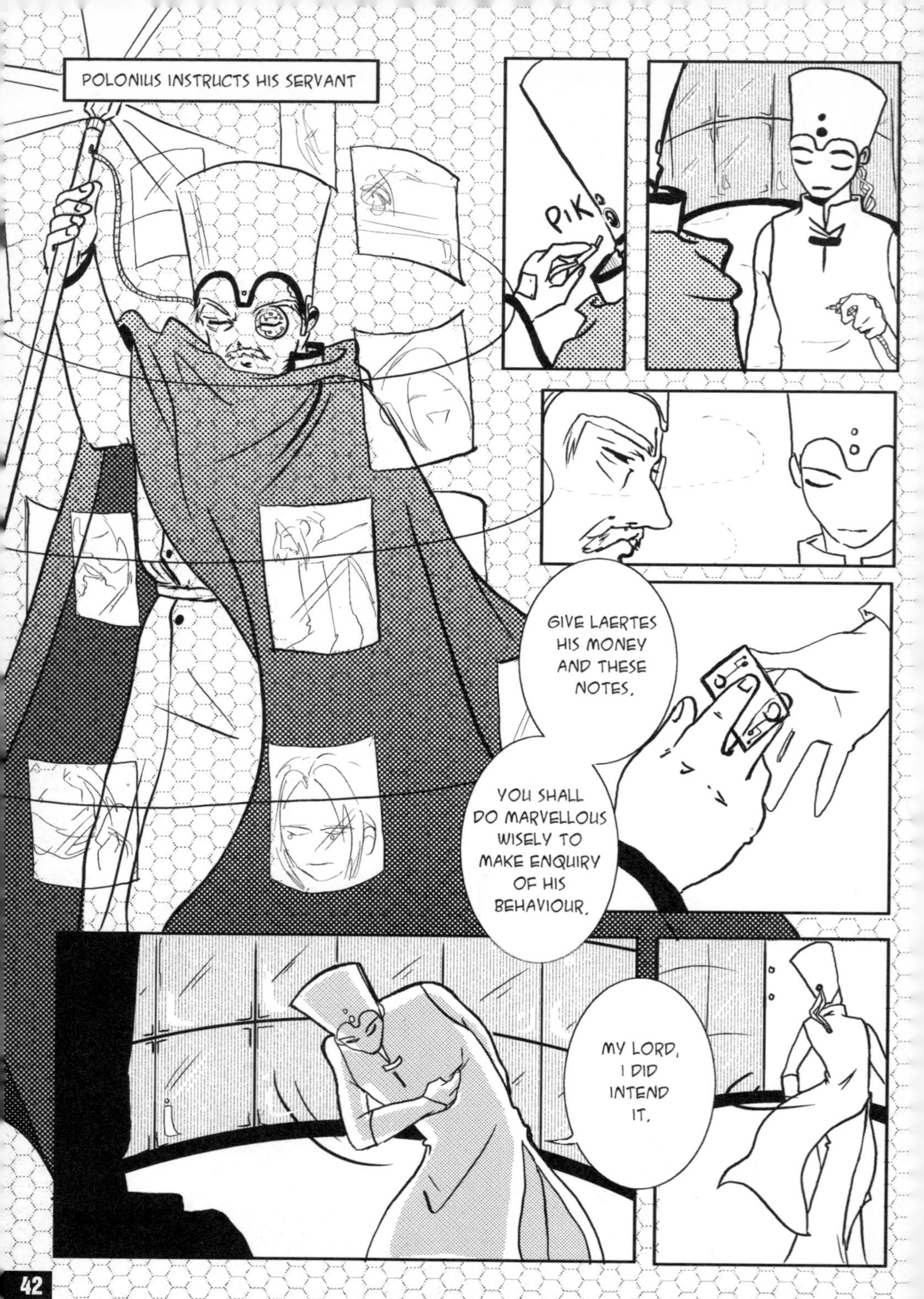
POLONIUS INSTRUCTS HIS SERVANT
PIK
GIVE LAERTES HIS MONEY AND THESE NOTES.
YOU SHALL DO MARVELLOUS WISELY TO MAKE ENQUIRY OF HIS BEHAVIOUR.
MY LORD, I DID INTEND IT.

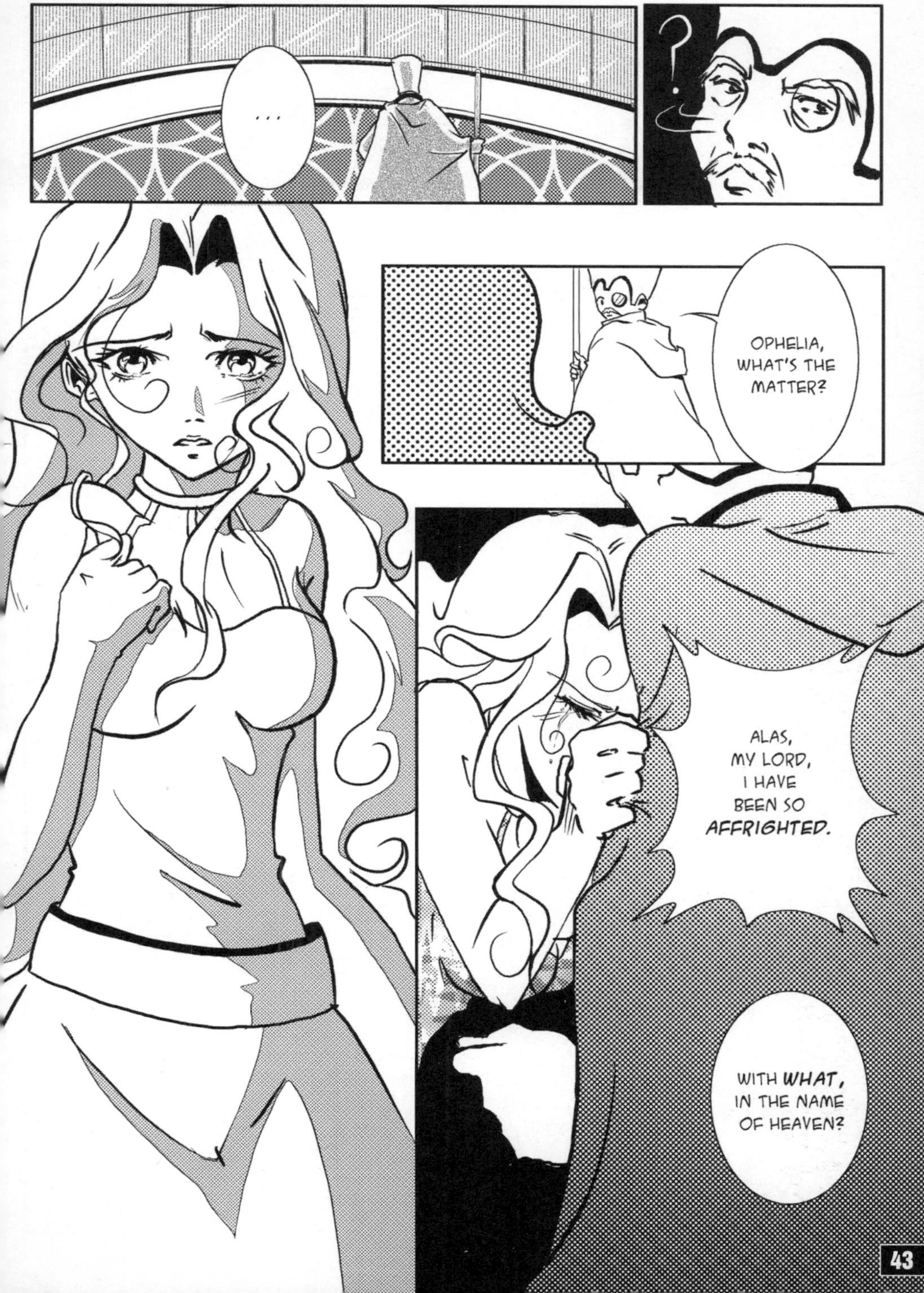

...
?
OPHELIA, WHAT'S THE MATTER?
ALAS, MY LORD, I HAVE BEEN SO AFFRIGHTED.
WITH WHAT, IN THE NAME OF HEAVEN?

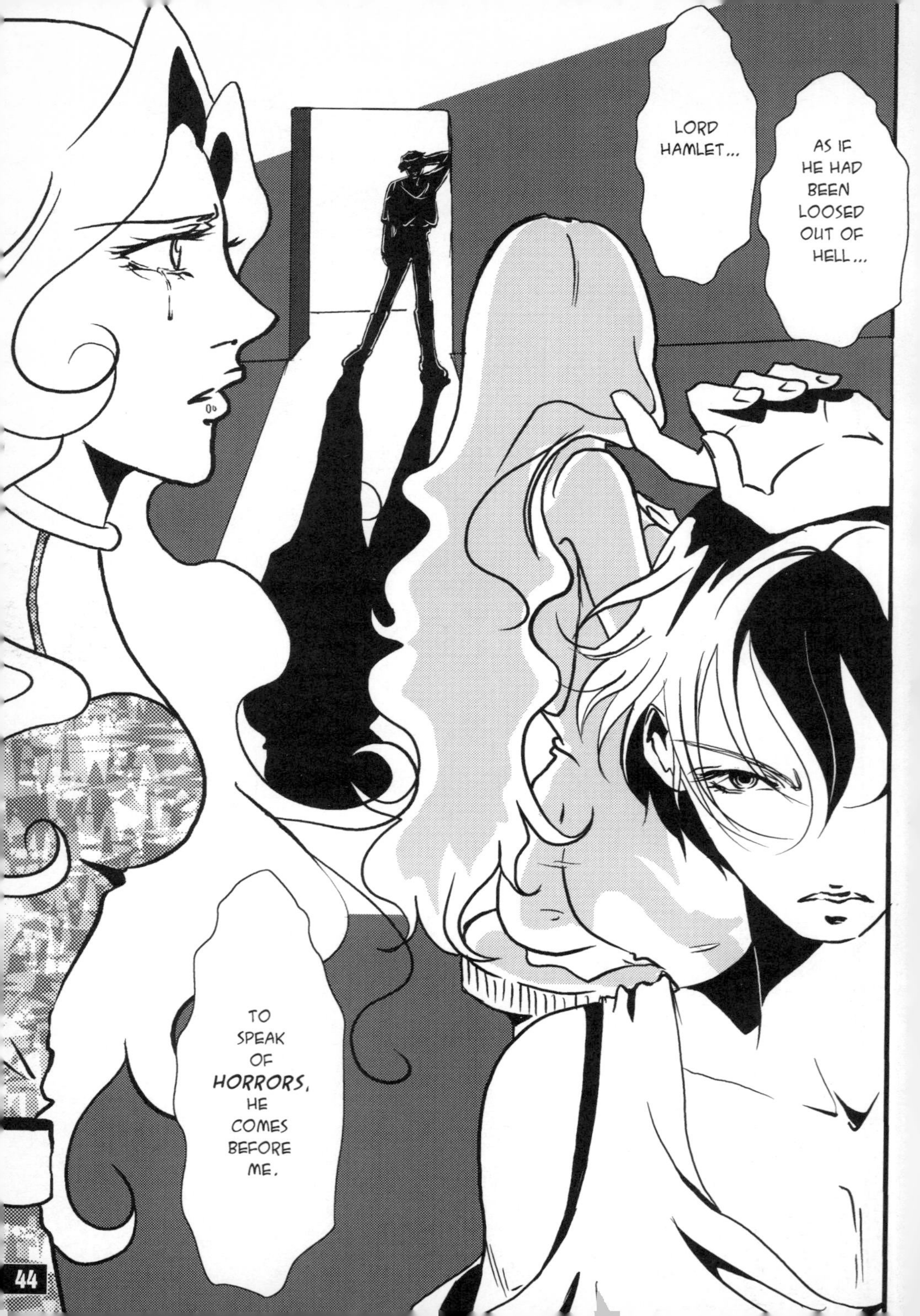
LORD HAMLET...
AS IF HE HAD BEEN LOOSED OUT OF HELL...
TO SPEAK OF HORRORS, HE COMES BEFORE ME.

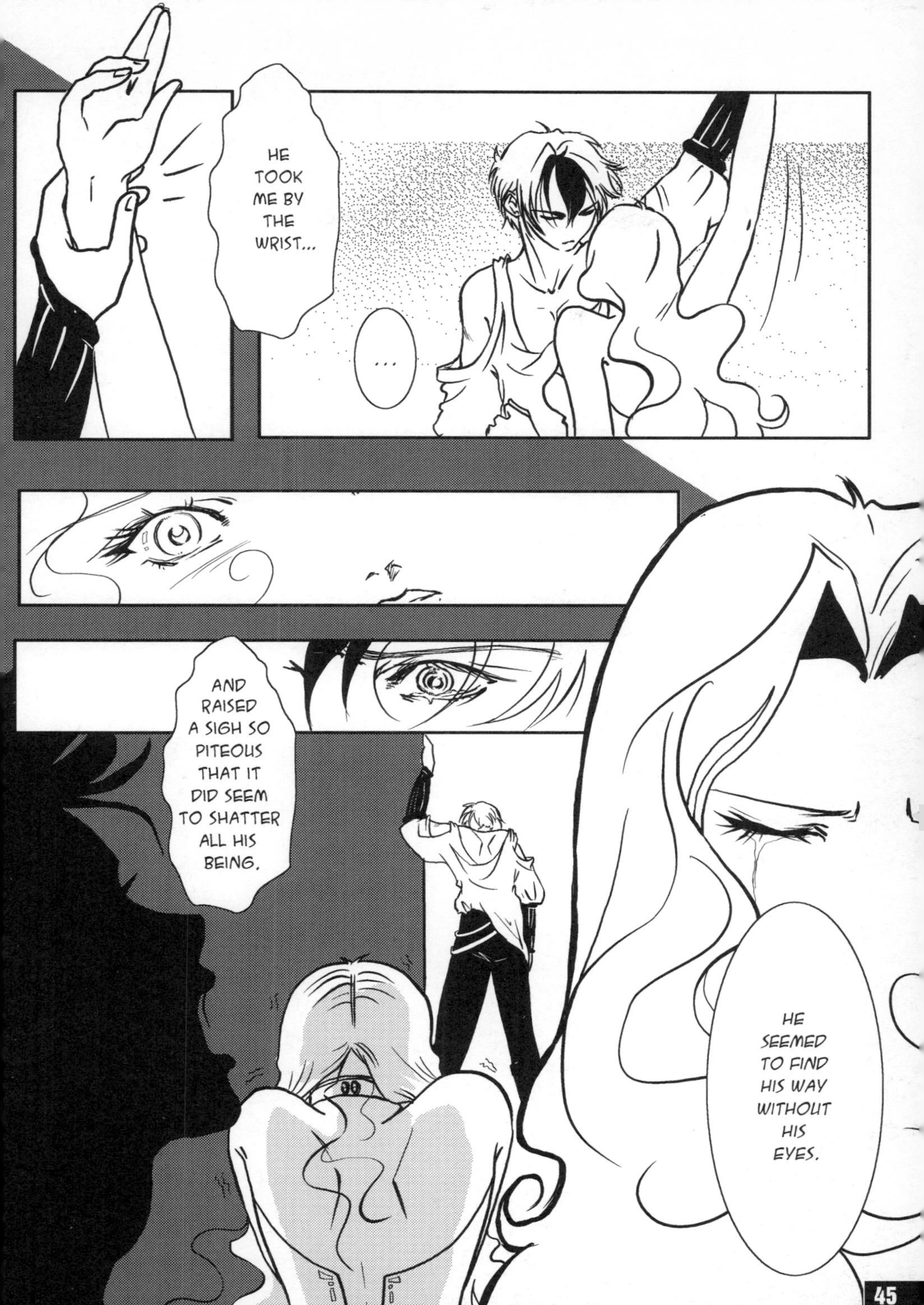
HE TOOK ME BY THE WRIST...
...
AND RAISED A SIGH SO PITEOUS THAT IT DID SEEM TO SHATTER ALL HIS BEING.
HE SEEMED TO FIND HIS WAY WITHOUT HIS EYES.

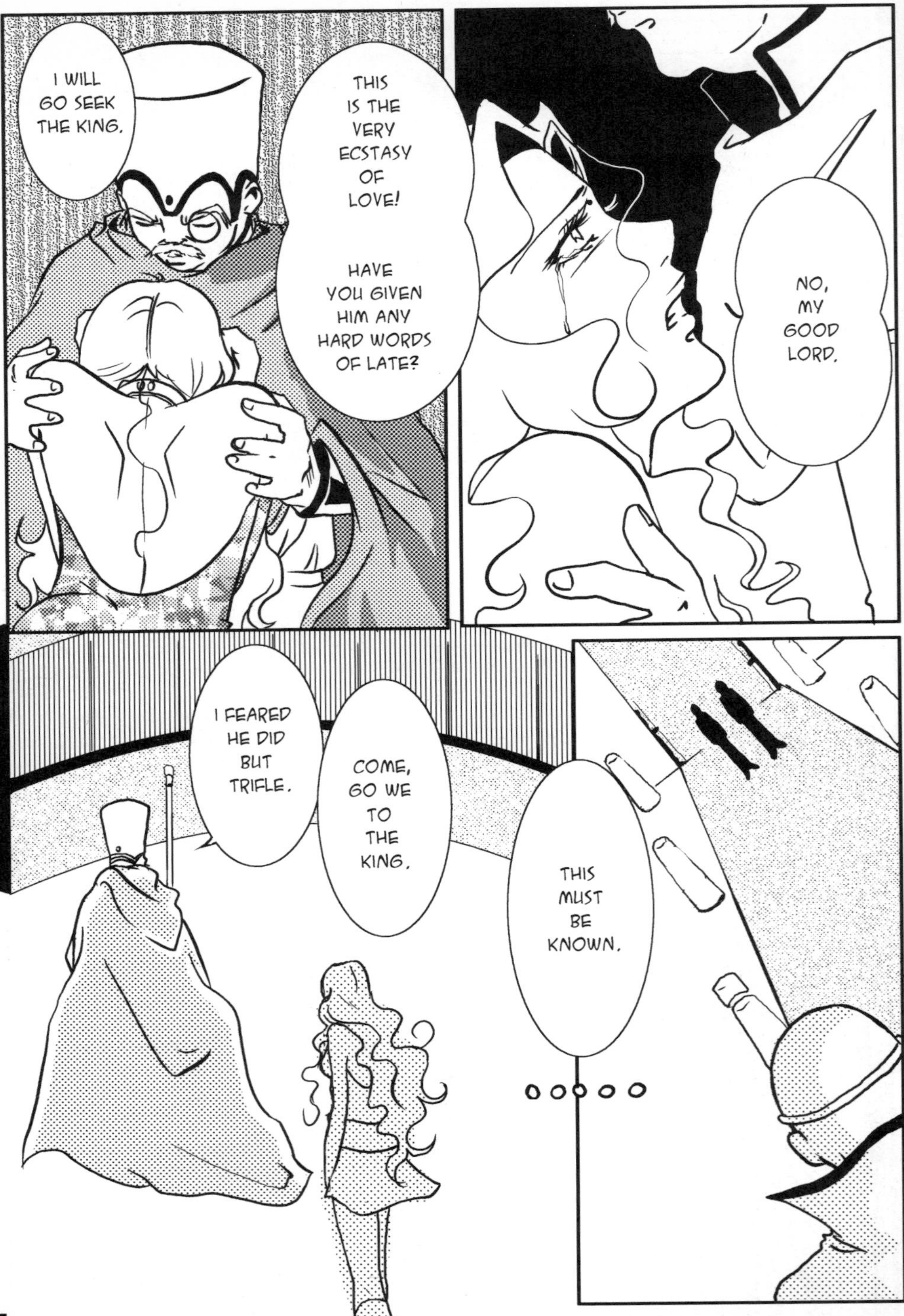
I WILL GO SEEK THE KING.
THIS IS THE VERY ECSTASY OF LOVE!
HAVE YOU GIVEN HIM ANY HARD WORDS OF LATE?
NO, MY GOOD LORD.
I FEARED HE DID BUT TRIFLE.
COME, GO WE TO THE KING.
THIS MUST BE KNOWN.
OOOOO

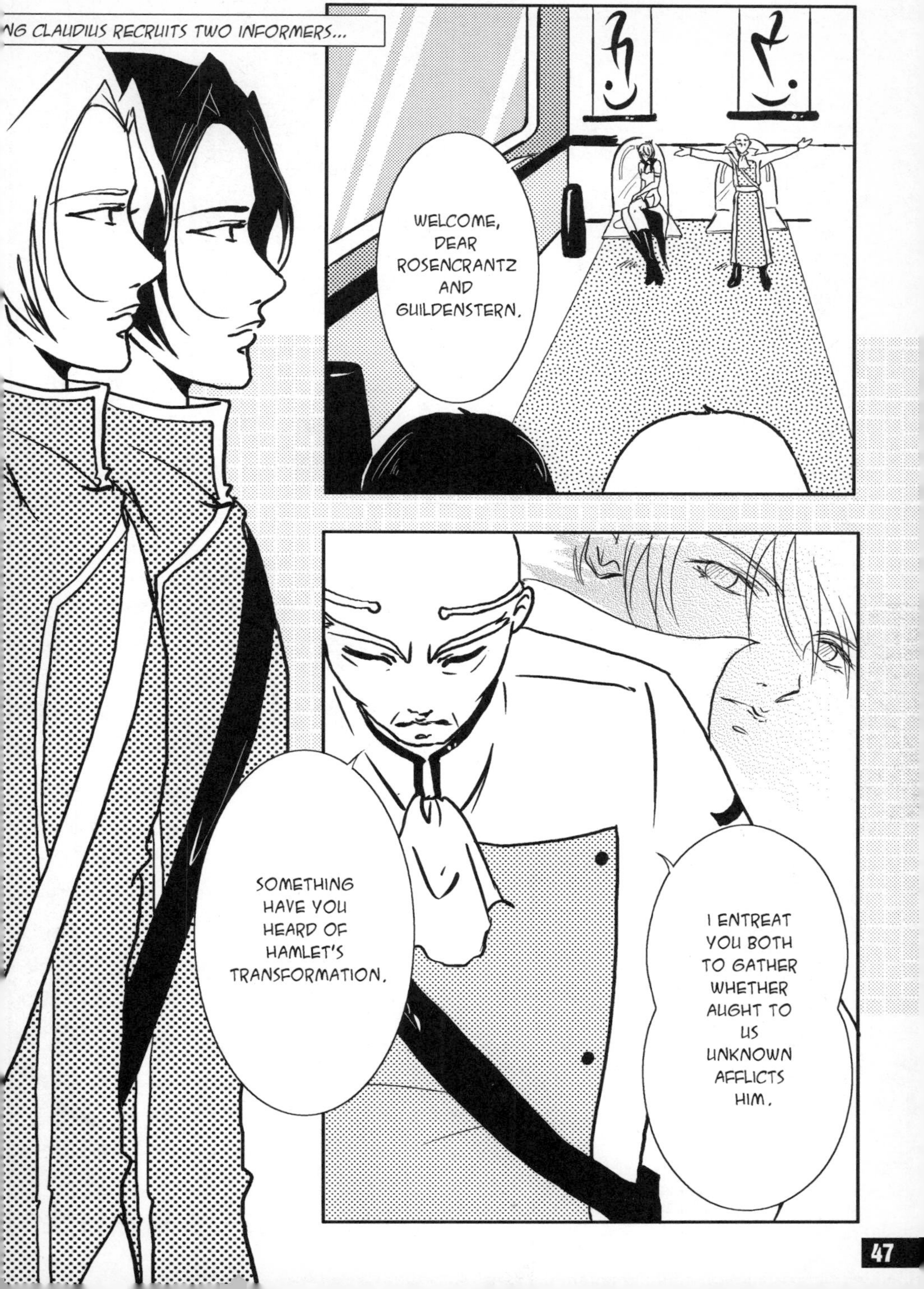
NG CLAUDIUS RECRUITS TWO INFORMERS...
WELCOME, DEAR ROSENCRANTZ AND GUILDENSTERN.
SOMETHING HAVE YOU HEARD OF HAMLET'S TRANSFORMATION.
I ENTREAT YOU BOTH TO GATHER WHETHER AUGHT TO US UNKNOWN AFFLICTS HIM.

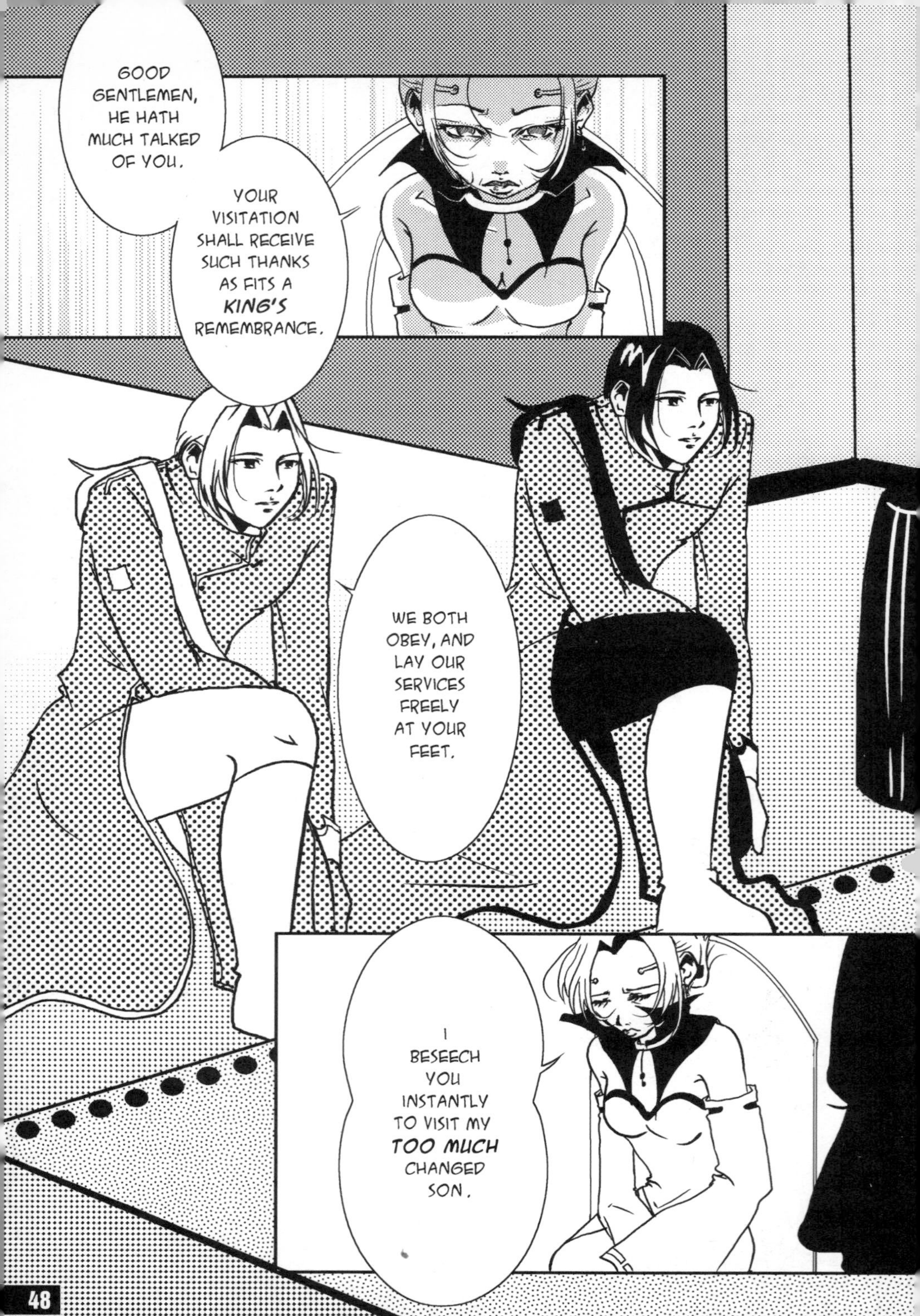
GOOD GENTLEMEN, HE HATH MUCH TALKED OF YOU.
YOUR VISITATION SHALL RECEIVE SUCH THANKS AS FITS A **KING'S** REMEMBRANCE.
WE BOTH OBEY, AND LAY OUR SERVICES FREELY AT YOUR FEET.
I BESEECH YOU INSTANTLY TO VISIT MY **TOO MUCH** CHANGED SON.

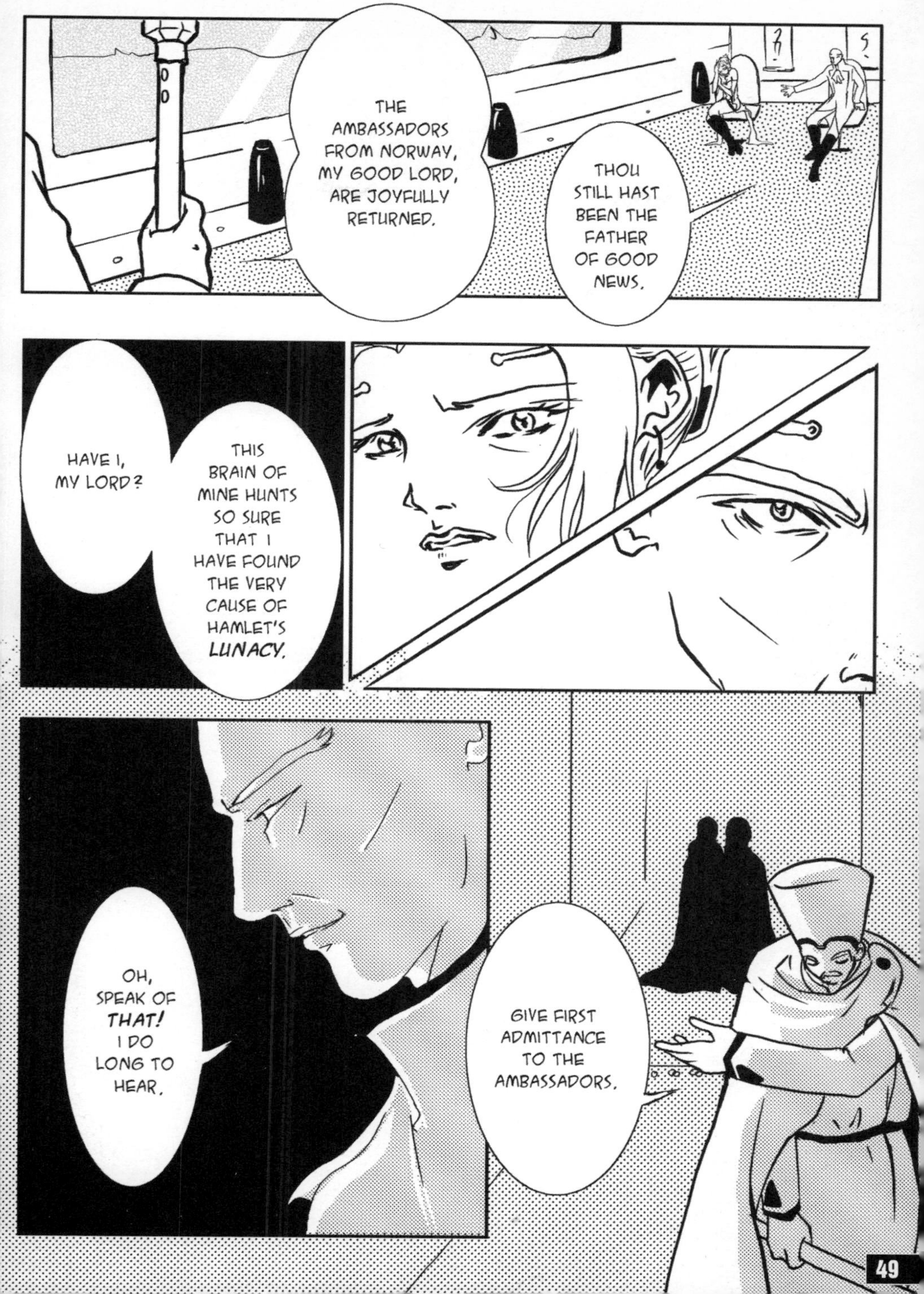
THE AMBASSADORS FROM NORWAY, MY GOOD LORD, ARE JOYFULLY RETURNED.
THOU STILL HAST BEEN THE FATHER OF GOOD NEWS.
HAVE I, MY LORD?
THIS BRAIN OF MINE HUNTS SO SURE THAT I HAVE FOUND THE VERY CAUSE OF HAMLET'S *LUNACY.*
OH, SPEAK OF *THAT!* I DO LONG TO HEAR.
GIVE FIRST ADMITTANCE TO THE AMBASSADORS.

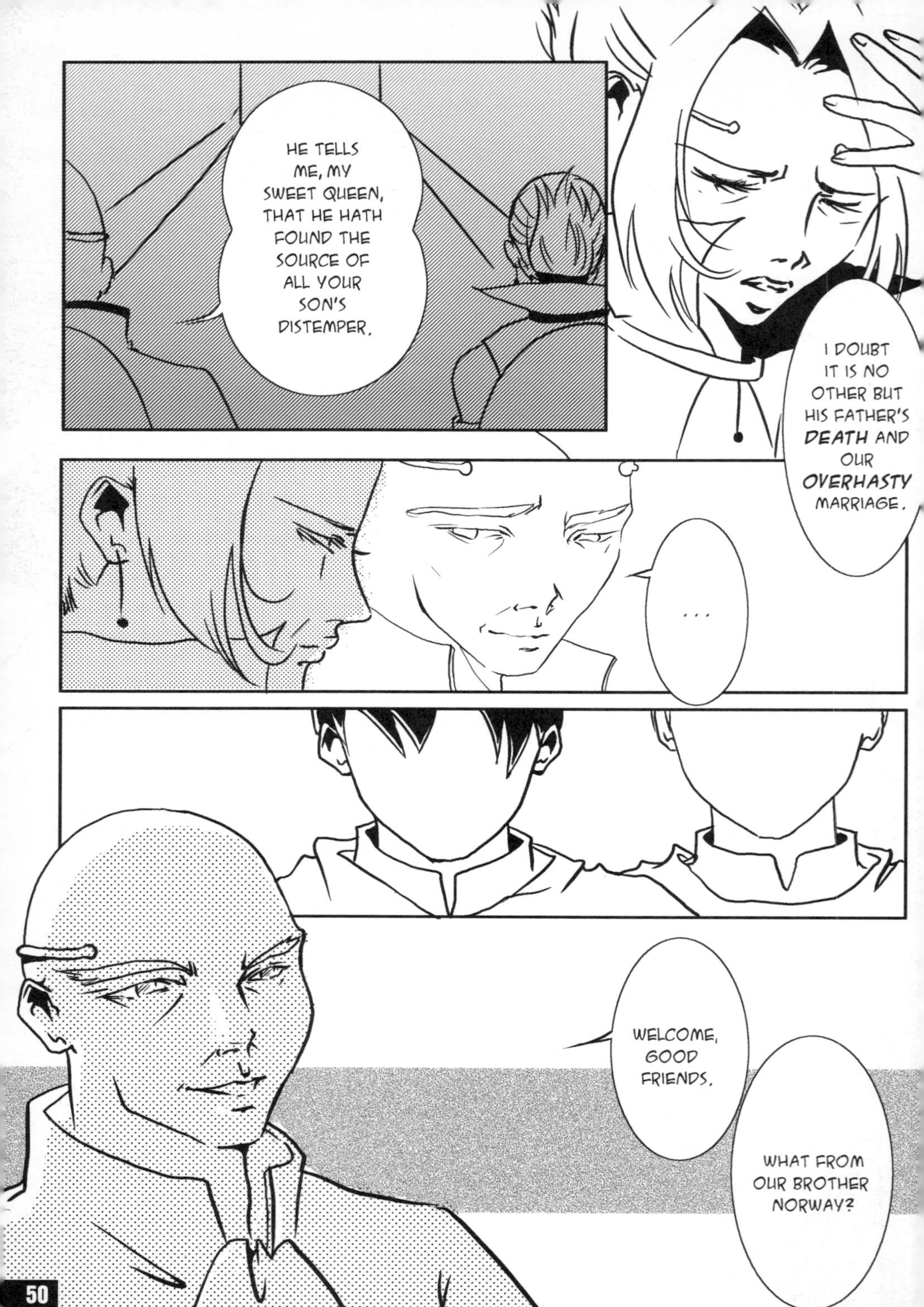
HE TELLS ME, MY SWEET QUEEN, THAT HE HATH FOUND THE SOURCE OF ALL YOUR SON'S DISTEMPER.
I DOUBT IT IS NO OTHER BUT HIS FATHER'S DEATH AND OUR OVERHASTY MARRIAGE.
...
WELCOME, GOOD FRIENDS.
WHAT FROM OUR BROTHER NORWAY?

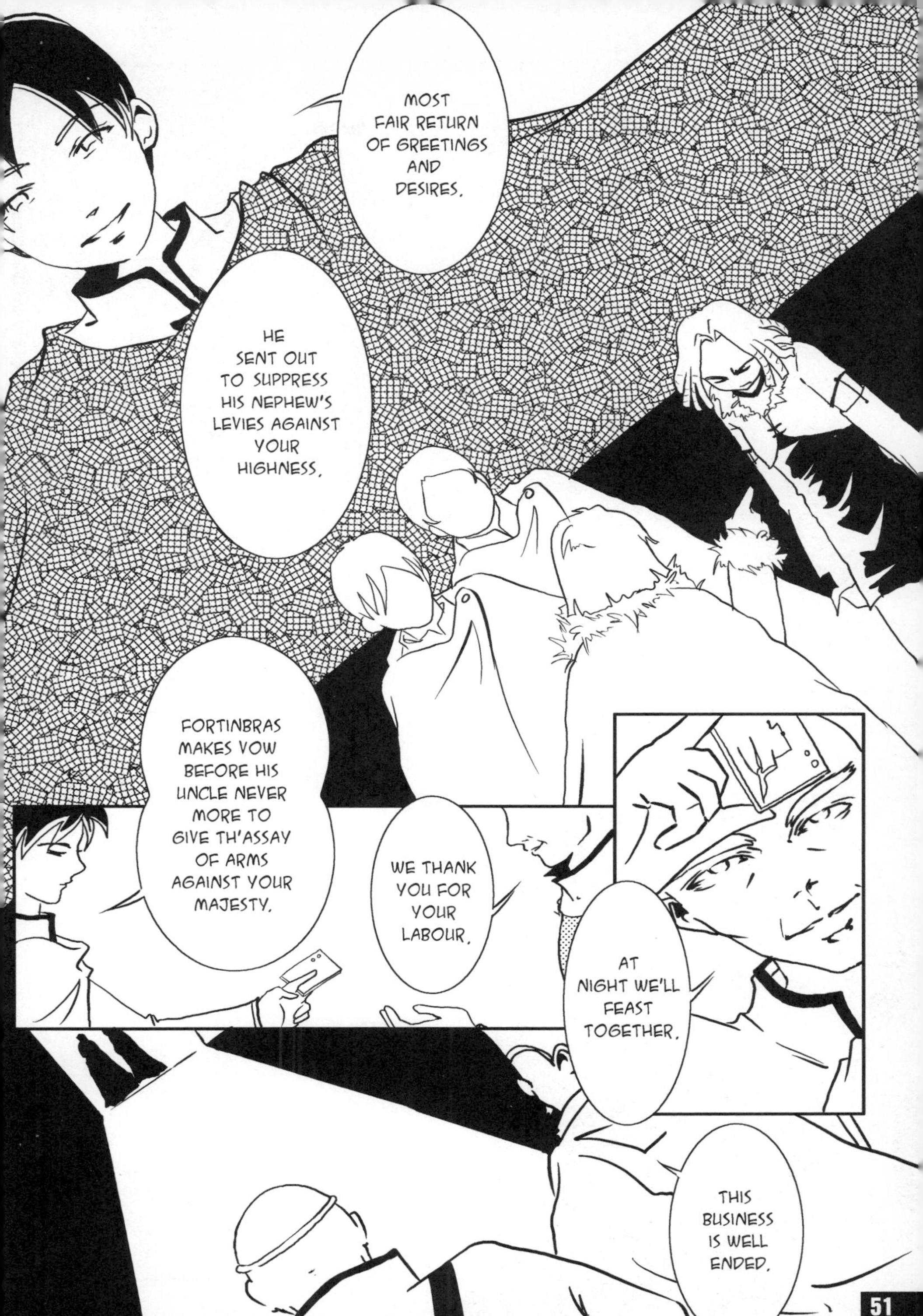
MOST FAIR RETURN OF GREETINGS AND DESIRES.
HE SENT OUT TO SUPPRESS HIS NEPHEW'S LEVIES AGAINST YOUR HIGHNESS.
FORTINBRAS MAKES VOW BEFORE HIS UNCLE NEVER MORE TO GIVE TH'ASSAY OF ARMS AGAINST YOUR MAJESTY.
WE THANK YOU FOR YOUR LABOUR.
AT NIGHT WE'LL FEAST TOGETHER.
THIS BUSINESS IS WELL ENDED.

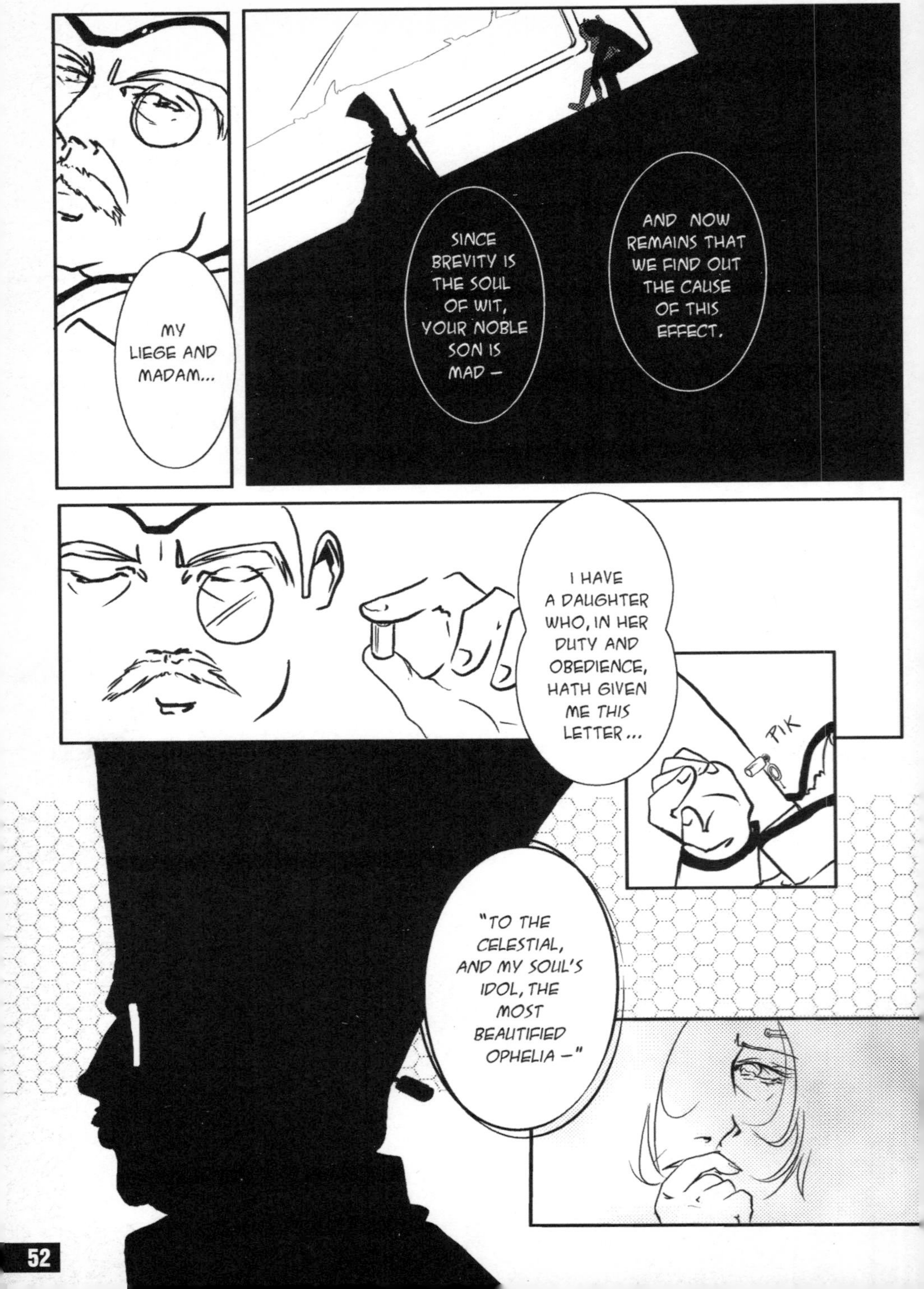
MY LIEGE AND MADAM...
SINCE BREVITY IS THE SOUL OF WIT, YOUR NOBLE SON IS MAD –
AND NOW REMAINS THAT WE FIND OUT THE CAUSE OF THIS EFFECT.
I HAVE A DAUGHTER WHO, IN HER DUTY AND OBEDIENCE, HATH GIVEN ME THIS LETTER...
PIK
"TO THE CELESTIAL, AND MY SOUL'S IDOL, THE MOST BEAUTIFIED OPHELIA –"

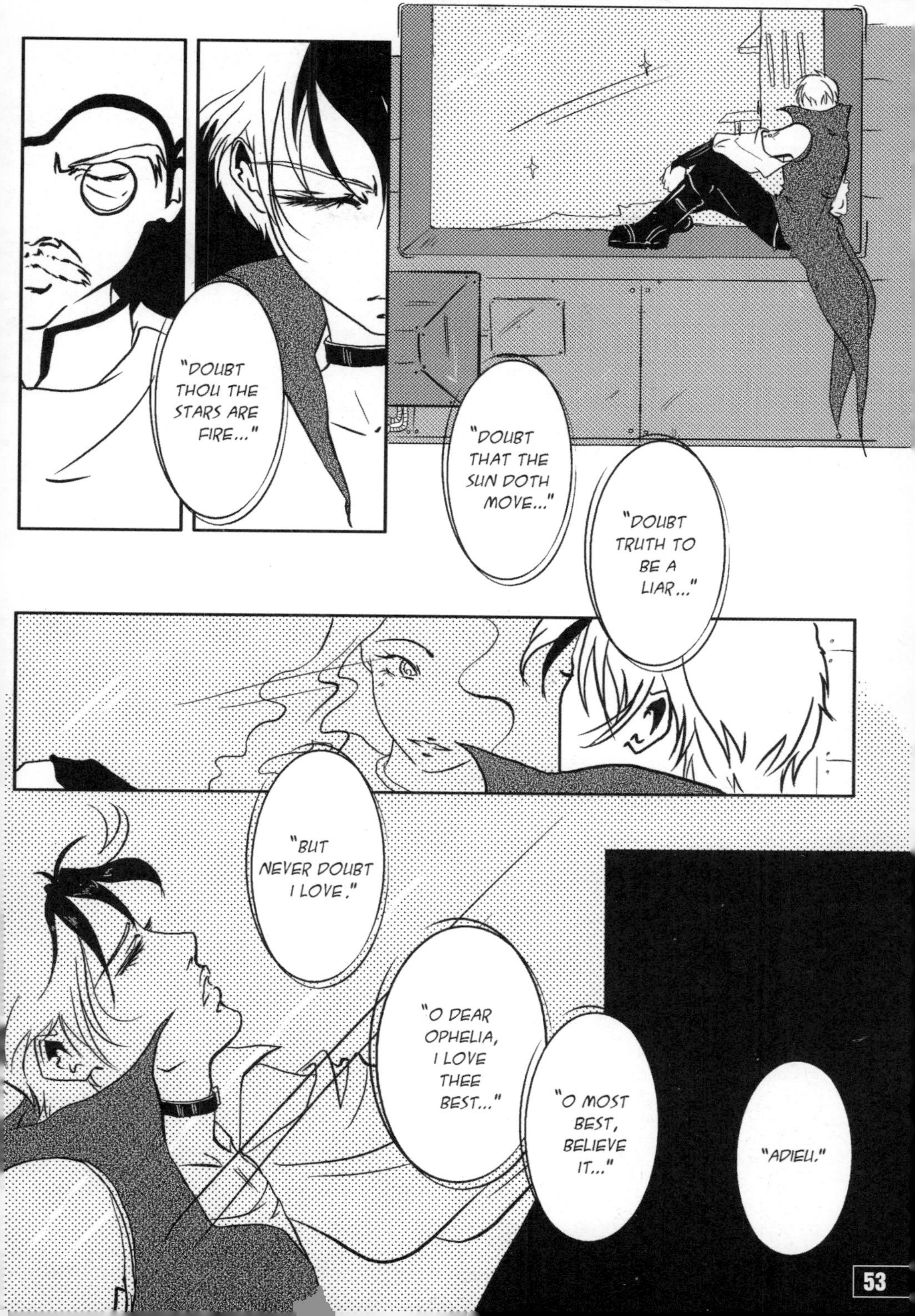
"DOUBT THOU THE STARS ARE FIRE..."
"DOUBT THAT THE SUN DOTH MOVE..."
"DOUBT TRUTH TO BE A LIAR..."
"BUT NEVER DOUBT I LOVE."
"O DEAR OPHELIA, I LOVE THEE BEST..."
"O MOST BEST, BELIEVE IT..."
"ADIEU."

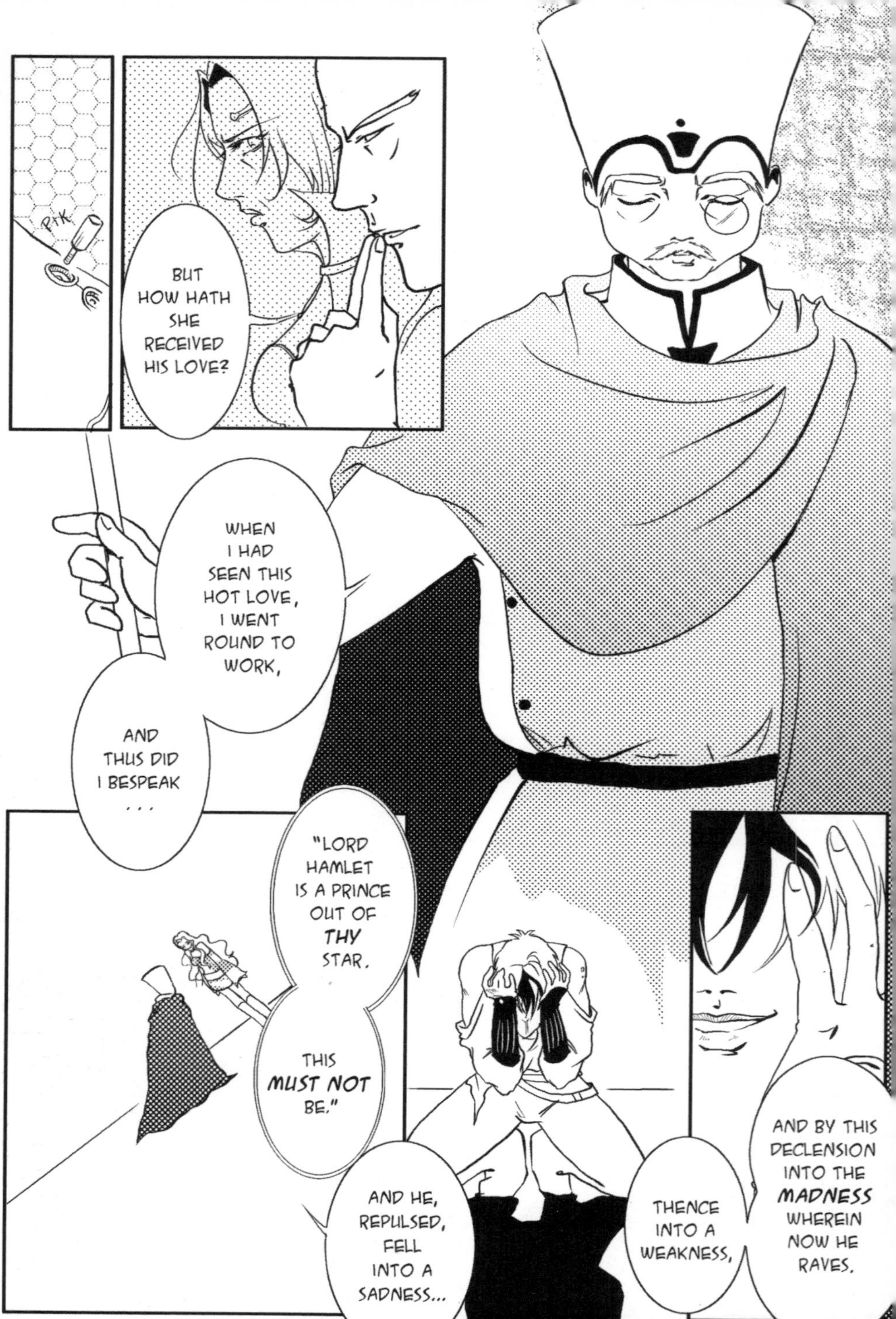
P+K
BUT HOW HATH SHE RECEIVED HIS LOVE?
WHEN I HAD SEEN THIS HOT LOVE, I WENT ROUND TO WORK,
AND THUS DID I BESPEAK . . .
"LORD HAMLET IS A PRINCE OUT OF **THY** STAR.
THIS ***MUST NOT*** BE."
AND HE, REPULSED, FELL INTO A SADNESS...
THENCE INTO A WEAKNESS,
AND BY THIS DECLENSION INTO THE ***MADNESS*** WHEREIN NOW HE RAVES.

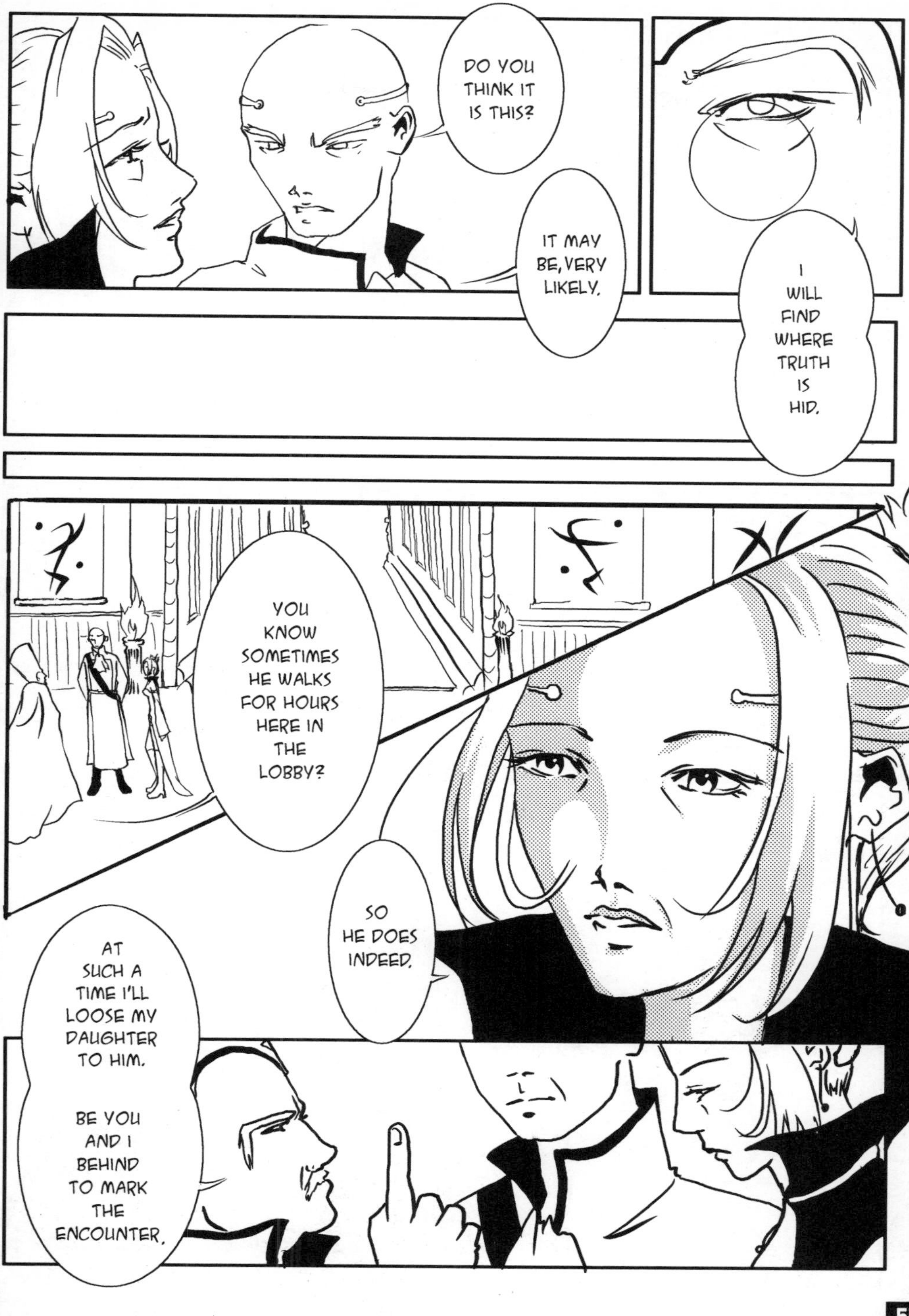
DO YOU THINK IT IS THIS?
IT MAY BE, VERY LIKELY.
I WILL FIND WHERE TRUTH IS HID.
YOU KNOW SOMETIMES HE WALKS FOR HOURS HERE IN THE LOBBY?
SO HE DOES INDEED.
AT SUCH A TIME I'LL LOOSE MY DAUGHTER TO HIM.
BE YOU AND I BEHIND TO MARK THE ENCOUNTER.

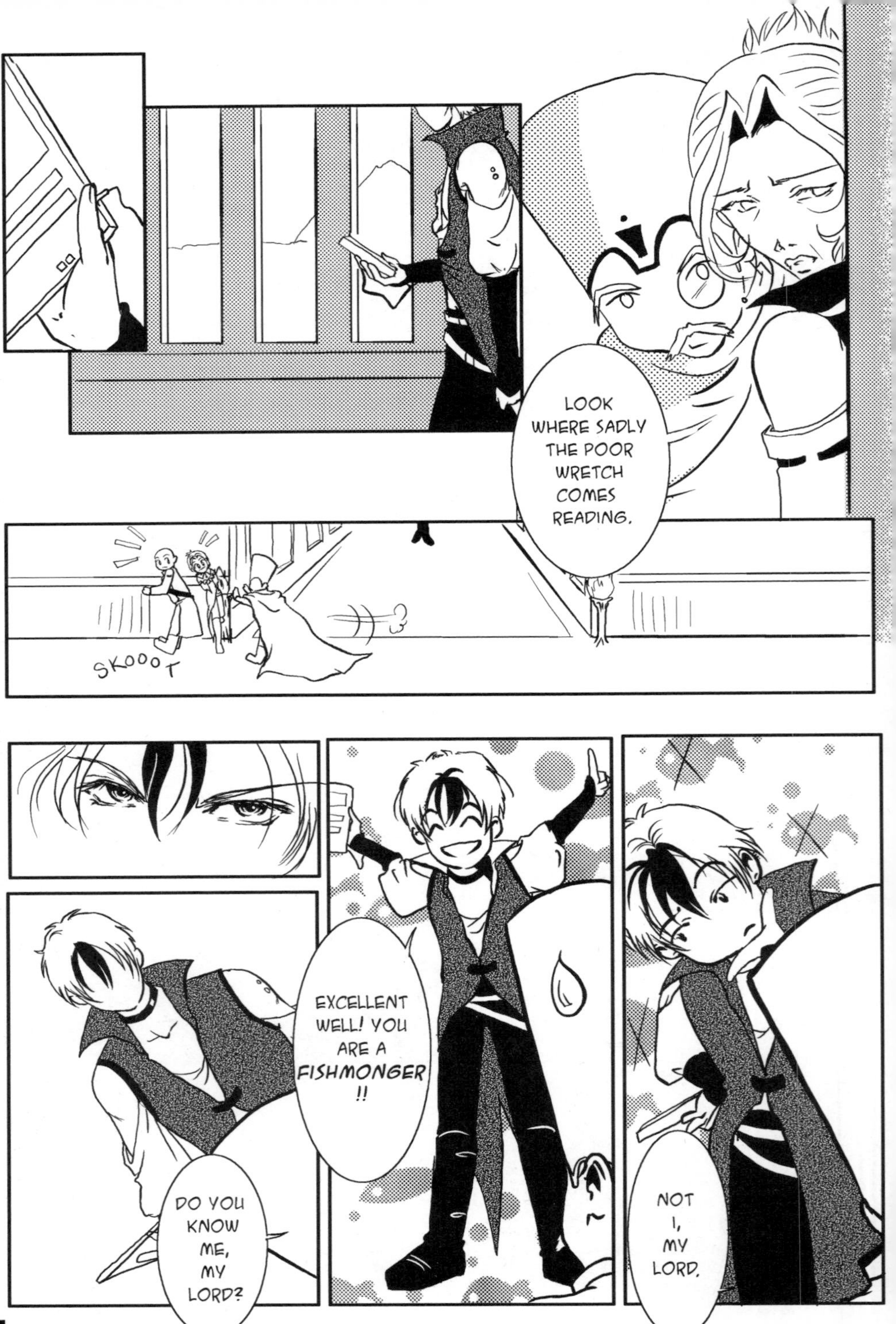
LOOK WHERE SADLY THE POOR WRETCH COMES READING.
SKOOOT
DO YOU KNOW ME, MY LORD?
EXCELLENT WELL! YOU ARE A FISHMONGER !!
NOT I, MY LORD.

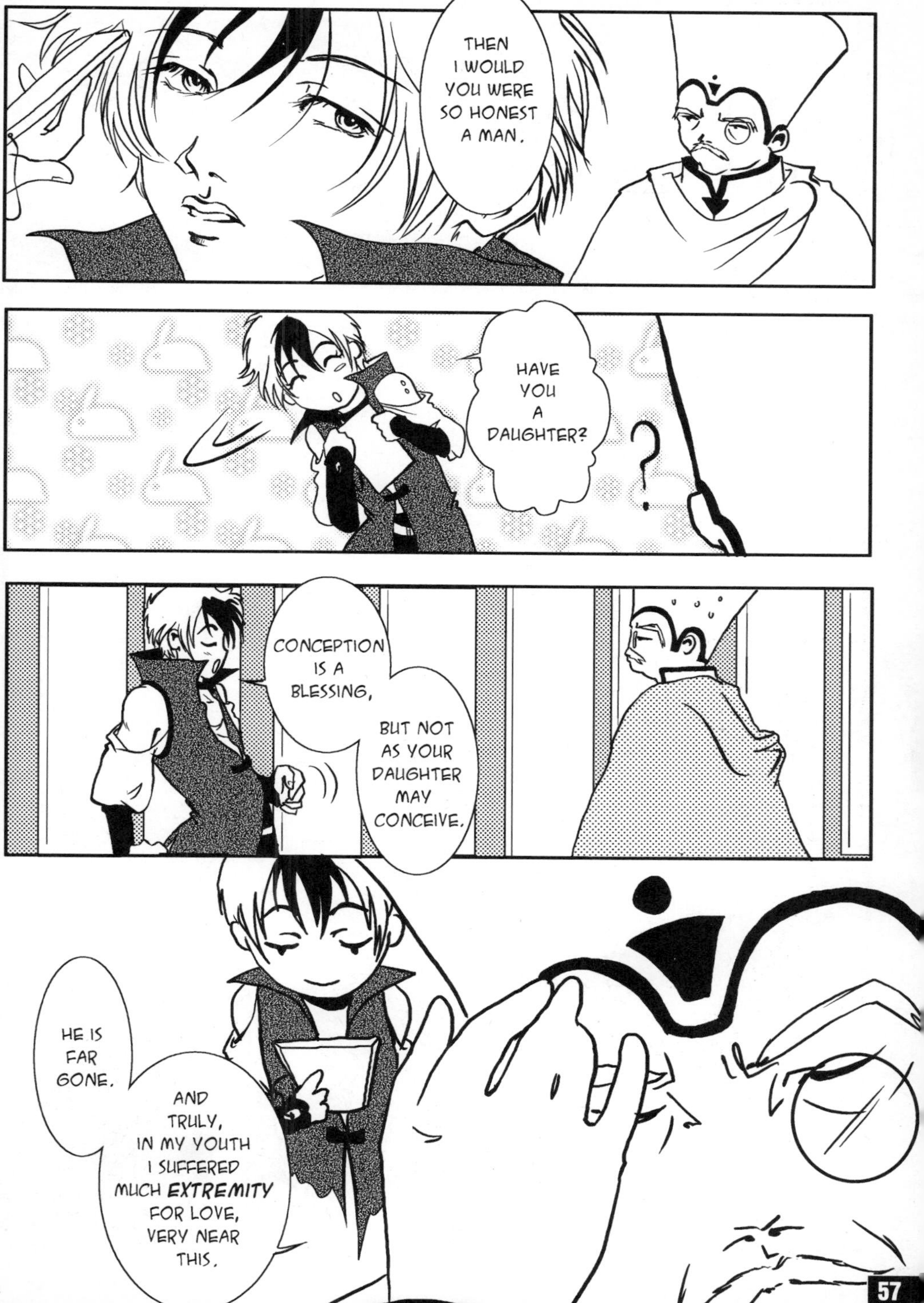
THEN I WOULD YOU WERE SO HONEST A MAN.
HAVE YOU A DAUGHTER?
?
CONCEPTION IS A BLESSING,
BUT NOT AS YOUR DAUGHTER MAY CONCEIVE.
HE IS FAR GONE.
AND TRULY, IN MY YOUTH I SUFFERED MUCH **EXTREMITY** FOR LOVE, VERY NEAR THIS.

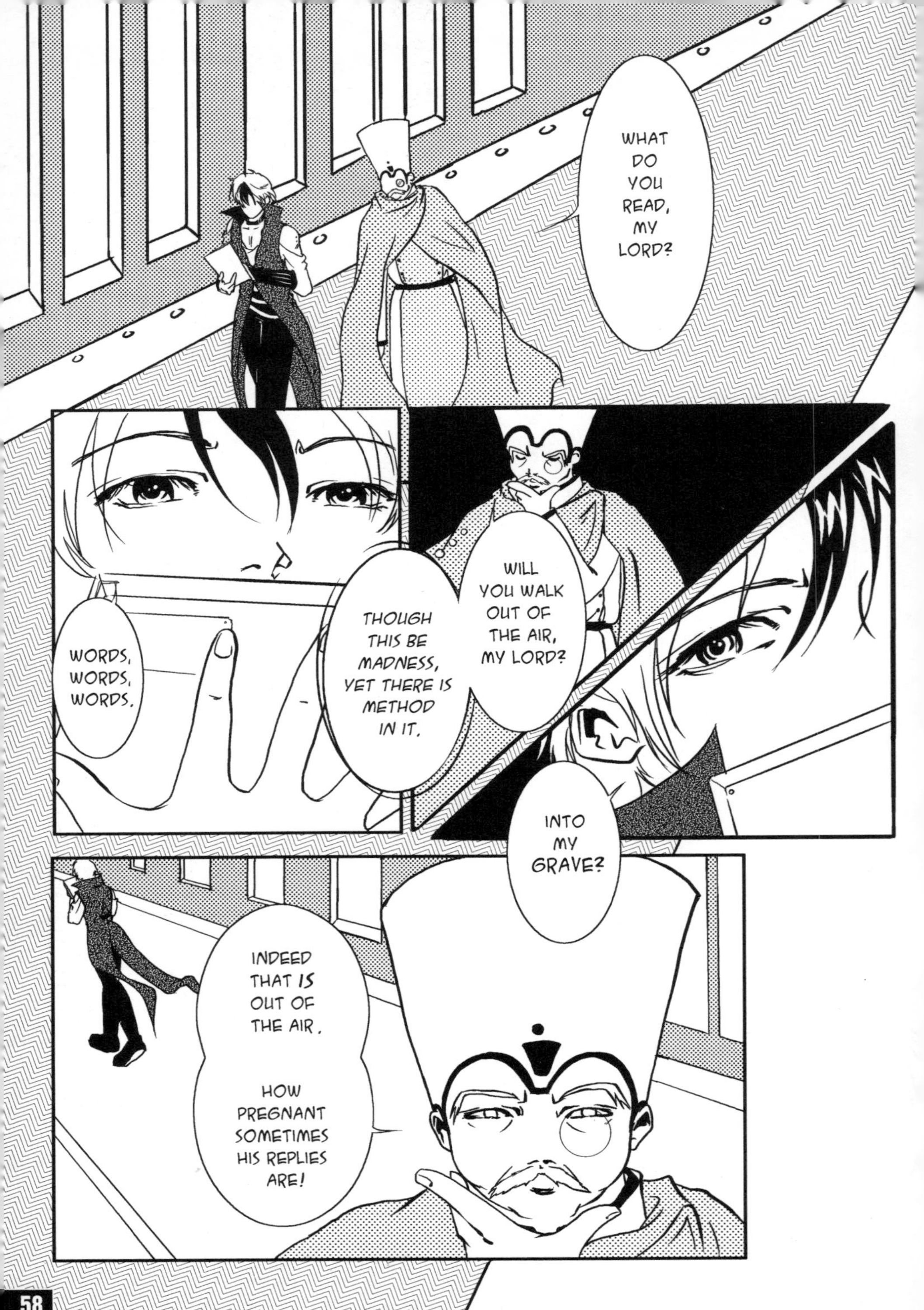
WHAT DO YOU READ, MY LORD?
WORDS, WORDS, WORDS.
WILL YOU WALK OUT OF THE AIR, MY LORD?
THOUGH THIS BE MADNESS, YET THERE IS METHOD IN IT.
INTO MY GRAVE?
INDEED THAT IS OUT OF THE AIR.
HOW PREGNANT SOMETIMES HIS REPLIES ARE!

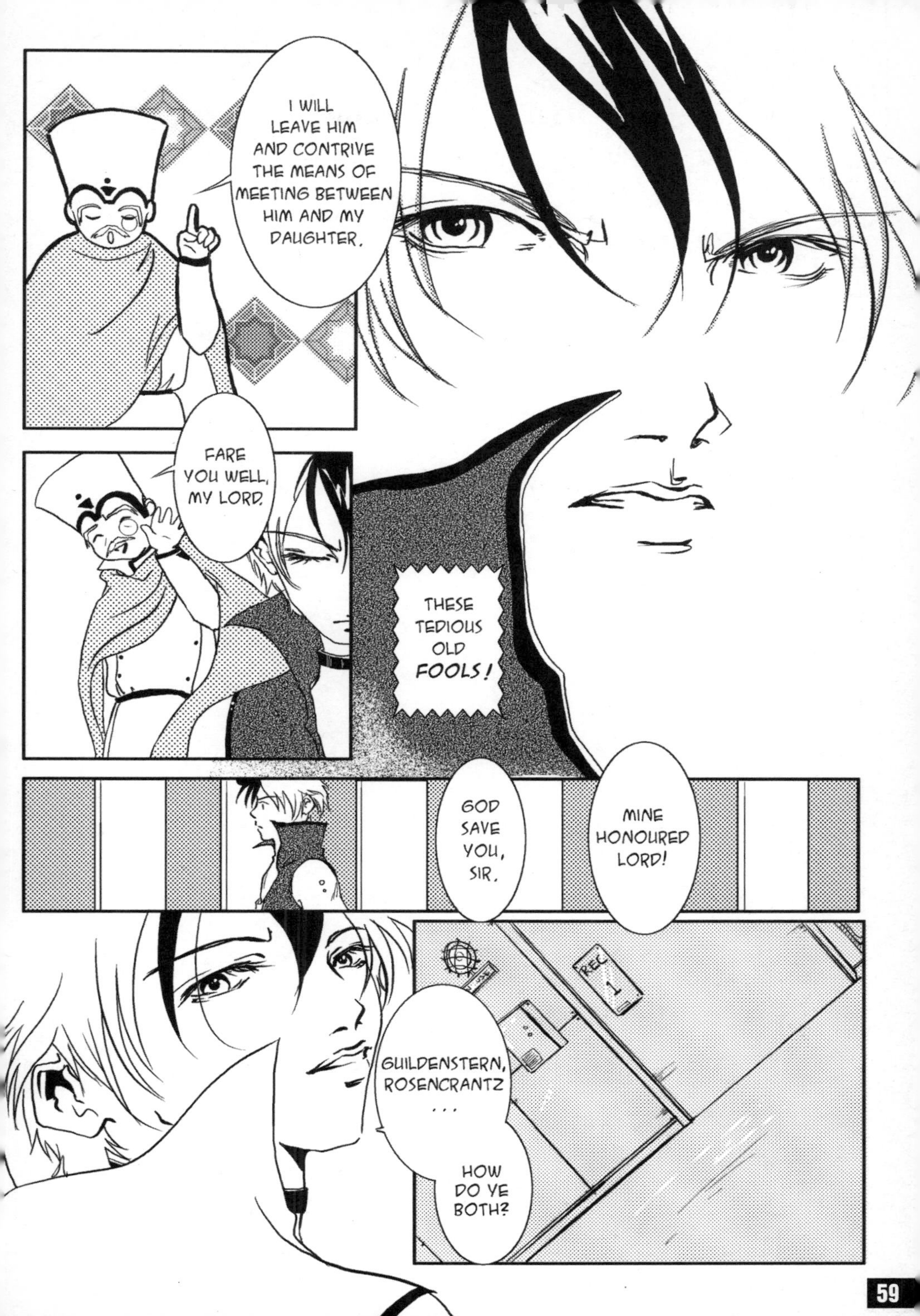
I WILL LEAVE HIM AND CONTRIVE THE MEANS OF MEETING BETWEEN HIM AND MY DAUGHTER.
FARE YOU WELL, MY LORD.
THESE TEDIOUS OLD FOOLS!
GOD SAVE YOU, SIR.
MINE HONOURED LORD!
REC. 1
GUILDENSTERN, ROSENCRANTZ . . .
HOW DO YE BOTH?

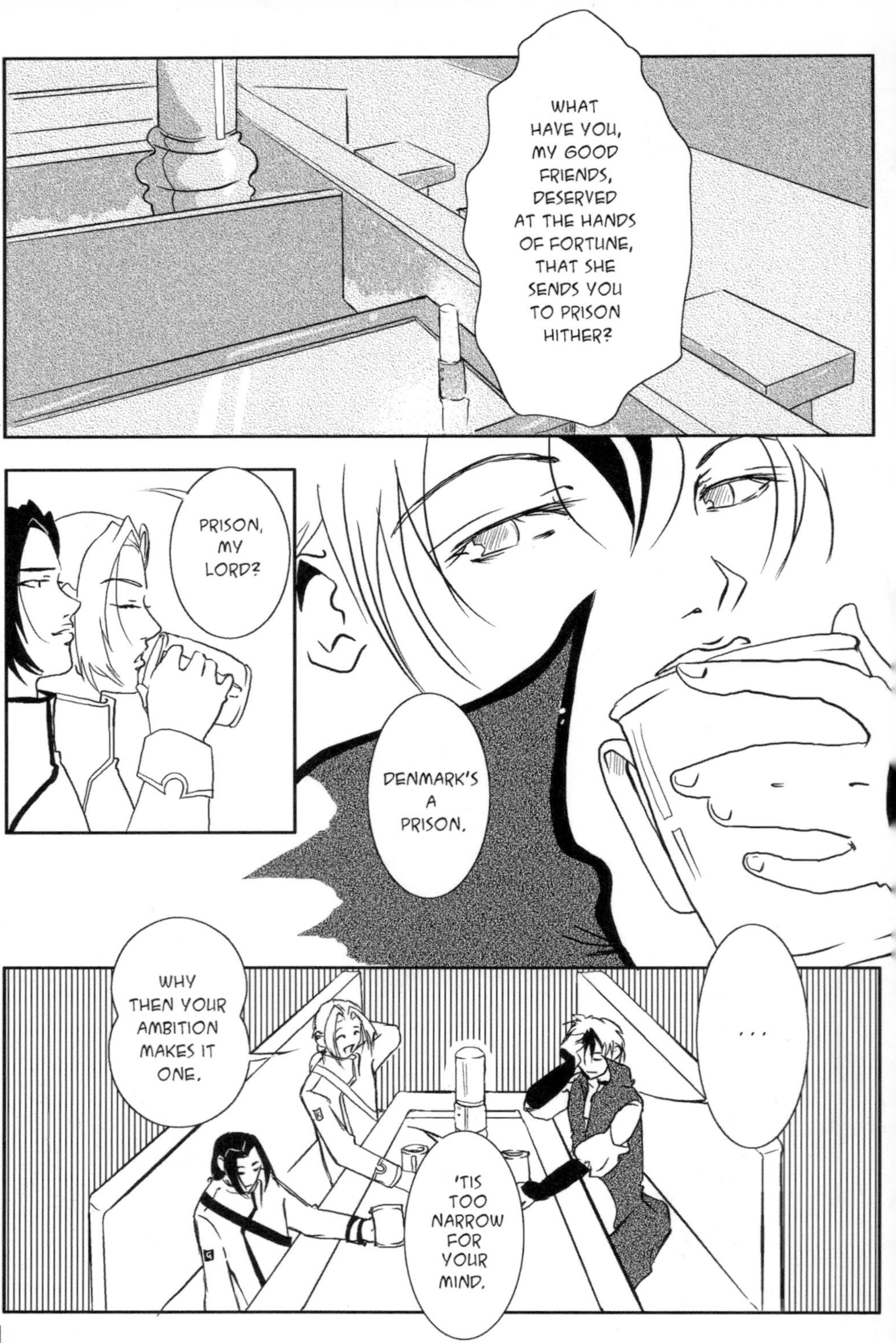
WHAT HAVE YOU, MY GOOD FRIENDS, DESERVED AT THE HANDS OF FORTUNE, THAT SHE SENDS YOU TO PRISON HITHER?
PRISON, MY LORD?
DENMARK'S A PRISON.
WHY THEN YOUR AMBITION MAKES IT ONE.
'TIS TOO NARROW FOR YOUR MIND.
. . .

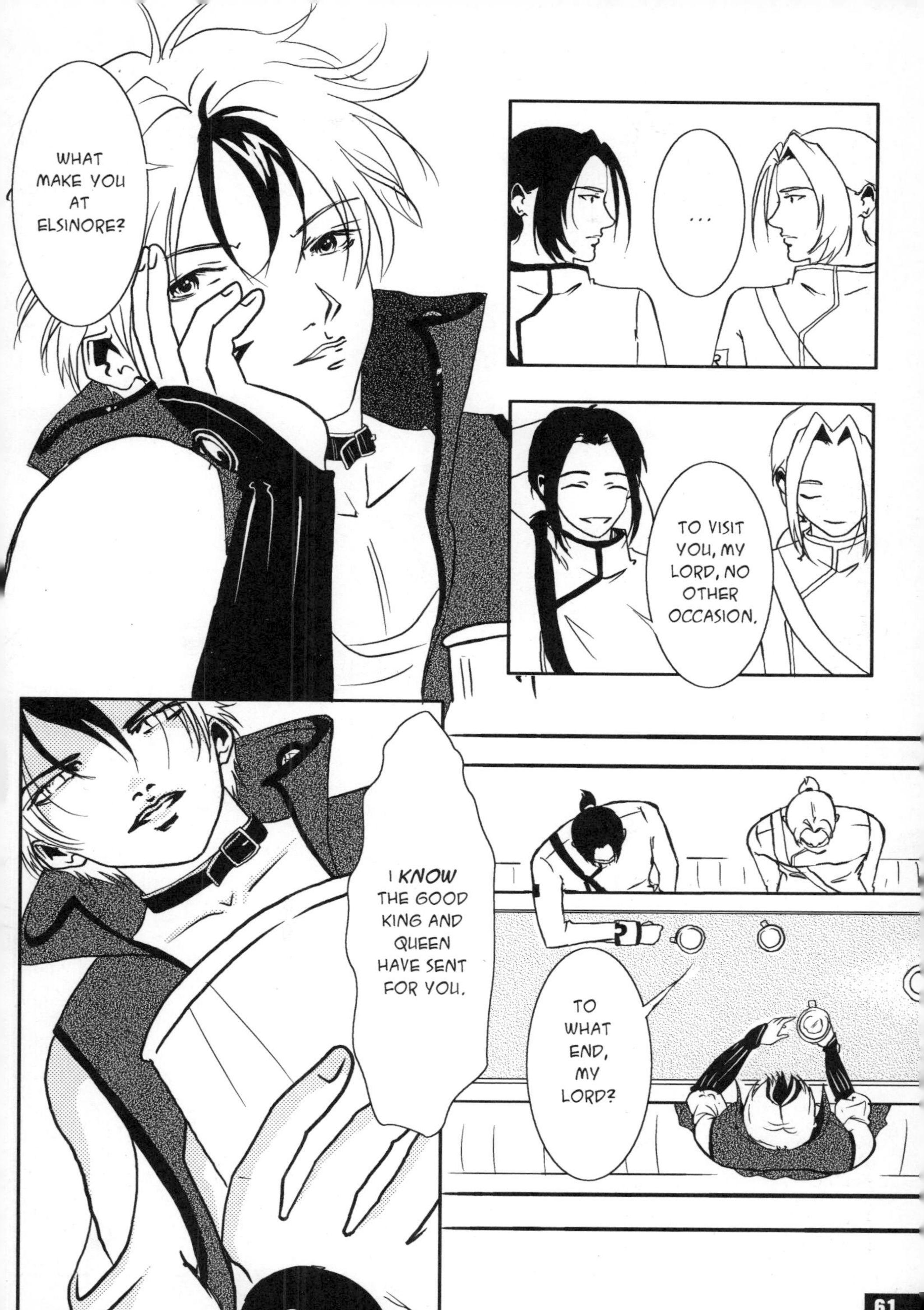
WHAT MAKE YOU AT ELSINORE?
...
TO VISIT YOU, MY LORD, NO OTHER OCCASION.
I KNOW THE GOOD KING AND QUEEN HAVE SENT FOR YOU.
TO WHAT END, MY LORD?

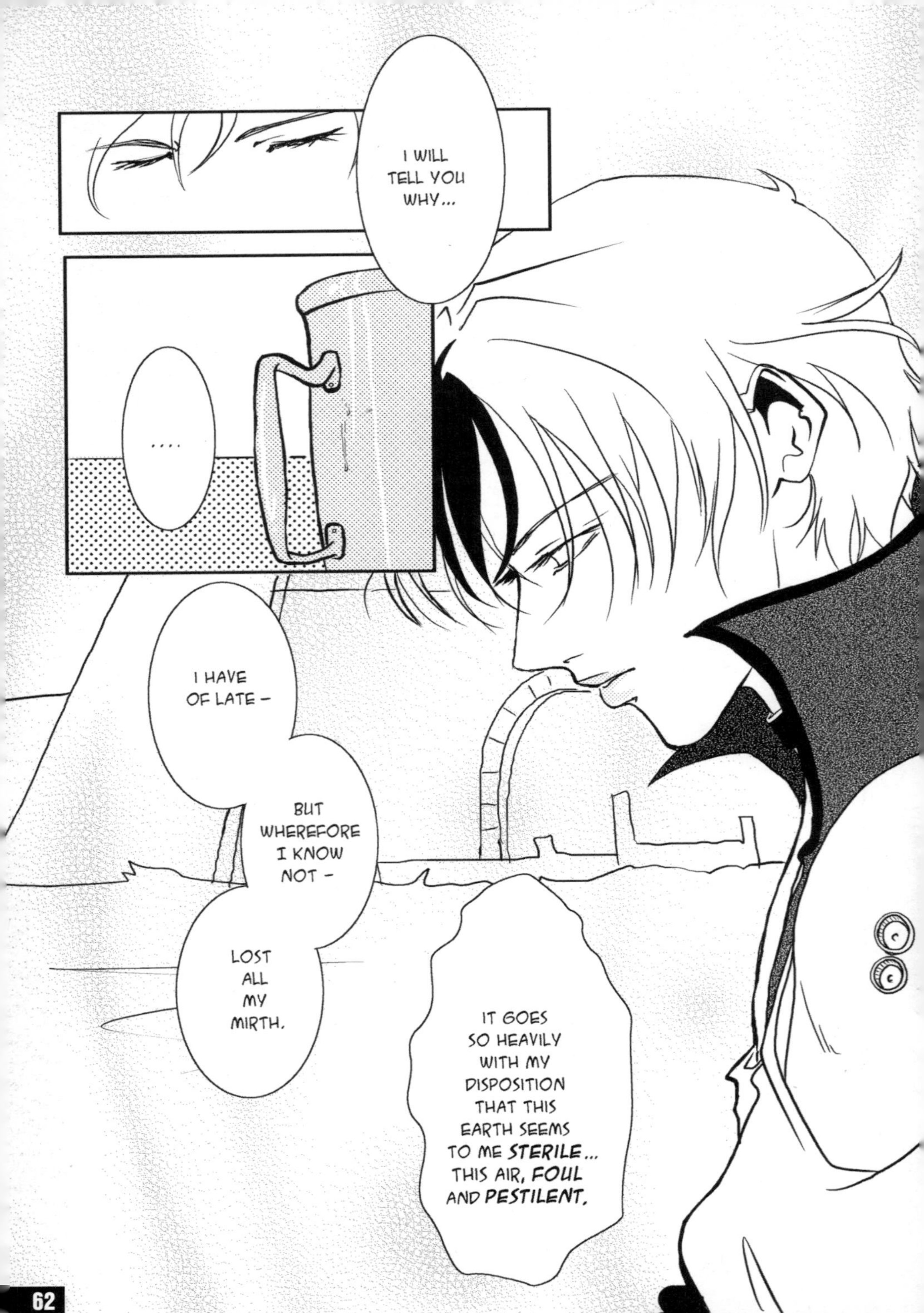
I WILL TELL YOU WHY...
....
I HAVE OF LATE -
BUT WHEREFORE I KNOW NOT -
LOST ALL MY MIRTH.
IT GOES SO HEAVILY WITH MY DISPOSITION THAT THIS EARTH SEEMS TO ME STERILE... THIS AIR, FOUL AND PESTILENT.

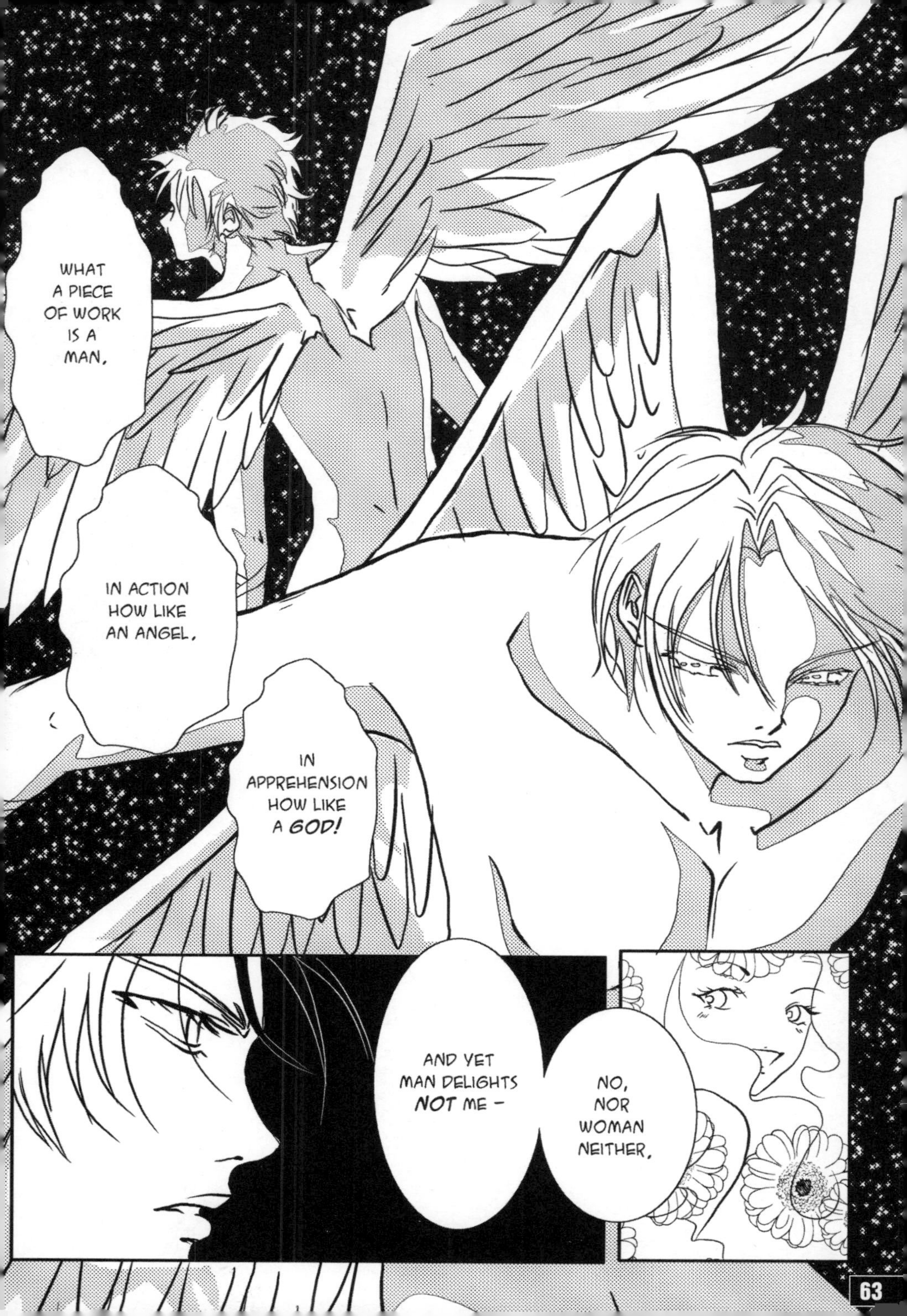

WHAT A PIECE OF WORK IS A MAN.
IN ACTION HOW LIKE AN ANGEL.
IN APPREHENSION HOW LIKE A GOD!
AND YET MAN DELIGHTS NOT ME -
NO, NOR WOMAN NEITHER.

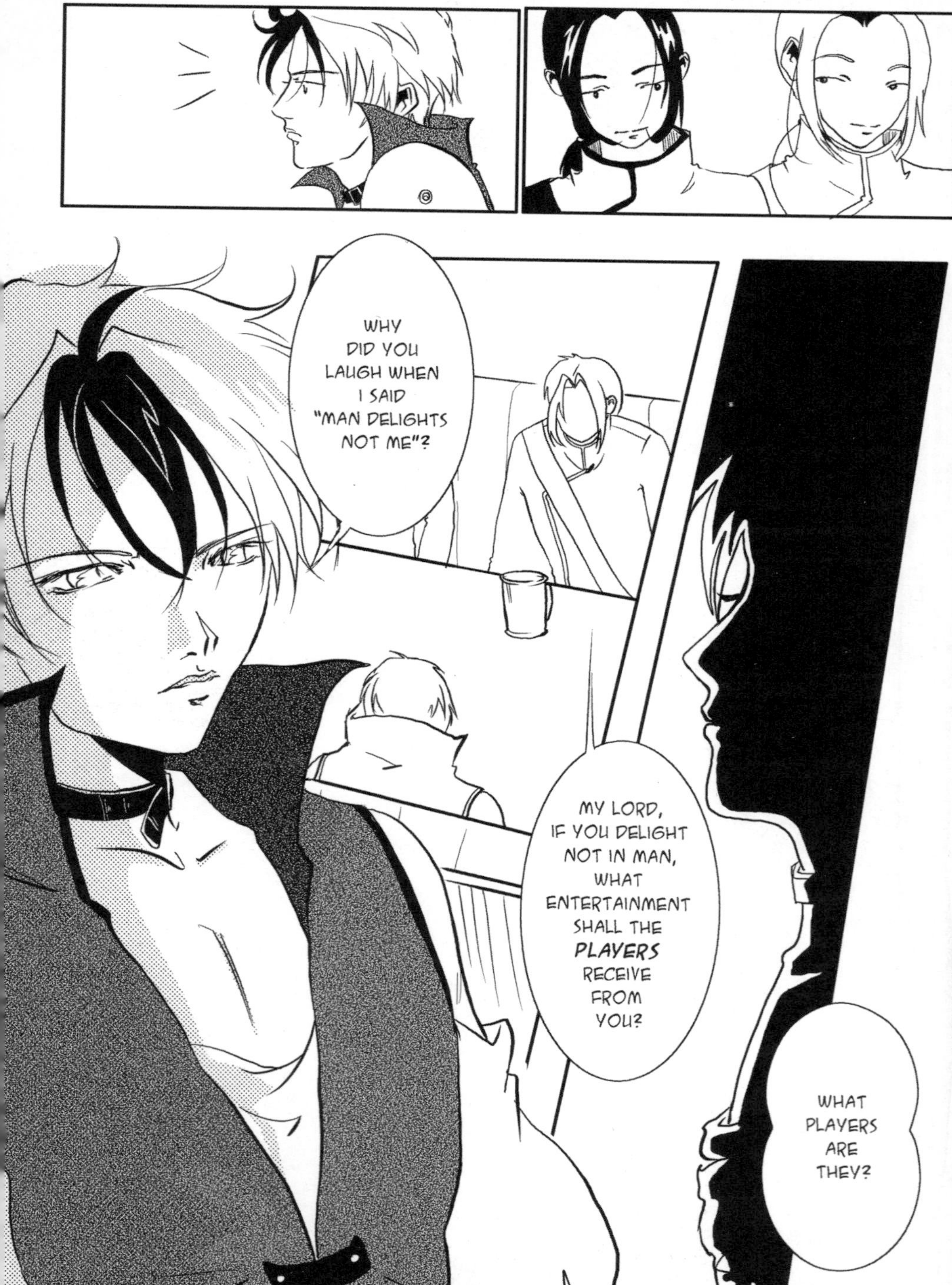

WHY DID YOU LAUGH WHEN I SAID "MAN DELIGHTS NOT ME"?
MY LORD, IF YOU DELIGHT NOT IN MAN, WHAT ENTERTAINMENT SHALL THE **PLAYERS** RECEIVE FROM YOU?
WHAT PLAYERS ARE THEY?

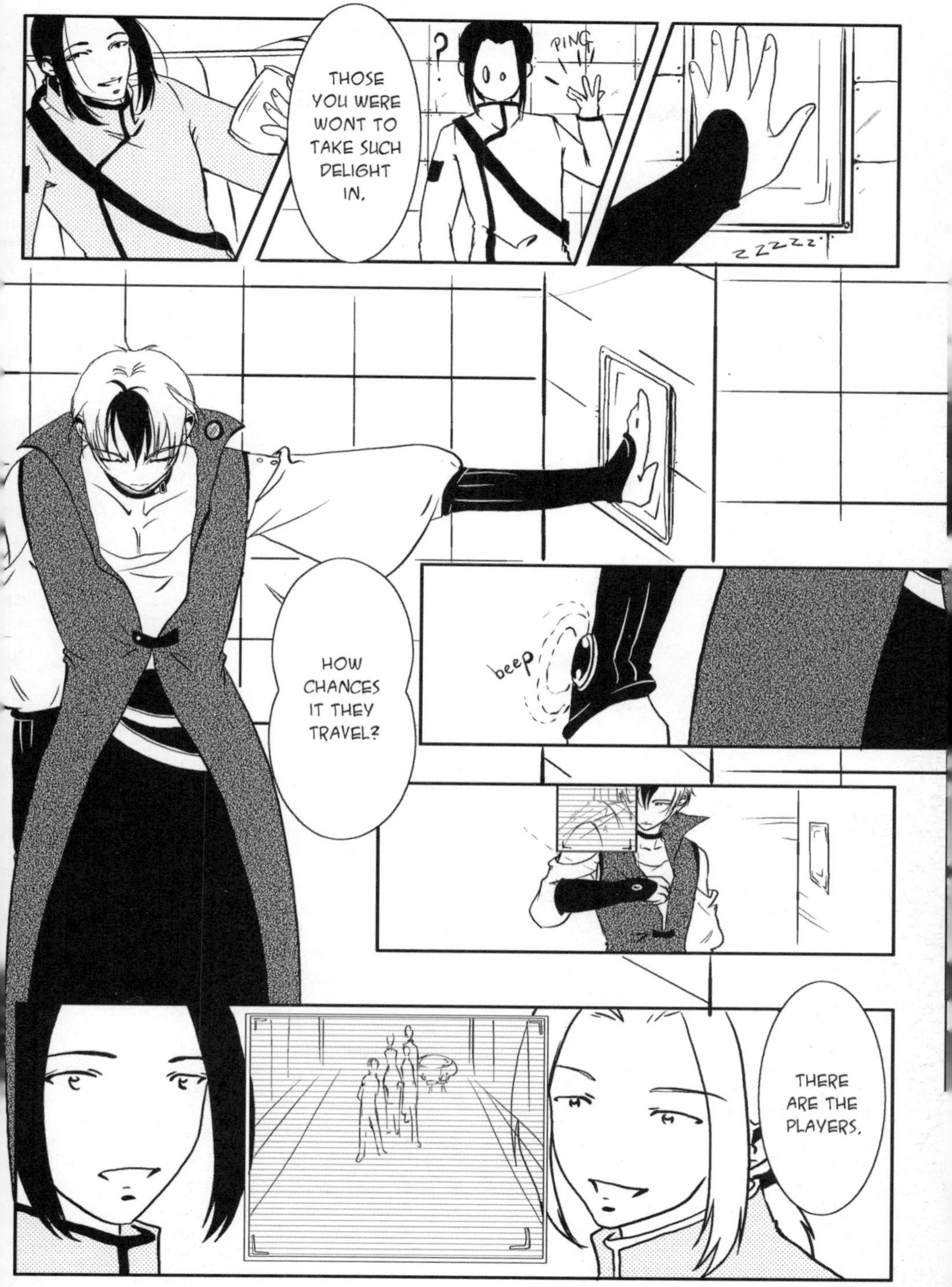
THOSE YOU WERE WONT TO TAKE SUCH DELIGHT IN.
?
PING
ZZZZZZ
HOW CHANCES IT THEY TRAVEL?
beep
THERE ARE THE PLAYERS.

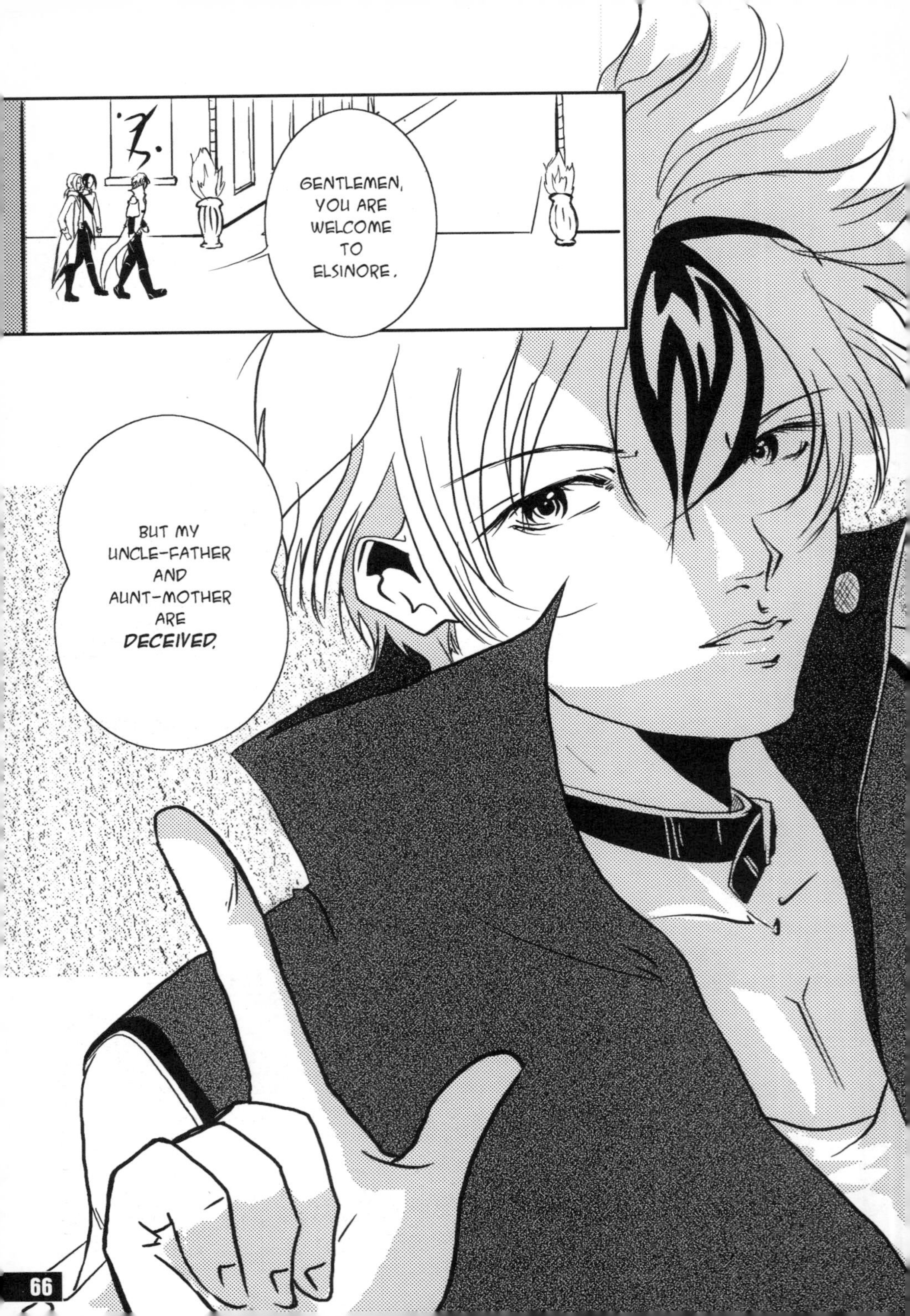
GENTLEMEN, YOU ARE WELCOME TO ELSINORE.
BUT MY UNCLE-FATHER AND AUNT-MOTHER ARE **DECEIVED**.

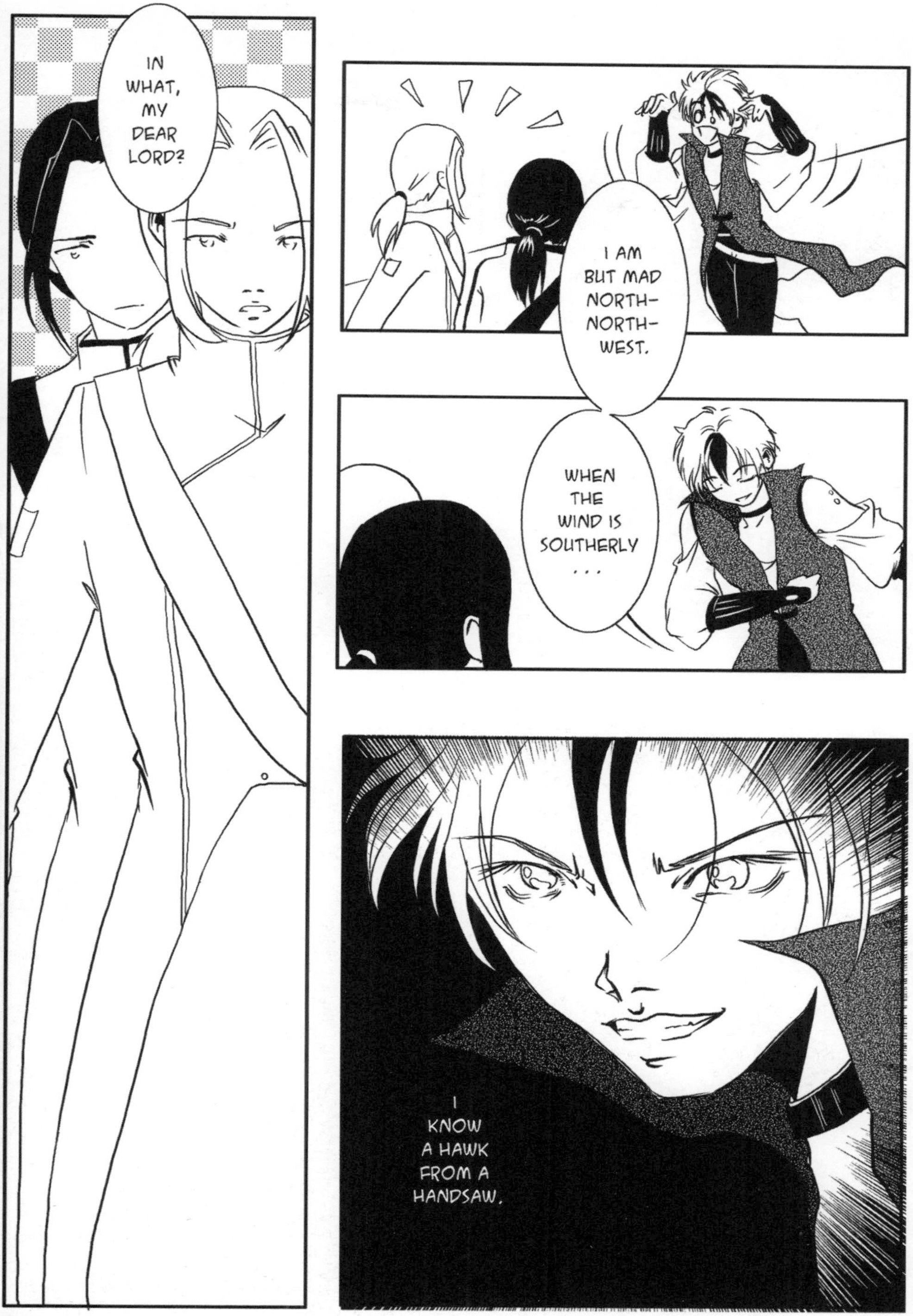
IN WHAT, MY DEAR LORD?
I AM BUT MAD NORTH-NORTH-WEST.
WHEN THE WIND IS SOUTHERLY . . .
I KNOW A HAWK FROM A HANDSAW.

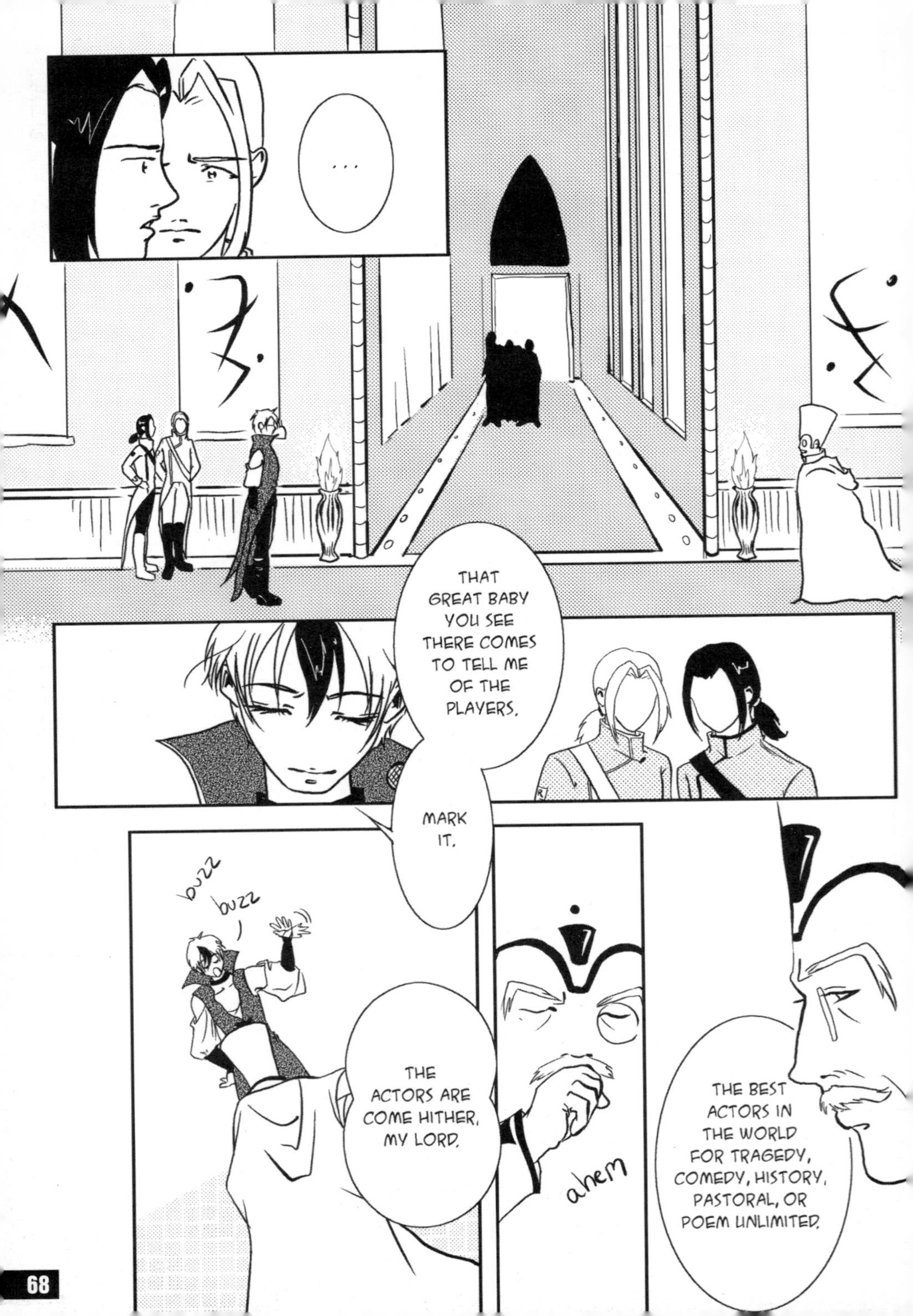
...
THAT GREAT BABY YOU SEE THERE COMES TO TELL ME OF THE PLAYERS.
MARK IT.
buzz
buzz
THE ACTORS ARE COME HITHER, MY LORD.
ahem
THE BEST ACTORS IN THE WORLD FOR TRAGEDY, COMEDY, HISTORY, PASTORAL, OR POEM UNLIMITED.

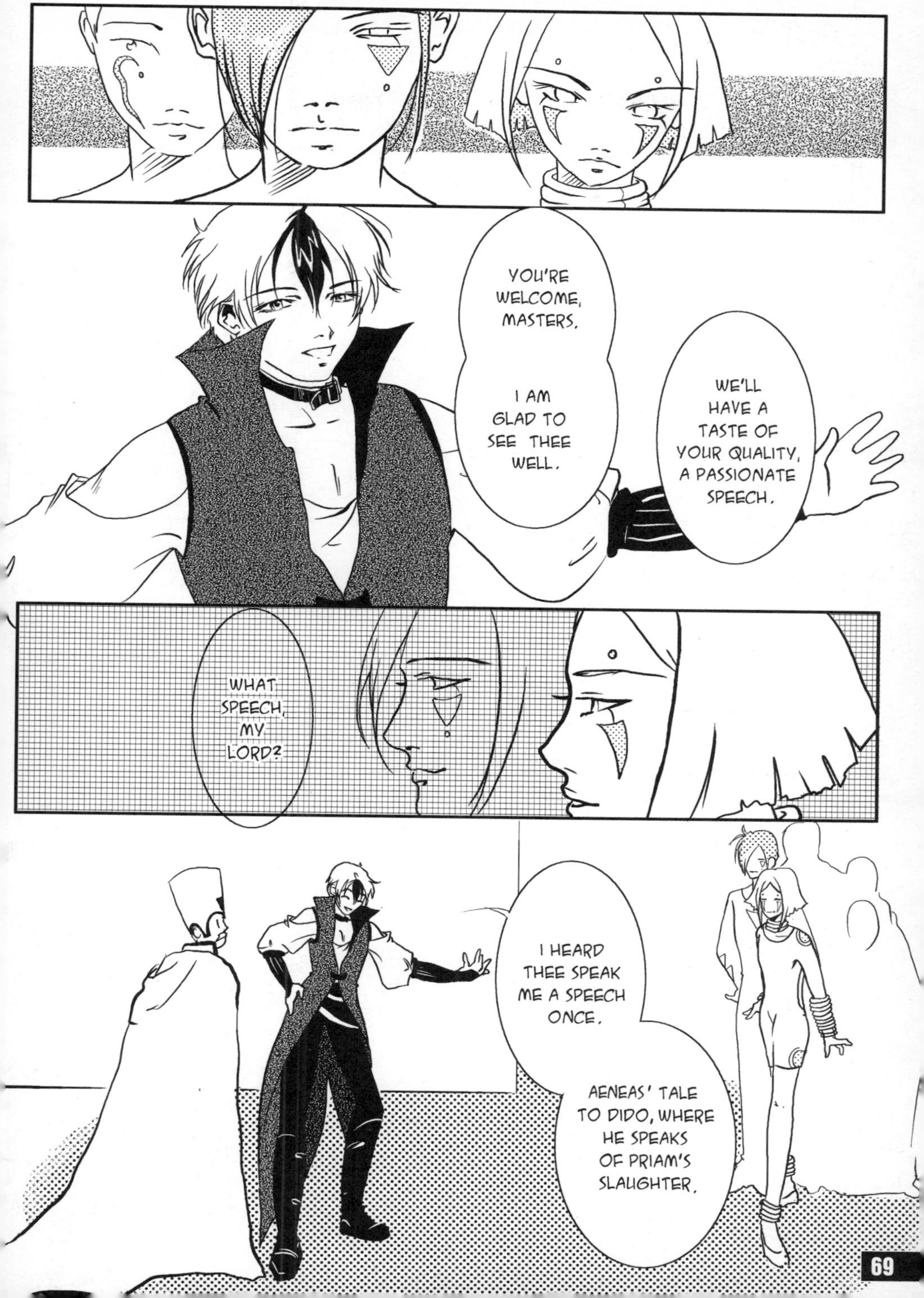

YOU'RE WELCOME, MASTERS.
I AM GLAD TO SEE THEE WELL.
WE'LL HAVE A TASTE OF YOUR QUALITY, A PASSIONATE SPEECH.
WHAT SPEECH, MY LORD?
I HEARD THEE SPEAK ME A SPEECH ONCE.
AENEAS' TALE TO DIDO, WHERE HE SPEAKS OF PRIAM'S SLAUGHTER.

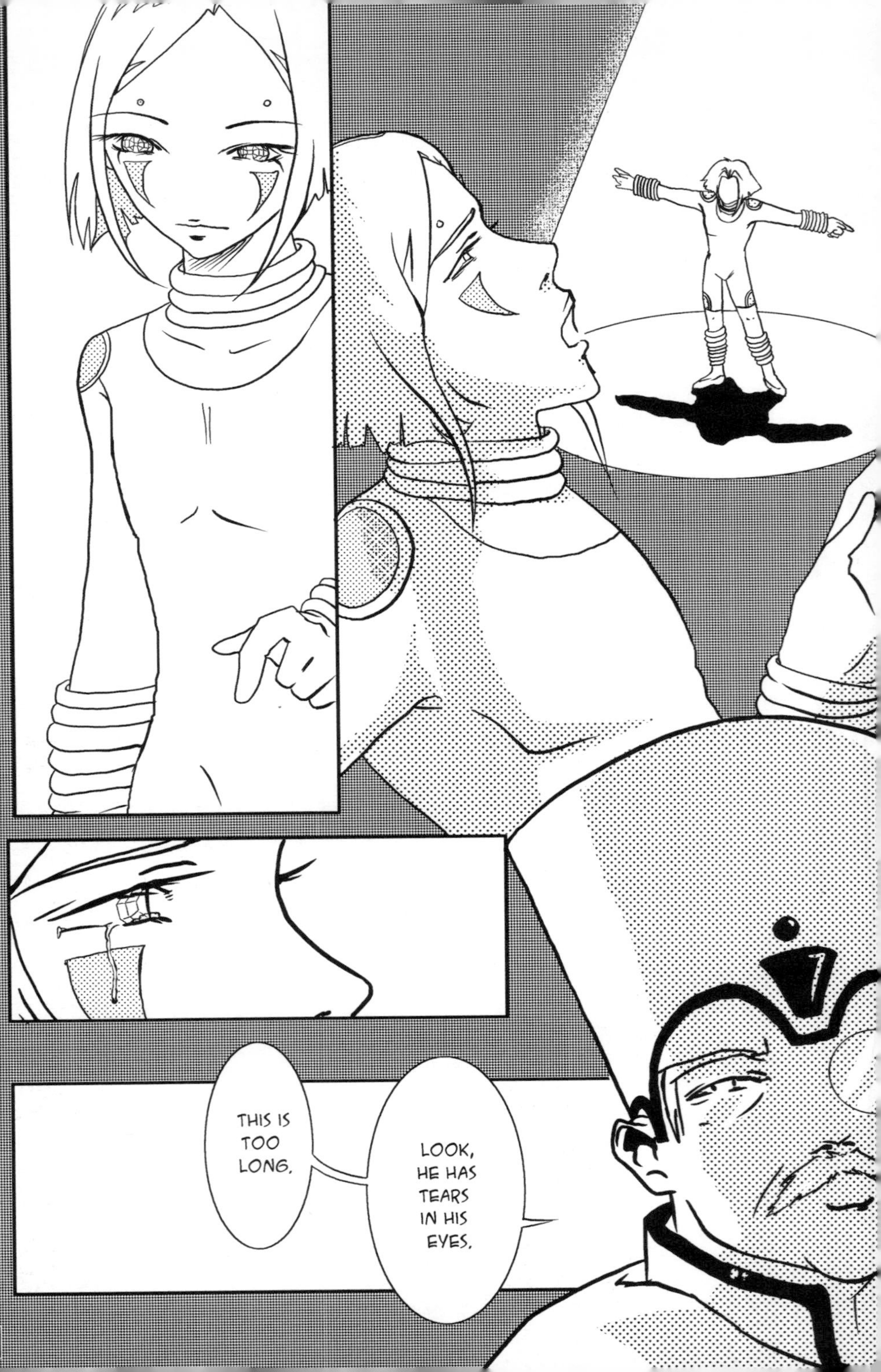
THIS IS TOO LONG.
LOOK, HE HAS TEARS IN HIS EYES.

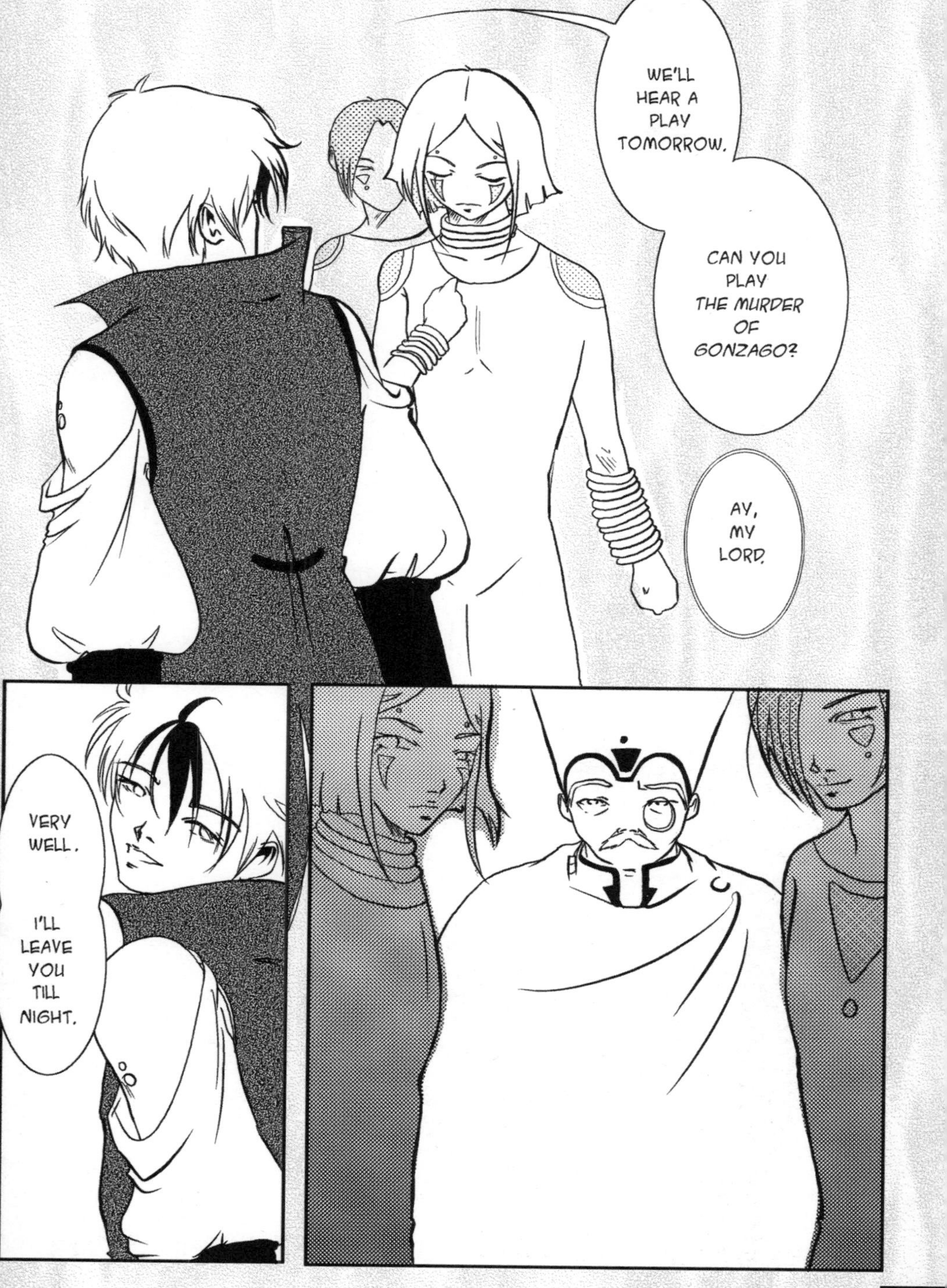
WE'LL HEAR A PLAY TOMORROW.
CAN YOU PLAY THE MURDER OF GONZAGO?
AY, MY LORD.
VERY WELL.
I'LL LEAVE YOU TILL NIGHT.

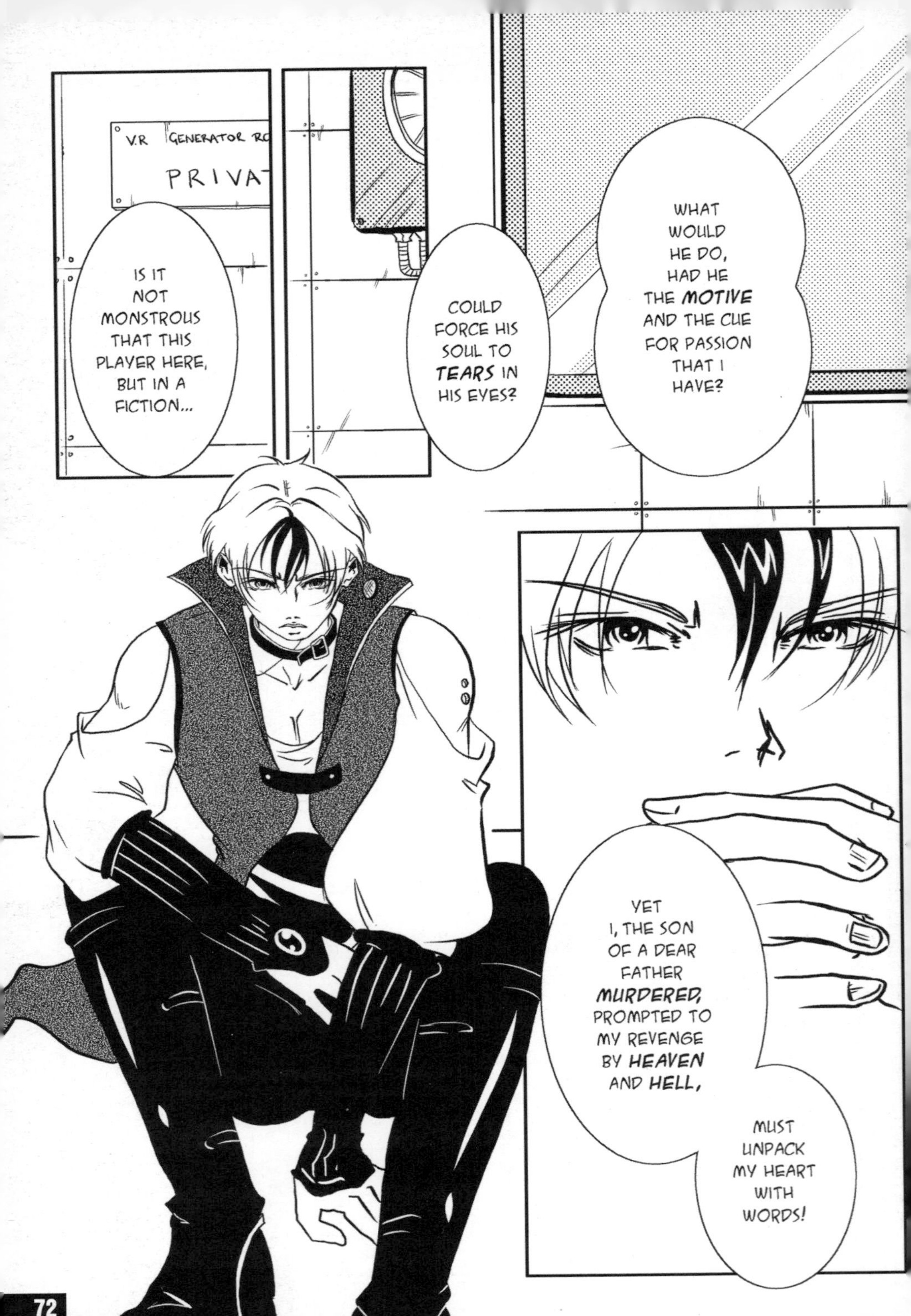
V.R GENERATOR RO
PRIVAT
IS IT NOT MONSTROUS THAT THIS PLAYER HERE, BUT IN A FICTION...
COULD FORCE HIS SOUL TO **TEARS** IN HIS EYES?
WHAT WOULD HE DO, HAD HE THE **MOTIVE** AND THE CUE FOR PASSION THAT I HAVE?
YET I, THE SON OF A DEAR FATHER **MURDERED**, PROMPTED TO MY REVENGE BY **HEAVEN** AND **HELL**,
MUST UNPACK MY HEART WITH WORDS!

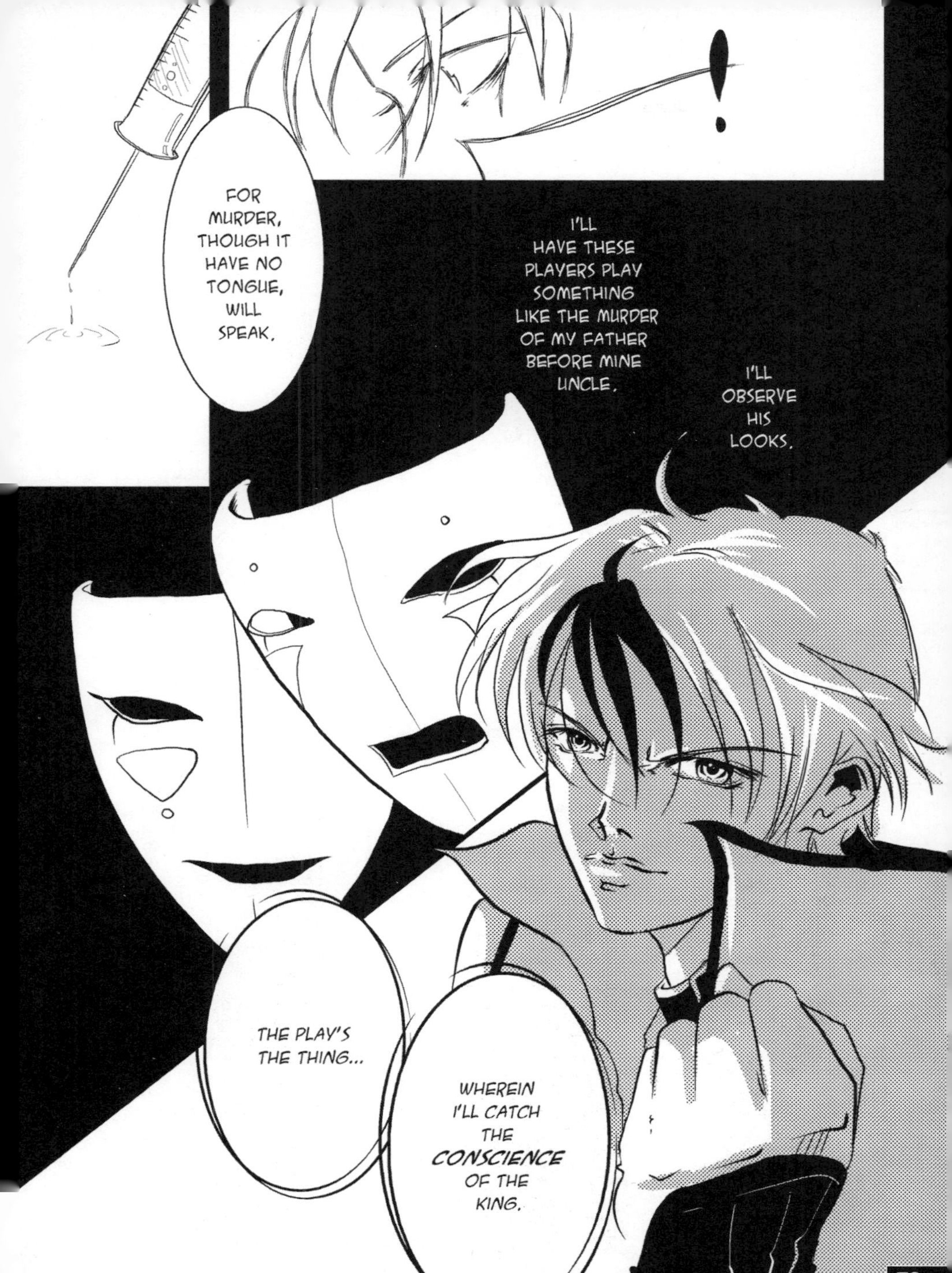

!
FOR MURDER, THOUGH IT HAVE NO TONGUE, WILL SPEAK.
I'LL HAVE THESE PLAYERS PLAY SOMETHING LIKE THE MURDER OF MY FATHER BEFORE MINE UNCLE.
I'LL OBSERVE HIS LOOKS.
THE PLAY'S THE THING...
WHEREIN I'LL CATCH THE *CONSCIENCE* OF THE KING.

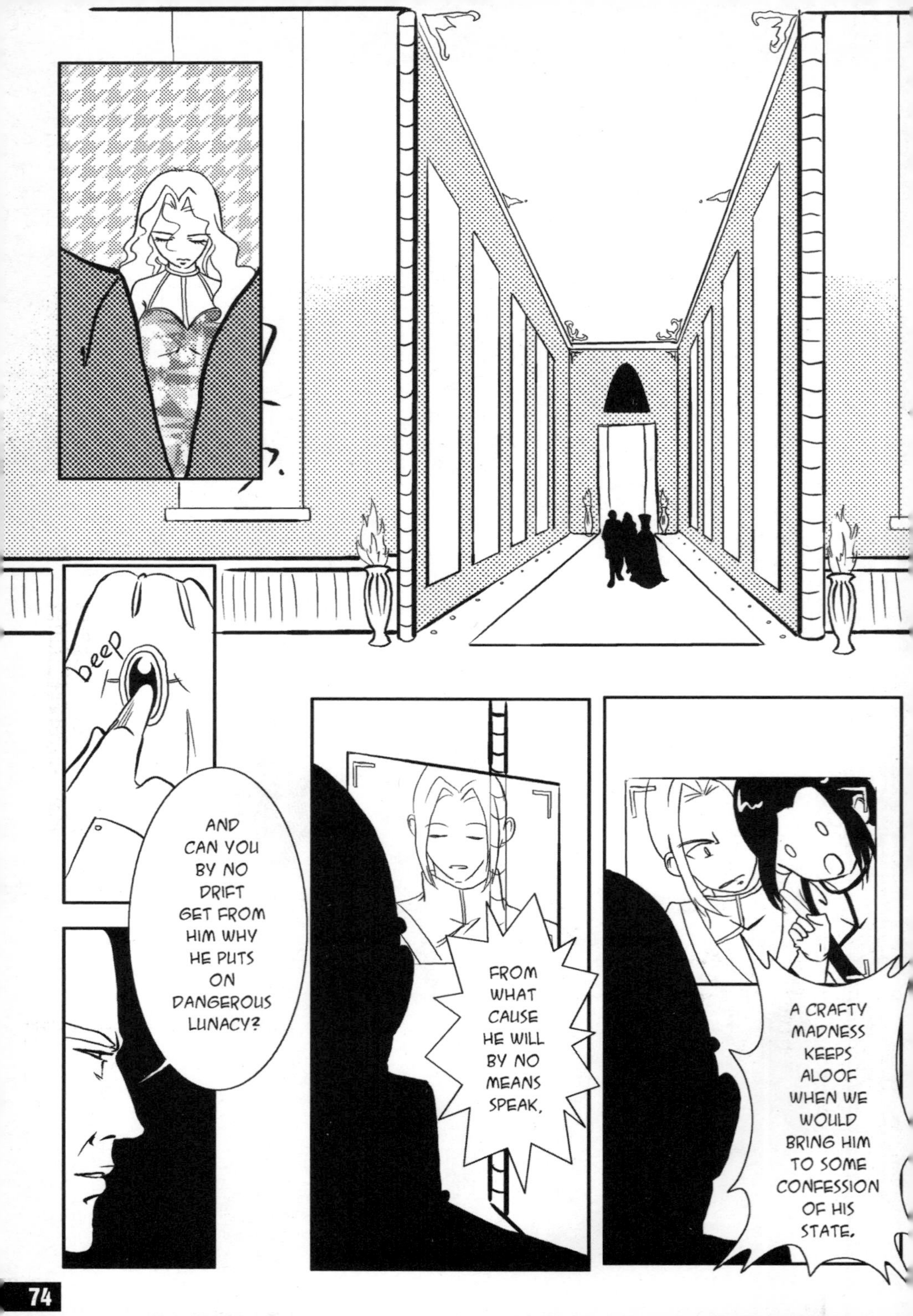
beep
AND CAN YOU BY NO DRIFT GET FROM HIM WHY HE PUTS ON DANGEROUS LUNACY?
FROM WHAT CAUSE HE WILL BY NO MEANS SPEAK,
A CRAFTY MADNESS KEEPS ALOOF WHEN WE WOULD BRING HIM TO SOME CONFESSION OF HIS STATE.

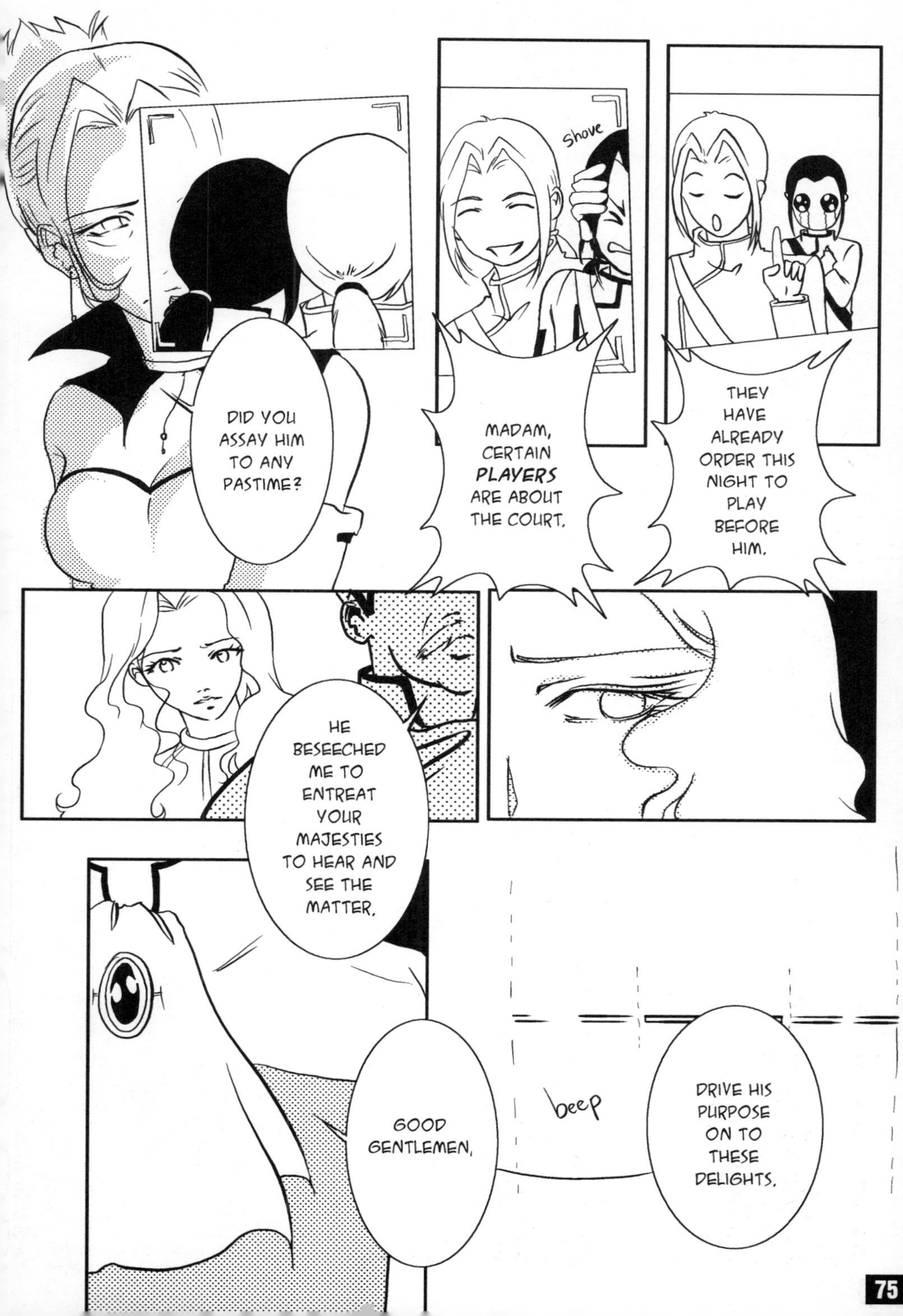

Shove
DID YOU ASSAY HIM TO ANY PASTIME?
MADAM, CERTAIN **PLAYERS** ARE ABOUT THE COURT.
THEY HAVE ALREADY ORDER THIS NIGHT TO PLAY BEFORE HIM.
HE BESEECHED ME TO ENTREAT YOUR MAJESTIES TO HEAR AND SEE THE MATTER.
GOOD GENTLEMEN,
beep
DRIVE HIS PURPOSE ON TO THESE DELIGHTS.

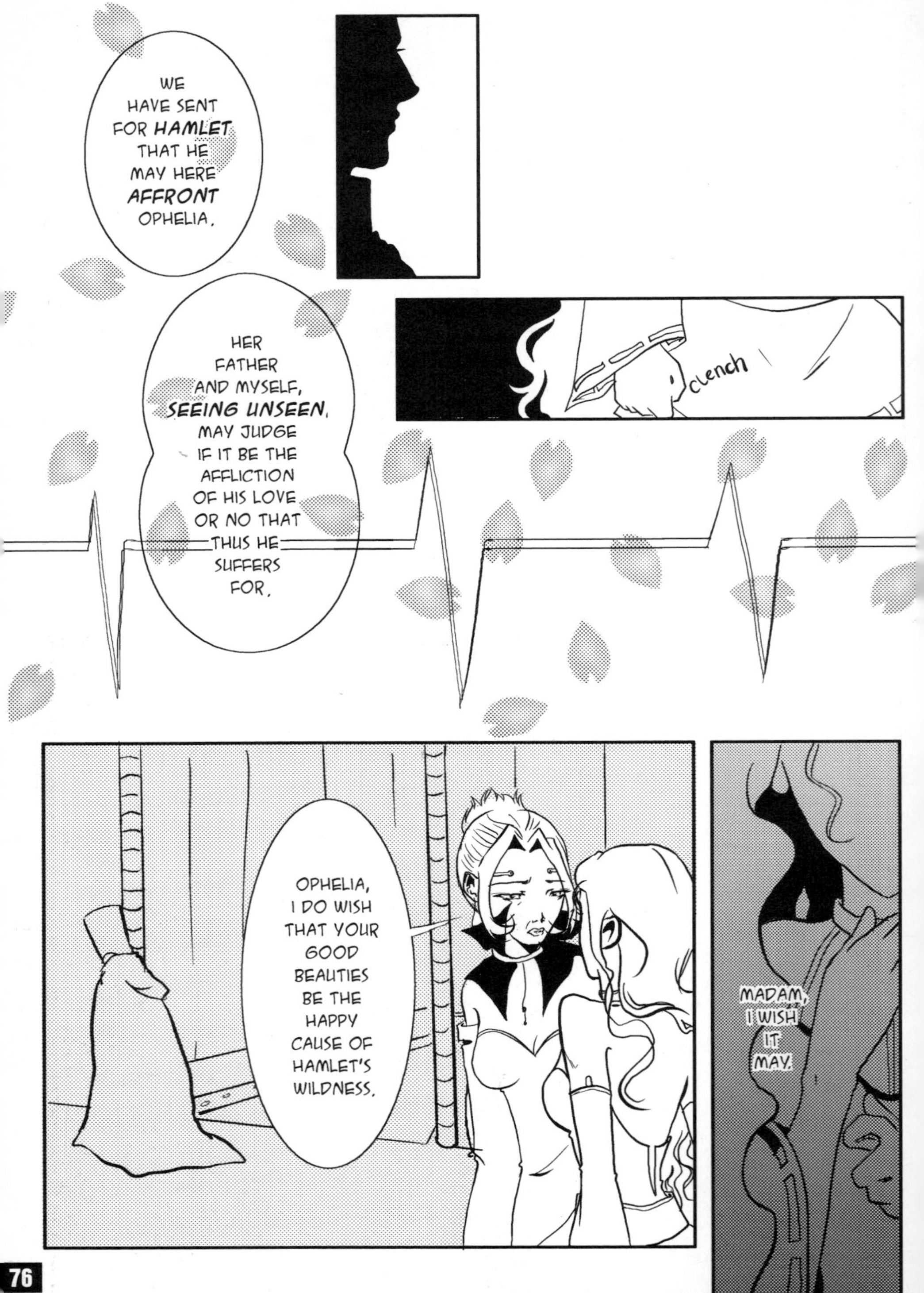

WE HAVE SENT FOR HAMLET THAT HE MAY HERE AFFRONT OPHELIA.
HER FATHER AND MYSELF, SEEING UNSEEN, MAY JUDGE IF IT BE THE AFFLICTION OF HIS LOVE OR NO THAT THUS HE SUFFERS FOR.
clench
OPHELIA, I DO WISH THAT YOUR GOOD BEAUTIES BE THE HAPPY CAUSE OF HAMLET'S WILDNESS.
MADAM, I WISH IT MAY.

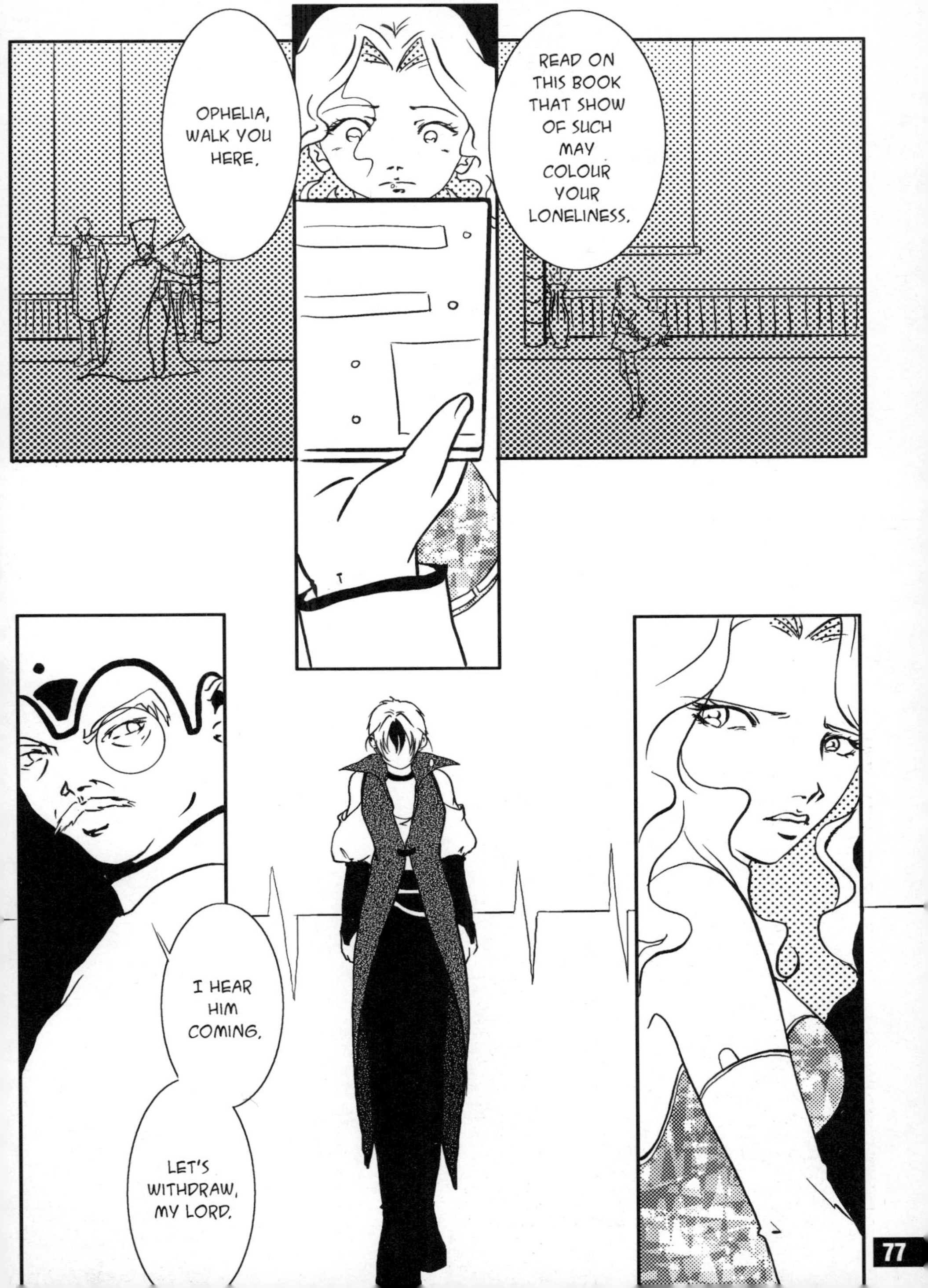

OPHELIA, WALK YOU HERE.
READ ON THIS BOOK THAT SHOW OF SUCH MAY COLOUR YOUR LONELINESS.
I HEAR HIM COMING.
LET'S WITHDRAW, MY LORD.

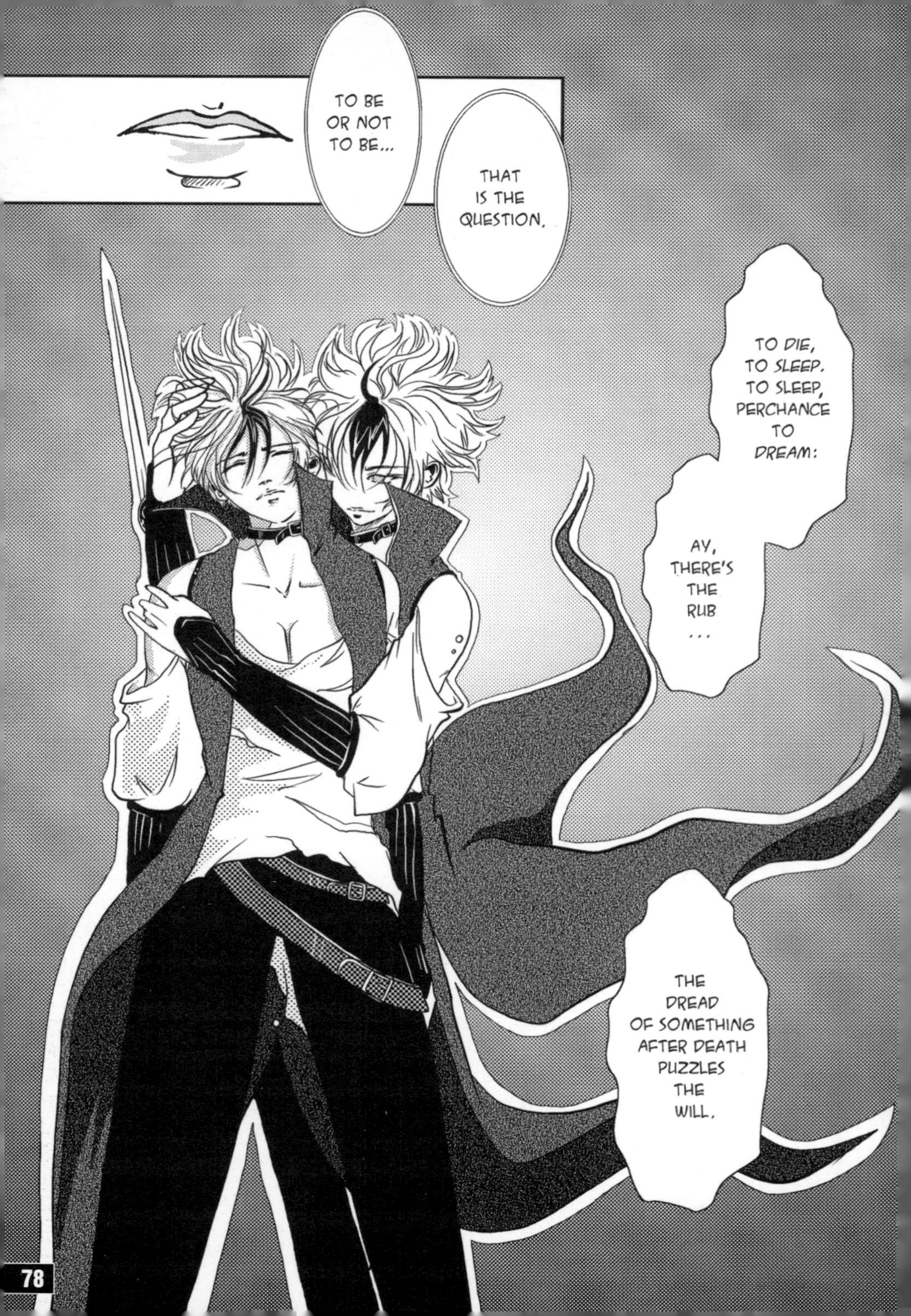
TO BE OR NOT TO BE...
THAT IS THE QUESTION.
TO DIE, TO SLEEP. TO SLEEP, PERCHANCE TO DREAM:
AY, THERE'S THE RUB ...
THE DREAD OF SOMETHING AFTER DEATH PUZZLES THE WILL.

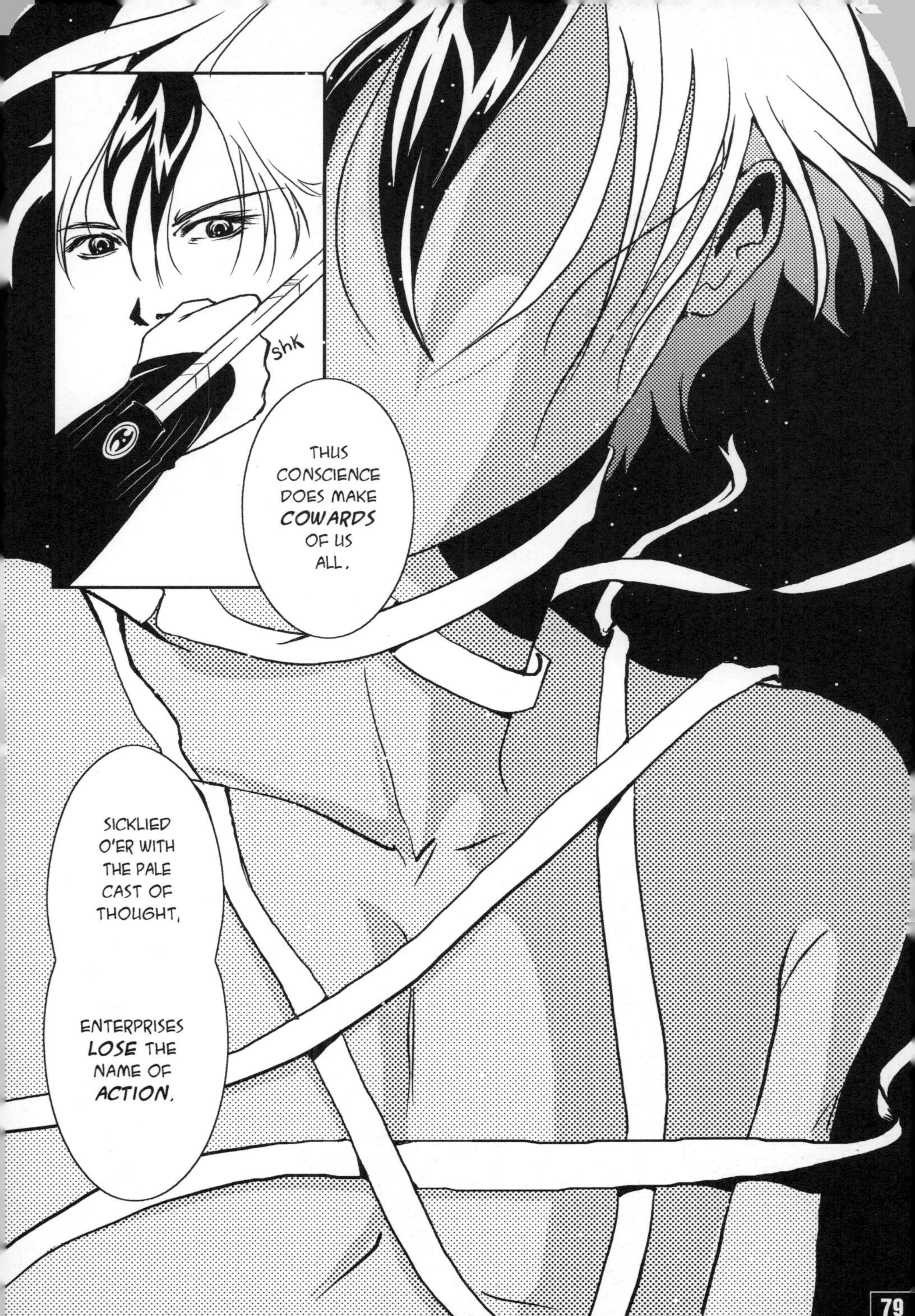

ShK
THUS CONSCIENCE DOES MAKE COWARDS OF US ALL.
SICKLIED O'ER WITH THE PALE CAST OF THOUGHT,
ENTERPRISES LOSE THE NAME OF ACTION.

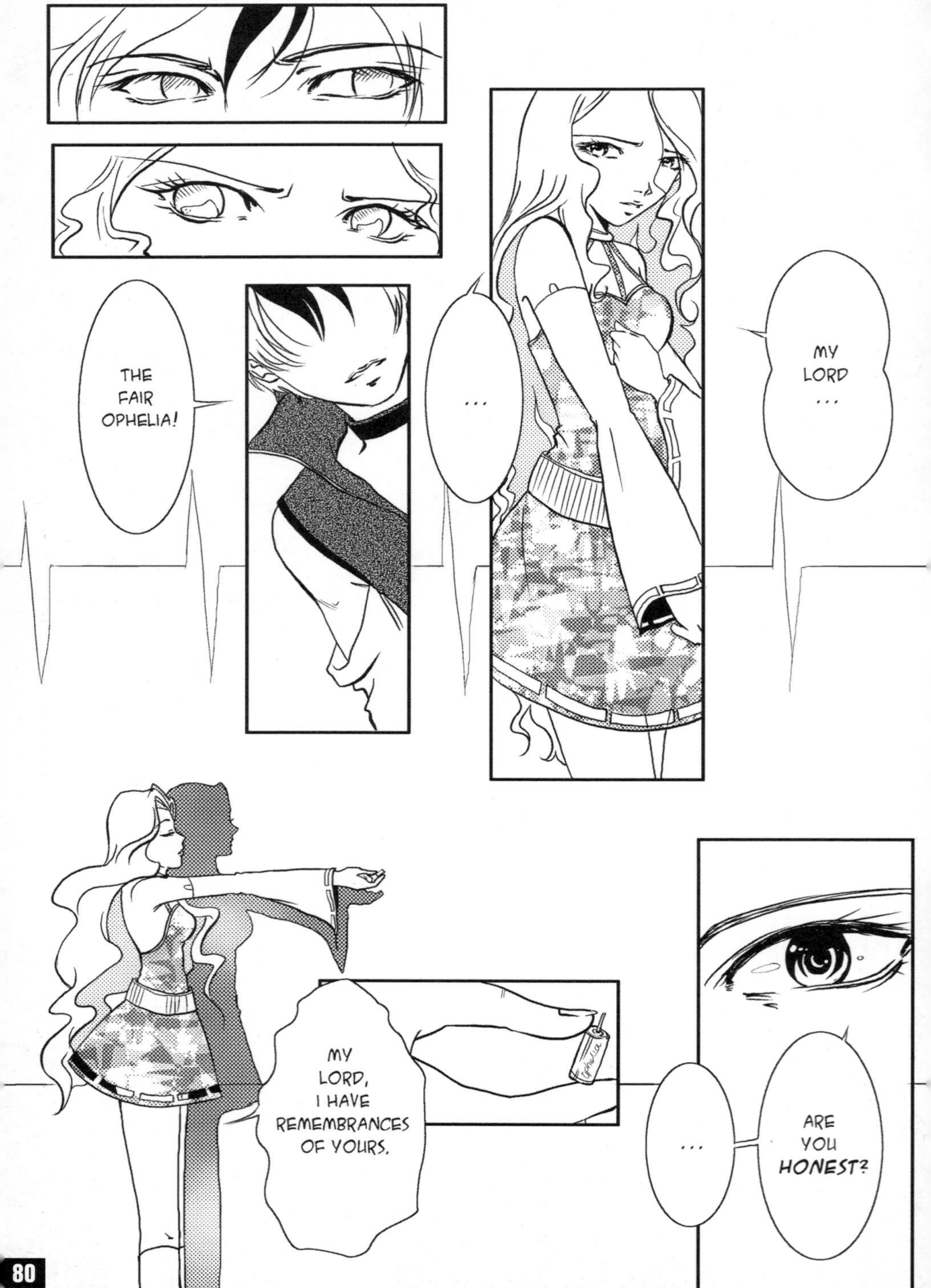

THE FAIR OPHELIA!
...
MY LORD ...
MY LORD, I HAVE REMEMBRANCES OF YOURS.
Ophelia
ARE YOU **HONEST**?
...

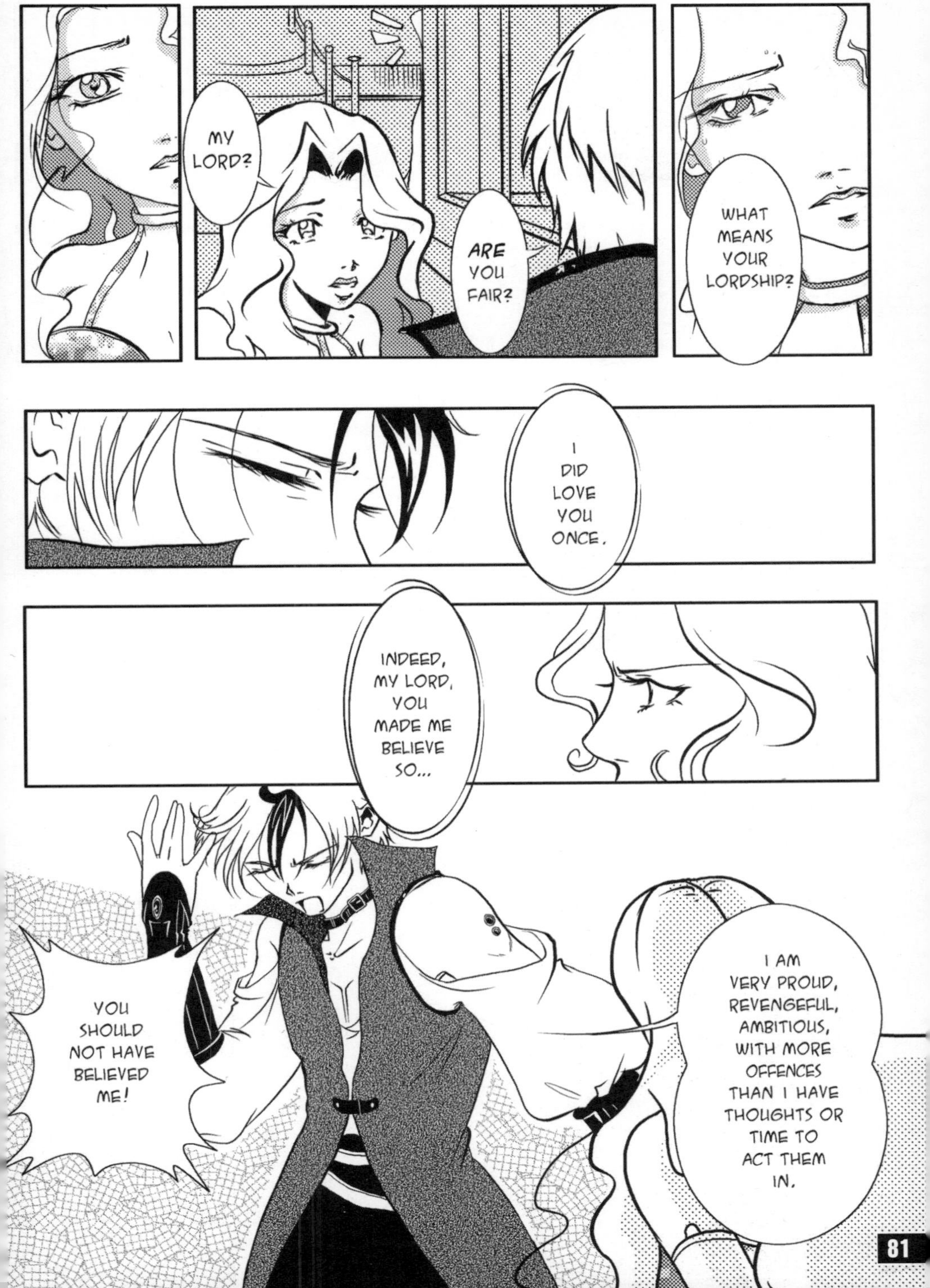
MY LORD?
ARE YOU FAIR?
WHAT MEANS YOUR LORDSHIP?
I DID LOVE YOU ONCE.
INDEED, MY LORD, YOU MADE ME BELIEVE SO...
YOU SHOULD NOT HAVE BELIEVED ME!
I AM VERY PROUD, REVENGEFUL, AMBITIOUS, WITH MORE OFFENCES THAN I HAVE THOUGHTS OR TIME TO ACT THEM IN.

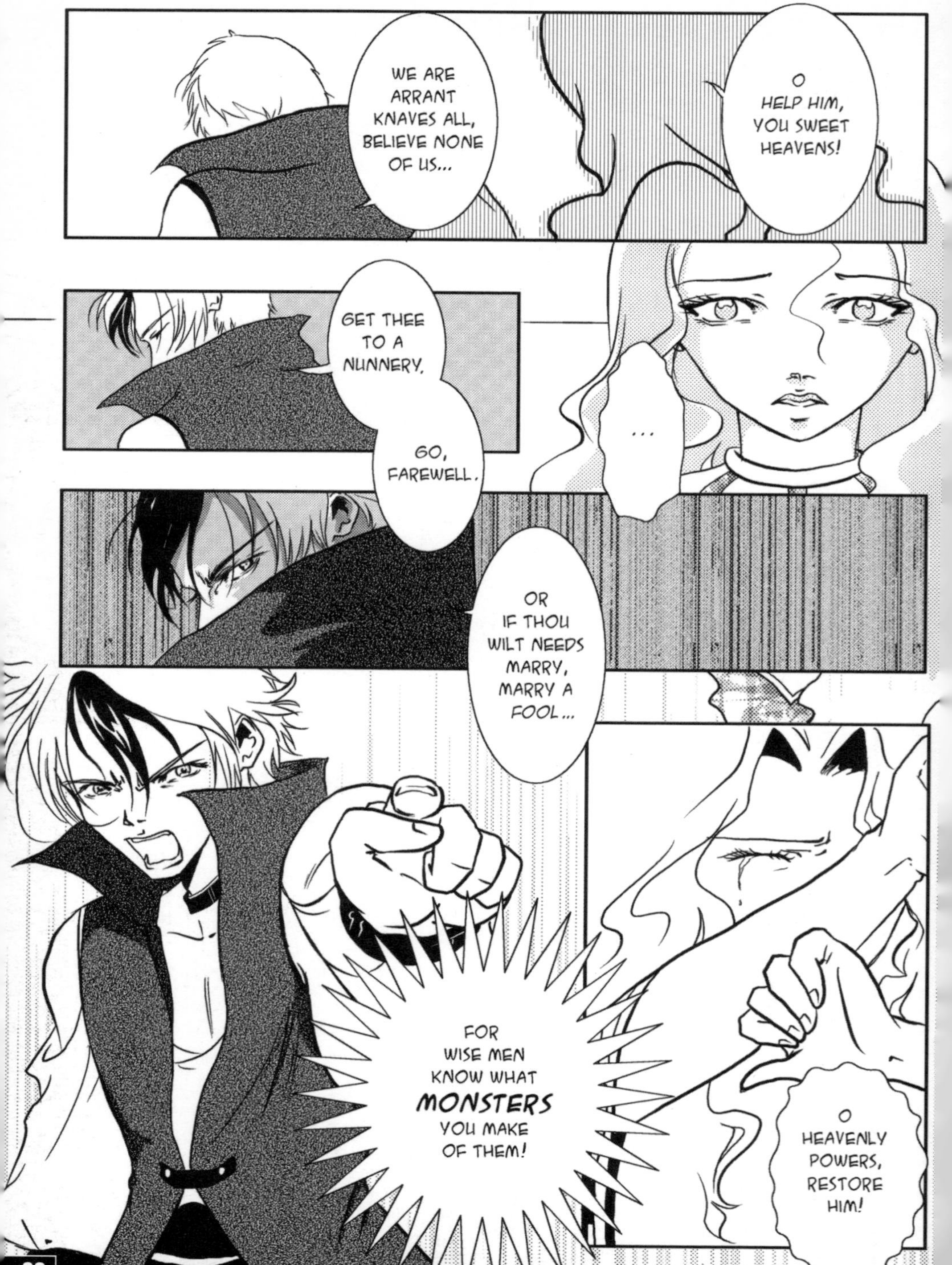
WE ARE ARRANT KNAVES ALL, BELIEVE NONE OF US...
O HELP HIM, YOU SWEET HEAVENS!
GET THEE TO A NUNNERY,
GO, FAREWELL.
...
OR IF THOU WILT NEEDS MARRY, MARRY A FOOL...
FOR WISE MEN KNOW WHAT MONSTERS YOU MAKE OF THEM!
O HEAVENLY POWERS, RESTORE HIM!

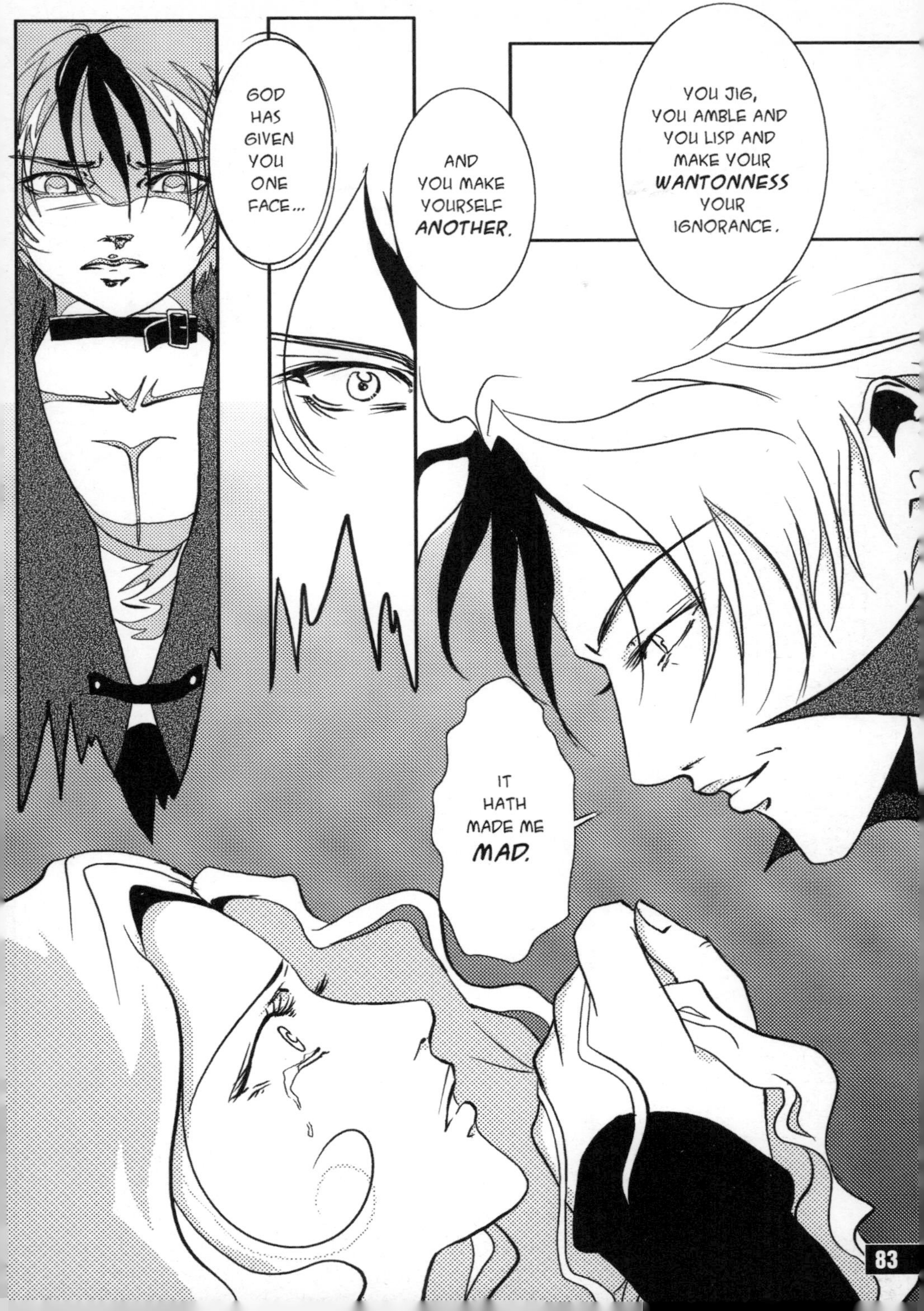
GOD HAS GIVEN YOU ONE FACE...
AND YOU MAKE YOURSELF ANOTHER.
YOU JIG, YOU AMBLE AND YOU LISP AND MAKE YOUR WANTONNESS YOUR IGNORANCE.
IT HATH MADE ME MAD.

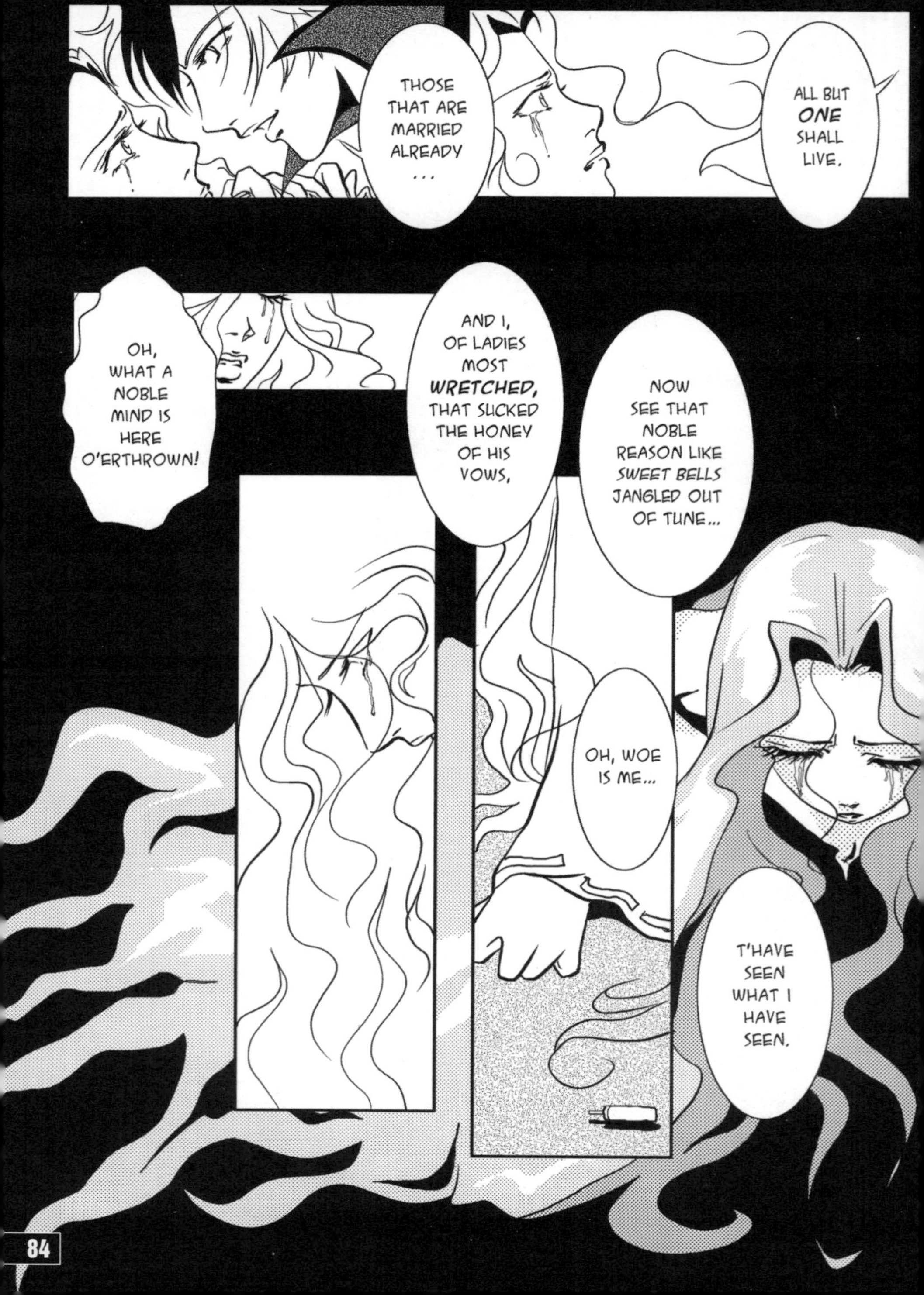
THOSE THAT ARE MARRIED ALREADY . . .
ALL BUT **ONE** SHALL LIVE.
OH, WHAT A NOBLE MIND IS HERE O'ERTHROWN!
AND I, OF LADIES MOST **WRETCHED,** THAT SUCKED THE HONEY OF HIS VOWS,
NOW SEE THAT NOBLE REASON LIKE *SWEET BELLS* JANGLED OUT OF TUNE...
OH, WOE IS ME...
T'HAVE SEEN WHAT I HAVE SEEN.

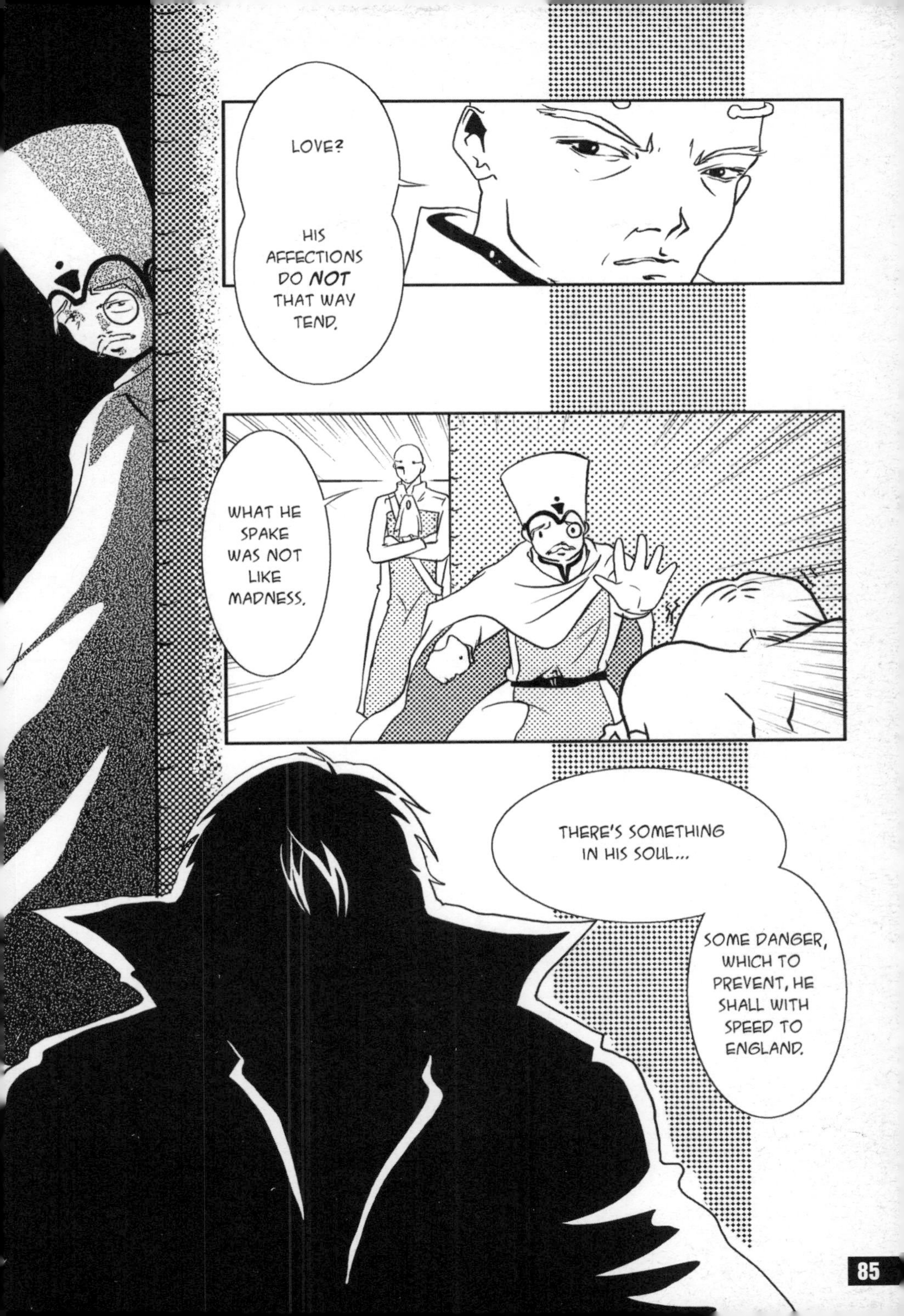

LOVE?
HIS AFFECTIONS DO **NOT** THAT WAY TEND.
WHAT HE SPAKE WAS NOT LIKE MADNESS.
THERE'S SOMETHING IN HIS SOUL...
SOME DANGER, WHICH TO PREVENT, HE SHALL WITH SPEED TO ENGLAND.

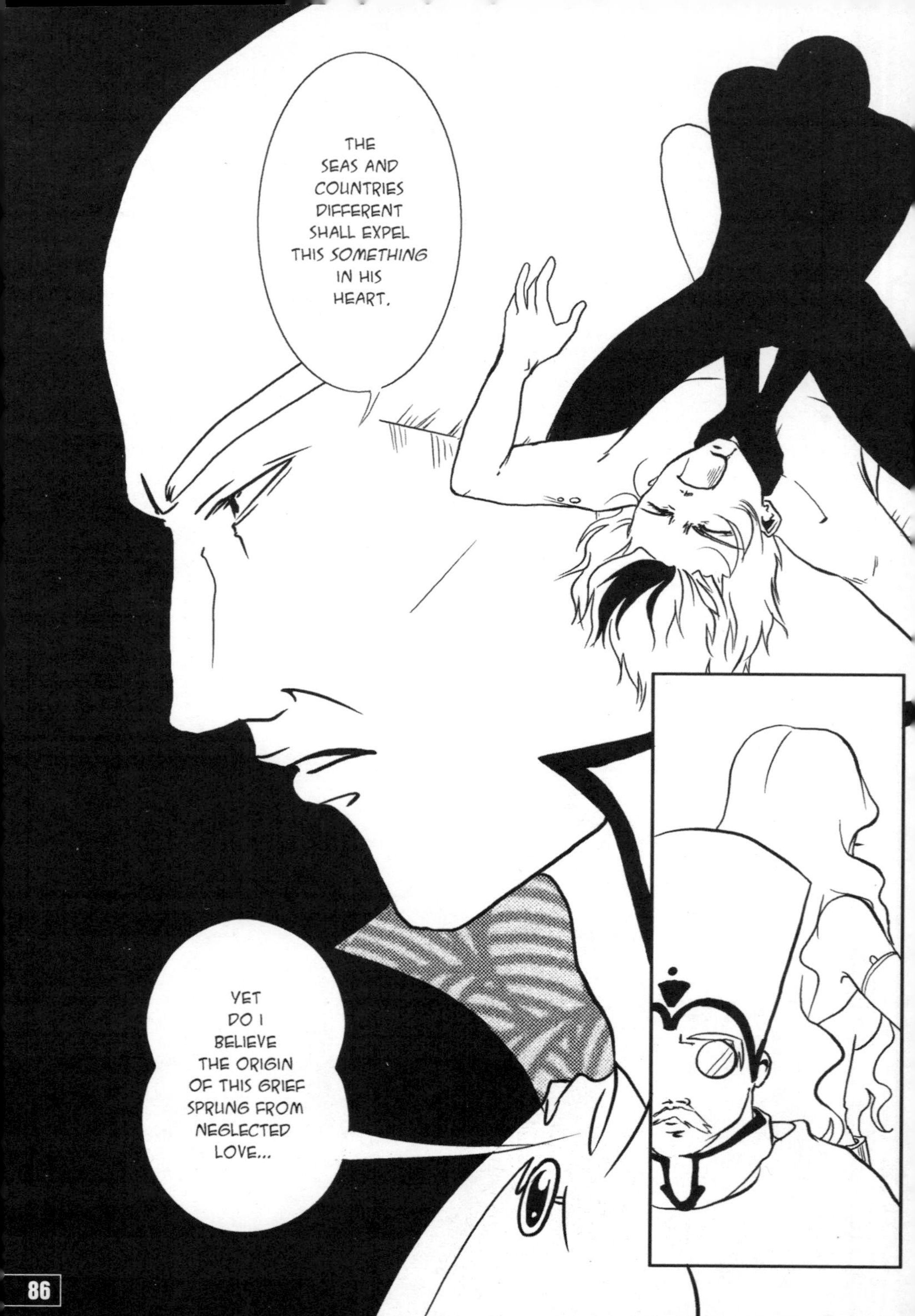
THE SEAS AND COUNTRIES DIFFERENT SHALL EXPEL THIS SOMETHING IN HIS HEART.
YET DO I BELIEVE THE ORIGIN OF THIS GRIEF SPRUNG FROM NEGLECTED LOVE...

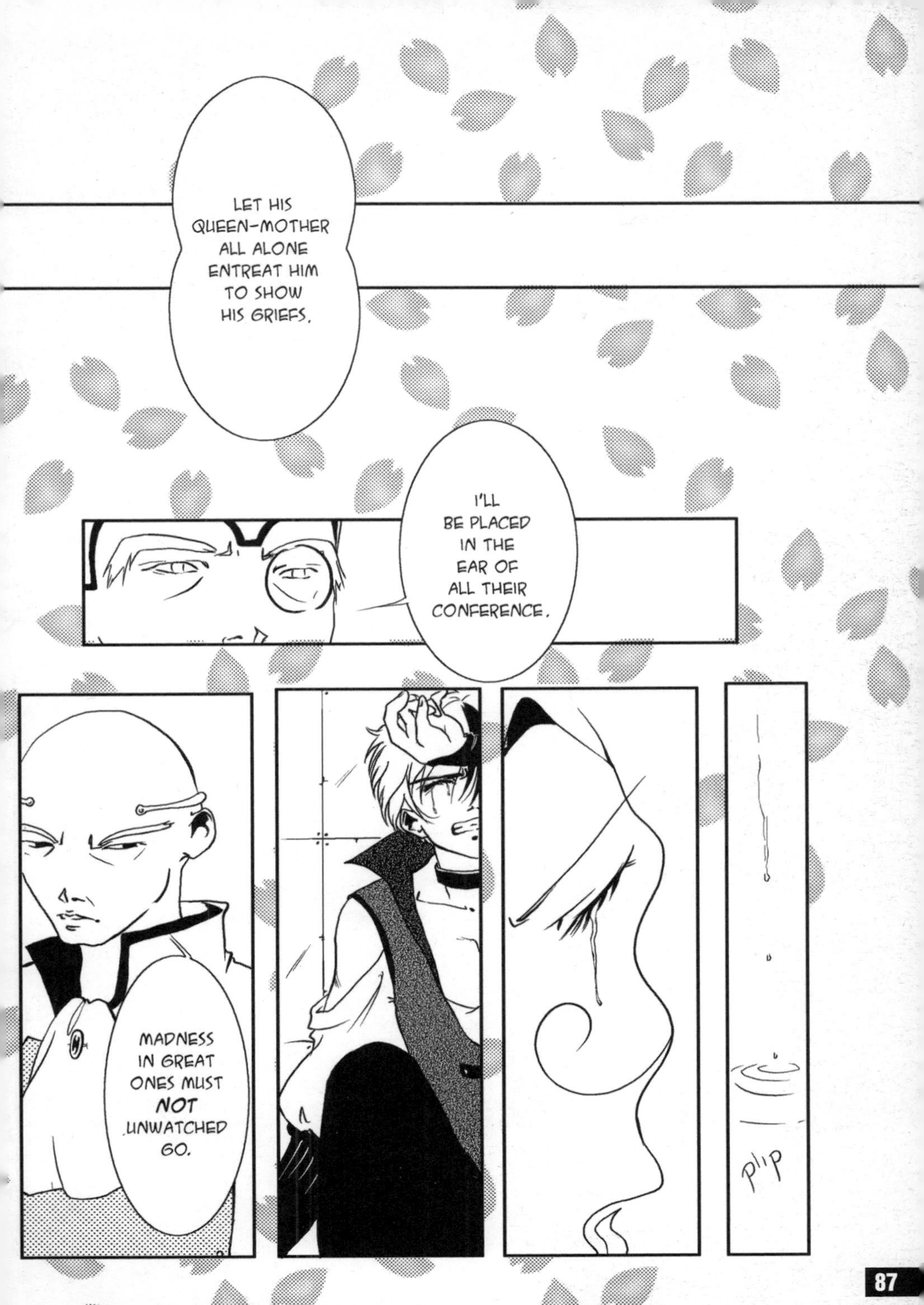
LET HIS QUEEN-MOTHER ALL ALONE ENTREAT HIM TO SHOW HIS GRIEFS.
I'LL BE PLACED IN THE EAR OF ALL THEIR CONFERENCE.
MADNESS IN GREAT ONES MUST **NOT** UNWATCHED GO.
plip

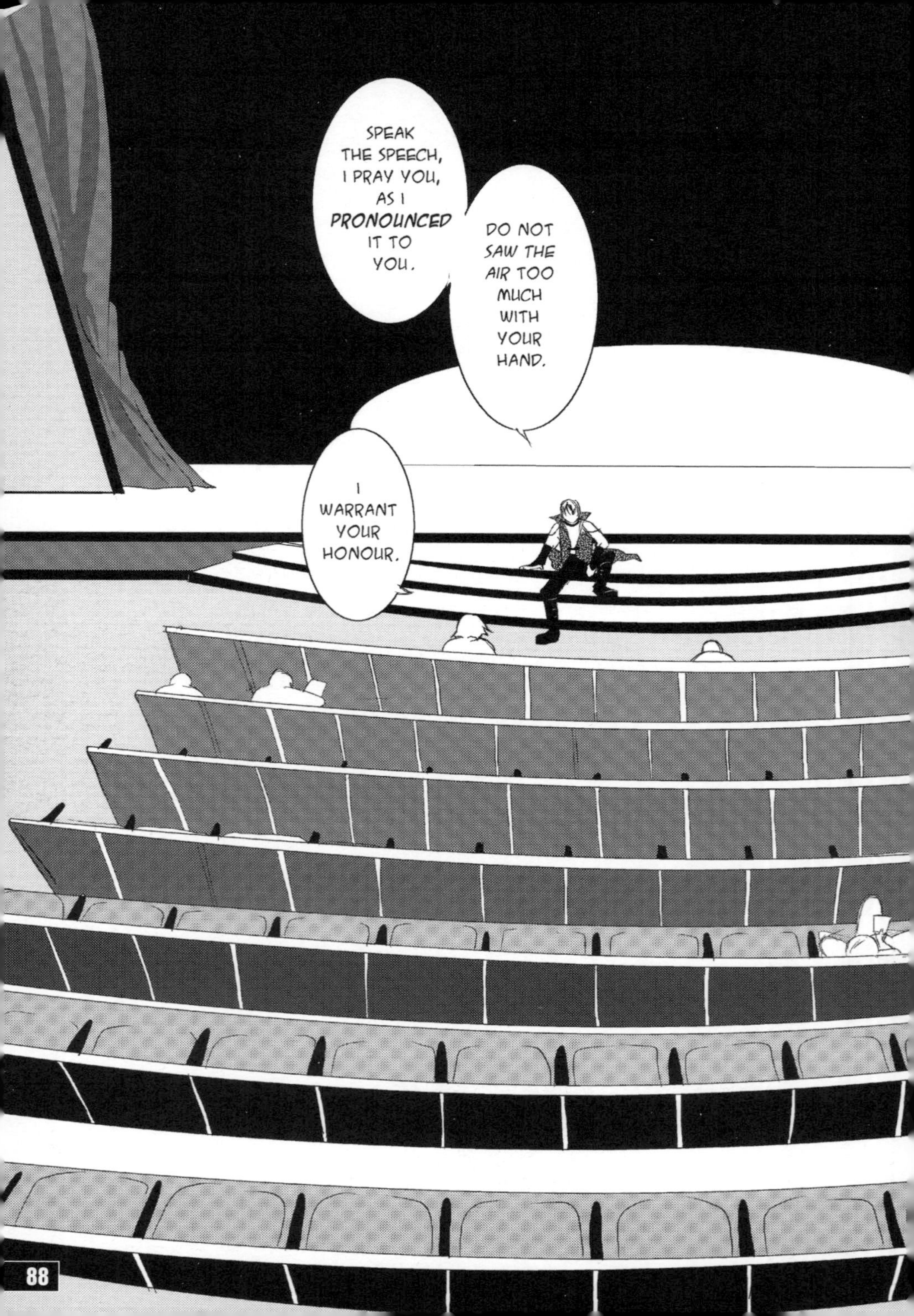
SPEAK THE SPEECH, I PRAY YOU, AS I PRONOUNCED IT TO YOU.
DO NOT SAW THE AIR TOO MUCH WITH YOUR HAND.
I WARRANT YOUR HONOUR.

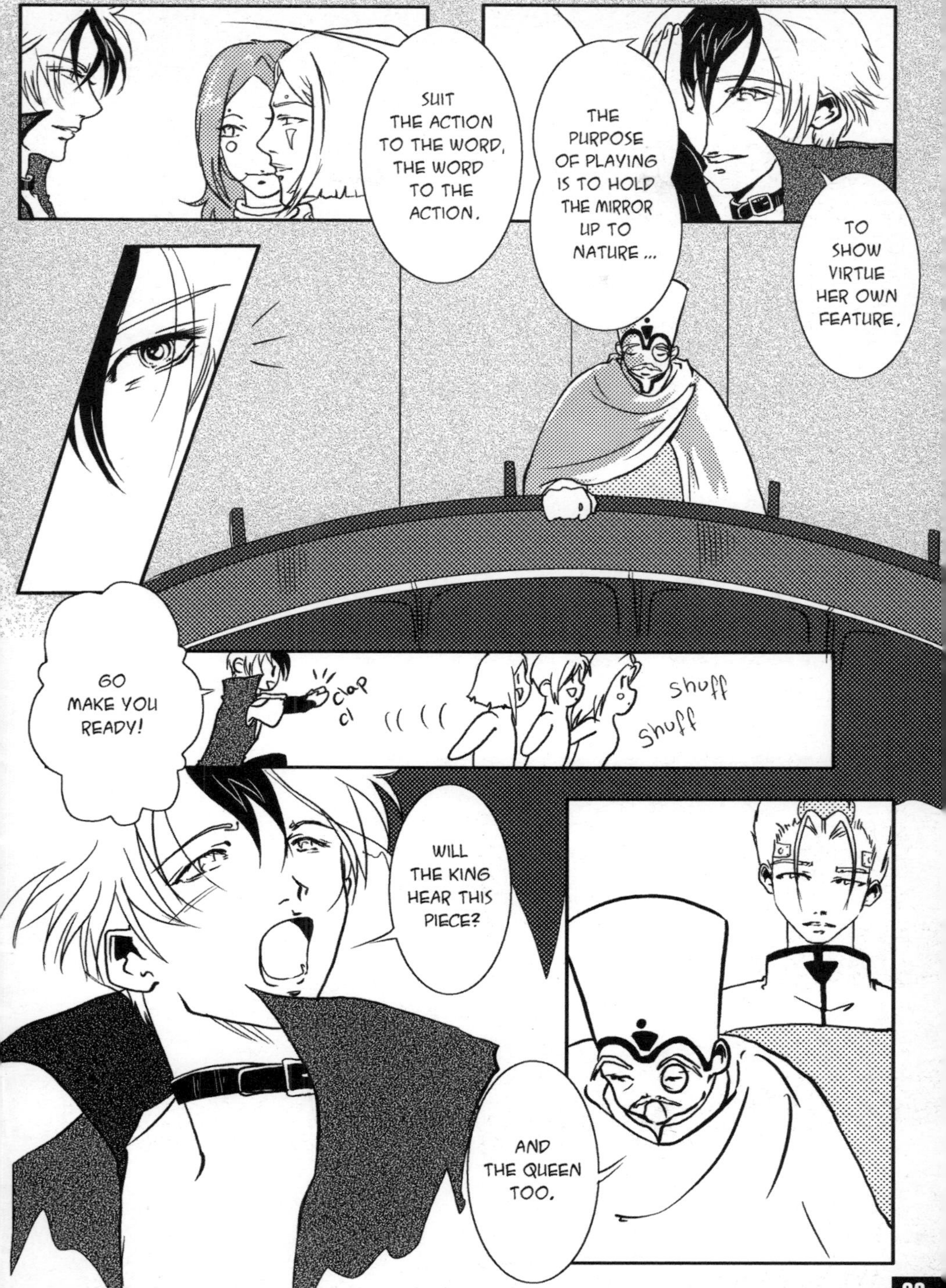
SUIT THE ACTION TO THE WORD, THE WORD TO THE ACTION.
THE PURPOSE OF PLAYING IS TO HOLD THE MIRROR UP TO NATURE ...
TO SHOW VIRTUE HER OWN FEATURE.
GO MAKE YOU READY!
clap cl
shuff
shuff
WILL THE KING HEAR THIS PIECE?
AND THE QUEEN TOO.

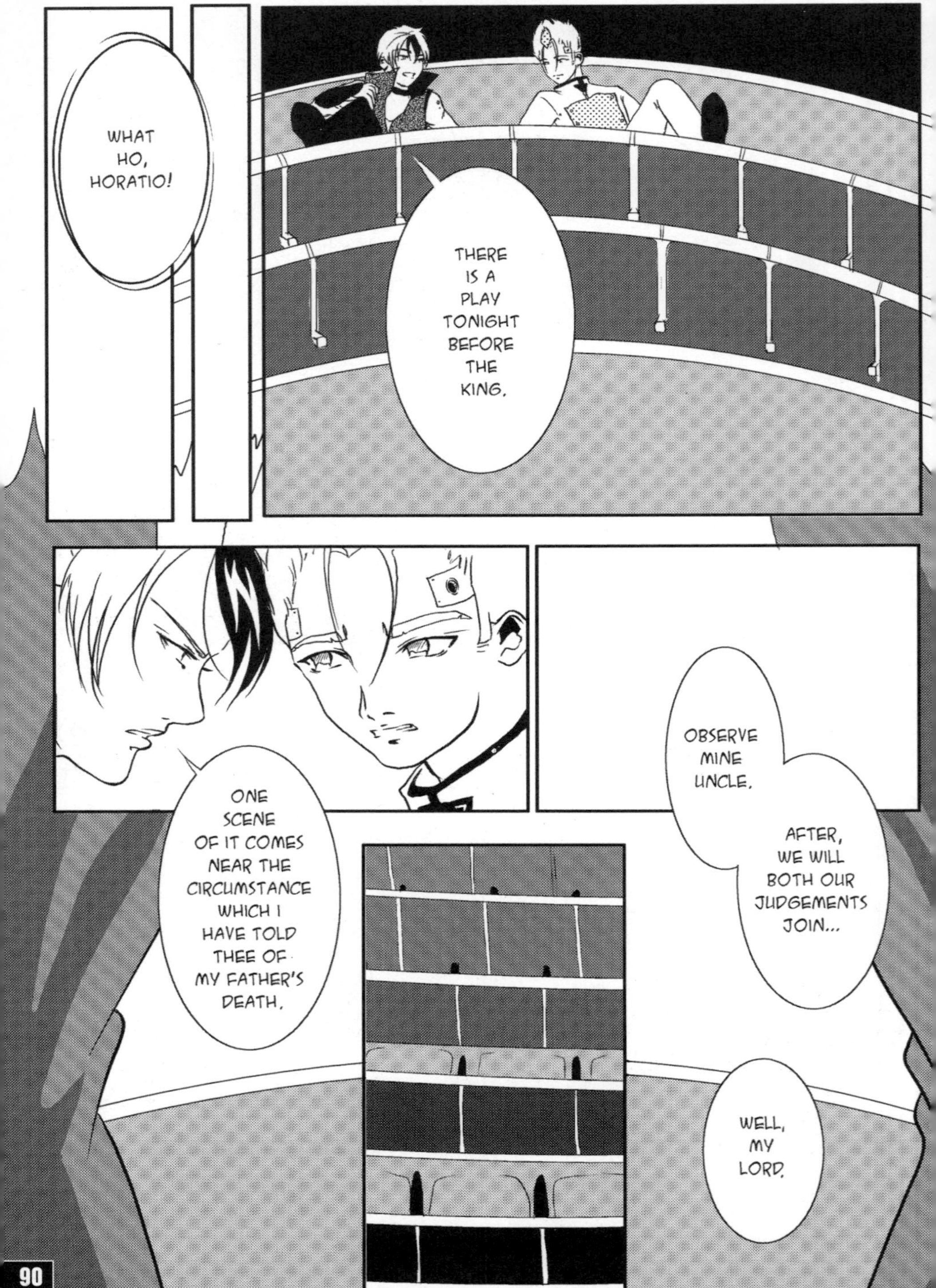
WHAT HO, HORATIO!
THERE IS A PLAY TONIGHT BEFORE THE KING.
ONE SCENE OF IT COMES NEAR THE CIRCUMSTANCE WHICH I HAVE TOLD THEE OF MY FATHER'S DEATH,
OBSERVE MINE UNCLE.
AFTER, WE WILL BOTH OUR JUDGEMENTS JOIN...
WELL, MY LORD.

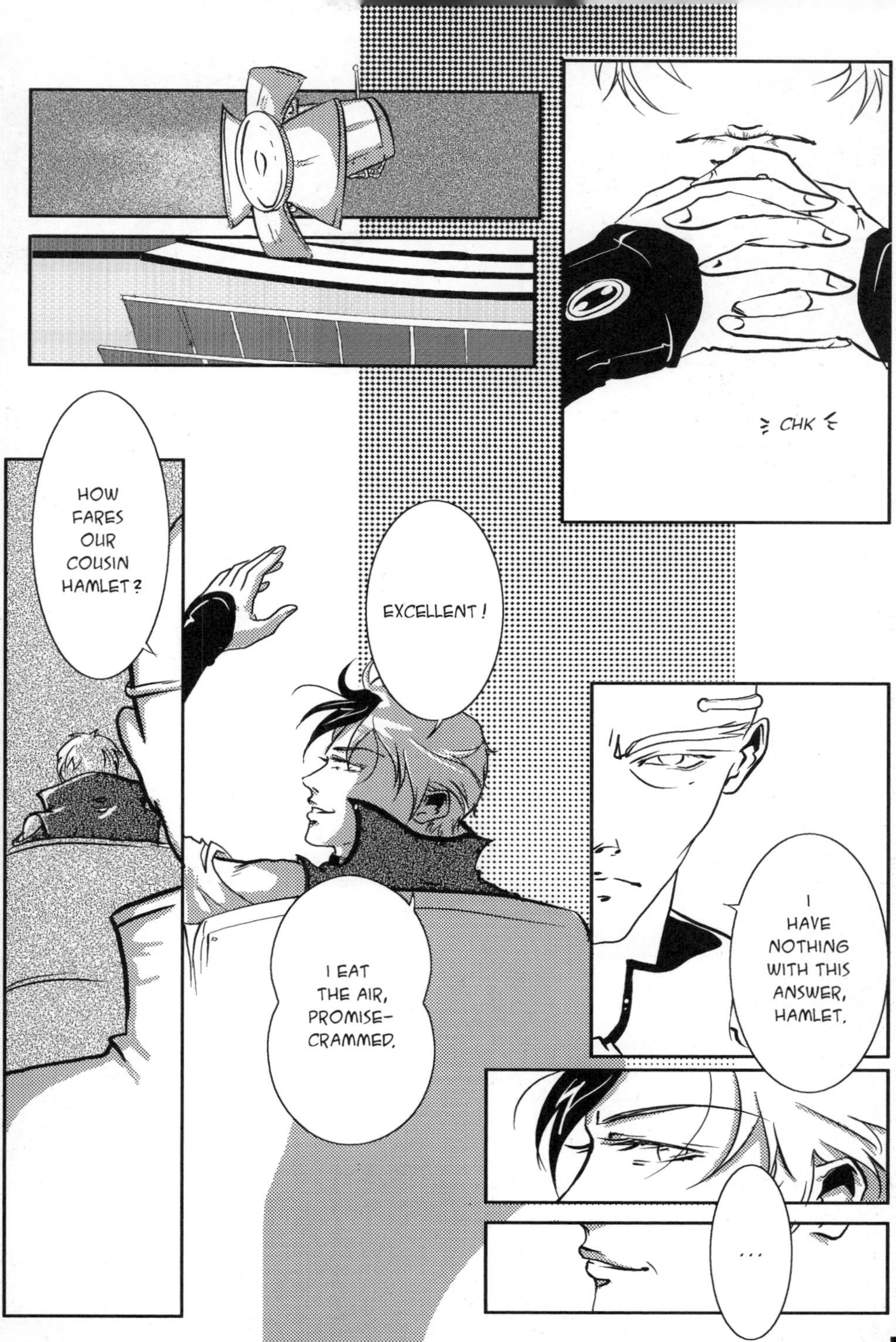
CHK
HOW FARES OUR COUSIN HAMLET?
EXCELLENT!
I EAT THE AIR, PROMISE-CRAMMED.
I HAVE NOTHING WITH THIS ANSWER, HAMLET.
...

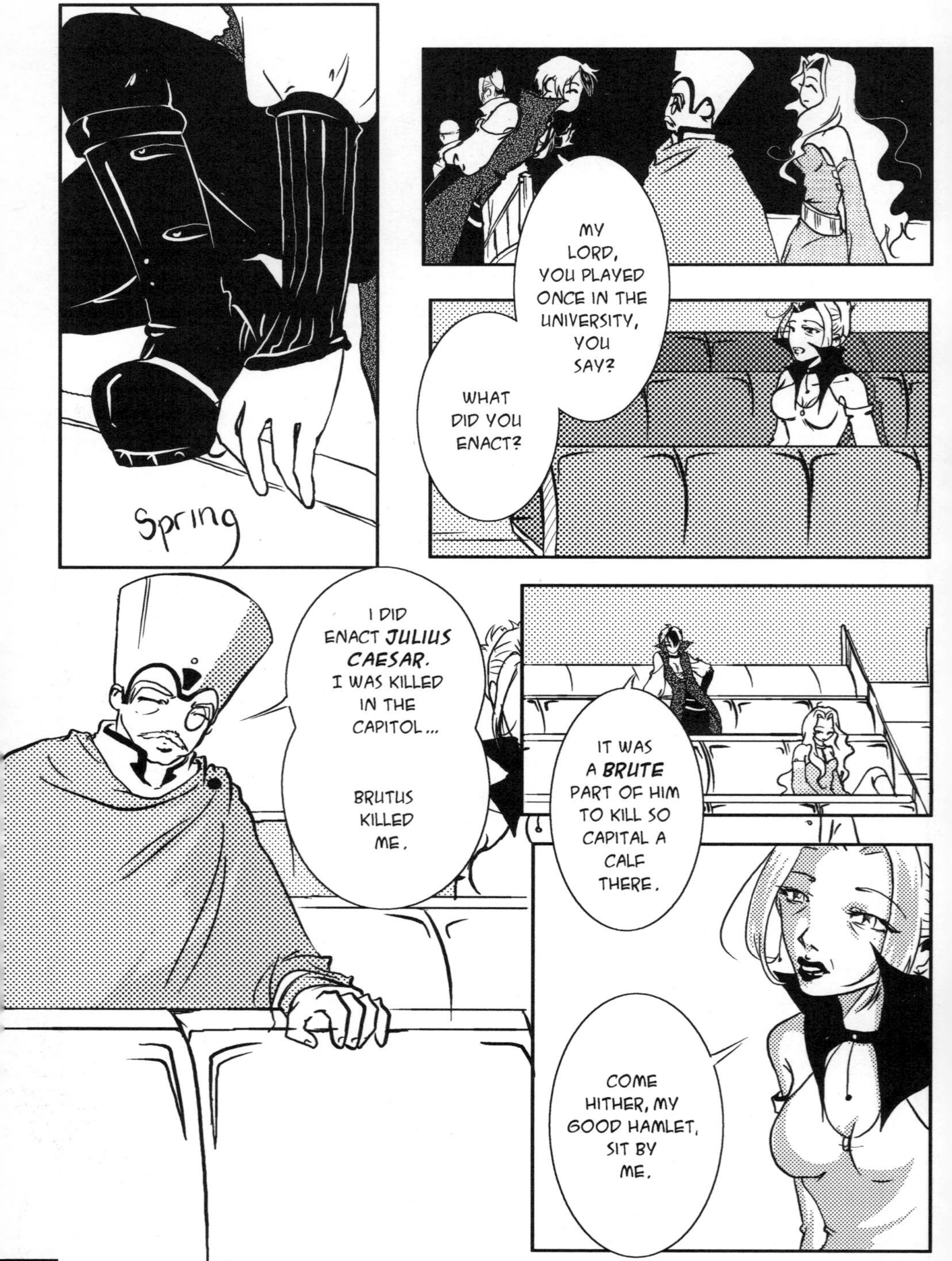
Spring
MY LORD, YOU PLAYED ONCE IN THE UNIVERSITY, YOU SAY?
WHAT DID YOU ENACT?
I DID ENACT JULIUS CAESAR. I WAS KILLED IN THE CAPITOL...
BRUTUS KILLED ME.
IT WAS A BRUTE PART OF HIM TO KILL SO CAPITAL A CALF THERE.
COME HITHER, MY GOOD HAMLET, SIT BY ME.

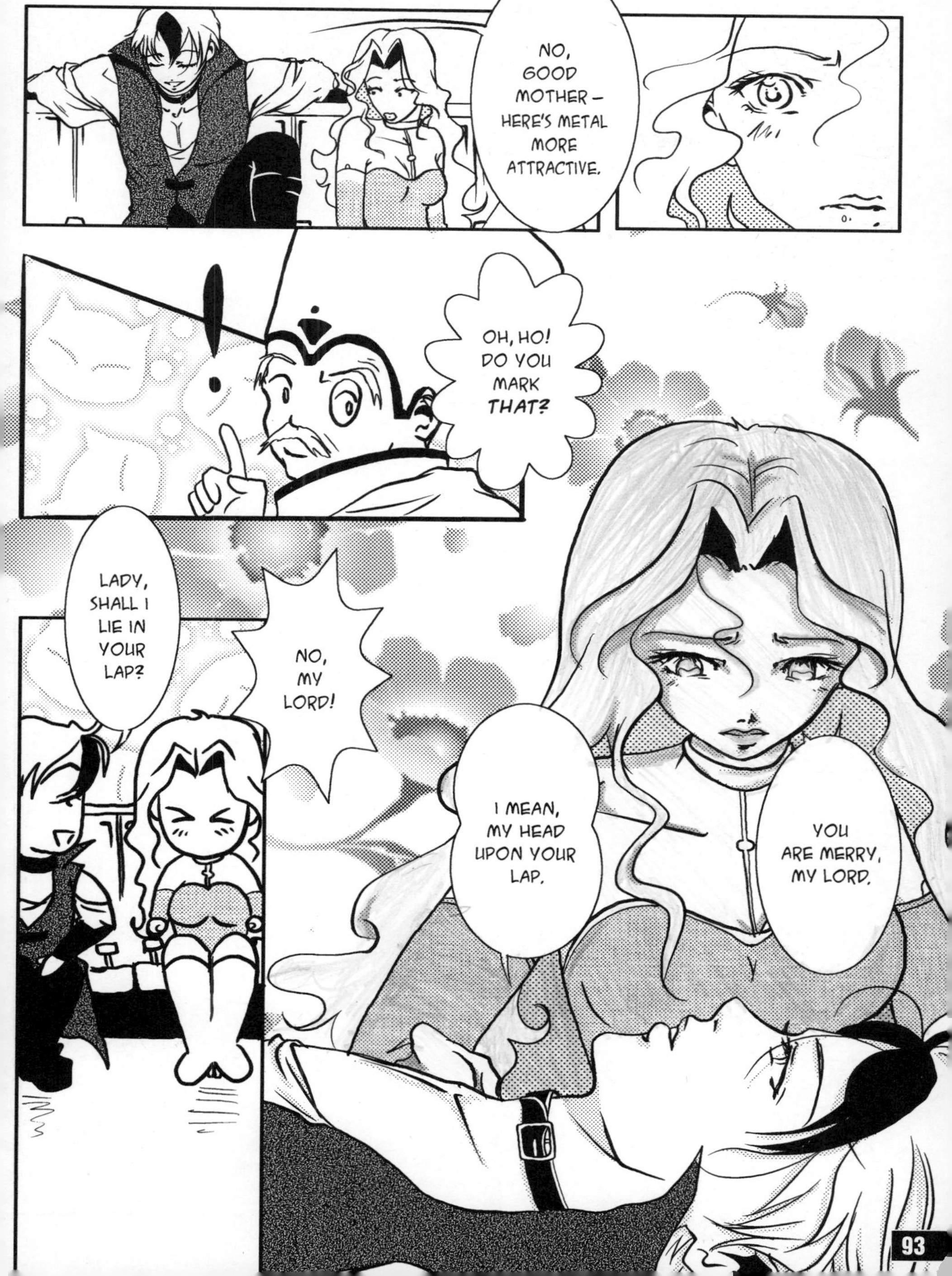
NO, GOOD MOTHER – HERE'S METAL MORE ATTRACTIVE.
!
OH, HO! DO YOU MARK THAT?
LADY, SHALL I LIE IN YOUR LAP?
NO, MY LORD!
I MEAN, MY HEAD UPON YOUR LAP.
YOU ARE MERRY, MY LORD.

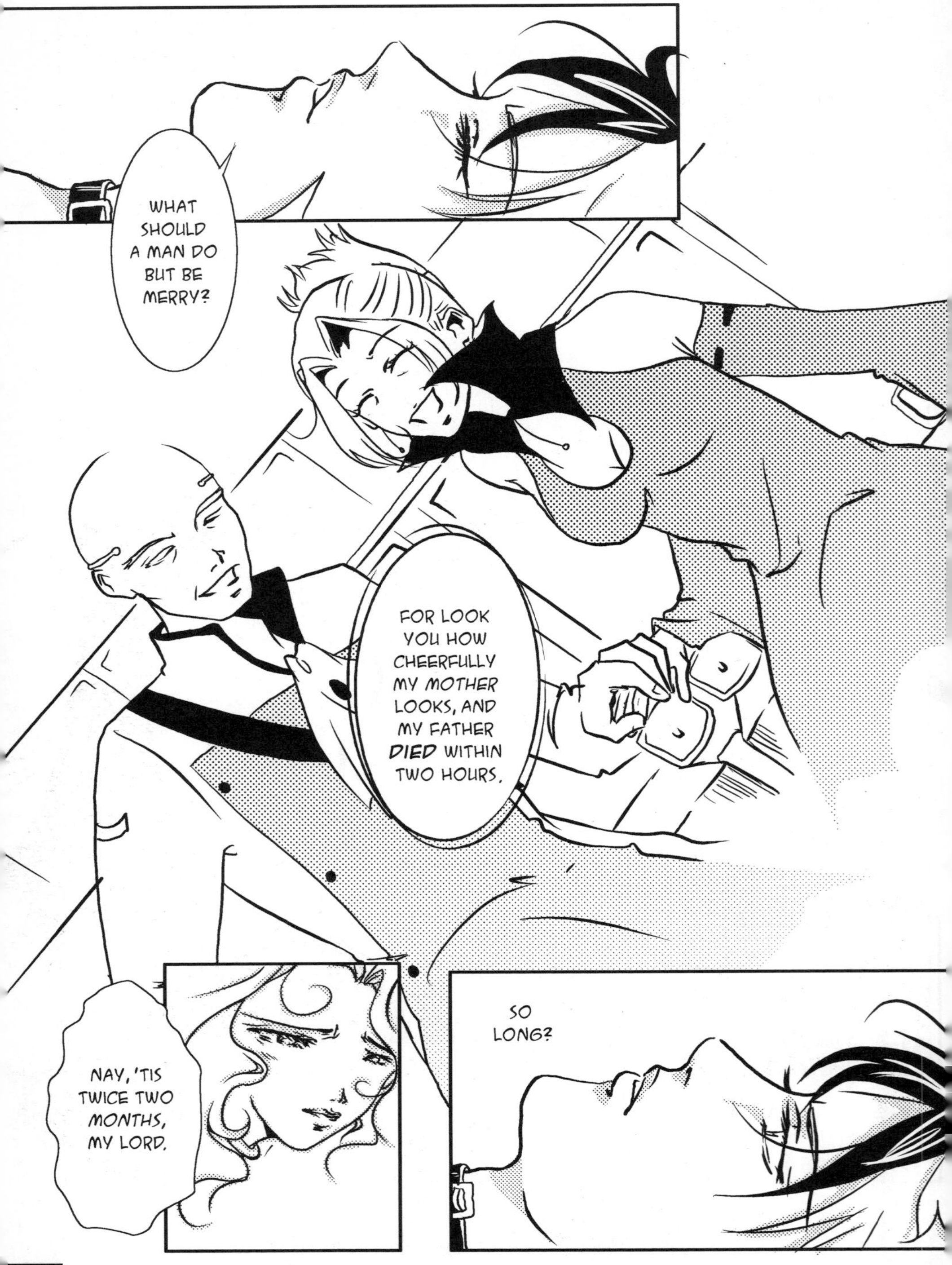
WHAT SHOULD A MAN DO BUT BE MERRY?
FOR LOOK YOU HOW CHEERFULLY MY *MOTHER* LOOKS, AND MY FATHER ***DIED*** WITHIN TWO HOURS.
NAY, 'TIS TWICE TWO MONTHS, MY LORD.
SO LONG?

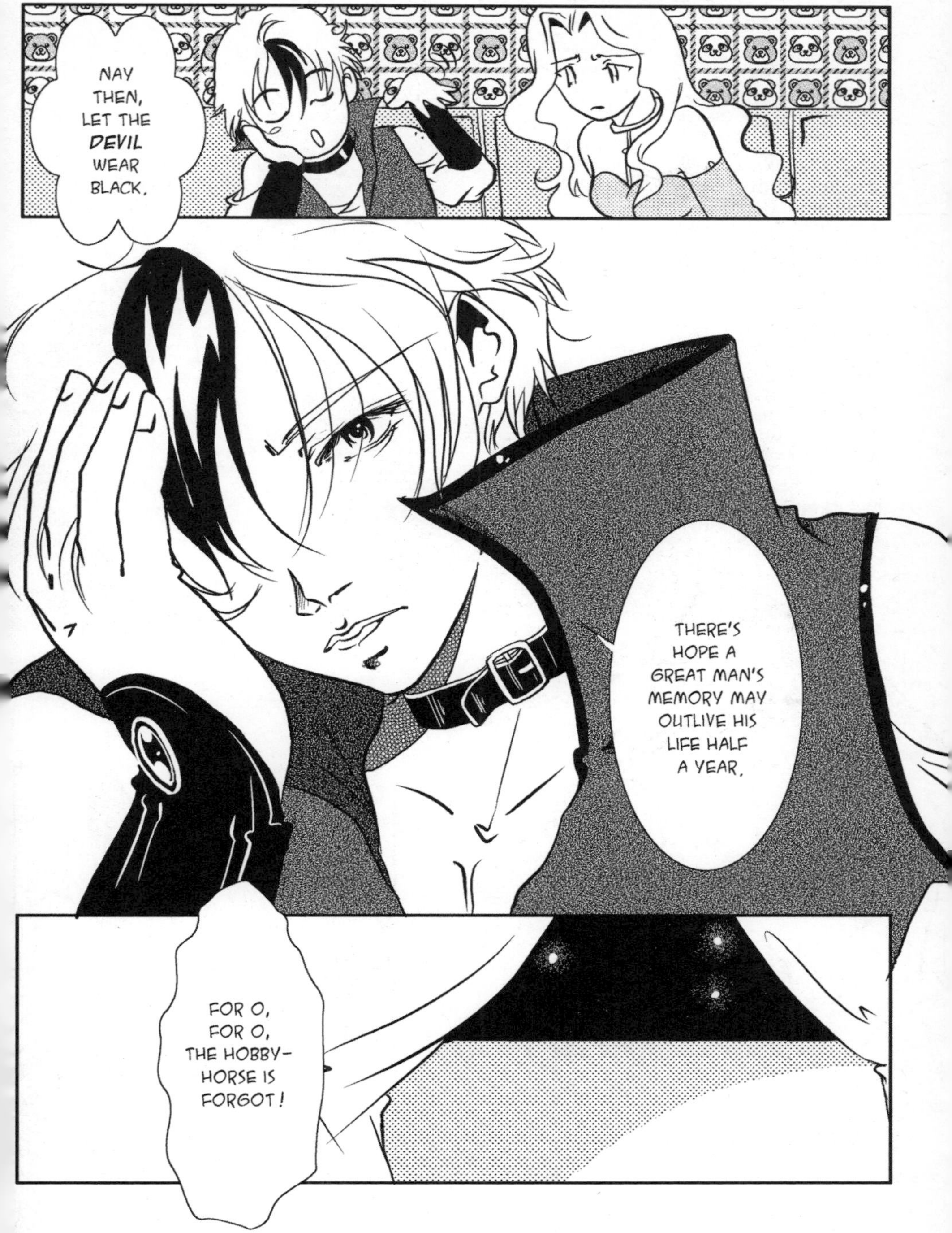
NAY THEN, LET THE DEVIL WEAR BLACK.
THERE'S HOPE A GREAT MAN'S MEMORY MAY OUTLIVE HIS LIFE HALF A YEAR.
FOR O, FOR O, THE HOBBY-HORSE IS FORGOT!

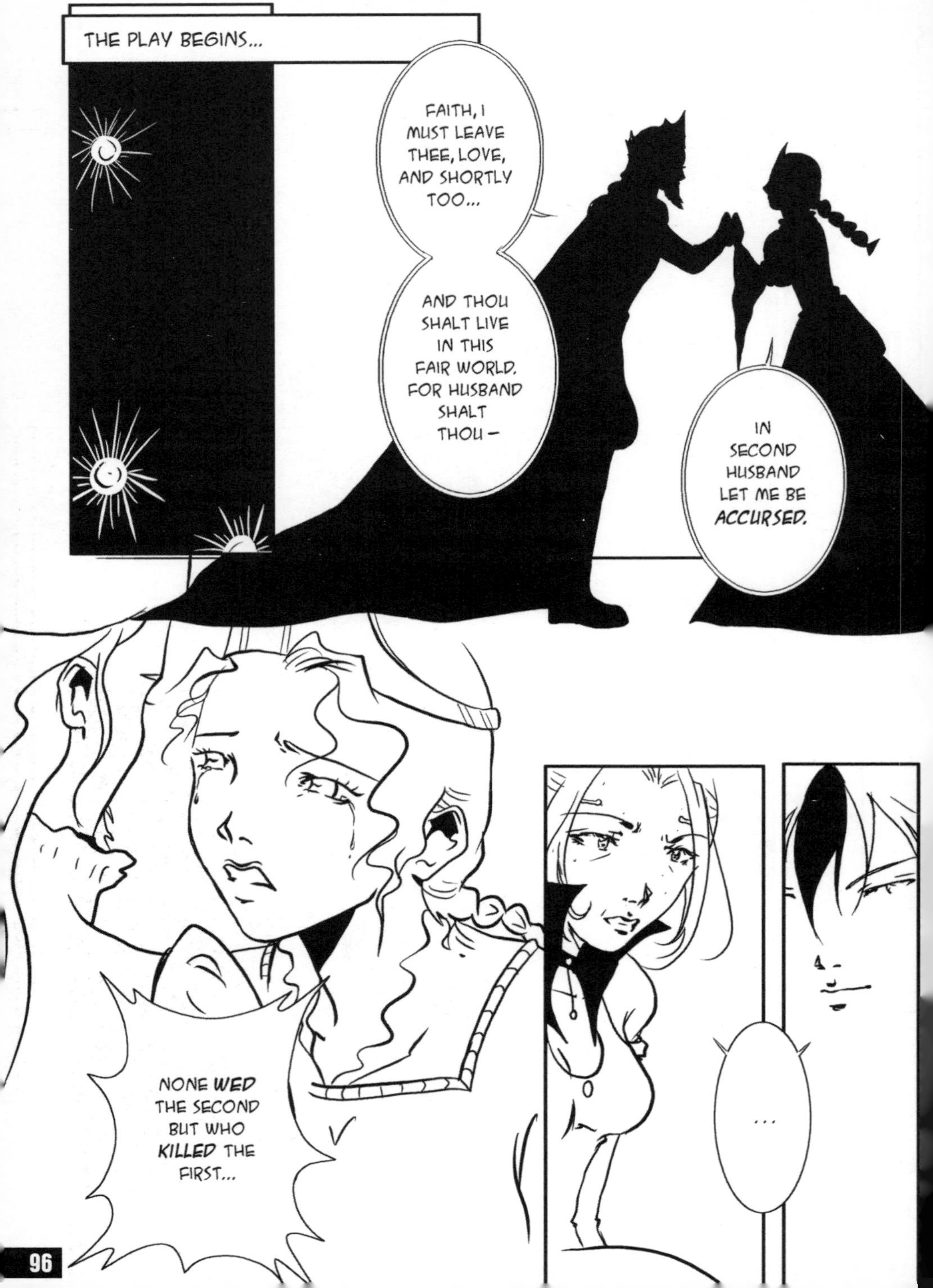
THE PLAY BEGINS...
FAITH, I MUST LEAVE THEE, LOVE, AND SHORTLY TOO...
AND THOU SHALT LIVE IN THIS FAIR WORLD. FOR HUSBAND SHALT THOU –
IN SECOND HUSBAND LET ME BE **ACCURSED.**
NONE **WED** THE SECOND BUT WHO **KILLED** THE FIRST...
...

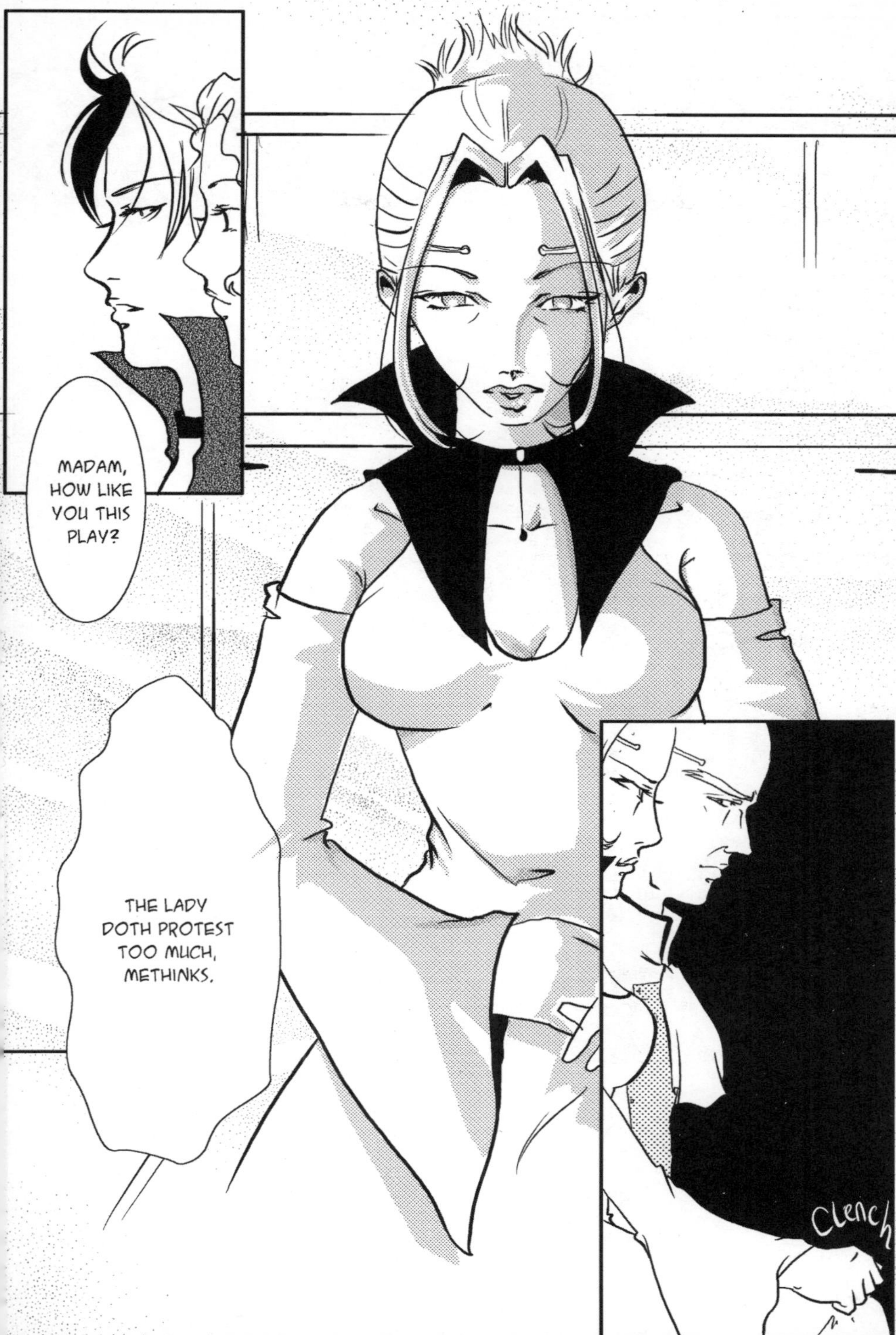
MADAM, HOW LIKE YOU THIS PLAY?
THE LADY DOTH PROTEST TOO MUCH, METHINKS.
Clench

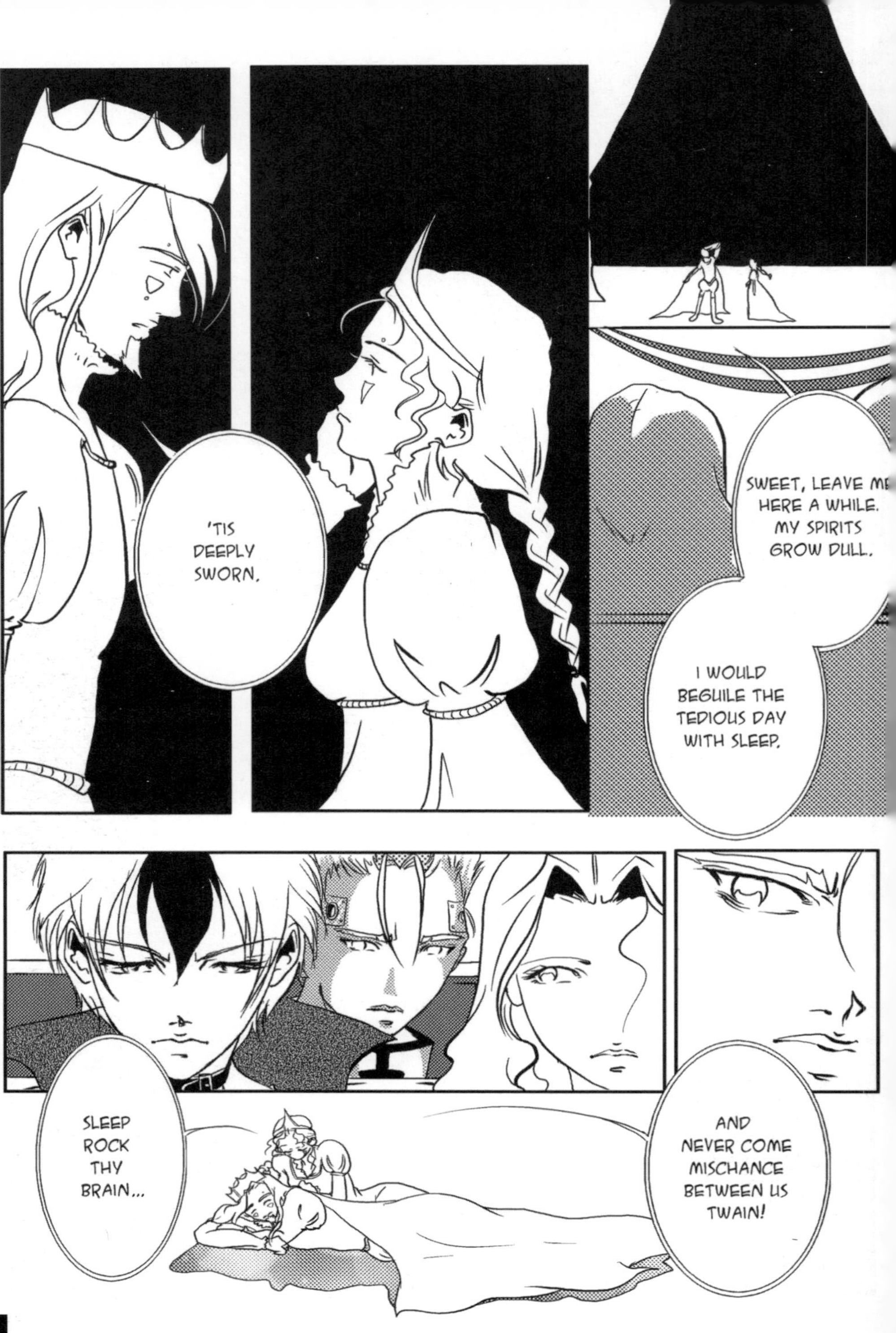
'TIS DEEPLY SWORN.
SWEET, LEAVE ME HERE A WHILE. MY SPIRITS GROW DULL.
I WOULD BEGUILE THE TEDIOUS DAY WITH SLEEP.
SLEEP ROCK THY BRAIN...
AND NEVER COME MISCHANCE BETWEEN US TWAIN!

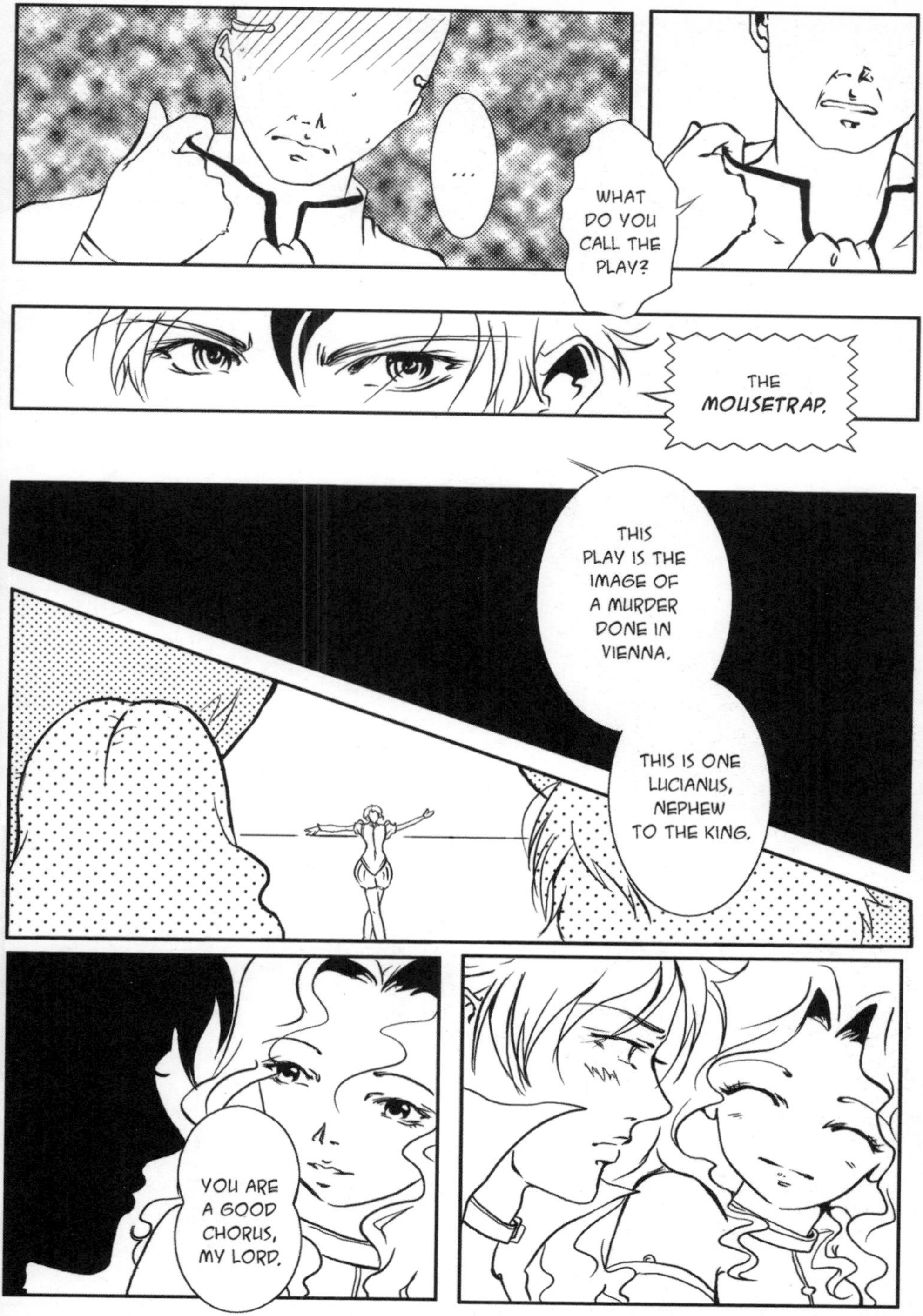
...
WHAT DO YOU CALL THE PLAY?
THE MOUSETRAP.
THIS PLAY IS THE IMAGE OF A MURDER DONE IN VIENNA.
THIS IS ONE LUCIANUS, NEPHEW TO THE KING.
YOU ARE A GOOD CHORUS, MY LORD.

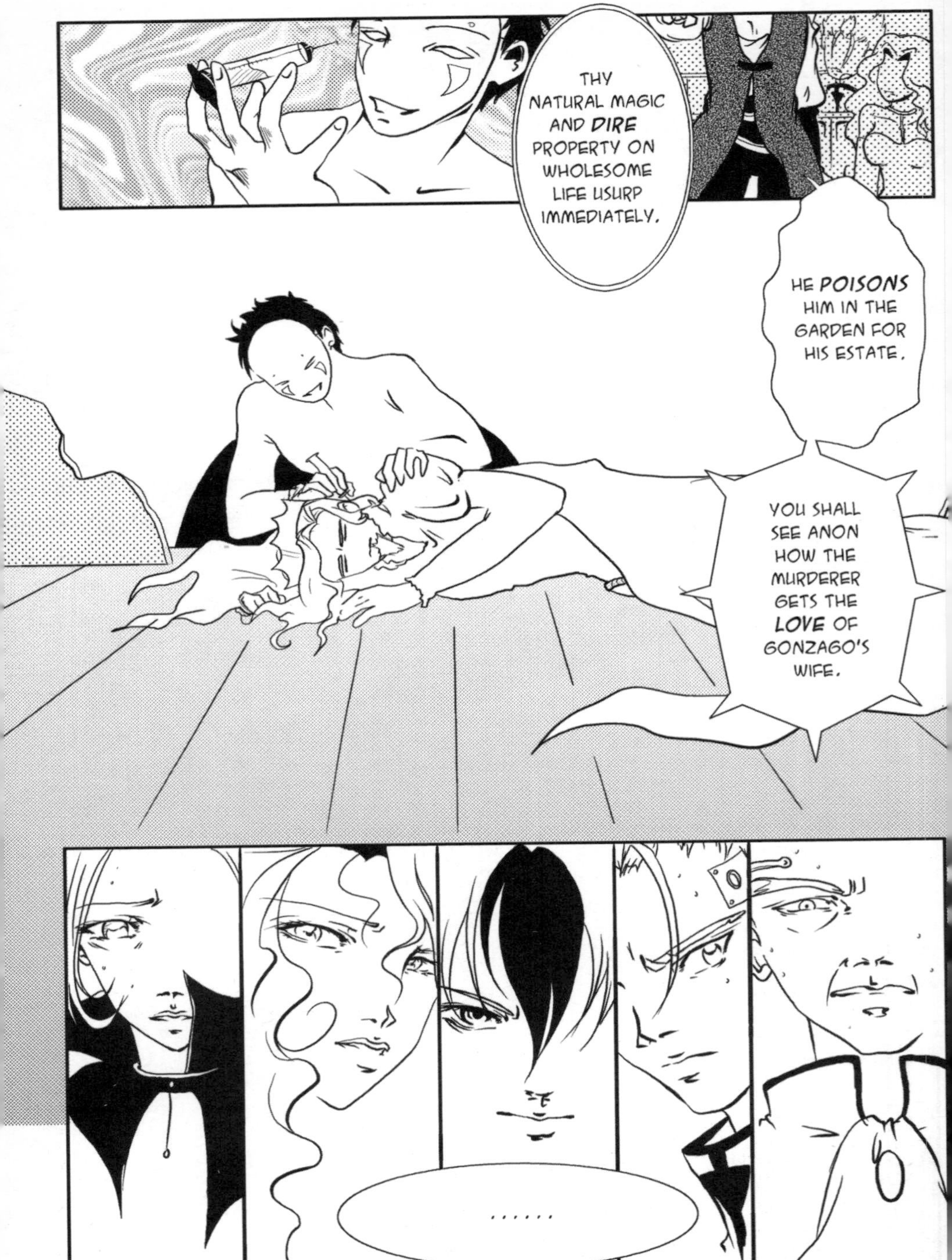
THY NATURAL MAGIC AND DIRE PROPERTY ON WHOLESOME LIFE USURP IMMEDIATELY.
HE POISONS HIM IN THE GARDEN FOR HIS ESTATE.
YOU SHALL SEE ANON HOW THE MURDERER GETS THE LOVE OF GONZAGO'S WIFE.
......

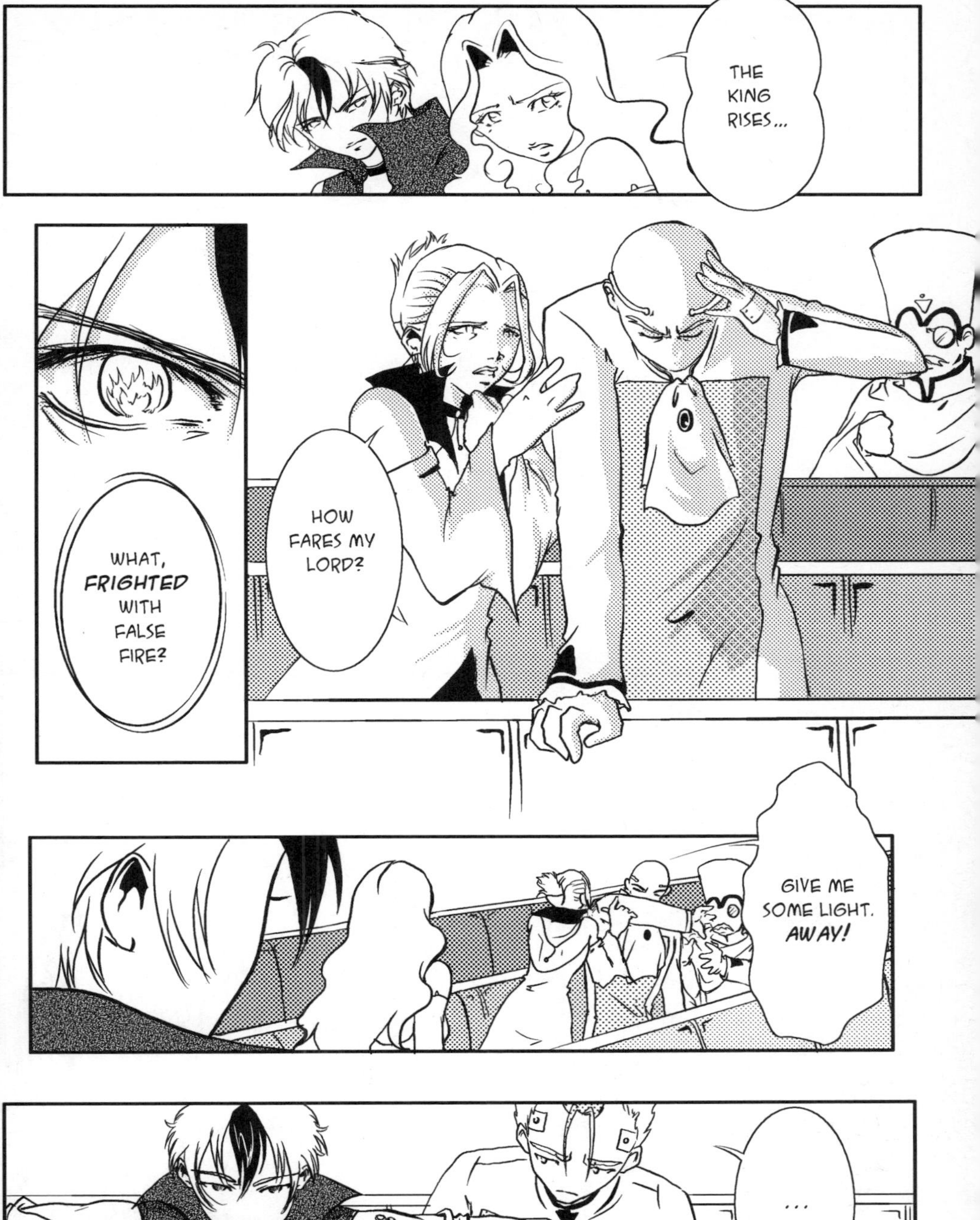
THE KING RISES...
HOW FARES MY LORD?
WHAT, **FRIGHTED** WITH FALSE FIRE?
GIVE ME SOME LIGHT. **AWAY!**
...

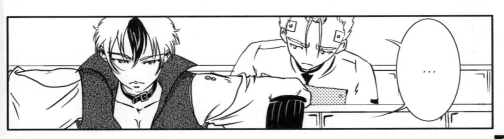

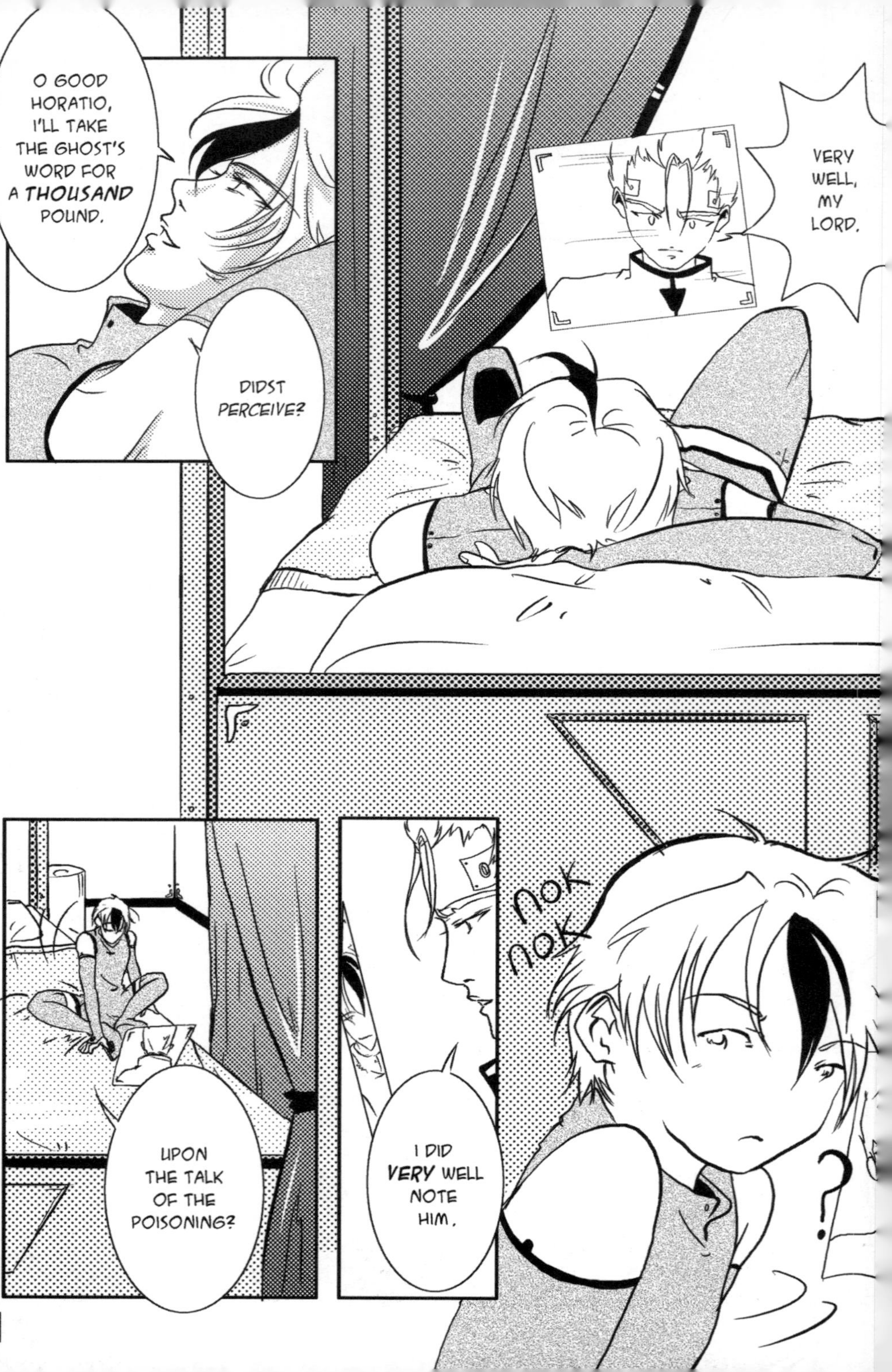
O GOOD HORATIO, I'LL TAKE THE GHOST'S WORD FOR A **THOUSAND** POUND.
VERY WELL, MY LORD.
DIDST PERCEIVE?
UPON THE TALK OF THE POISONING?
I DID **VERY** WELL NOTE HIM.
nok nok

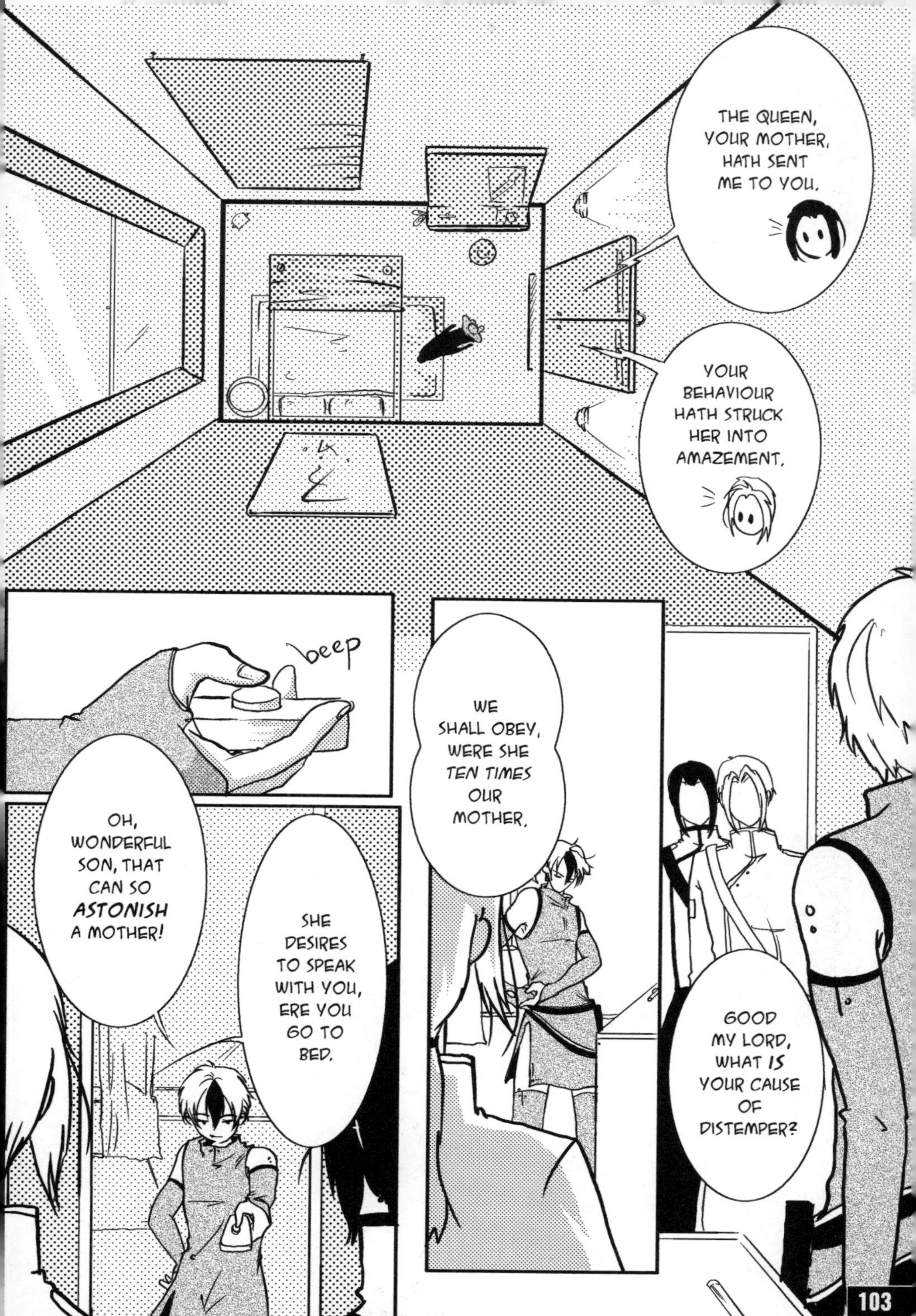
THE QUEEN, YOUR MOTHER, HATH SENT ME TO YOU.
YOUR BEHAVIOUR HATH STRUCK HER INTO AMAZEMENT.
beep
WE SHALL OBEY, WERE SHE *TEN TIMES* OUR MOTHER.
GOOD MY LORD, WHAT *IS* YOUR CAUSE OF DISTEMPER?
OH, WONDERFUL SON, THAT CAN SO ***ASTONISH*** A MOTHER!
SHE DESIRES TO SPEAK WITH YOU, ERE YOU GO TO BED.

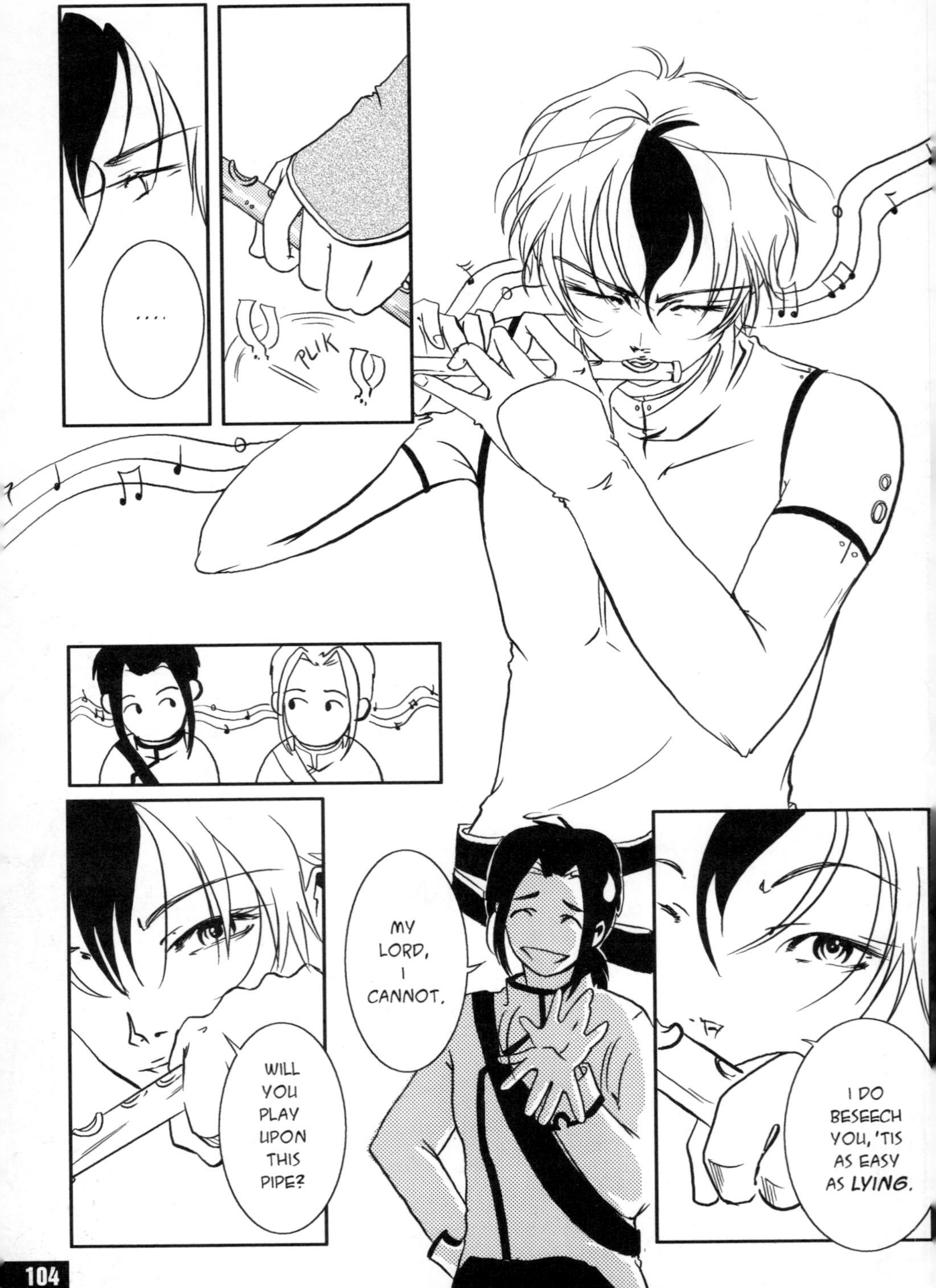
....
PLIK
WILL YOU PLAY UPON THIS PIPE?
MY LORD, I CANNOT.
I DO BESEECH YOU, 'TIS AS EASY AS LYING.

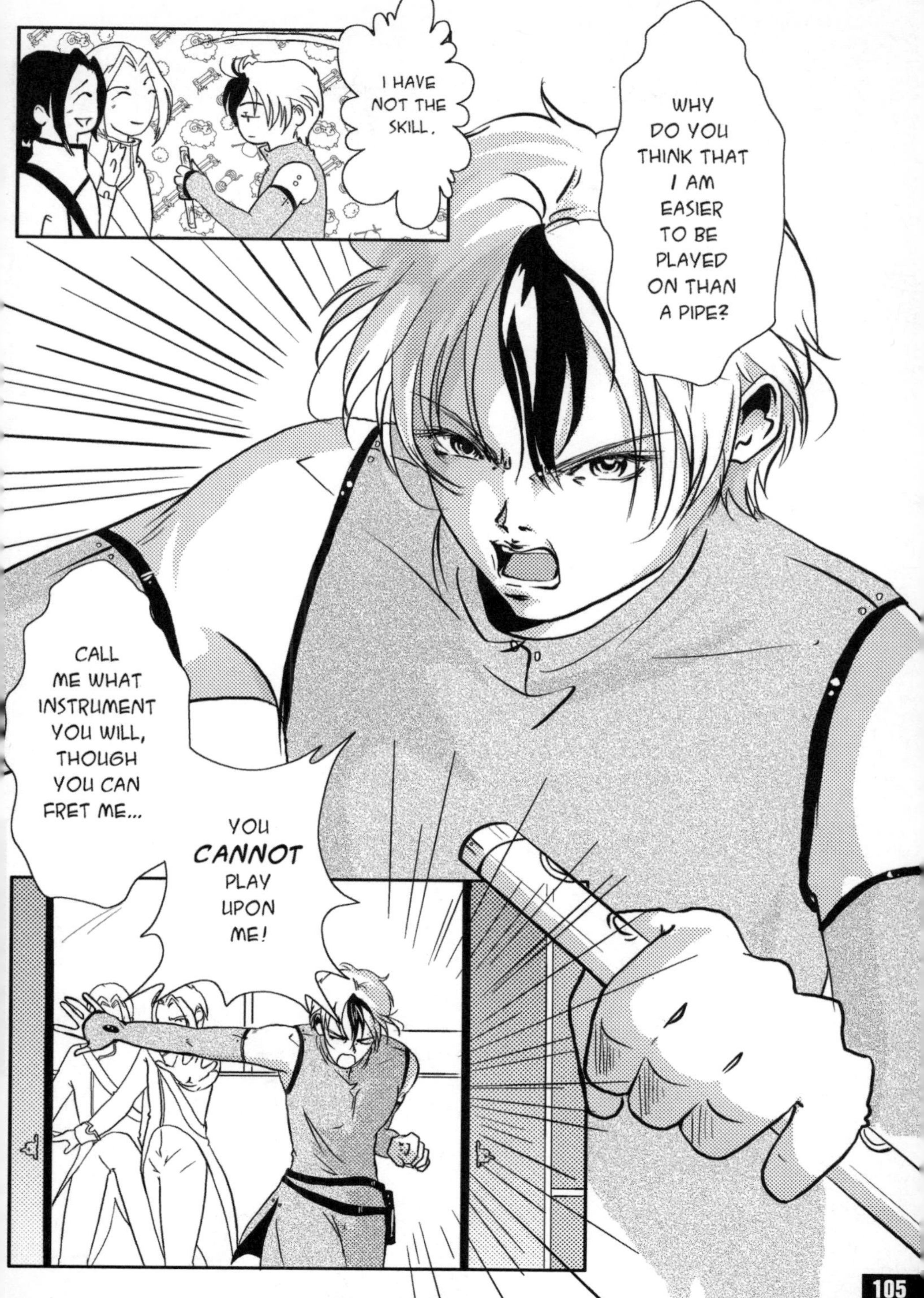
I HAVE NOT THE SKILL.
WHY DO YOU THINK THAT I AM EASIER TO BE PLAYED ON THAN A PIPE?
CALL ME WHAT INSTRUMENT YOU WILL, THOUGH YOU CAN FRET ME...
YOU CANNOT PLAY UPON ME!

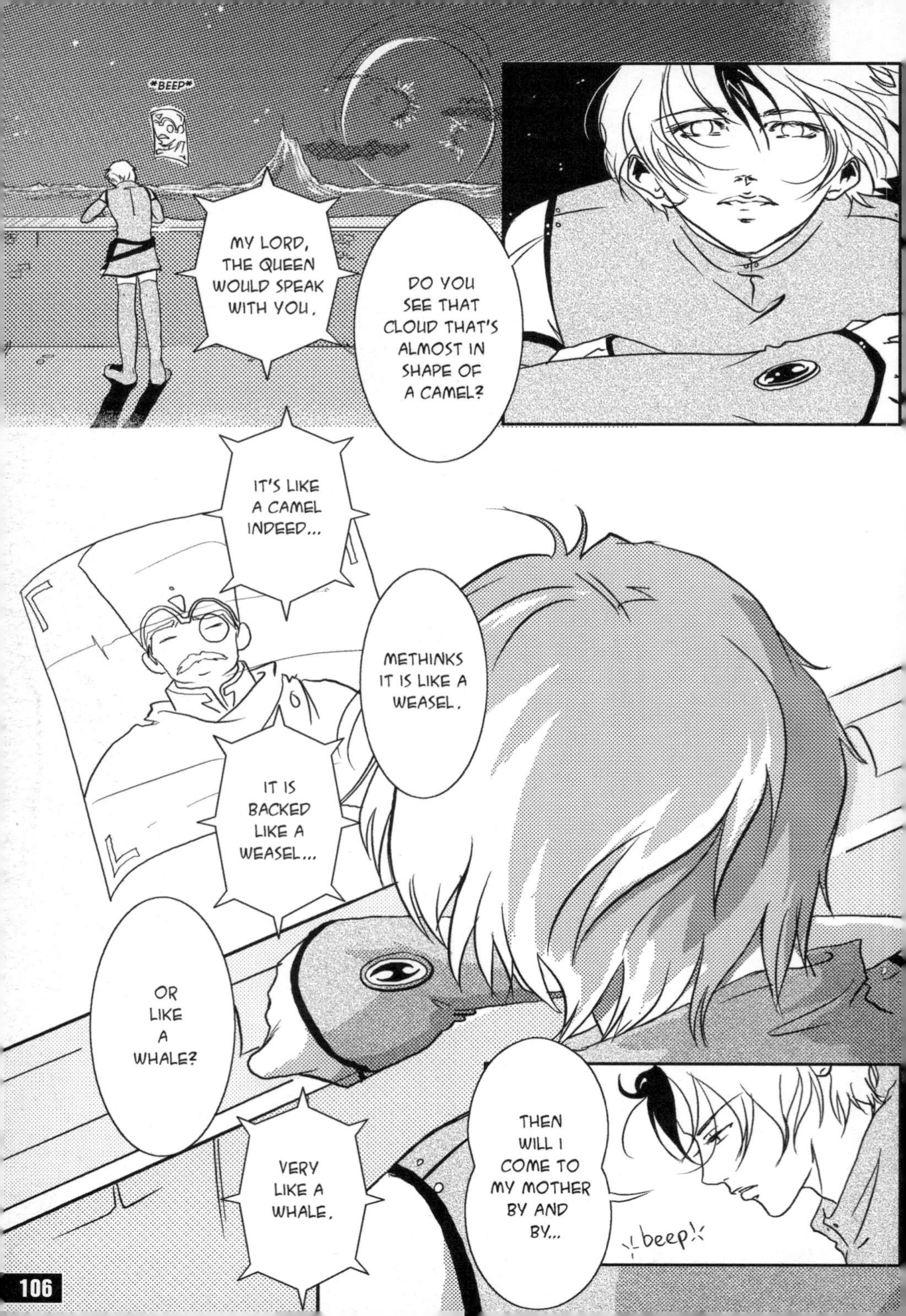
BEEP
MY LORD, THE QUEEN WOULD SPEAK WITH YOU.
DO YOU SEE THAT CLOUD THAT'S ALMOST IN SHAPE OF A CAMEL?
IT'S LIKE A CAMEL INDEED...
METHINKS IT IS LIKE A WEASEL.
IT IS BACKED LIKE A WEASEL...
OR LIKE A WHALE?
VERY LIKE A WHALE.
THEN WILL I COME TO MY MOTHER BY AND BY...
beep

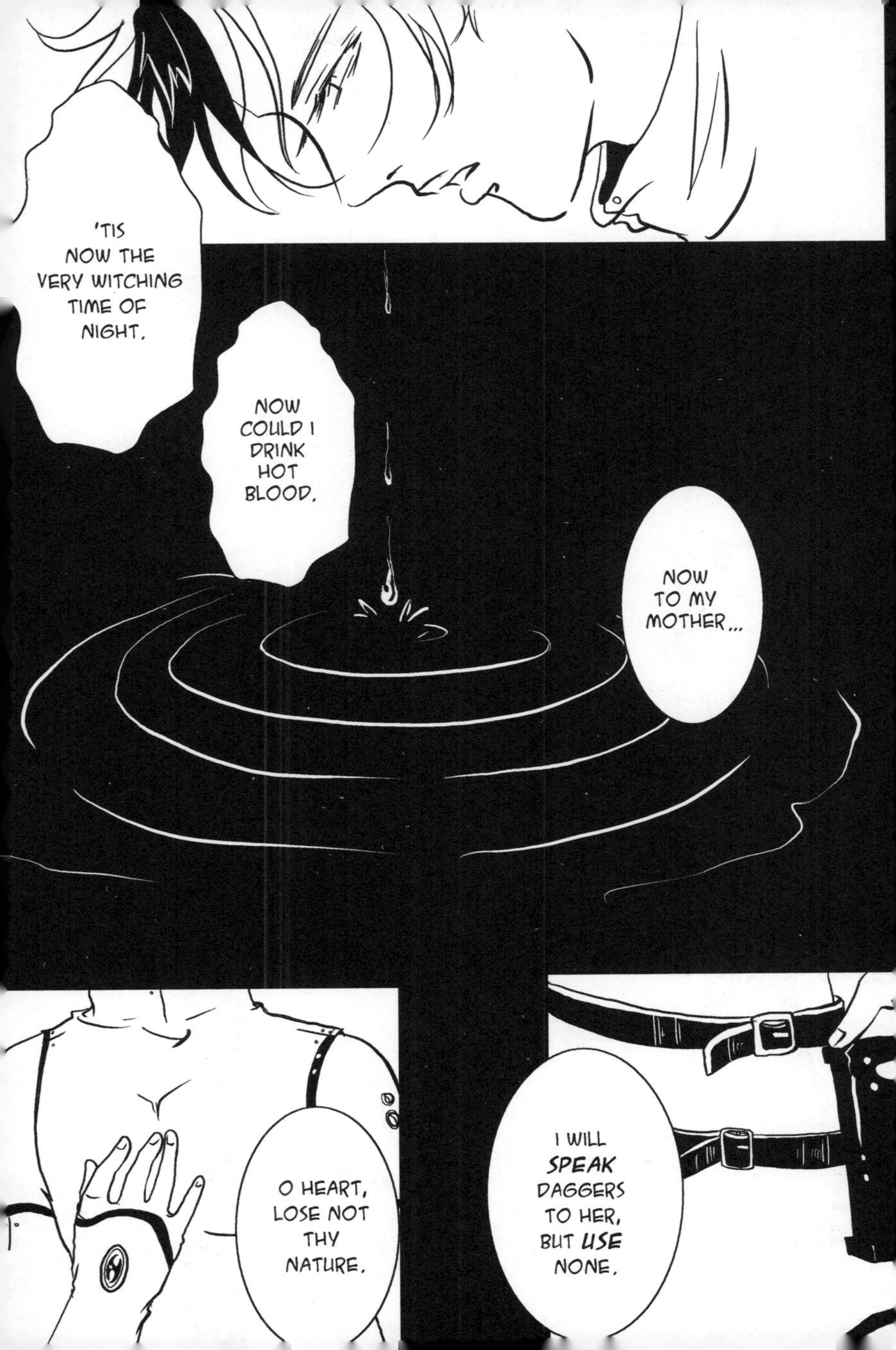
'TIS NOW THE VERY WITCHING TIME OF NIGHT.
NOW COULD I DRINK HOT BLOOD.
NOW TO MY MOTHER...
O HEART, LOSE NOT THY NATURE.
I WILL *SPEAK* DAGGERS TO HER, BUT *USE* NONE.

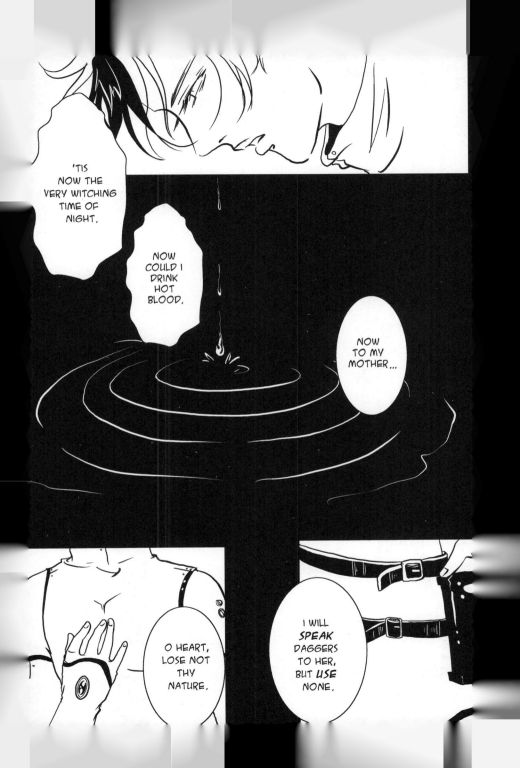

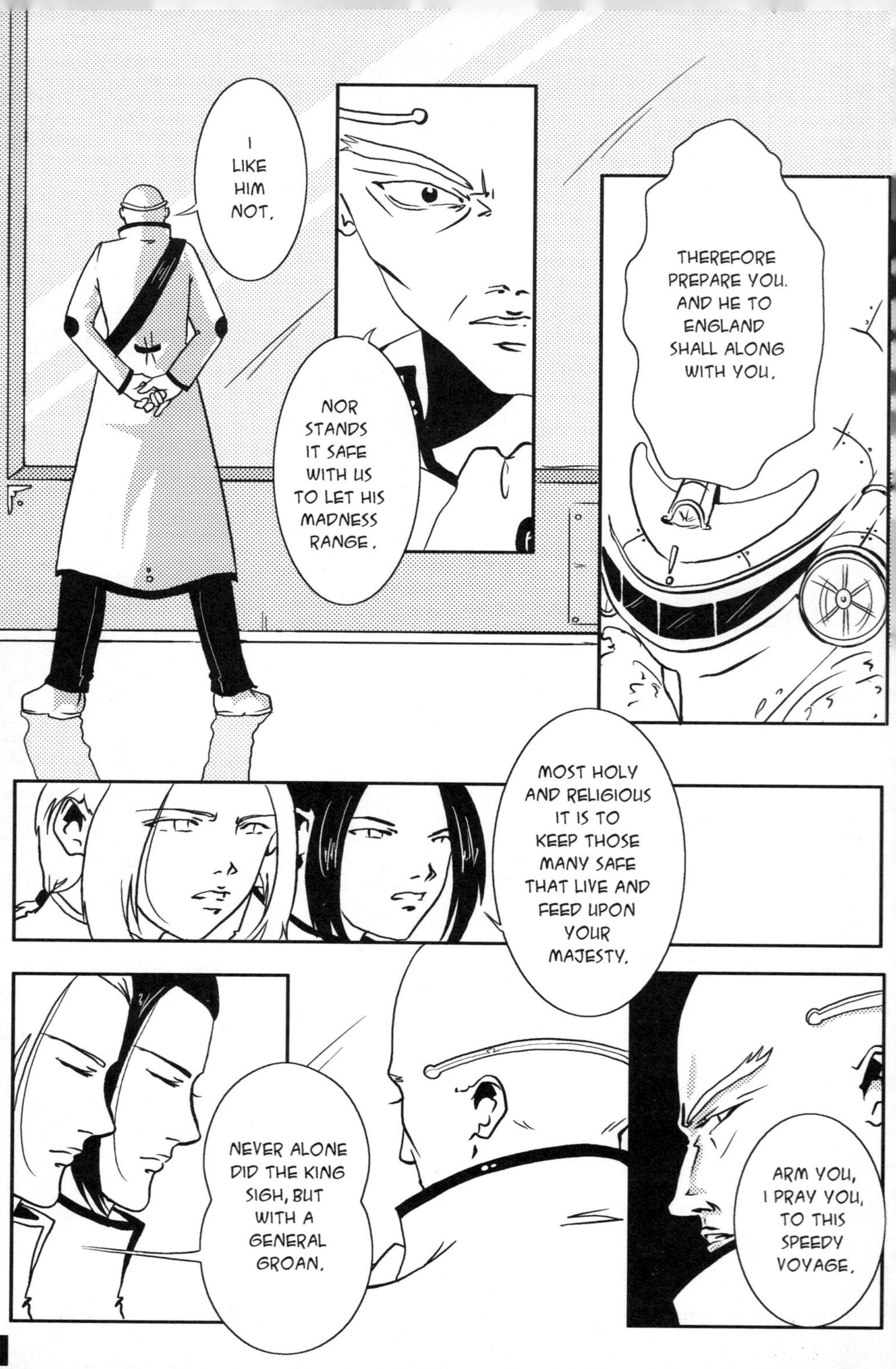

I LIKE HIM NOT.
NOR STANDS IT SAFE WITH US TO LET HIS MADNESS RANGE.
THEREFORE PREPARE YOU. AND HE TO ENGLAND SHALL ALONG WITH YOU.
MOST HOLY AND RELIGIOUS IT IS TO KEEP THOSE MANY SAFE THAT LIVE AND FEED UPON YOUR MAJESTY.
NEVER ALONE DID THE KING SIGH, BUT WITH A GENERAL GROAN.
ARM YOU, I PRAY YOU, TO THIS SPEEDY VOYAGE.

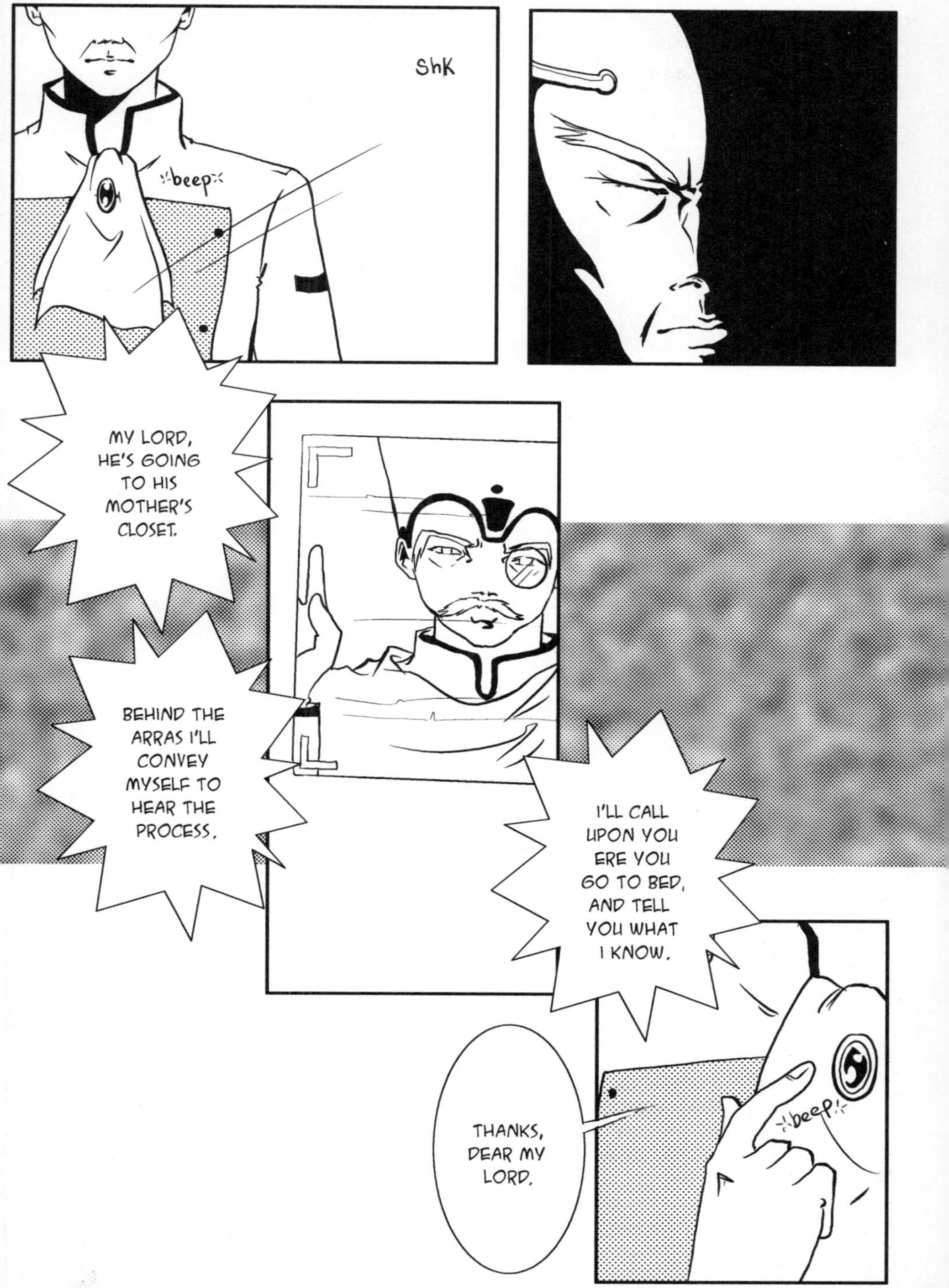
ShK
beep
MY LORD, HE'S GOING TO HIS MOTHER'S CLOSET.
BEHIND THE ARRAS I'LL CONVEY MYSELF TO HEAR THE PROCESS.
I'LL CALL UPON YOU ERE YOU GO TO BED, AND TELL YOU WHAT I KNOW.
beep
THANKS, DEAR MY LORD.

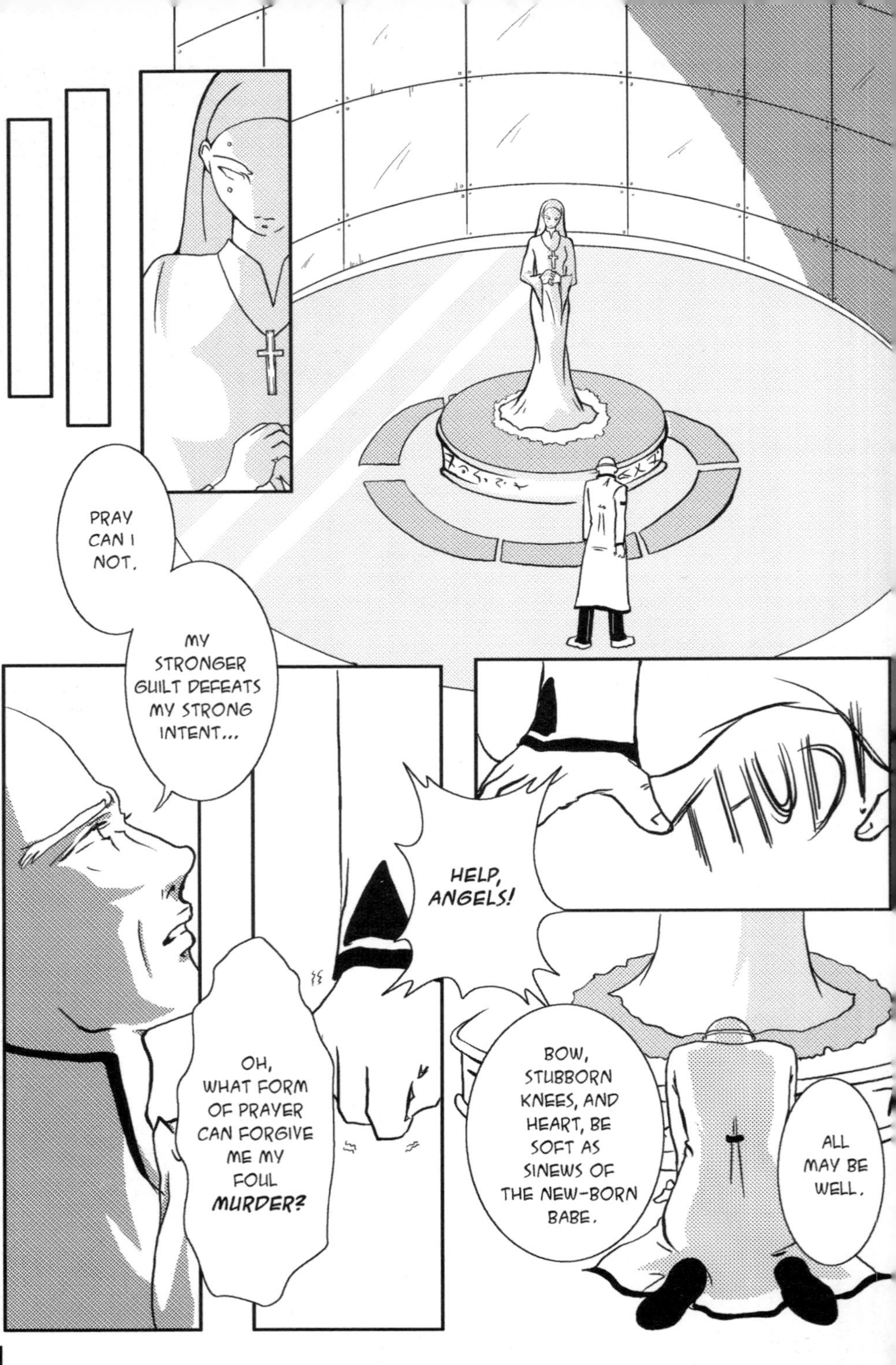
PRAY CAN I NOT.
MY STRONGER GUILT DEFEATS MY STRONG INTENT...
HELP, ANGELS!
THUD!
OH, WHAT FORM OF PRAYER CAN FORGIVE ME MY FOUL MURDER?
BOW, STUBBORN KNEES, AND HEART, BE SOFT AS SINEWS OF THE NEW-BORN BABE.
ALL MAY BE WELL.

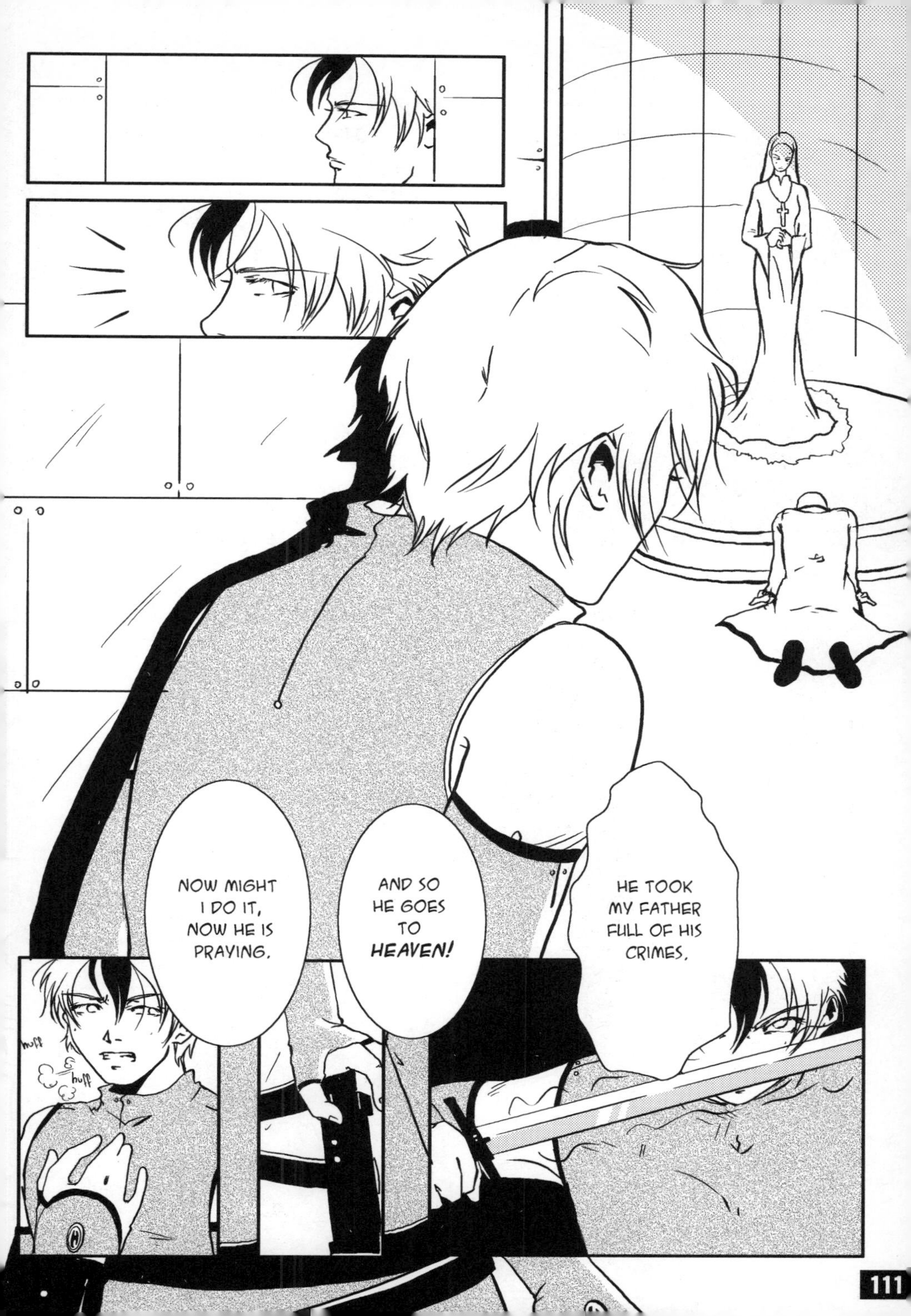

HE TOOK MY FATHER FULL OF HIS CRIMES.
AND SO HE GOES TO HEAVEN!
NOW MIGHT I DO IT, NOW HE IS PRAYING.
huff
huff

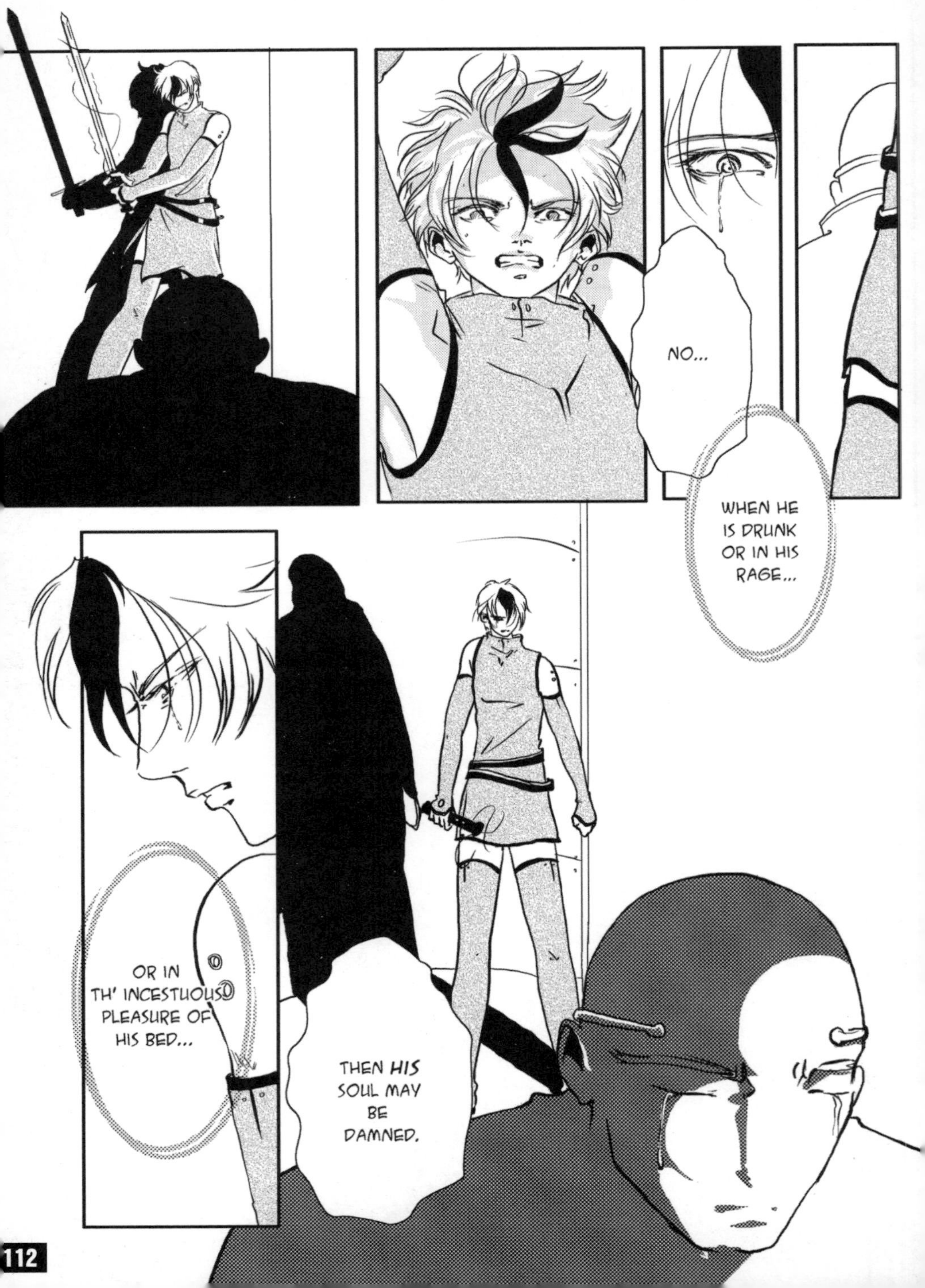
NO...
WHEN HE IS DRUNK OR IN HIS RAGE...
OR IN TH' INCESTUOUS PLEASURE OF HIS BED...
THEN HIS SOUL MAY BE DAMNED.

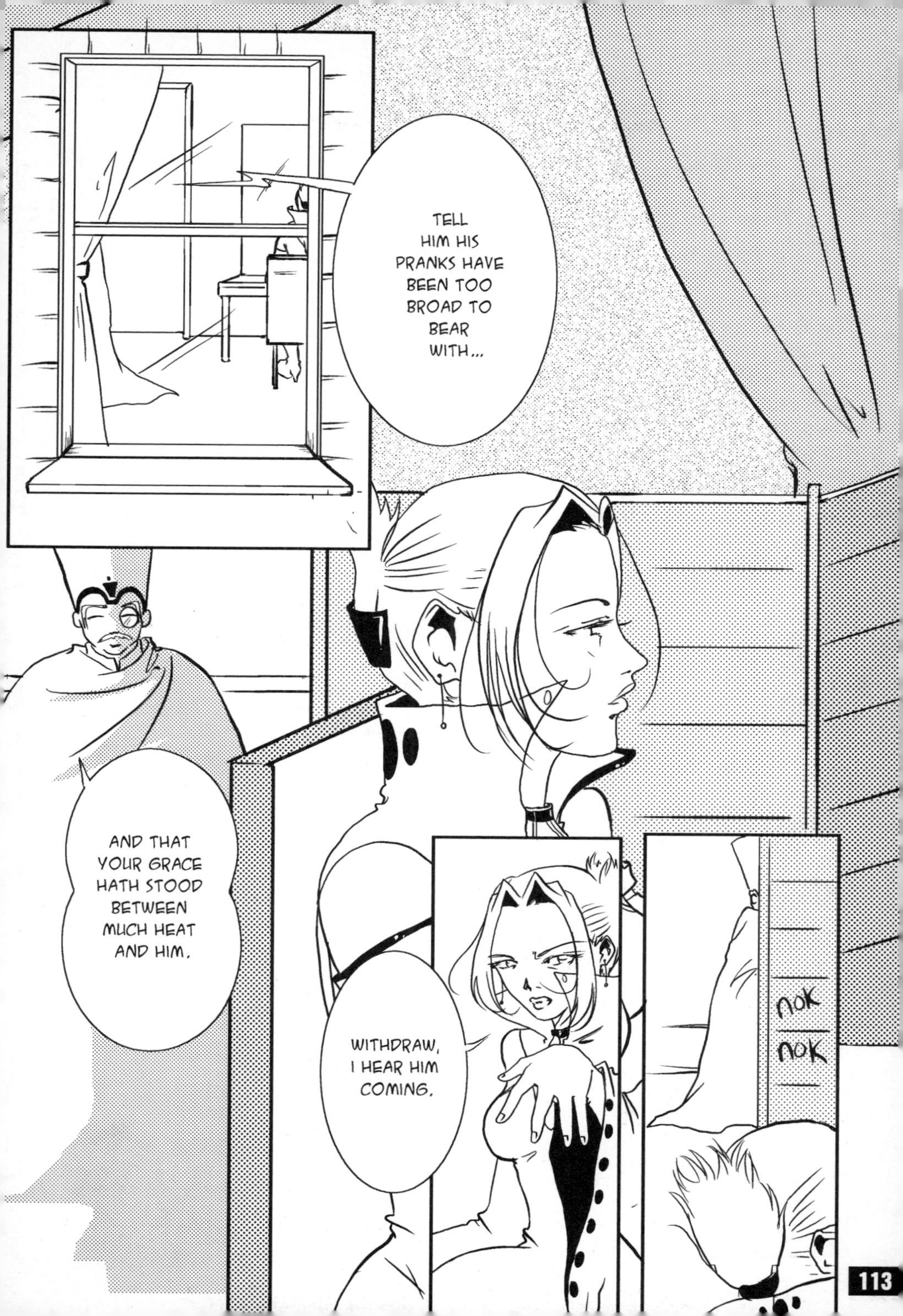
TELL HIM HIS PRANKS HAVE BEEN TOO BROAD TO BEAR WITH...
AND THAT YOUR GRACE HATH STOOD BETWEEN MUCH HEAT AND HIM.
WITHDRAW, I HEAR HIM COMING.
NOK
NOK

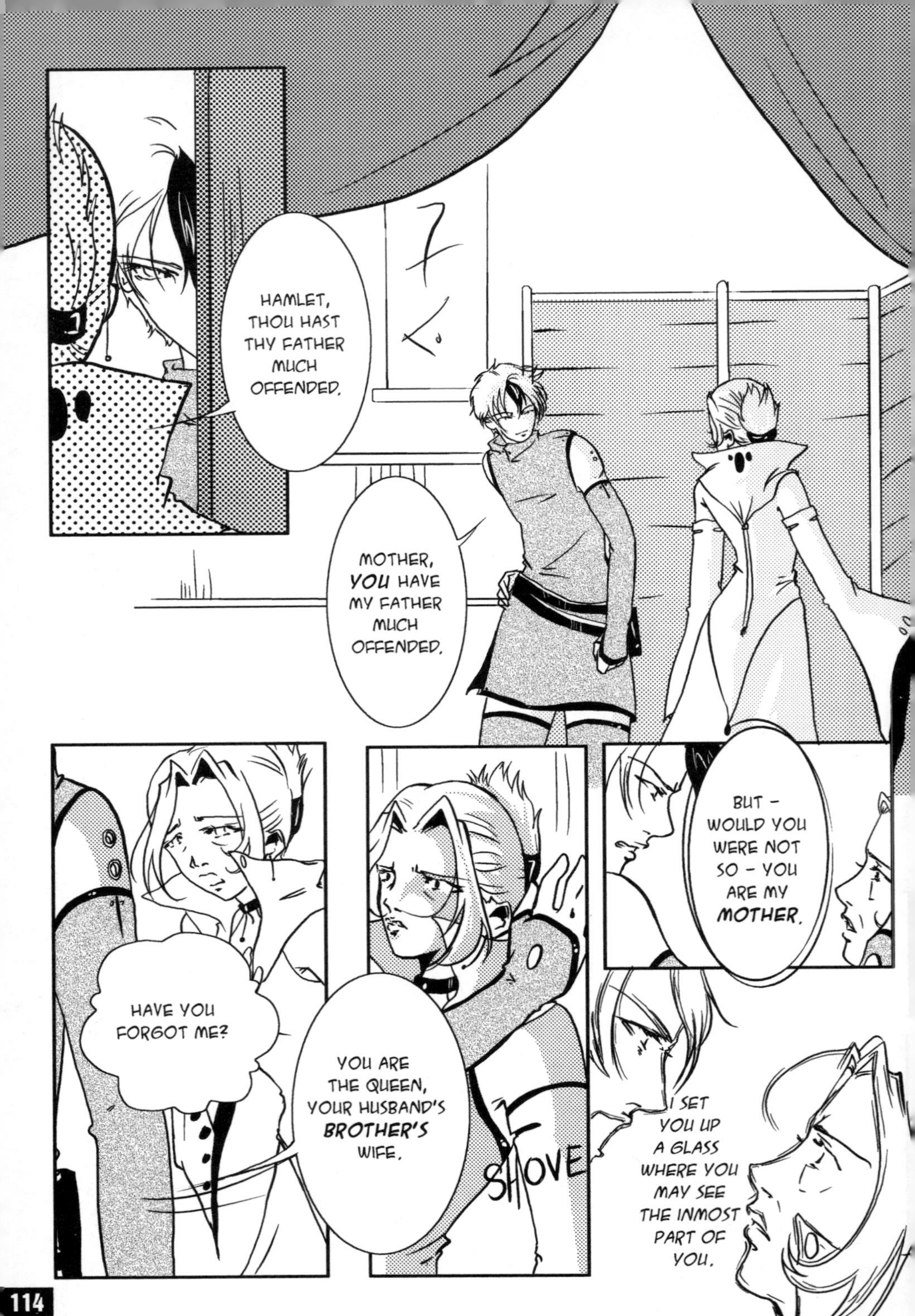

HAMLET, THOU HAST THY FATHER MUCH OFFENDED.
MOTHER, *YOU* HAVE MY FATHER MUCH OFFENDED.
HAVE YOU FORGOT ME?
YOU ARE THE QUEEN, YOUR HUSBAND'S **BROTHER'S** WIFE.
BUT - WOULD YOU WERE NOT SO - YOU ARE MY **MOTHER.**
SHOVE
I SET YOU UP A GLASS WHERE YOU MAY SEE THE INMOST PART OF YOU.

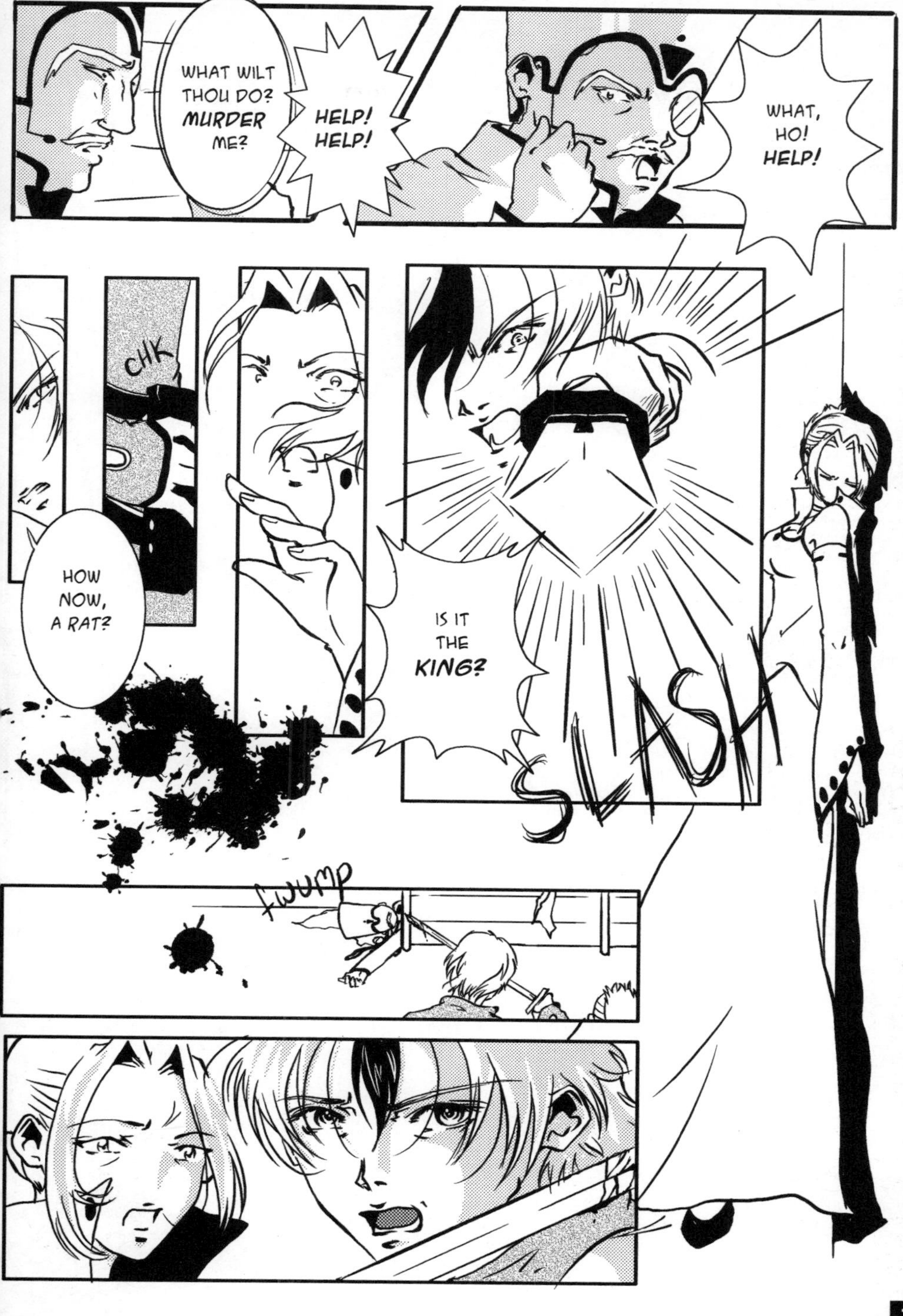
WHAT WILT THOU DO? MURDER ME?
HELP! HELP!
WHAT, HO! HELP!
CHK
HOW NOW, A RAT?
IS IT THE KING?
SLASH
fwump

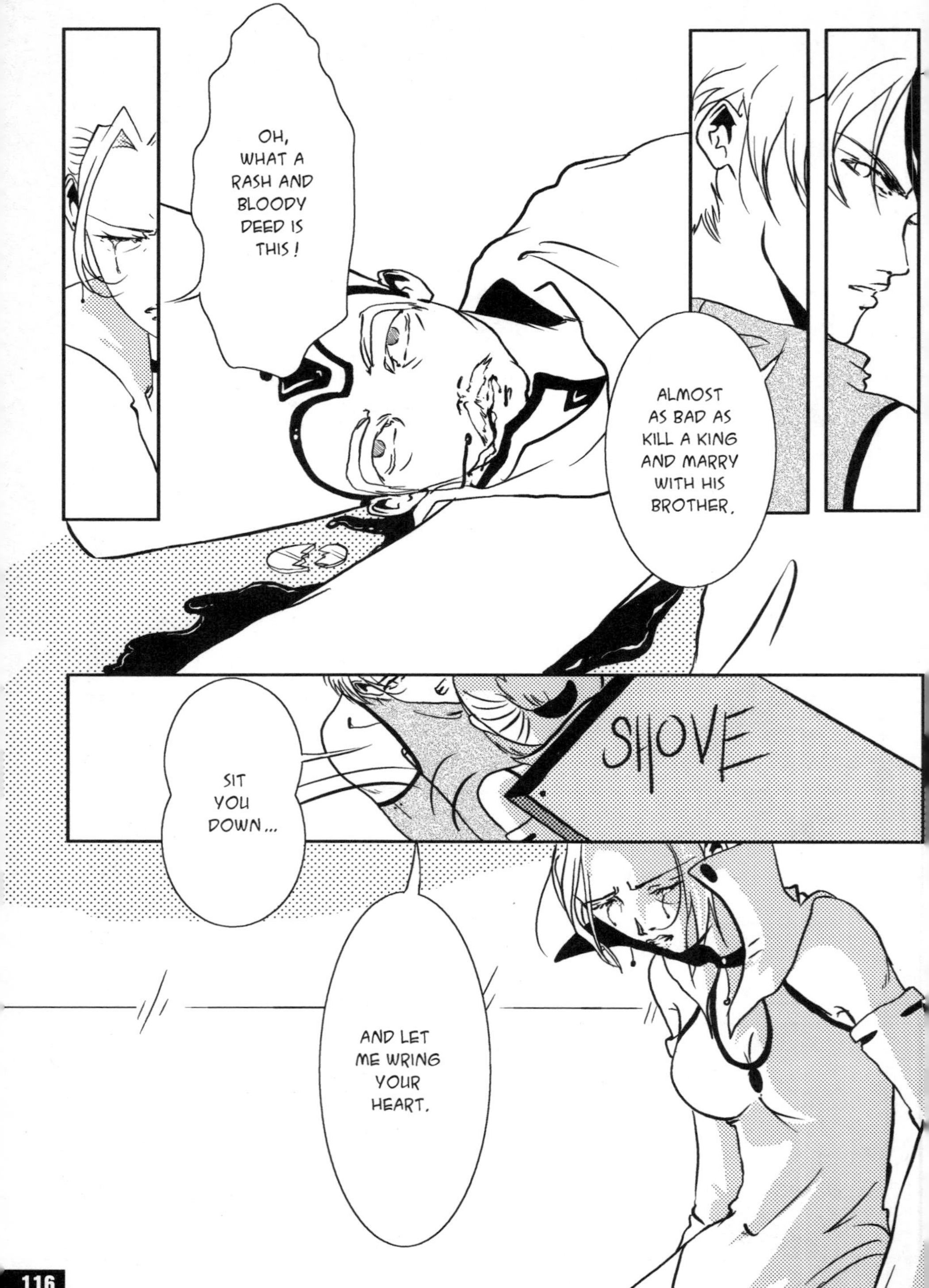
OH, WHAT A RASH AND BLOODY DEED IS THIS !
ALMOST AS BAD AS KILL A KING AND MARRY WITH HIS BROTHER.
SHOVE
SIT YOU DOWN...
AND LET ME WRING YOUR HEART.

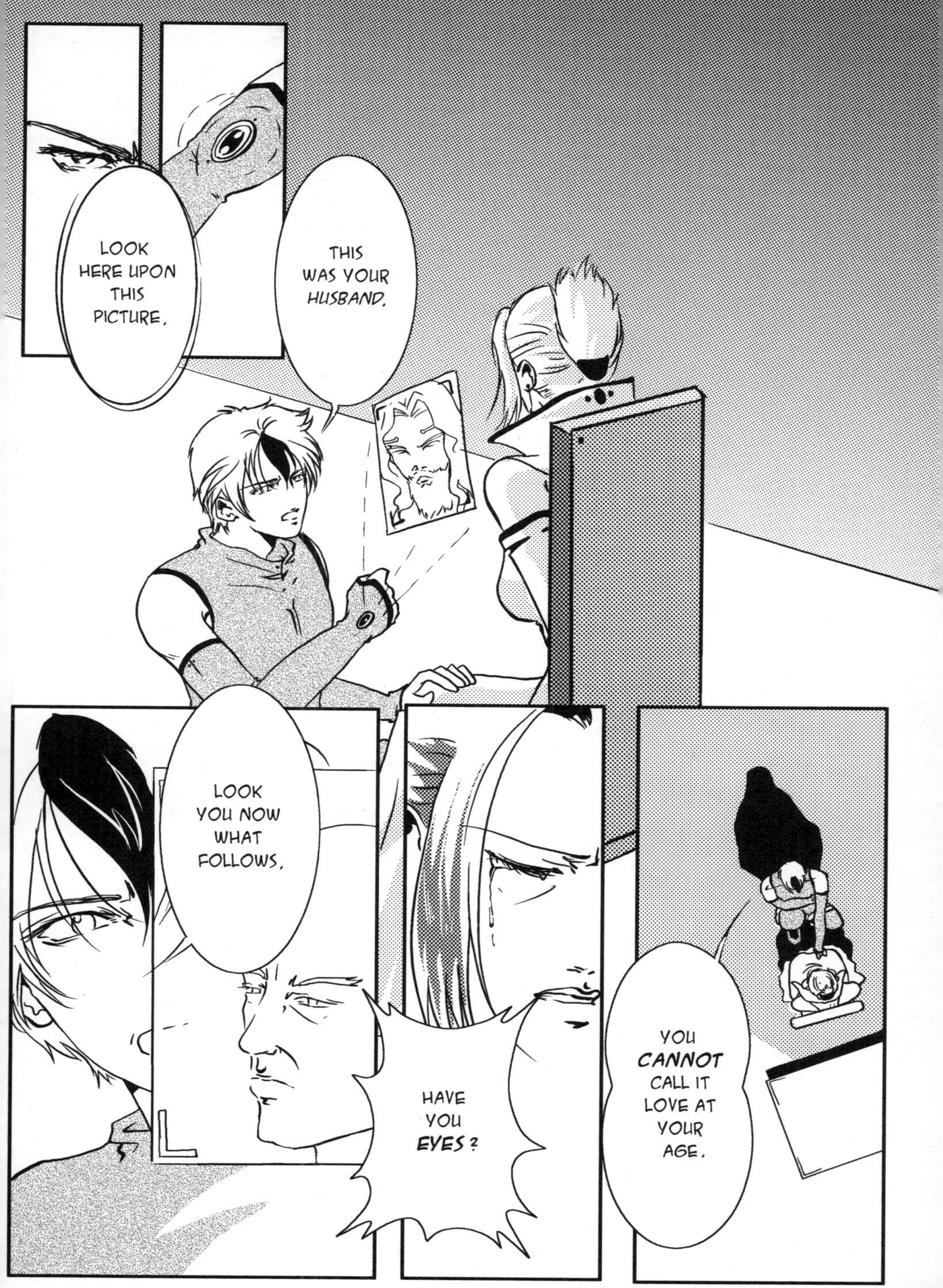
LOOK HERE UPON THIS PICTURE.
THIS WAS YOUR HUSBAND.
LOOK YOU NOW WHAT FOLLOWS.
HAVE YOU **EYES**?
YOU **CANNOT** CALL IT LOVE AT YOUR AGE.

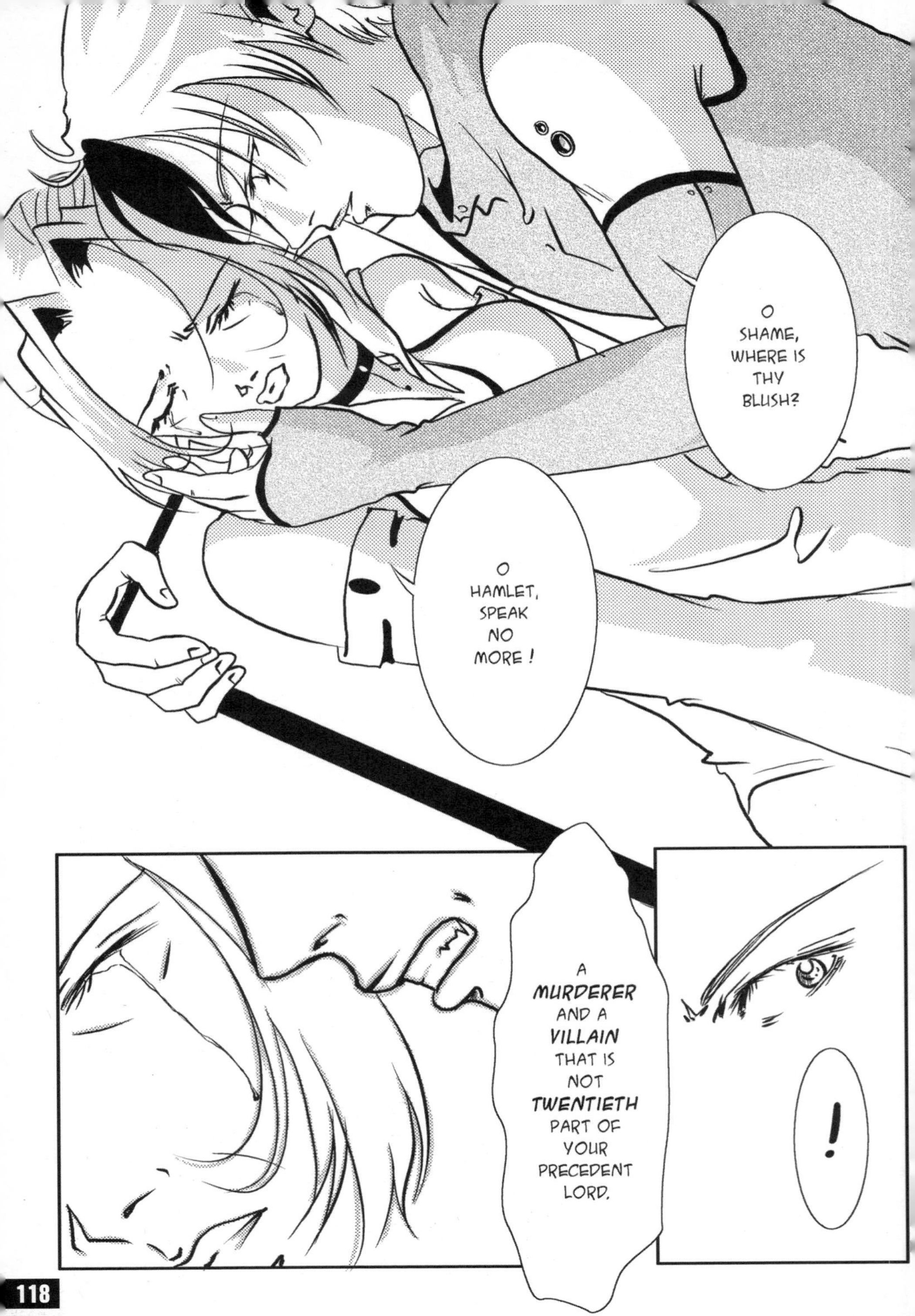
O SHAME, WHERE IS THY BLUSH?
O HAMLET, SPEAK NO MORE!
A MURDERER AND A VILLAIN THAT IS NOT TWENTIETH PART OF YOUR PRECEDENT LORD.
!

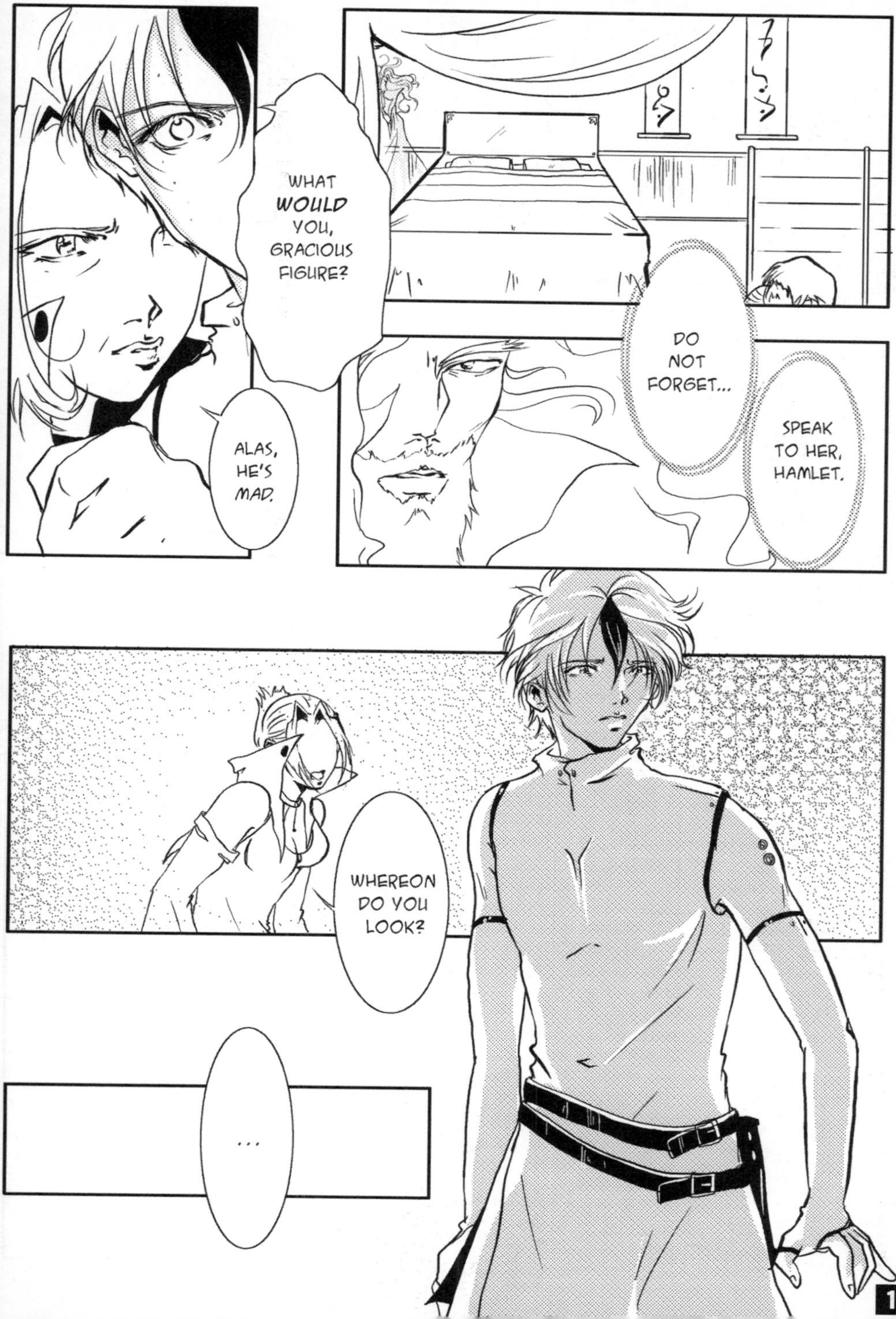
WHAT **WOULD** YOU, GRACIOUS FIGURE?
ALAS, HE'S MAD.
DO NOT FORGET...
SPEAK TO HER, HAMLET.
WHEREON DO YOU LOOK?
...

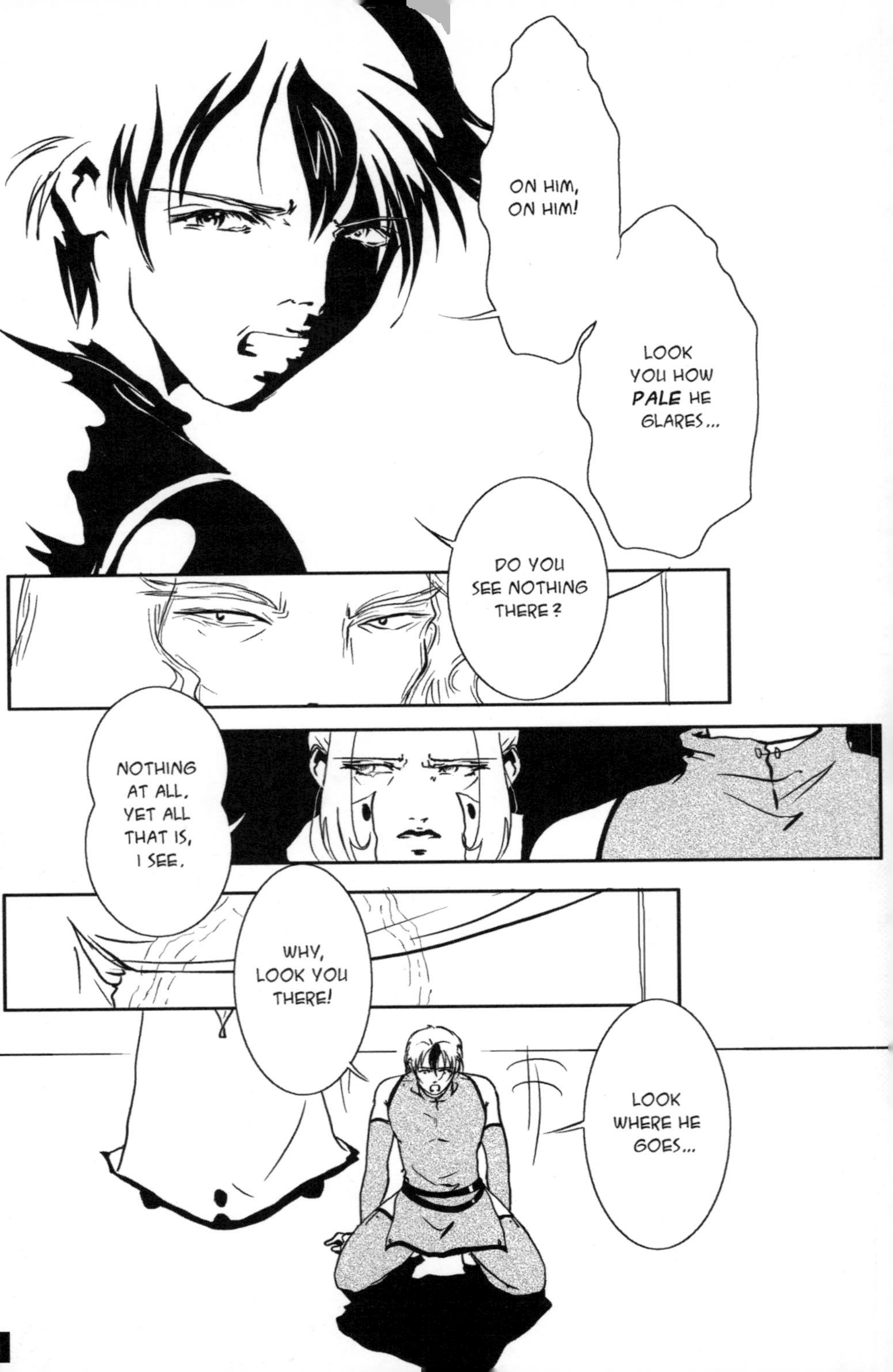

ON HIM, ON HIM!
LOOK YOU HOW PALE HE GLARES...
DO YOU SEE NOTHING THERE?
NOTHING AT ALL, YET ALL THAT IS, I SEE.
WHY, LOOK YOU THERE!
LOOK WHERE HE GOES...

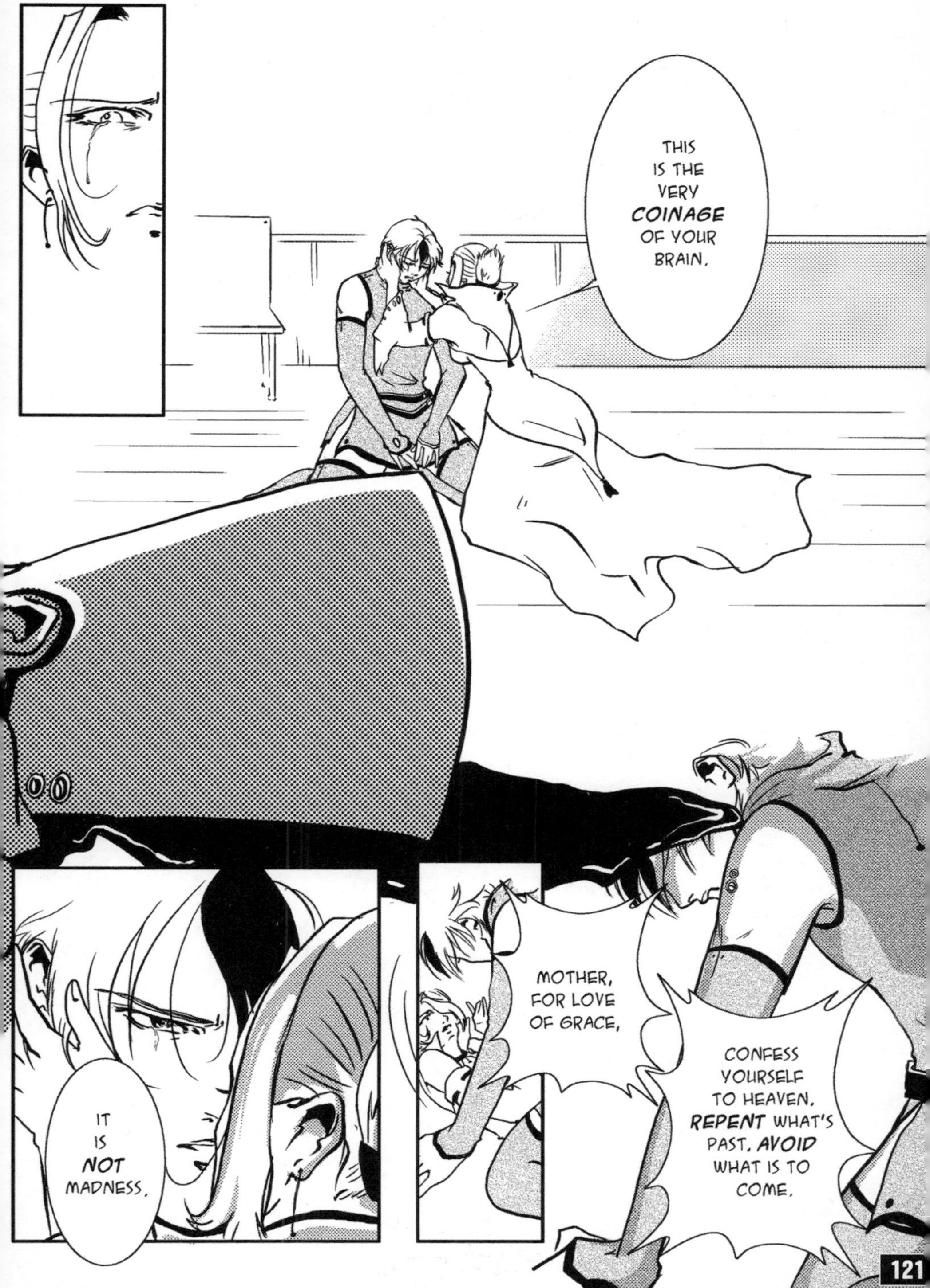
THIS IS THE VERY COINAGE OF YOUR BRAIN.
IT IS NOT MADNESS.
MOTHER, FOR LOVE OF GRACE,
CONFESS YOURSELF TO HEAVEN. REPENT WHAT'S PAST. AVOID WHAT IS TO COME.

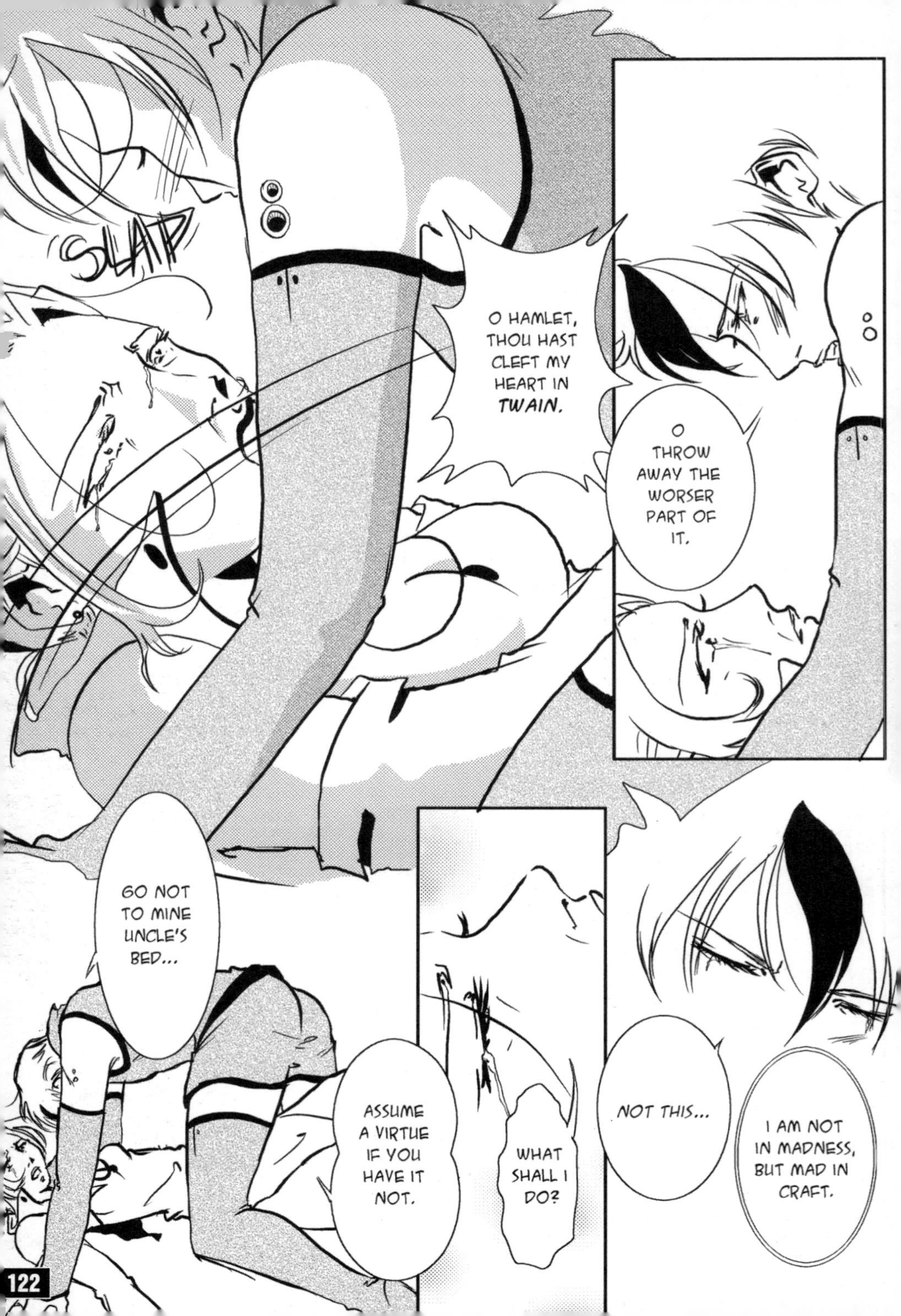
SLAP
O HAMLET, THOU HAST CLEFT MY HEART IN TWAIN.
O THROW AWAY THE WORSER PART OF IT.
GO NOT TO MINE UNCLE'S BED...
ASSUME A VIRTUE IF YOU HAVE IT NOT.
WHAT SHALL I DO?
NOT THIS...
I AM NOT IN MADNESS, BUT MAD IN CRAFT.

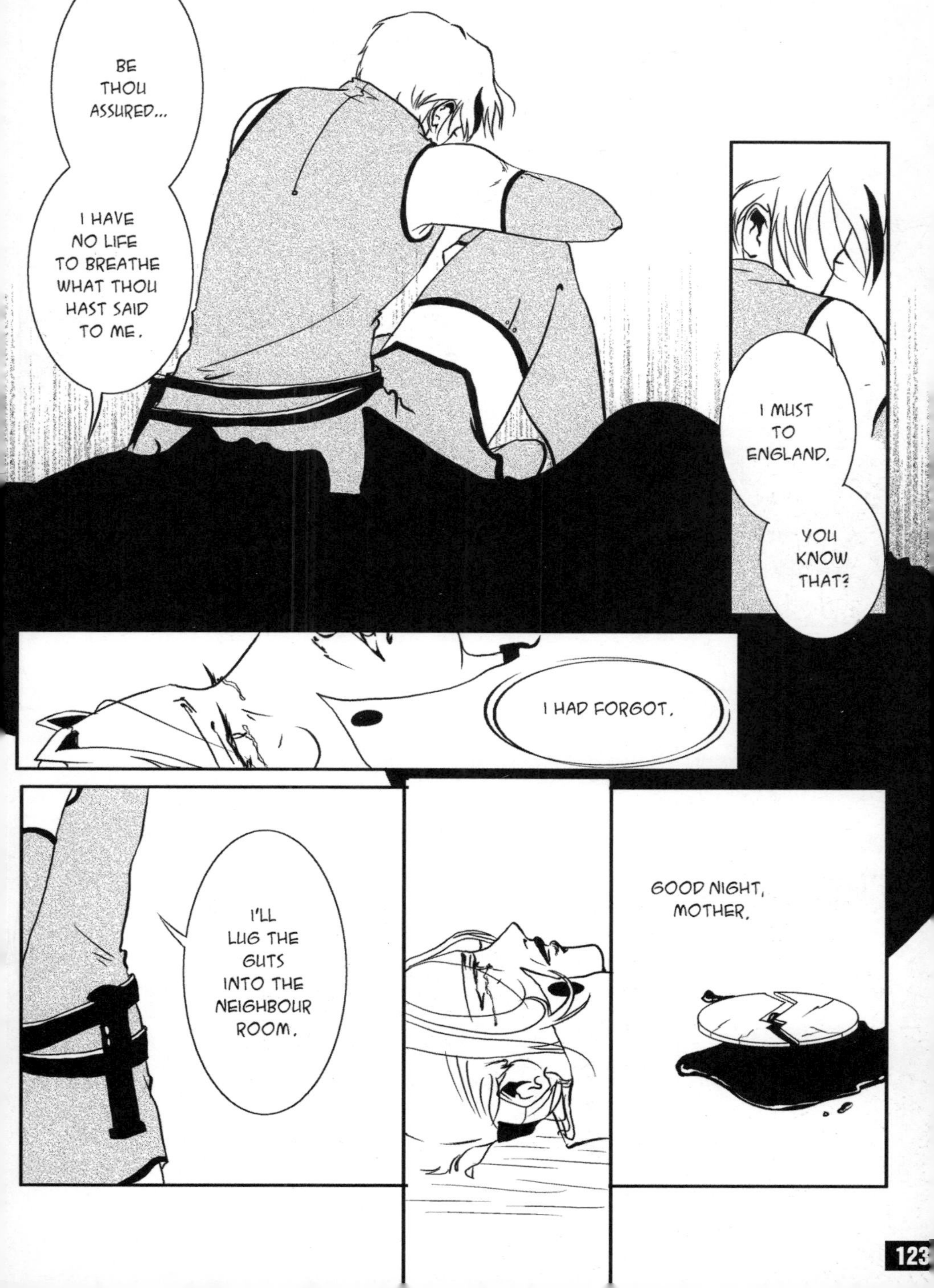

BE THOU ASSURED...
I HAVE NO LIFE TO BREATHE WHAT THOU HAST SAID TO ME.
I MUST TO ENGLAND.
YOU KNOW THAT?
I HAD FORGOT.
I'LL LUG THE GUTS INTO THE NEIGHBOUR ROOM.
GOOD NIGHT, MOTHER.

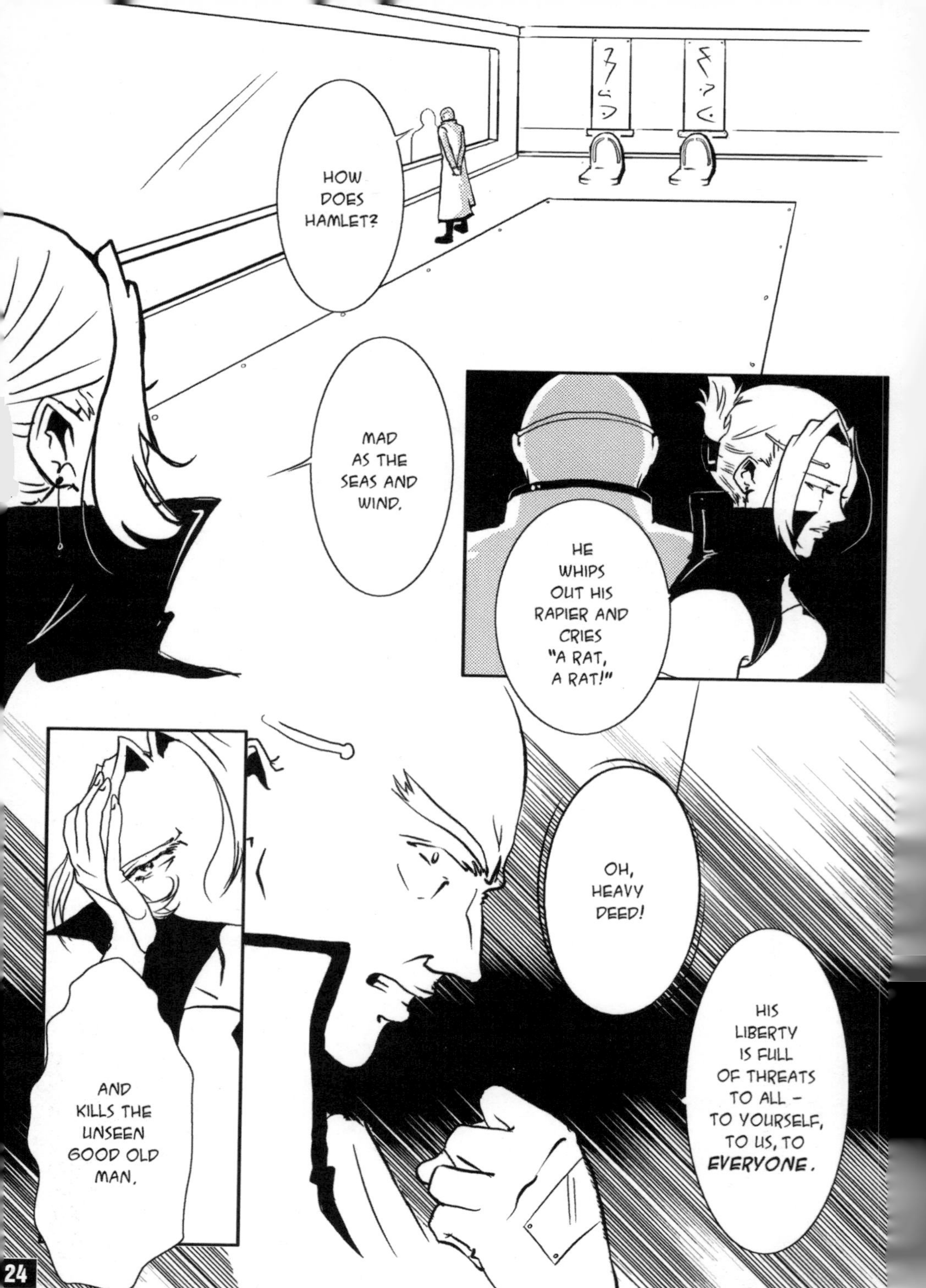
HOW DOES HAMLET?
MAD AS THE SEAS AND WIND.
HE WHIPS OUT HIS RAPIER AND CRIES "A RAT, A RAT!"
OH, HEAVY DEED!
AND KILLS THE UNSEEN GOOD OLD MAN.
HIS LIBERTY IS FULL OF THREATS TO ALL - TO YOURSELF, TO US, TO EVERYONE.

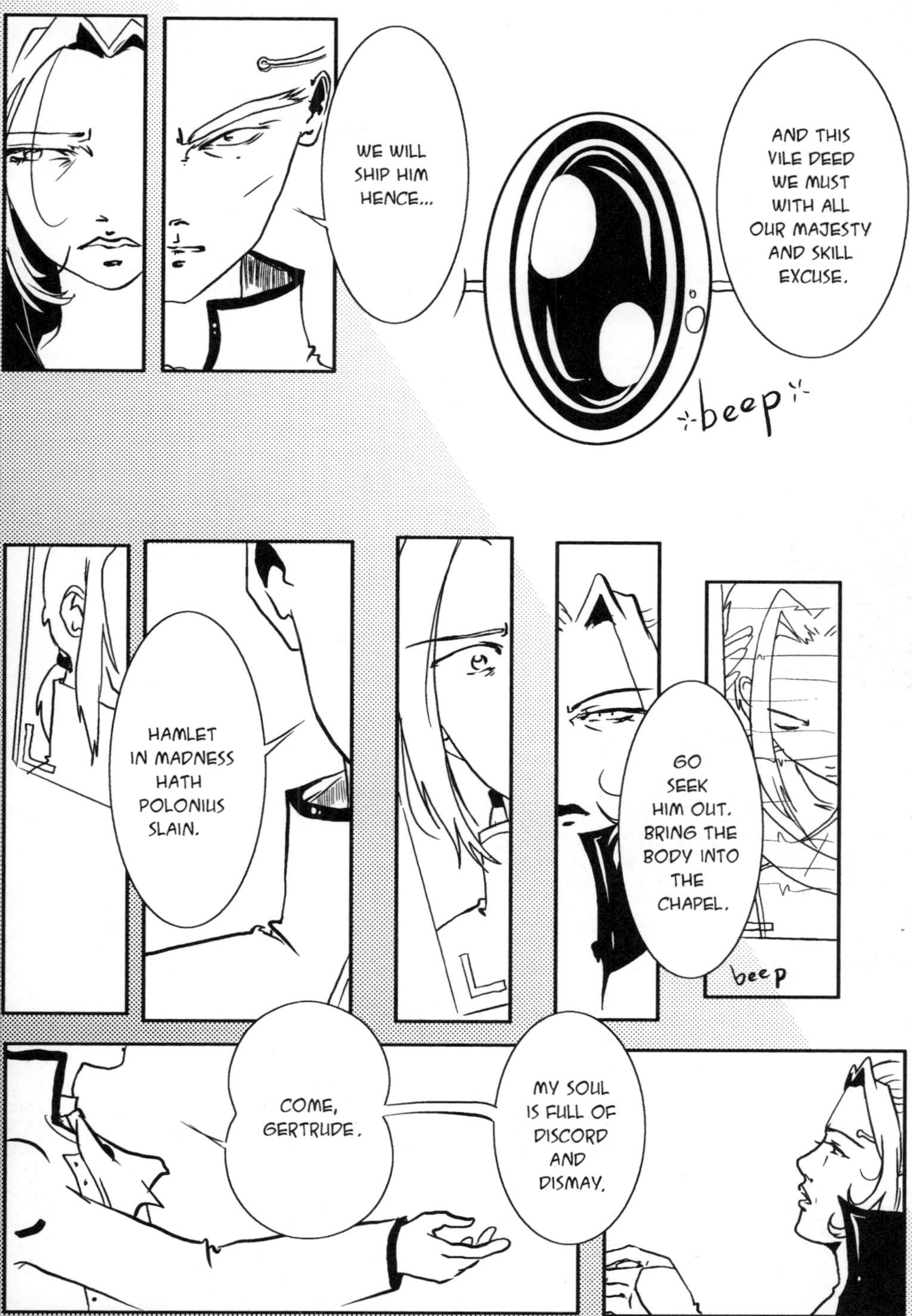
WE WILL SHIP HIM HENCE...
AND THIS VILE DEED WE MUST WITH ALL OUR MAJESTY AND SKILL EXCUSE.
beep
HAMLET IN MADNESS HATH POLONIUS SLAIN.
GO SEEK HIM OUT. BRING THE BODY INTO THE CHAPEL.
beep
COME, GERTRUDE.
MY SOUL IS FULL OF DISCORD AND DISMAY.

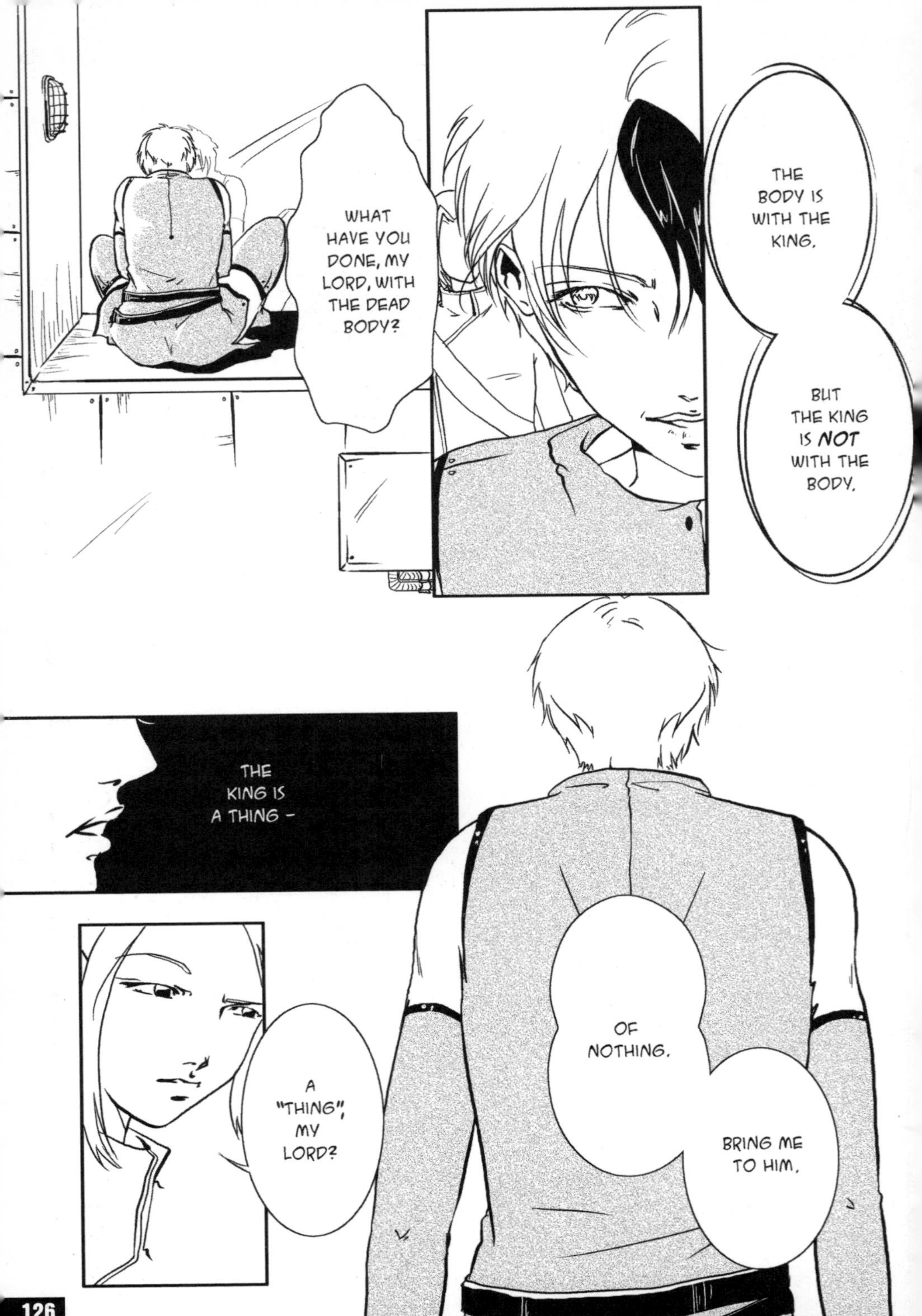
WHAT HAVE YOU DONE, MY LORD, WITH THE DEAD BODY?
THE BODY IS WITH THE KING.
BUT THE KING IS **NOT** WITH THE BODY.
THE KING IS A THING -
A "THING", MY LORD?
OF NOTHING.
BRING ME TO HIM.

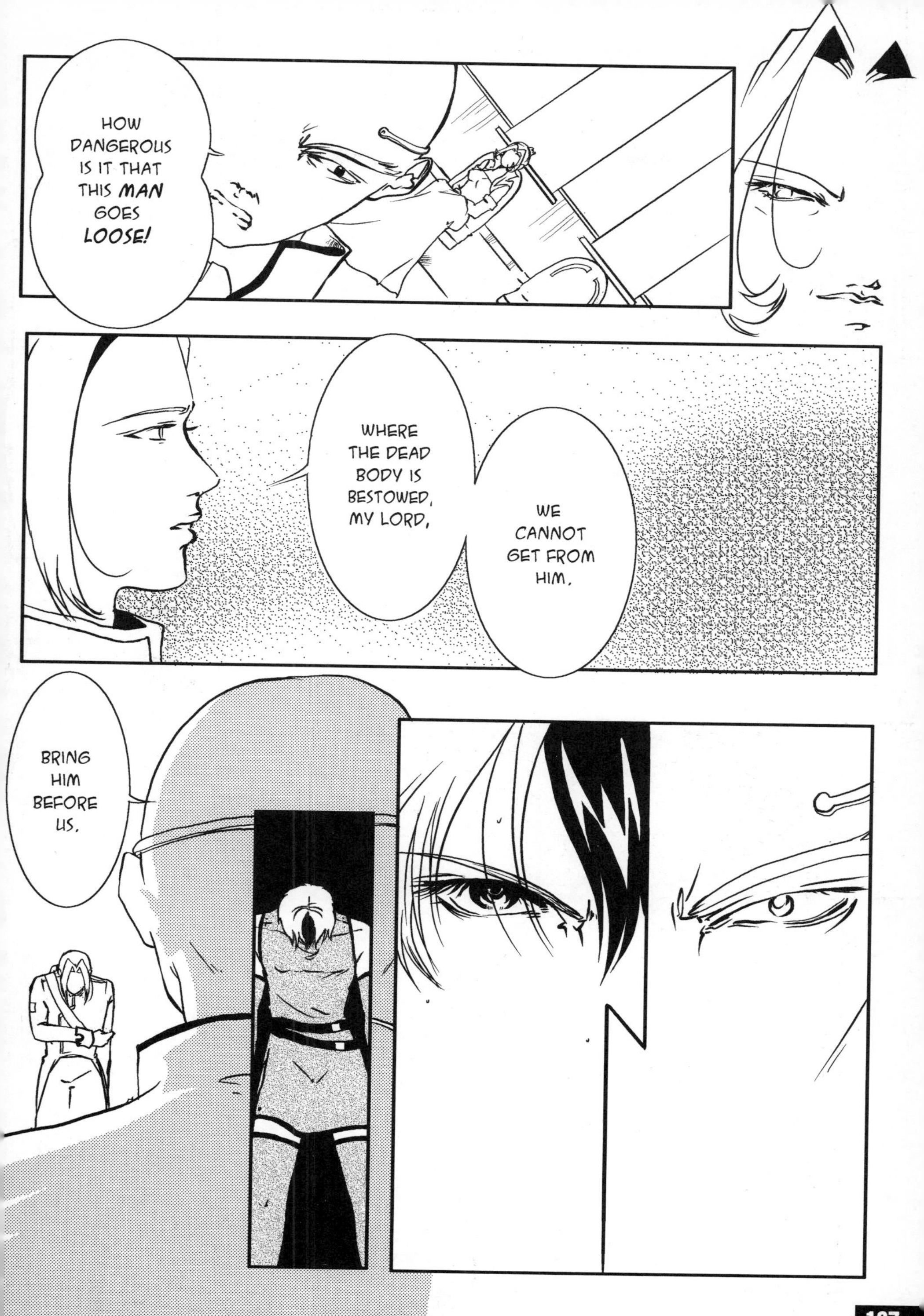

HOW DANGEROUS IS IT THAT THIS MAN GOES LOOSE!
WHERE THE DEAD BODY IS BESTOWED, MY LORD,
WE CANNOT GET FROM HIM.
BRING HIM BEFORE US.

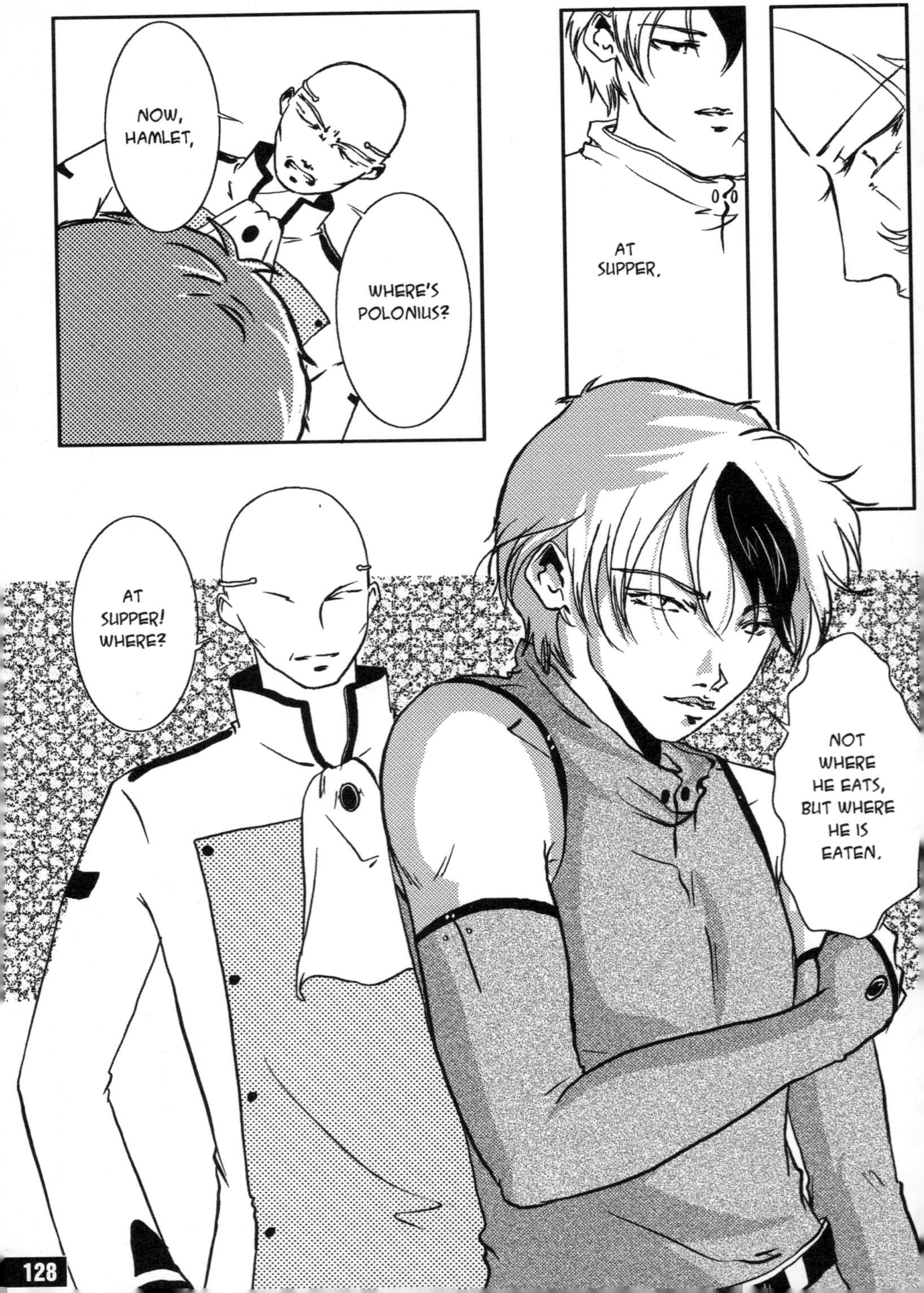
NOW, HAMLET,
WHERE'S POLONIUS?
AT SUPPER.
AT SUPPER! WHERE?
NOT WHERE HE EATS, BUT WHERE HE IS EATEN.

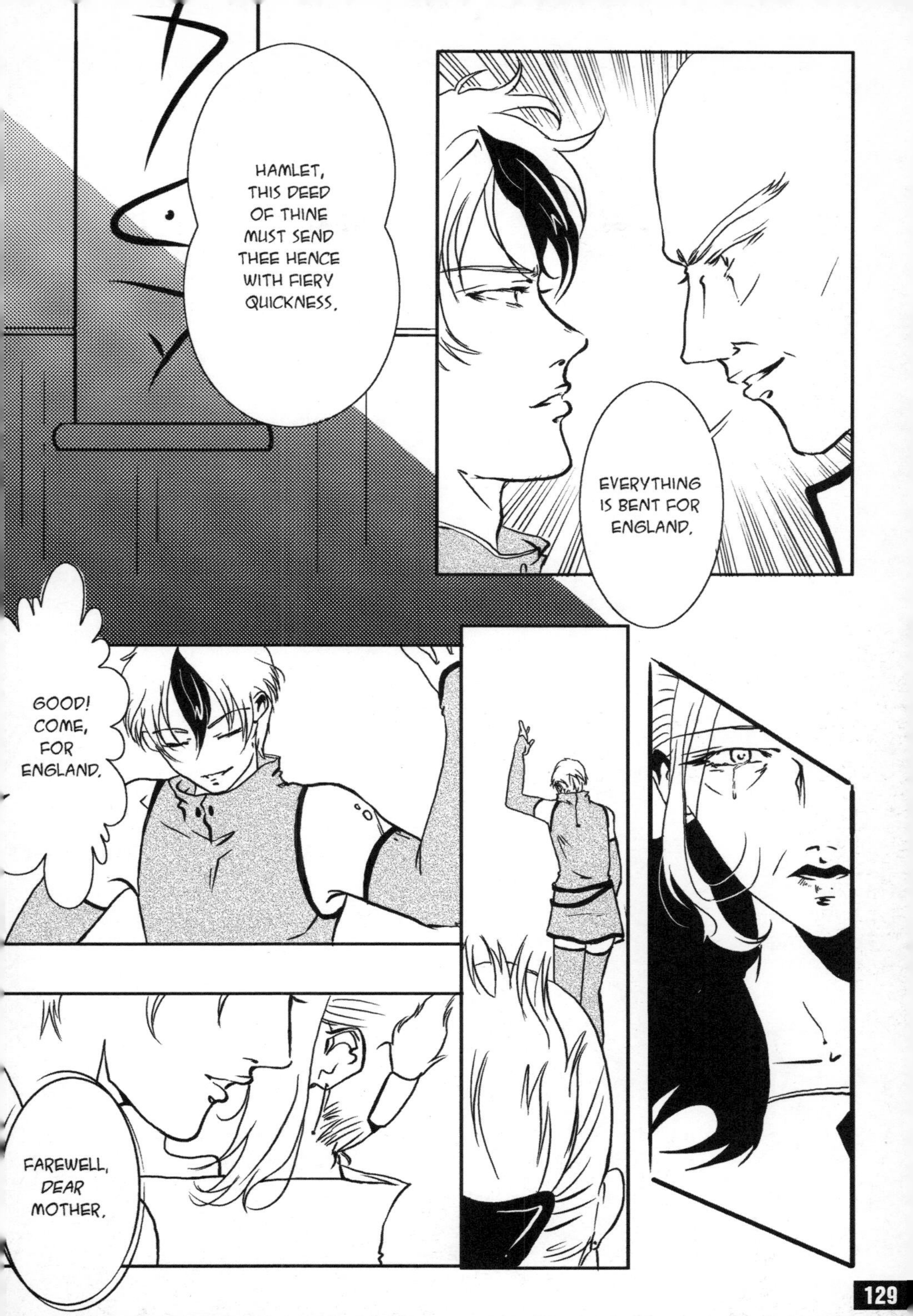

HAMLET, THIS DEED OF THINE MUST SEND THEE HENCE WITH FIERY QUICKNESS.
EVERYTHING IS BENT FOR ENGLAND.
GOOD! COME, FOR ENGLAND.
FAREWELL, DEAR MOTHER.

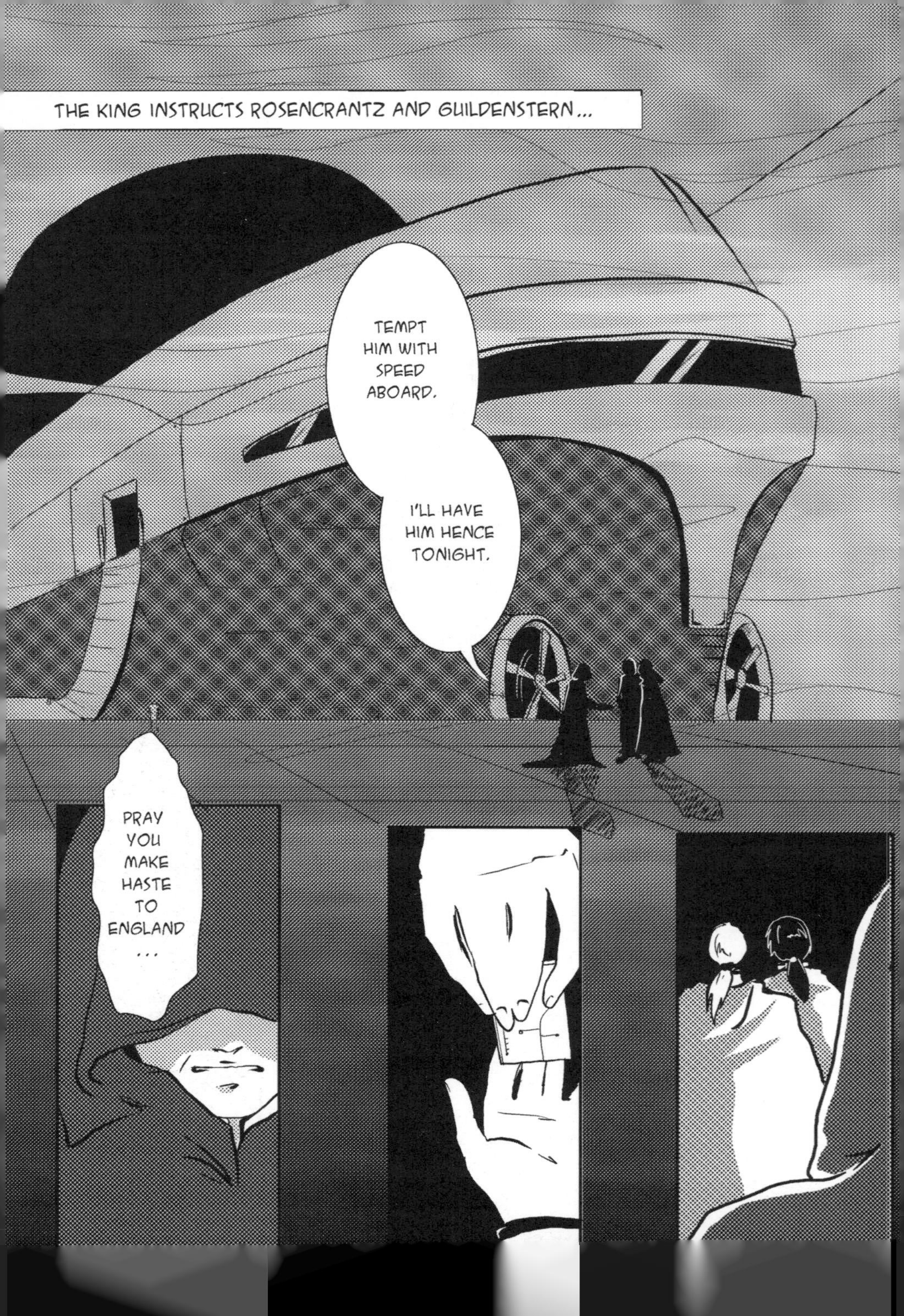

THE KING INSTRUCTS ROSENCRANTZ AND GUILDENSTERN...
TEMPT HIM WITH SPEED ABOARD.
I'LL HAVE HIM HENCE TONIGHT.
PRAY YOU MAKE HASTE TO ENGLAND ...

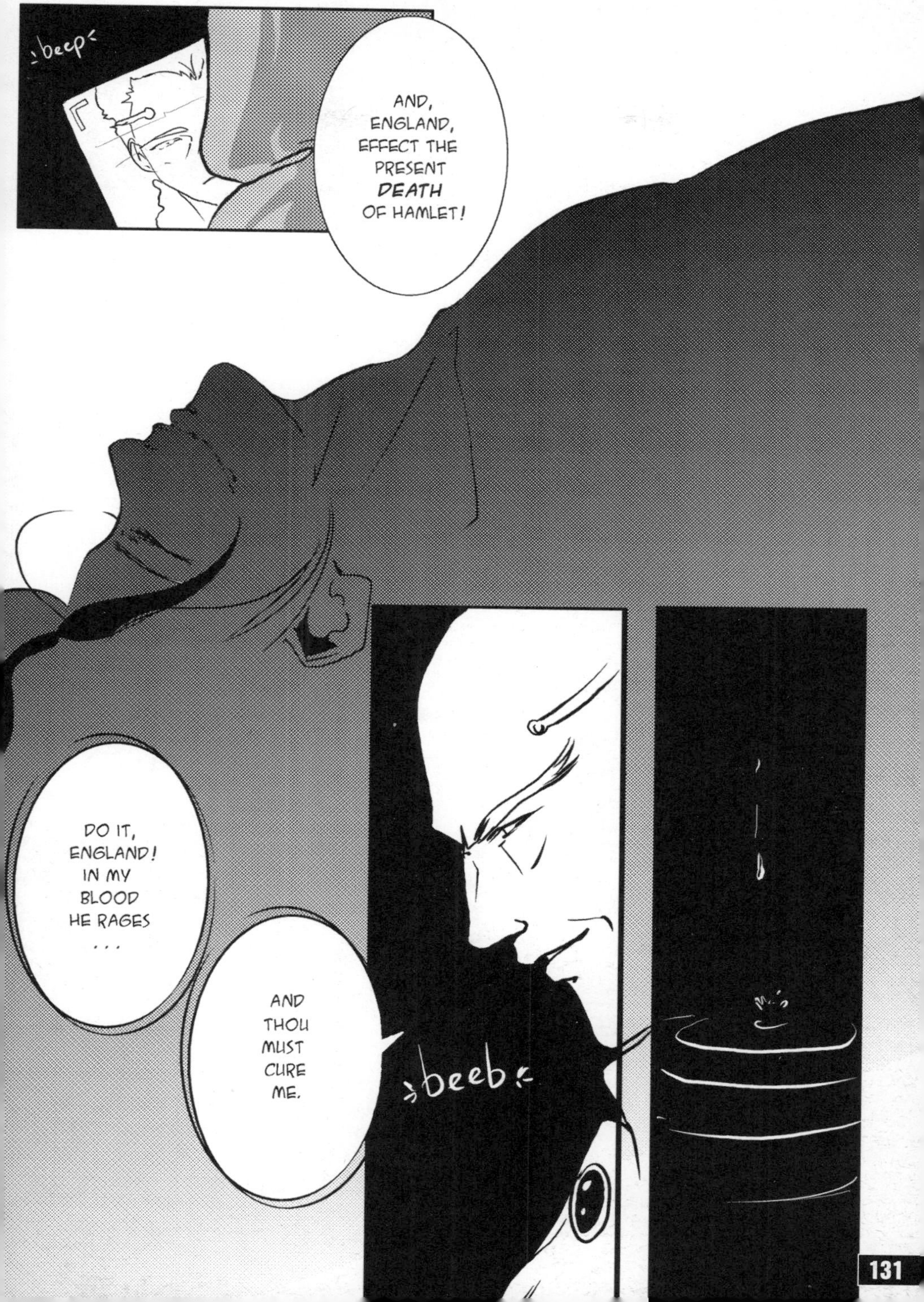
beep
AND, ENGLAND, EFFECT THE PRESENT DEATH OF HAMLET!
DO IT, ENGLAND! IN MY BLOOD HE RAGES . . .
AND THOU MUST CURE ME.
beeb

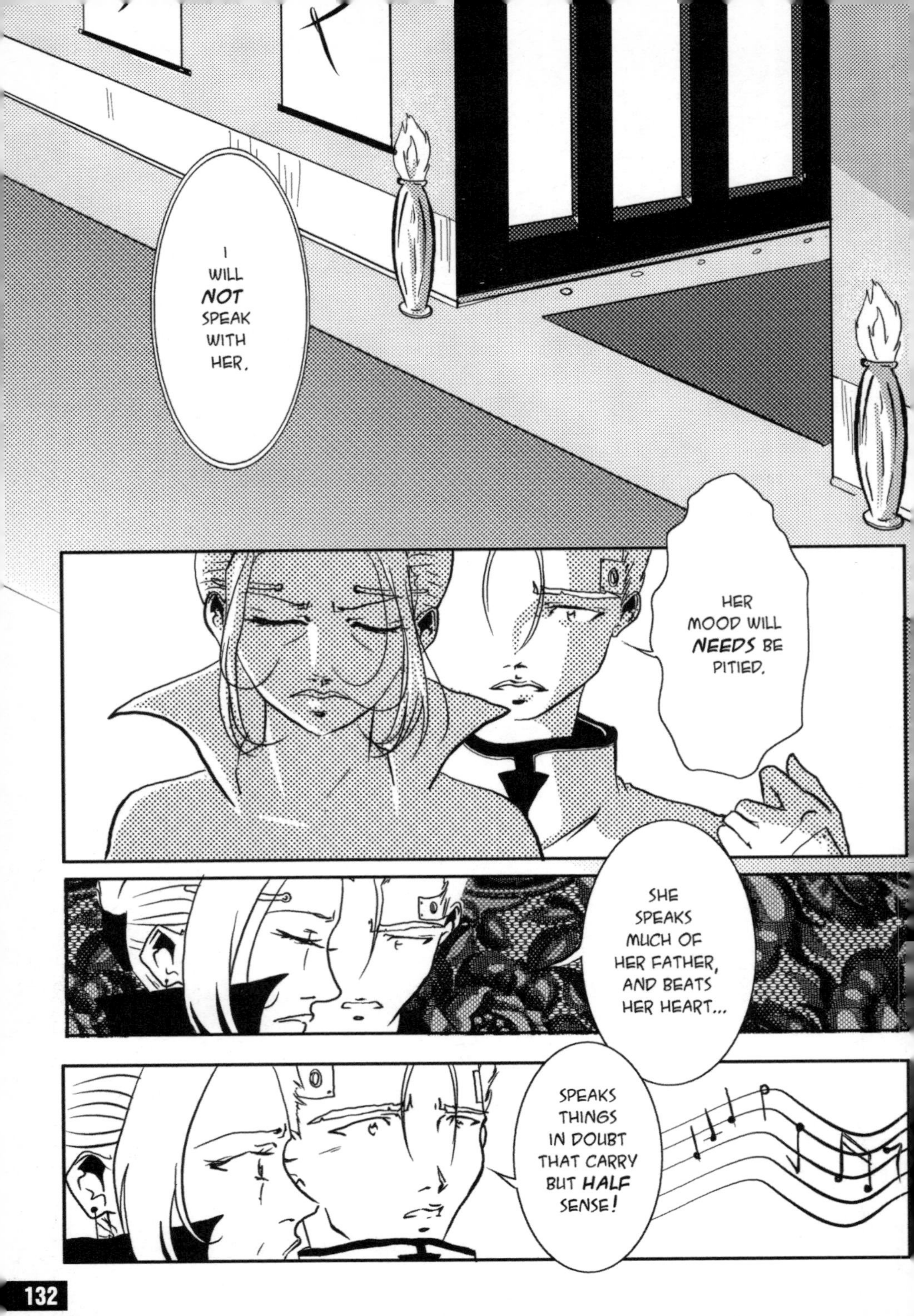
I WILL NOT SPEAK WITH HER.
HER MOOD WILL NEEDS BE PITIED.
SHE SPEAKS MUCH OF HER FATHER, AND BEATS HER HEART...
SPEAKS THINGS IN DOUBT THAT CARRY BUT HALF SENSE!

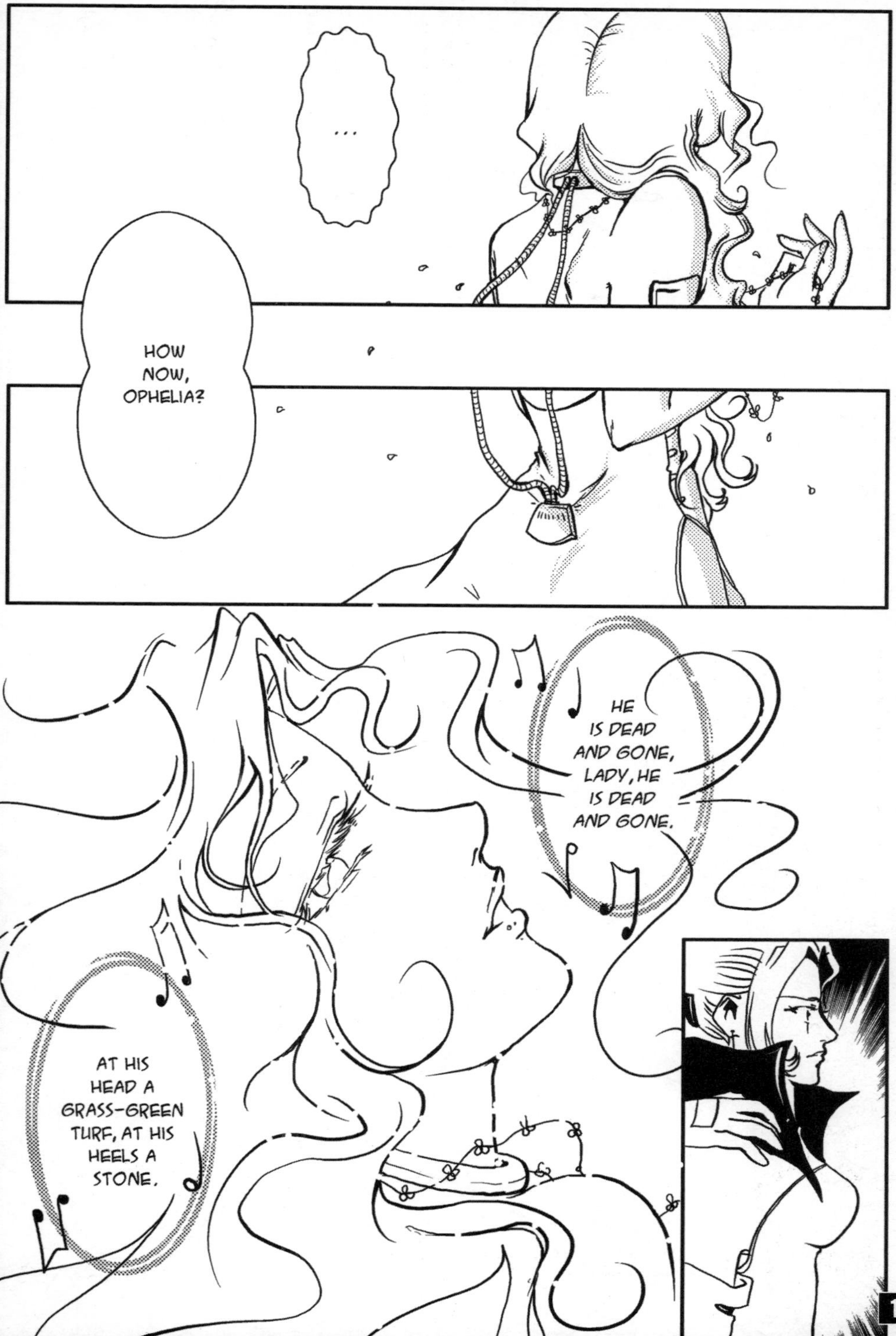
...
HOW NOW, OPHELIA?
HE IS DEAD AND GONE, LADY, HE IS DEAD AND GONE.
AT HIS HEAD A GRASS-GREEN TURF, AT HIS HEELS A STONE.

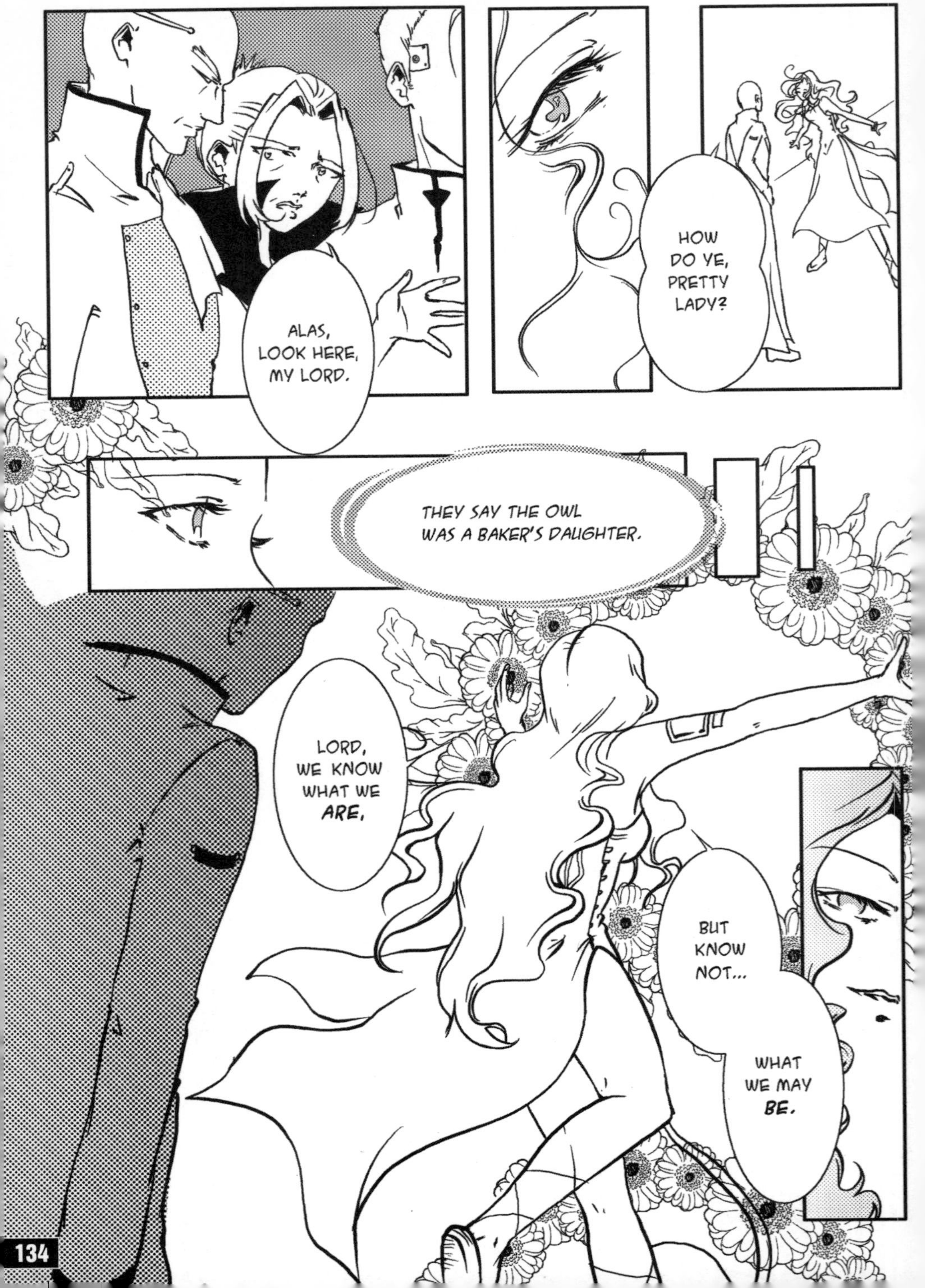
ALAS, LOOK HERE, MY LORD.
HOW DO YE, PRETTY LADY?
THEY SAY THE OWL WAS A BAKER'S DAUGHTER.
LORD, WE KNOW WHAT WE **ARE**,
BUT KNOW NOT...
WHAT WE MAY **BE**.

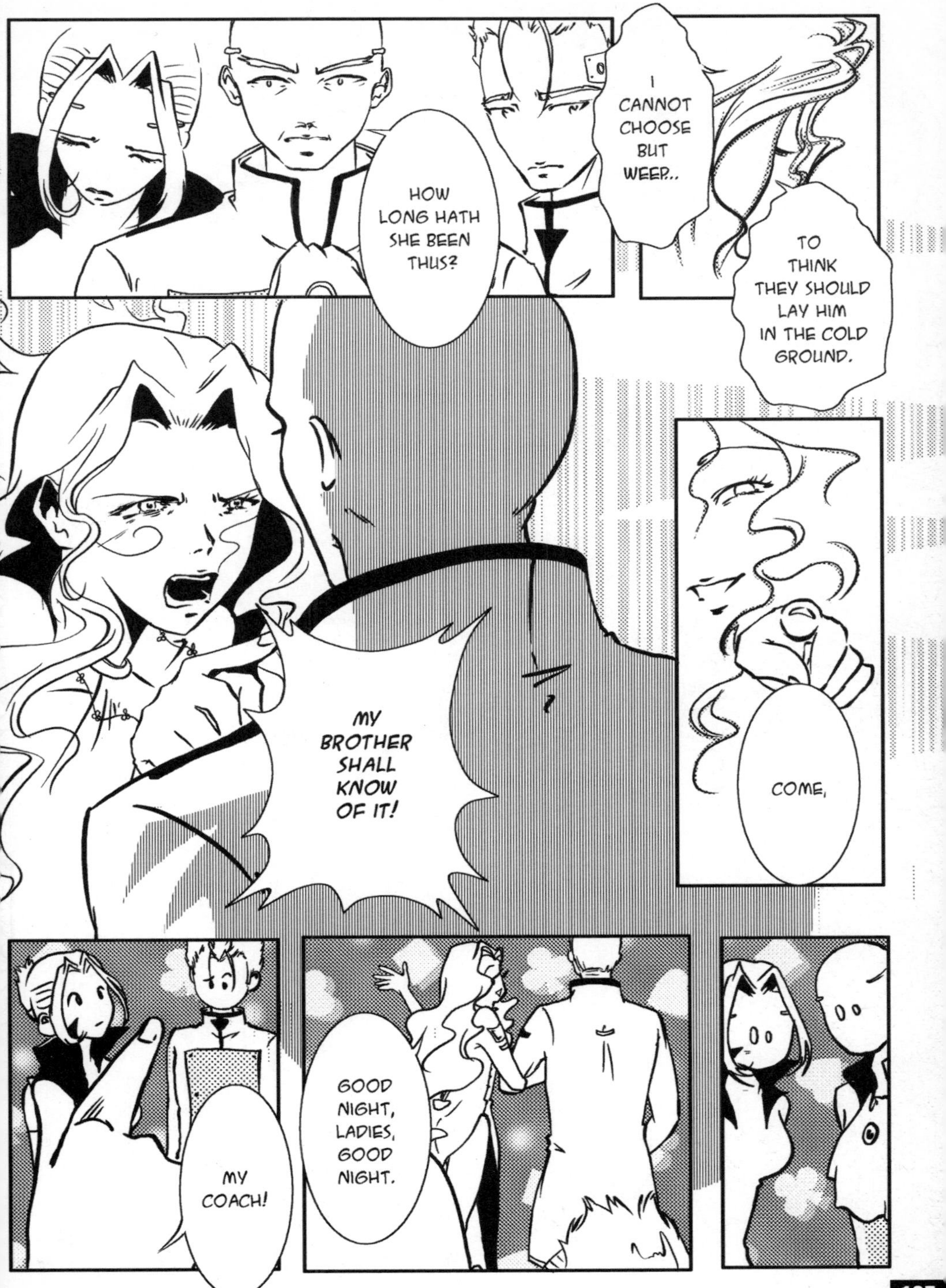
HOW LONG HATH SHE BEEN THUS?
I CANNOT CHOOSE BUT WEEP..
TO THINK THEY SHOULD LAY HIM IN THE COLD GROUND.
MY BROTHER SHALL KNOW OF IT!
COME,
MY COACH!
GOOD NIGHT, LADIES, GOOD NIGHT.

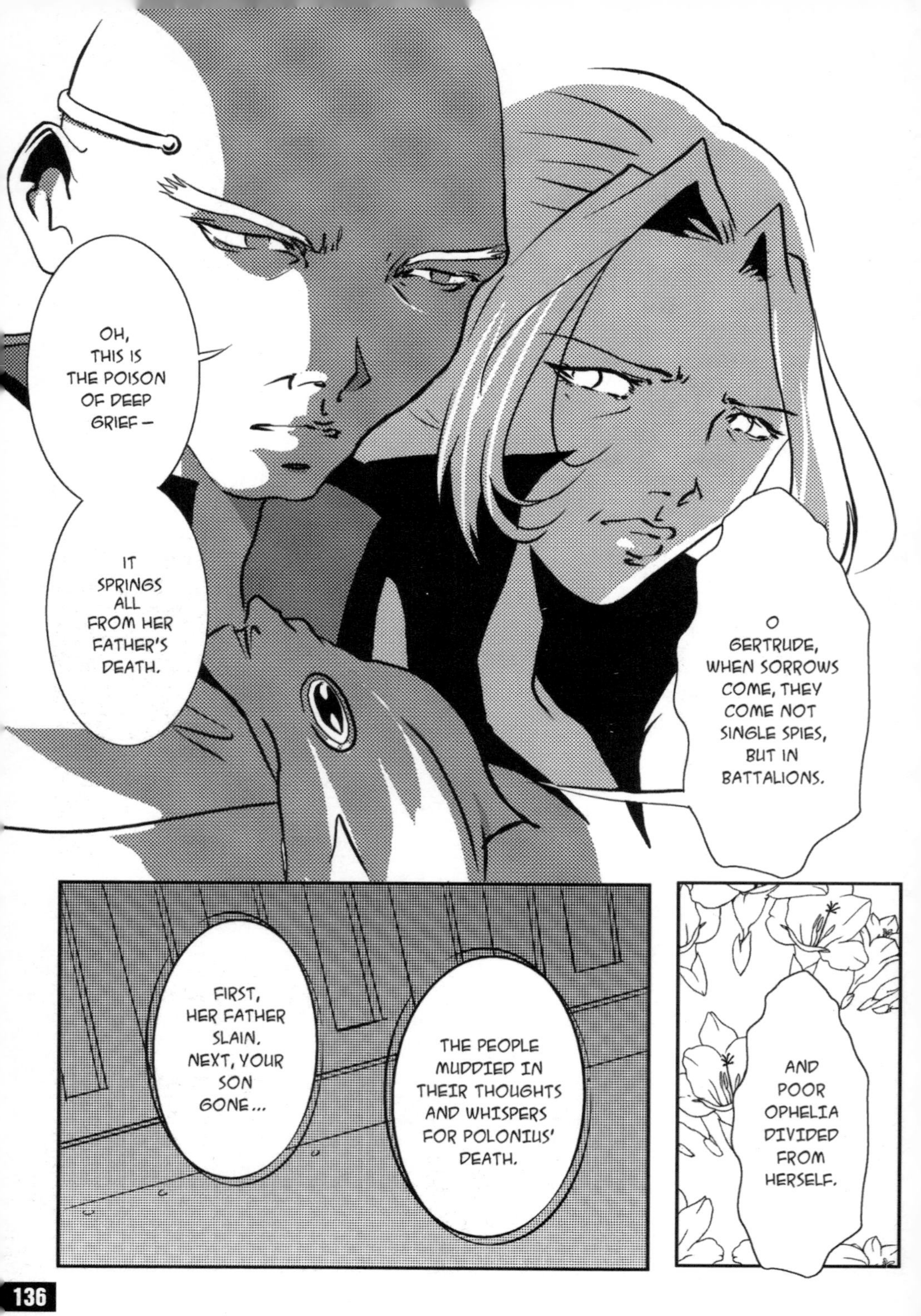

OH, THIS IS THE POISON OF DEEP GRIEF –
IT SPRINGS ALL FROM HER FATHER'S DEATH.
O GERTRUDE, WHEN SORROWS COME, THEY COME NOT SINGLE SPIES, BUT IN BATTALIONS.
FIRST, HER FATHER SLAIN. NEXT, YOUR SON GONE...
THE PEOPLE MUDDIED IN THEIR THOUGHTS AND WHISPERS FOR POLONIUS' DEATH.
AND POOR OPHELIA DIVIDED FROM HERSELF.

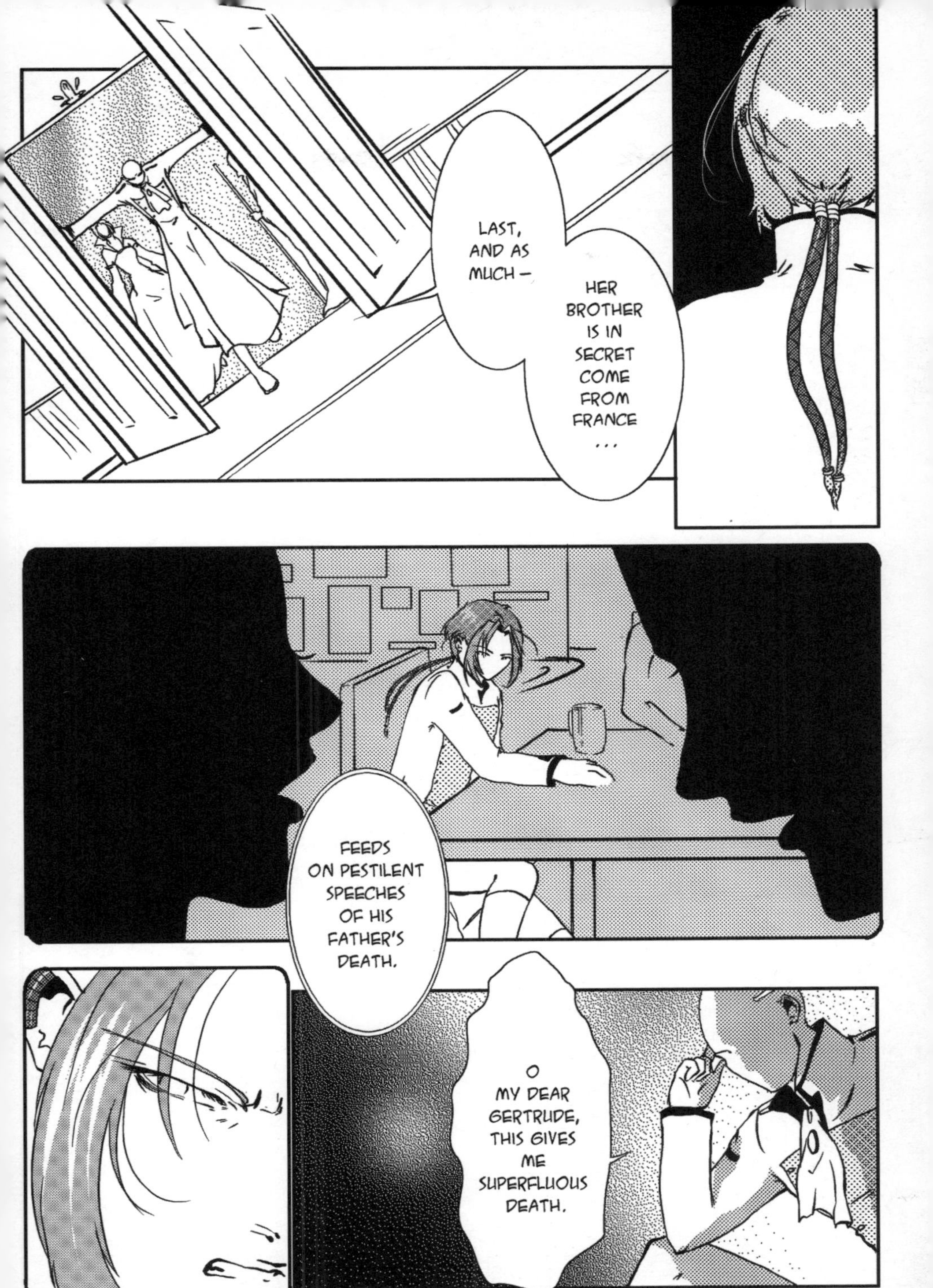
LAST, AND AS MUCH –
HER BROTHER IS IN SECRET COME FROM FRANCE . . .
FEEDS ON PESTILENT SPEECHES OF HIS FATHER'S DEATH.
O MY DEAR GERTRUDE, THIS GIVES ME SUPERFLUOUS DEATH.

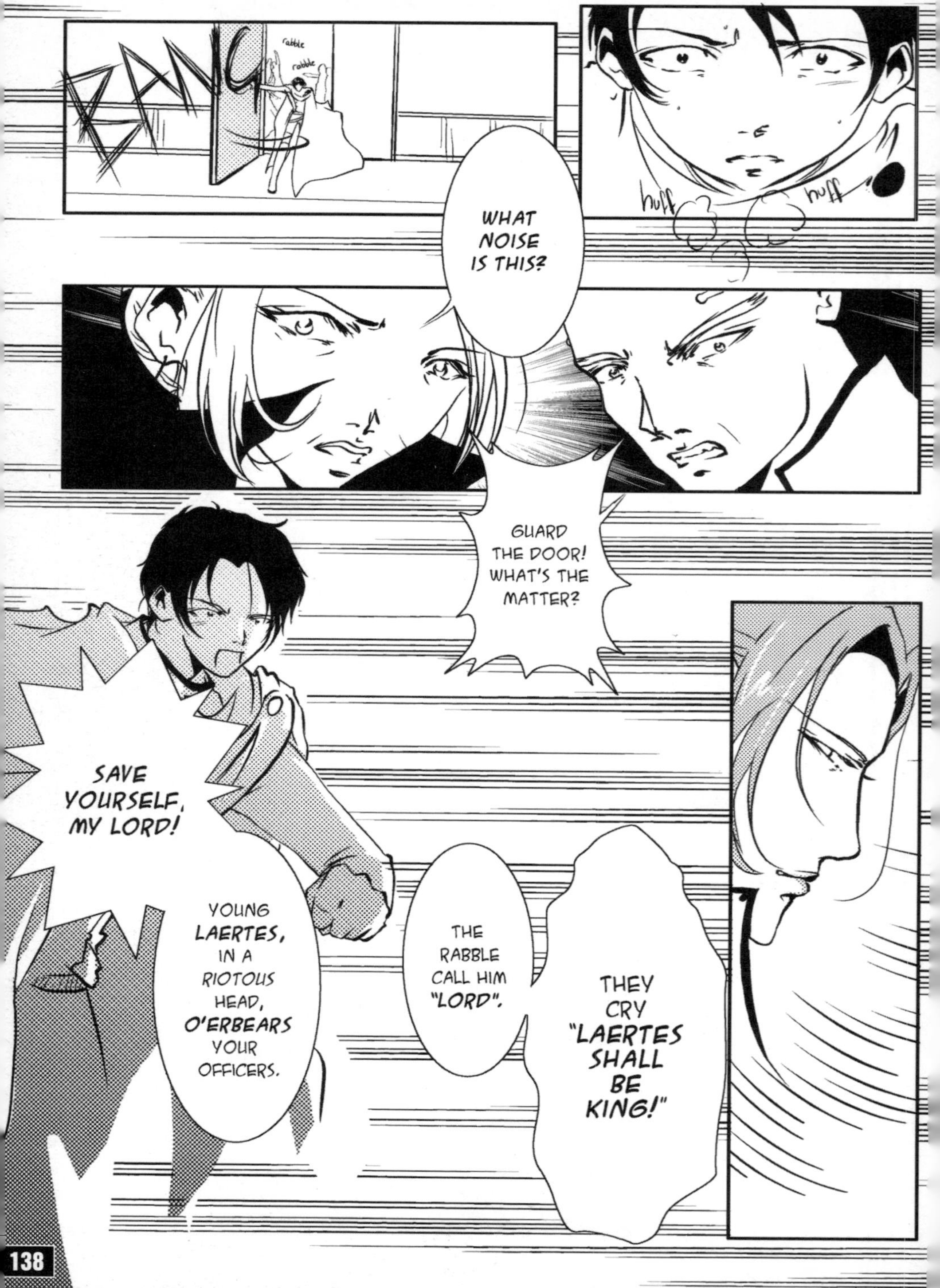
rabble
rabble
BANG
huff
huff
WHAT NOISE IS THIS?
GUARD THE DOOR! WHAT'S THE MATTER?
SAVE YOURSELF, MY LORD!
YOUNG LAERTES, IN A RIOTOUS HEAD, O'ERBEARS YOUR OFFICERS.
THE RABBLE CALL HIM "LORD".
THEY CRY "LAERTES SHALL BE KING!"

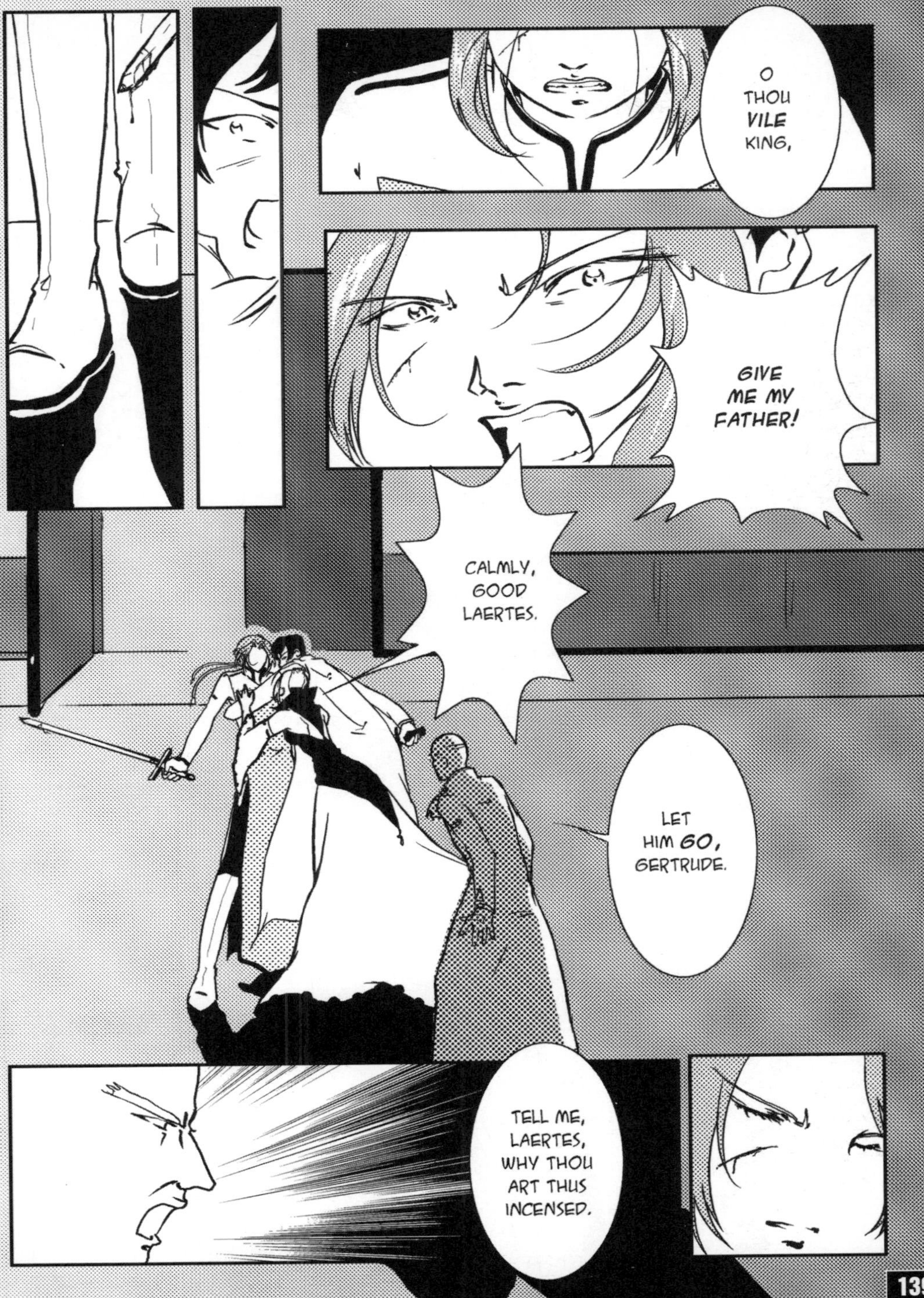
O THOU VILE KING,
GIVE ME MY FATHER!
CALMLY, GOOD LAERTES.
LET HIM GO, GERTRUDE.
TELL ME, LAERTES, WHY THOU ART THUS INCENSED.

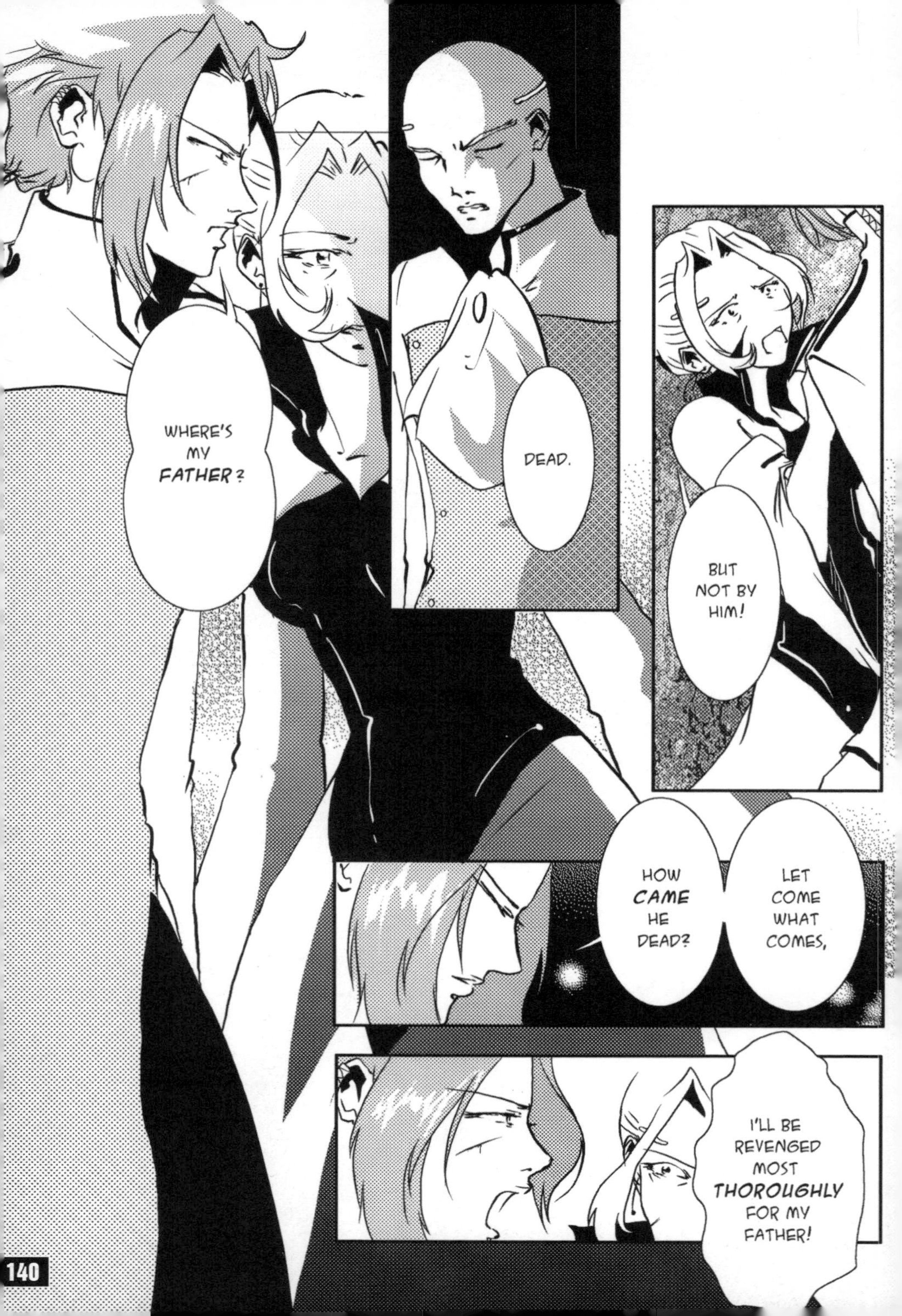
WHERE'S MY FATHER?
DEAD.
BUT NOT BY HIM!
HOW CAME HE DEAD?
LET COME WHAT COMES,
I'LL BE REVENGED MOST THOROUGHLY FOR MY FATHER!

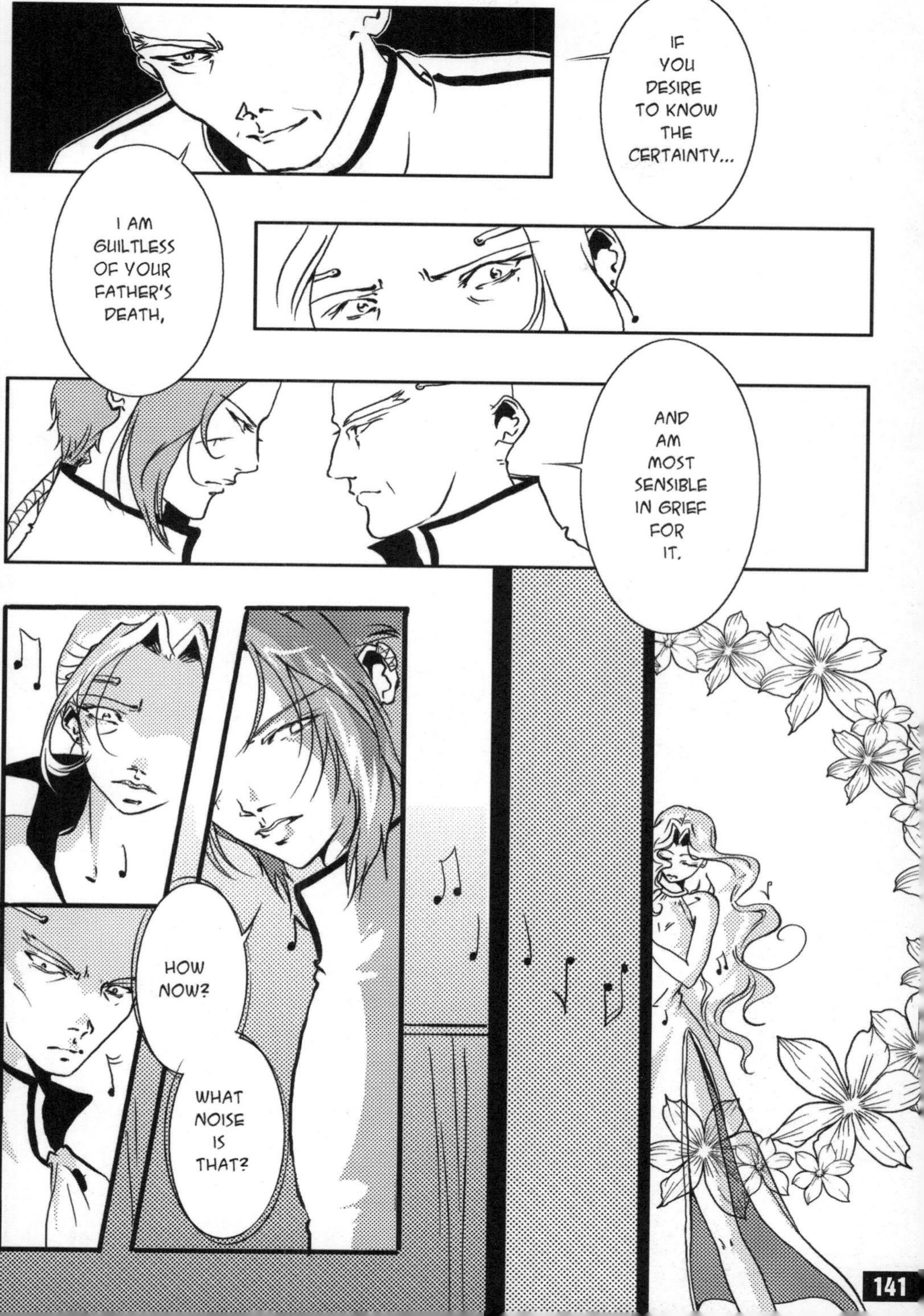
IF YOU DESIRE TO KNOW THE CERTAINTY...
I AM GUILTLESS OF YOUR FATHER'S DEATH,
AND AM MOST SENSIBLE IN GRIEF FOR IT.
HOW NOW?
WHAT NOISE IS THAT?

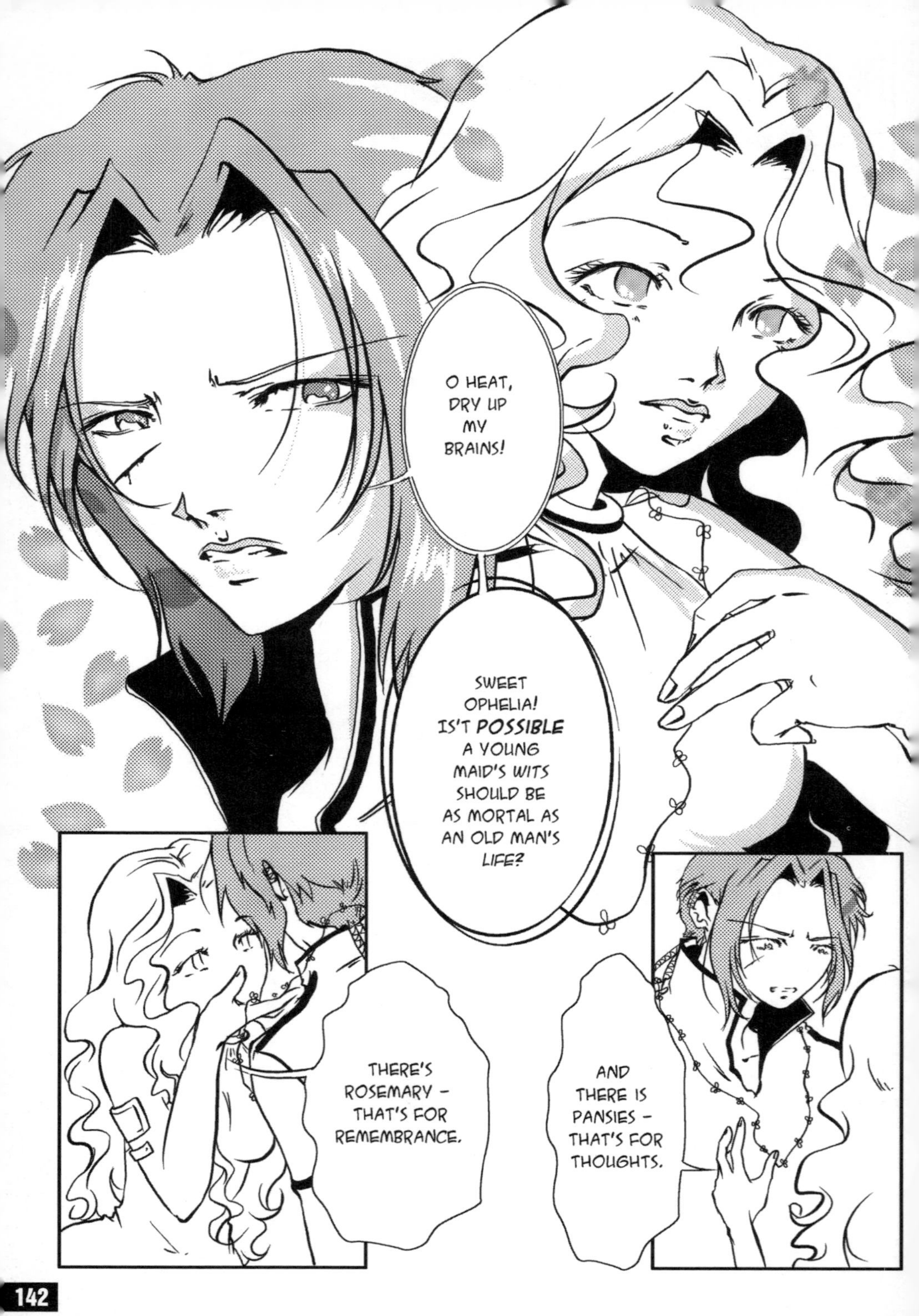
O HEAT, DRY UP MY BRAINS!
SWEET OPHELIA! IS'T **POSSIBLE** A YOUNG MAID'S WITS SHOULD BE AS MORTAL AS AN OLD MAN'S LIFE?
THERE'S ROSEMARY - THAT'S FOR REMEMBRANCE.
AND THERE IS PANSIES - THAT'S FOR THOUGHTS.

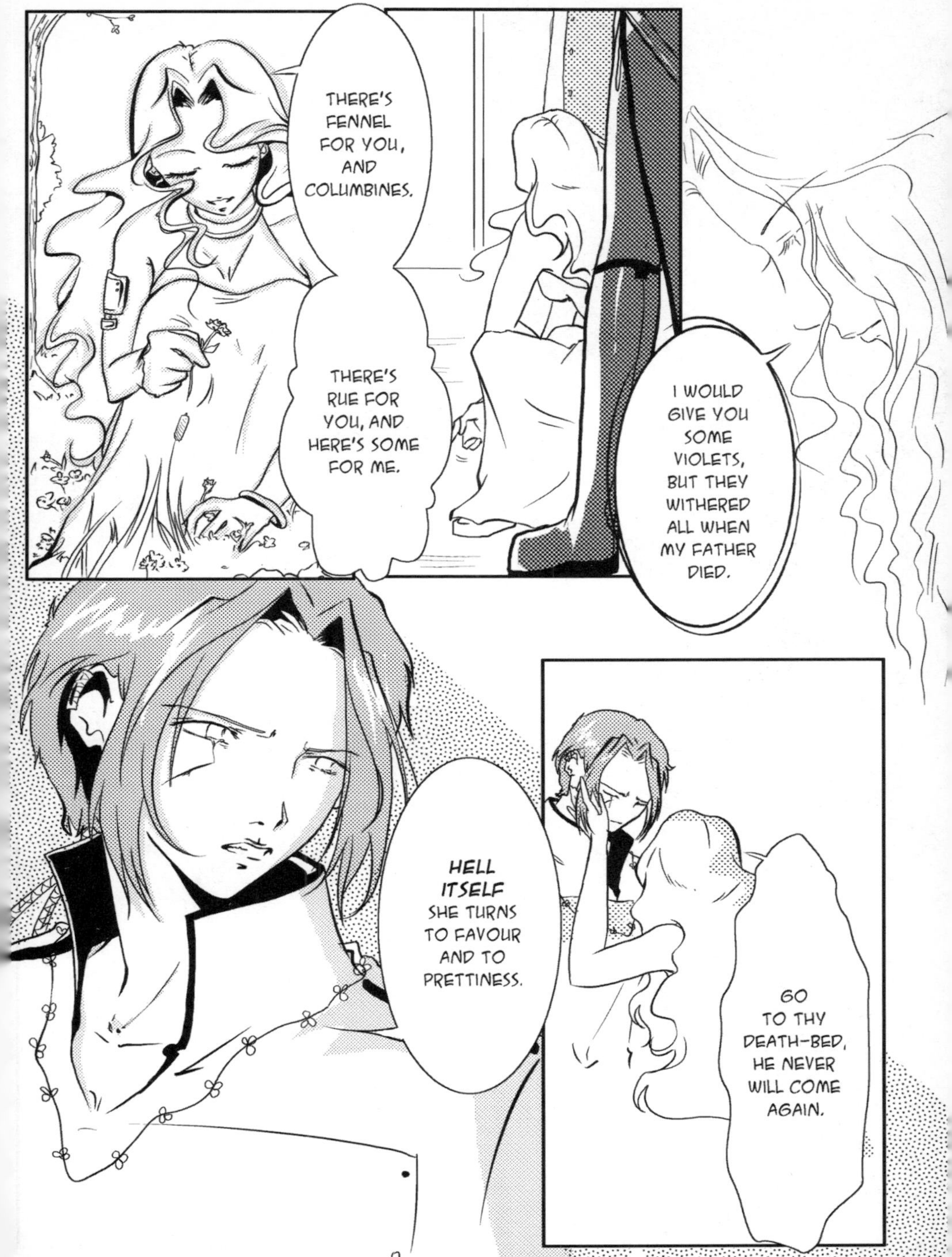
THERE'S FENNEL FOR YOU, AND COLUMBINES.
THERE'S RUE FOR YOU, AND HERE'S SOME FOR ME.
I WOULD GIVE YOU SOME VIOLETS, BUT THEY WITHERED ALL WHEN MY FATHER DIED.
HELL ITSELF SHE TURNS TO FAVOUR AND TO PRETTINESS.
GO TO THY DEATH-BED, HE NEVER WILL COME AGAIN.

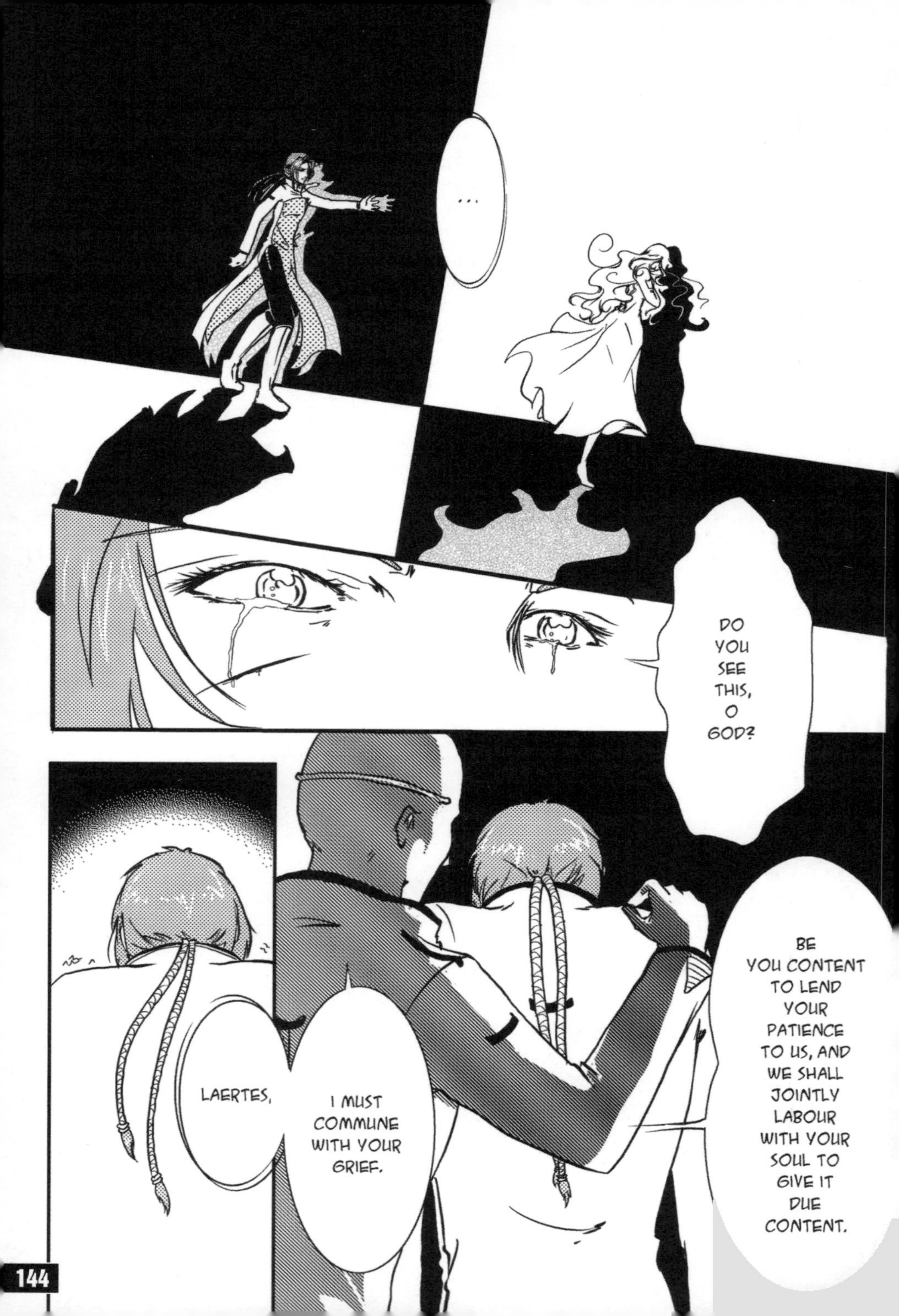
...
DO YOU SEE THIS, O GOD?
BE YOU CONTENT TO LEND YOUR PATIENCE TO US, AND WE SHALL JOINTLY LABOUR WITH YOUR SOUL TO GIVE IT DUE CONTENT.
LAERTES,
I MUST COMMUNE WITH YOUR GRIEF.

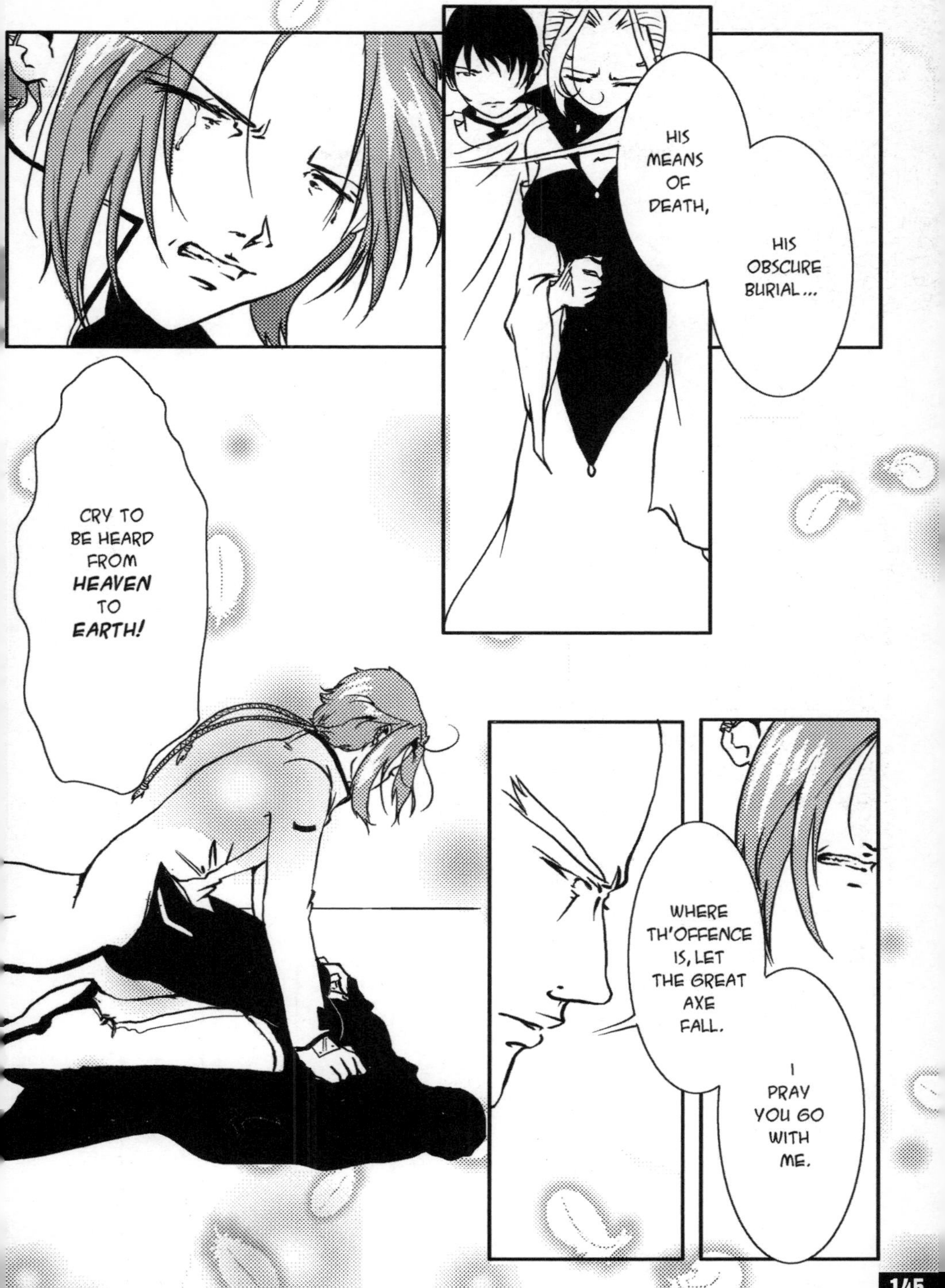
HIS MEANS OF DEATH,
HIS OBSCURE BURIAL...
CRY TO BE HEARD FROM **HEAVEN** TO **EARTH!**
WHERE TH'OFFENCE IS, LET THE GREAT AXE FALL.
I PRAY YOU GO WITH ME.

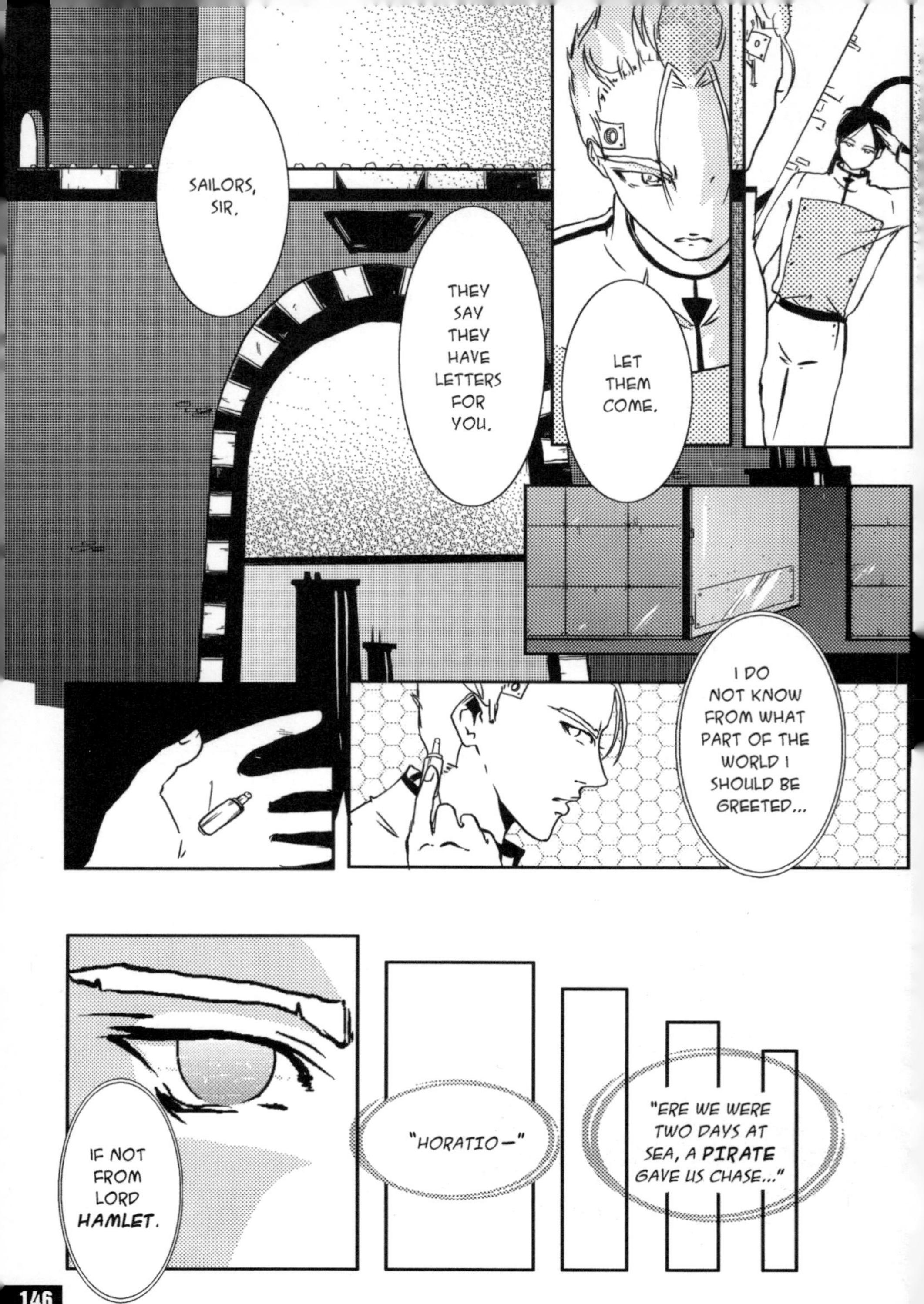
SAILORS, SIR.
THEY SAY THEY HAVE LETTERS FOR YOU.
LET THEM COME.
I DO NOT KNOW FROM WHAT PART OF THE WORLD I SHOULD BE GREETED...
IF NOT FROM LORD **HAMLET**.
"HORATIO—"
"ERE WE WERE TWO DAYS AT SEA, A **PIRATE** GAVE US CHASE..."

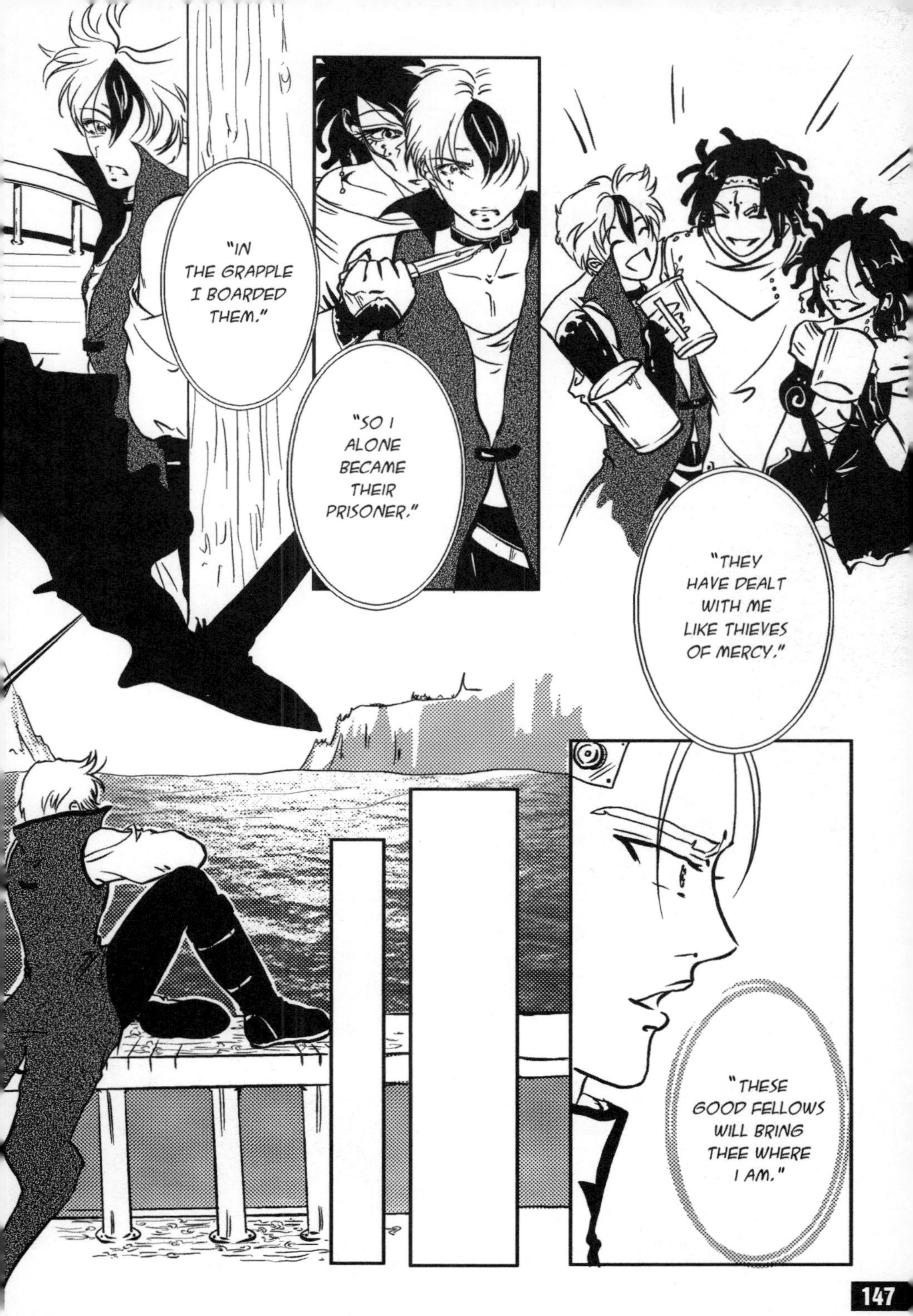
"IN THE GRAPPLE I BOARDED THEM."
"SO I ALONE BECAME THEIR PRISONER."
"THEY HAVE DEALT WITH ME LIKE THIEVES OF MERCY."
"THESE GOOD FELLOWS WILL BRING THEE WHERE I AM."

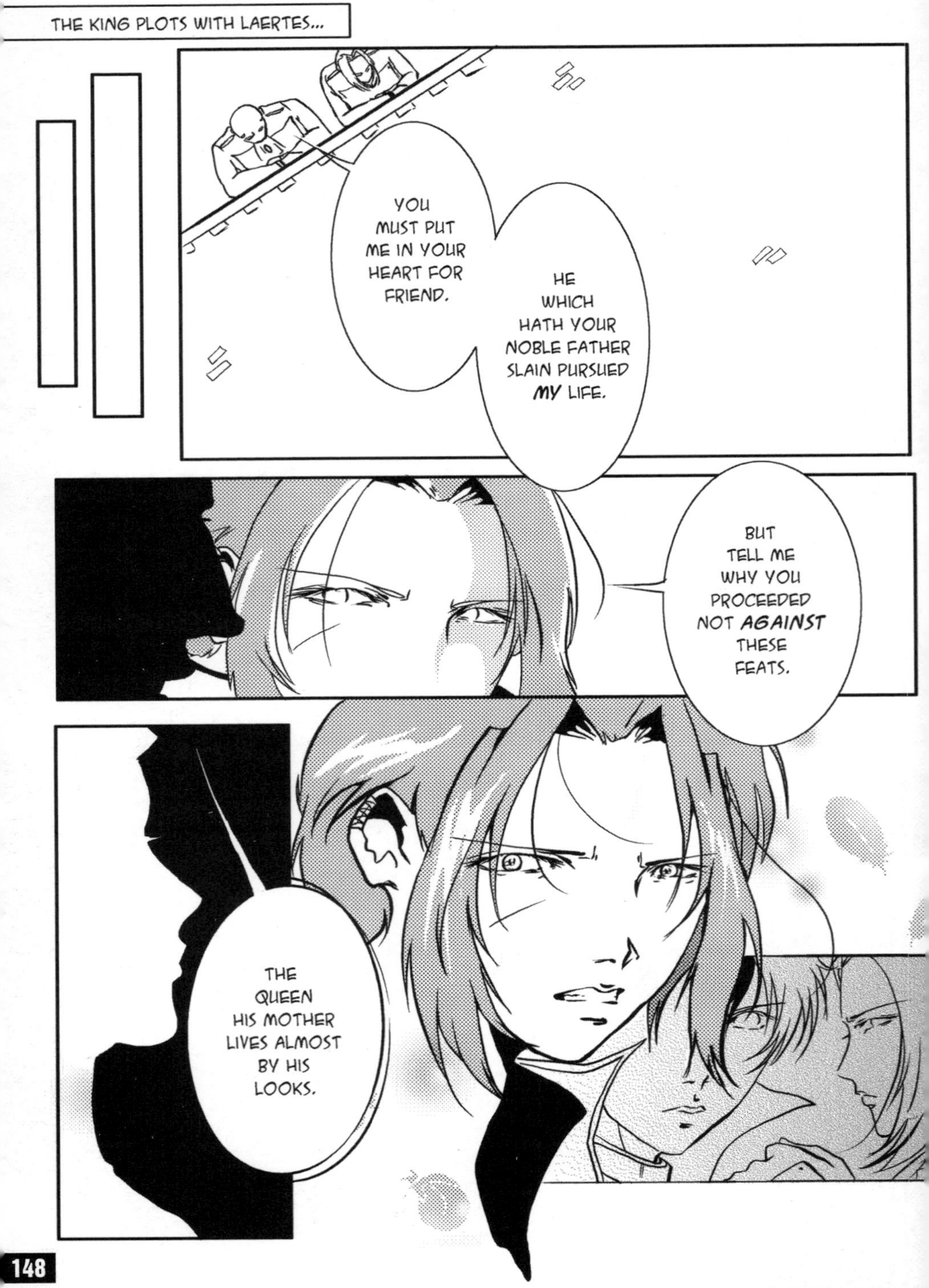
THE KING PLOTS WITH LAERTES...
YOU MUST PUT ME IN YOUR HEART FOR FRIEND.
HE WHICH HATH YOUR NOBLE FATHER SLAIN PURSUED MY LIFE.
BUT TELL ME WHY YOU PROCEEDED NOT AGAINST THESE FEATS.
THE QUEEN HIS MOTHER LIVES ALMOST BY HIS LOOKS.

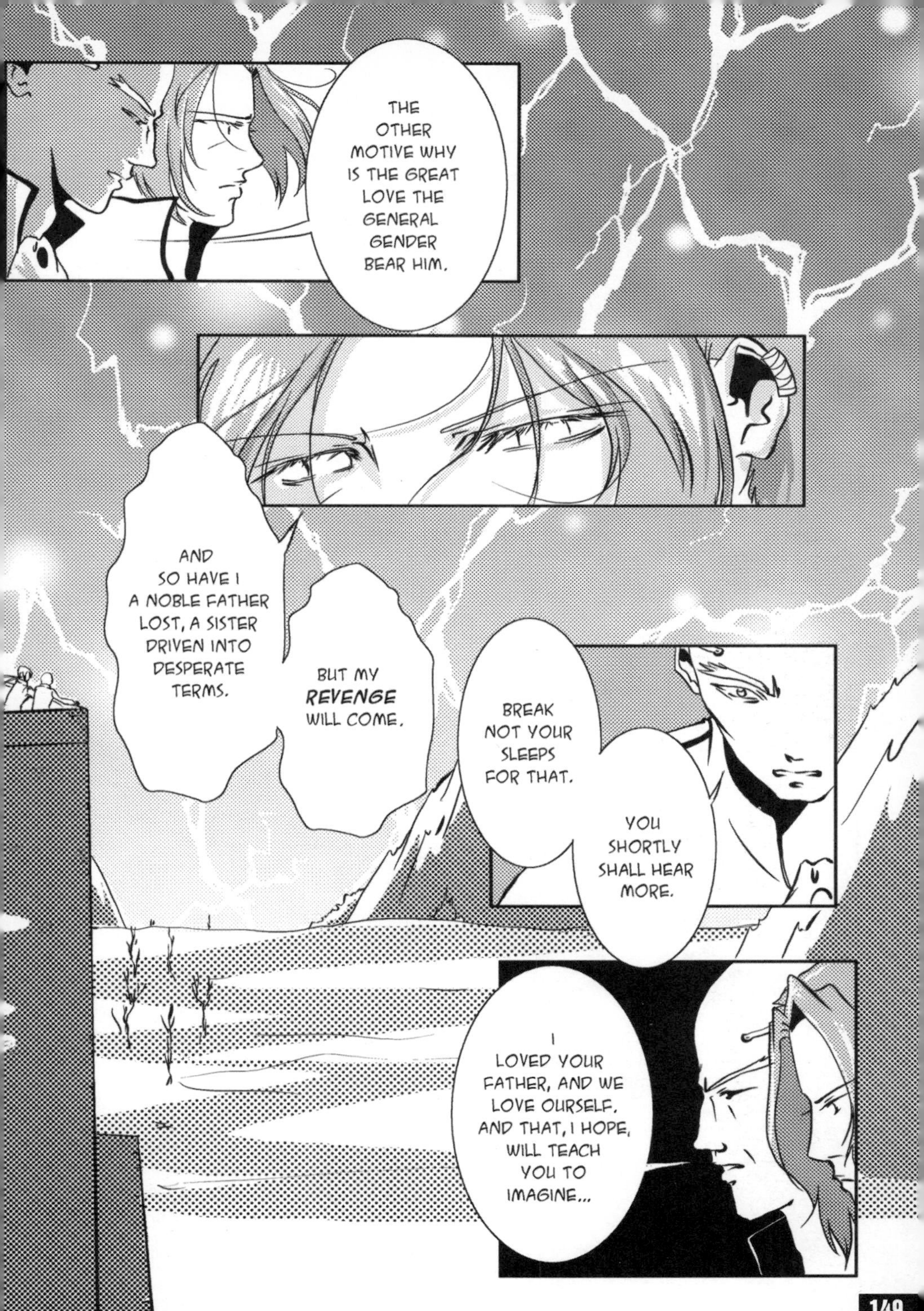

THE OTHER MOTIVE WHY IS THE GREAT LOVE THE GENERAL GENDER BEAR HIM.
AND SO HAVE I A NOBLE FATHER LOST, A SISTER DRIVEN INTO DESPERATE TERMS.
BUT MY **REVENGE** WILL COME.
BREAK NOT YOUR SLEEPS FOR THAT.
YOU SHORTLY SHALL HEAR MORE.
I LOVED YOUR FATHER, AND WE LOVE OURSELF. AND THAT, I HOPE, WILL TEACH YOU TO IMAGINE...

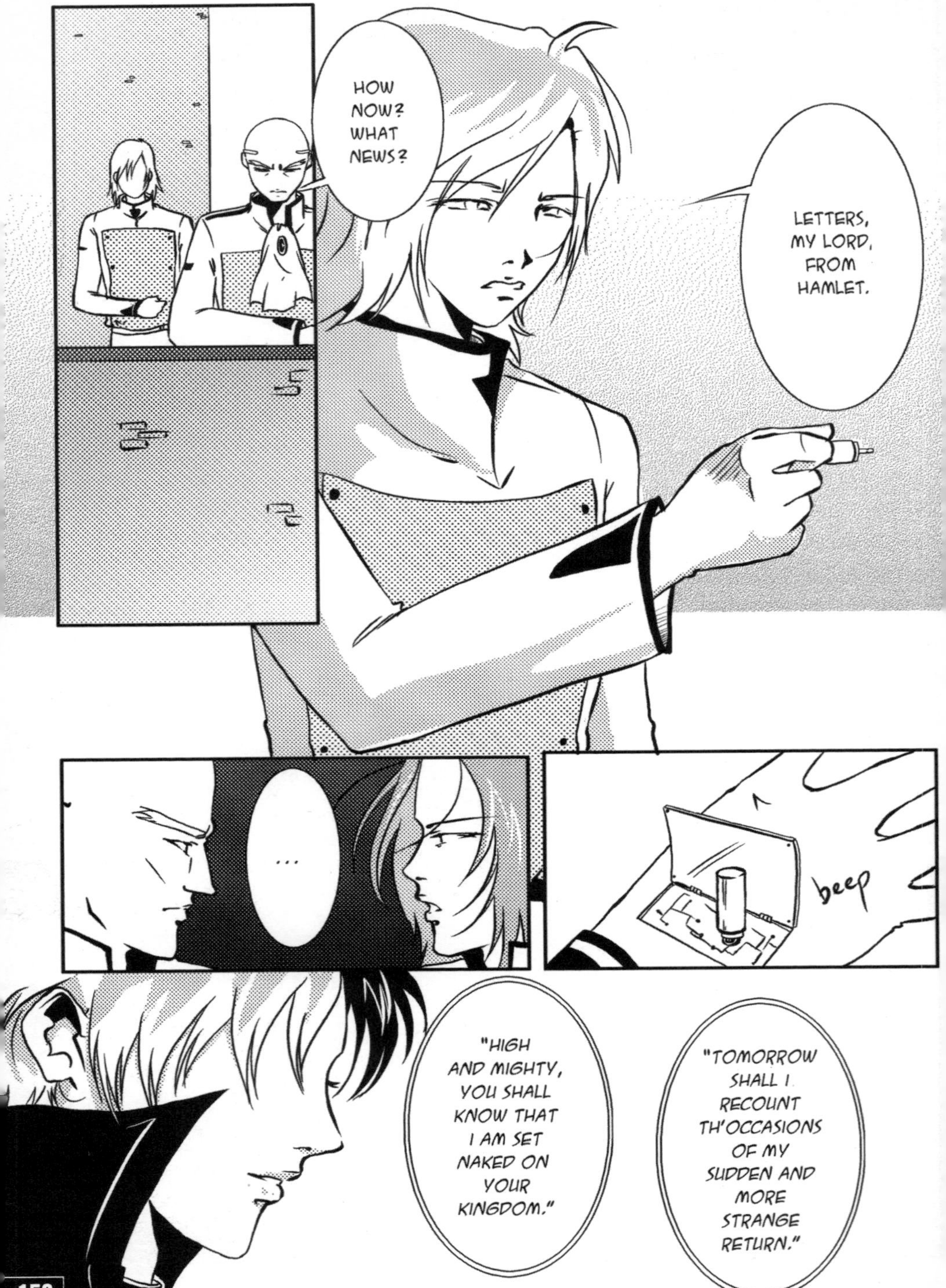
HOW NOW? WHAT NEWS?
LETTERS, MY LORD, FROM HAMLET.
...
beep
"HIGH AND MIGHTY, YOU SHALL KNOW THAT I AM SET NAKED ON YOUR KINGDOM."
"TOMORROW SHALL I RECOUNT TH'OCCASIONS OF MY SUDDEN AND MORE STRANGE RETURN."

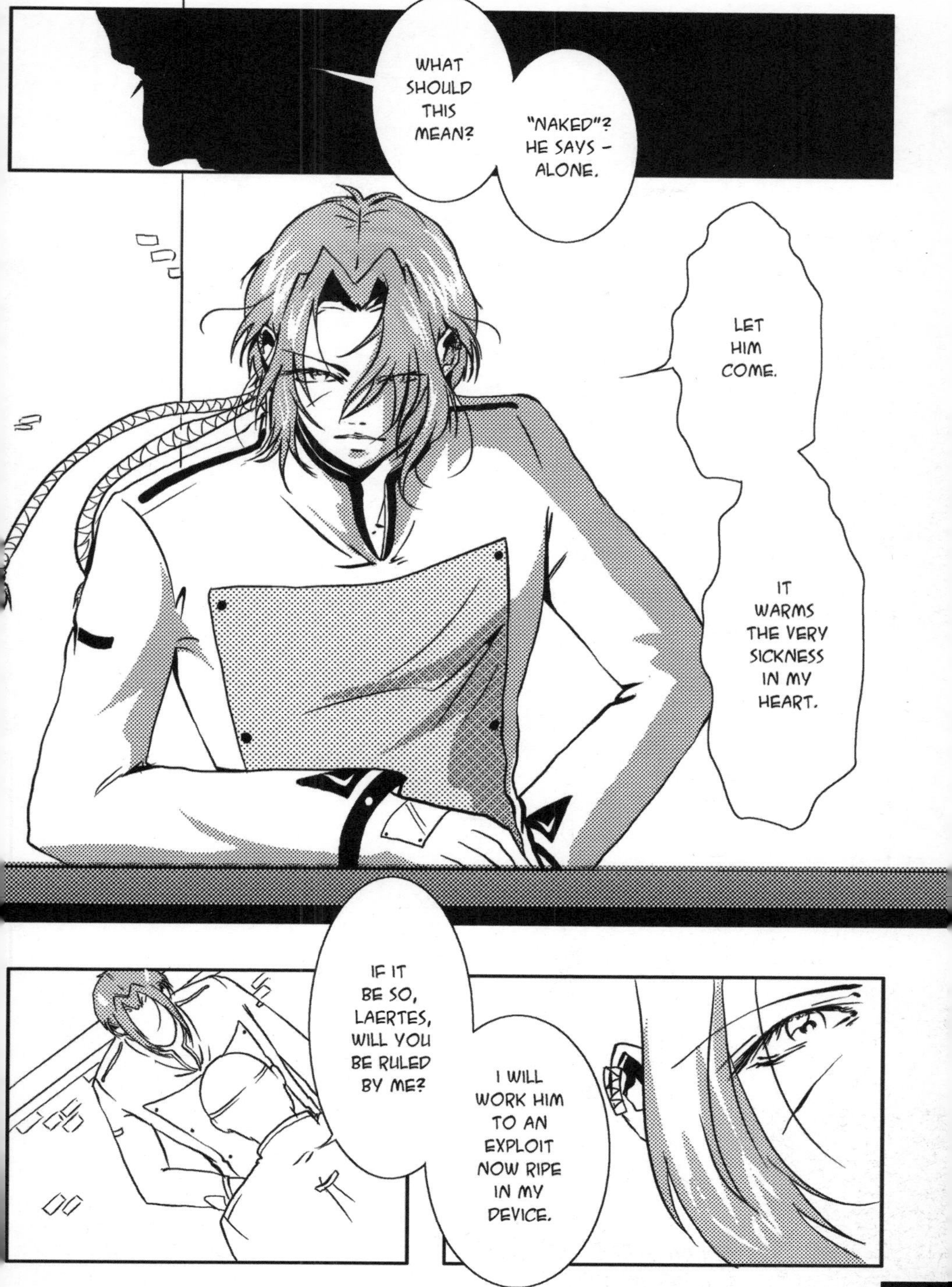
WHAT SHOULD THIS MEAN?
"NAKED"? HE SAYS - ALONE.
LET HIM COME.
IT WARMS THE VERY SICKNESS IN MY HEART.
IF IT BE SO, LAERTES, WILL YOU BE RULED BY ME?
I WILL WORK HIM TO AN EXPLOIT NOW RIPE IN MY DEVICE.

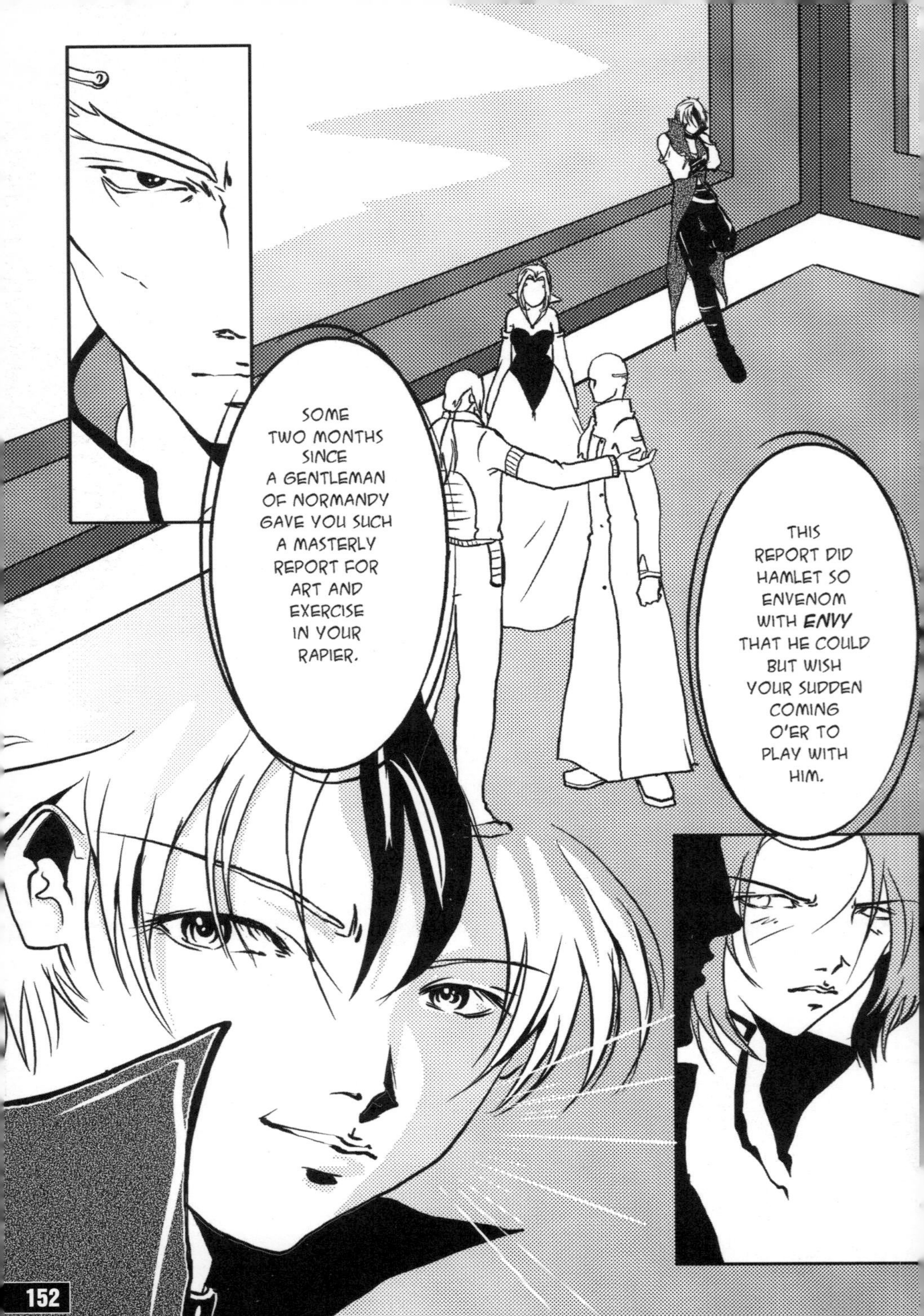
SOME TWO MONTHS SINCE A GENTLEMAN OF NORMANDY GAVE YOU SUCH A MASTERLY REPORT FOR ART AND EXERCISE IN YOUR RAPIER.
THIS REPORT DID HAMLET SO ENVENOM WITH **ENVY** THAT HE COULD BUT WISH YOUR SUDDEN COMING O'ER TO PLAY WITH HIM.

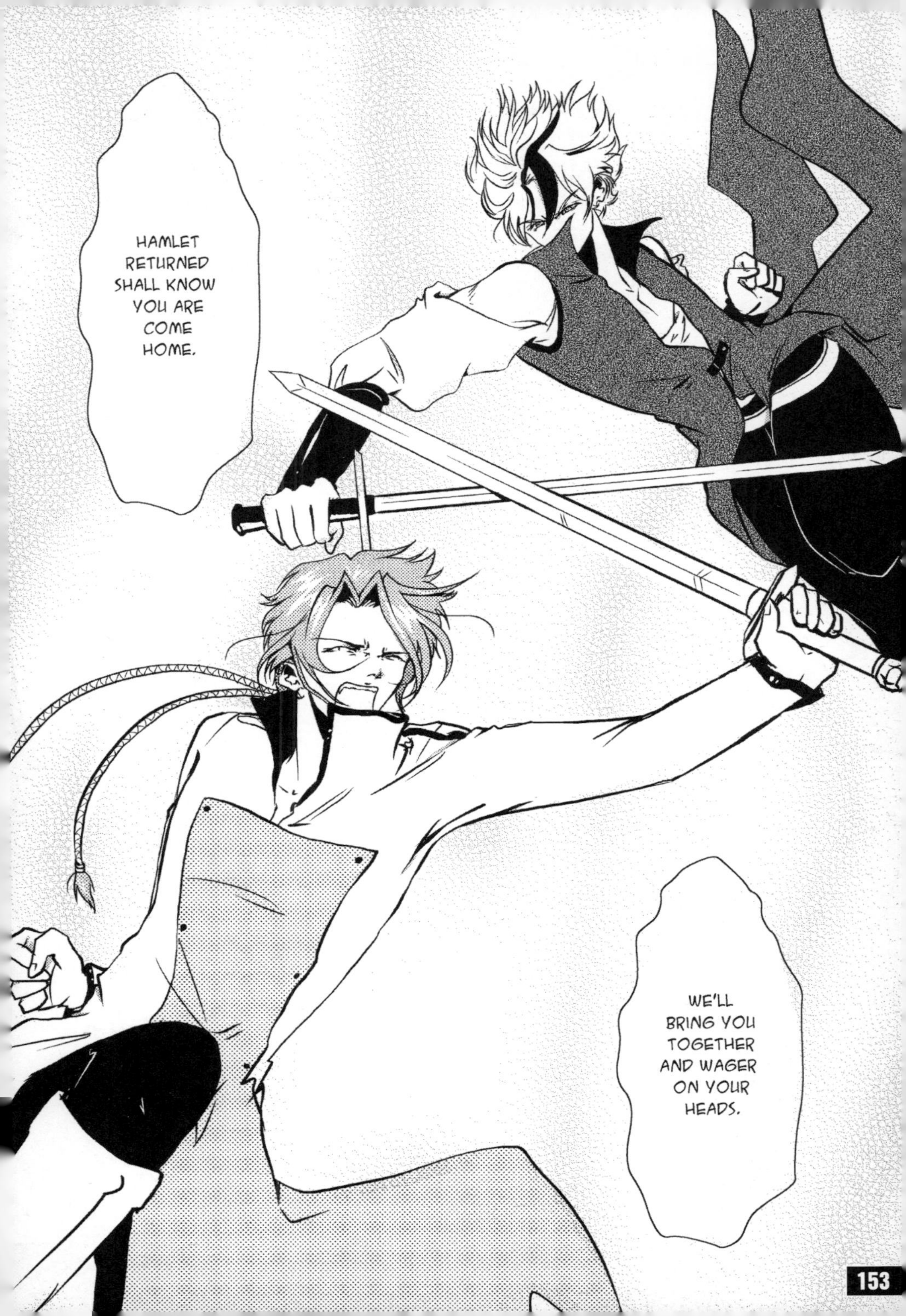
HAMLET RETURNED SHALL KNOW YOU ARE COME HOME.
WE'LL BRING YOU TOGETHER AND WAGER ON YOUR HEADS.

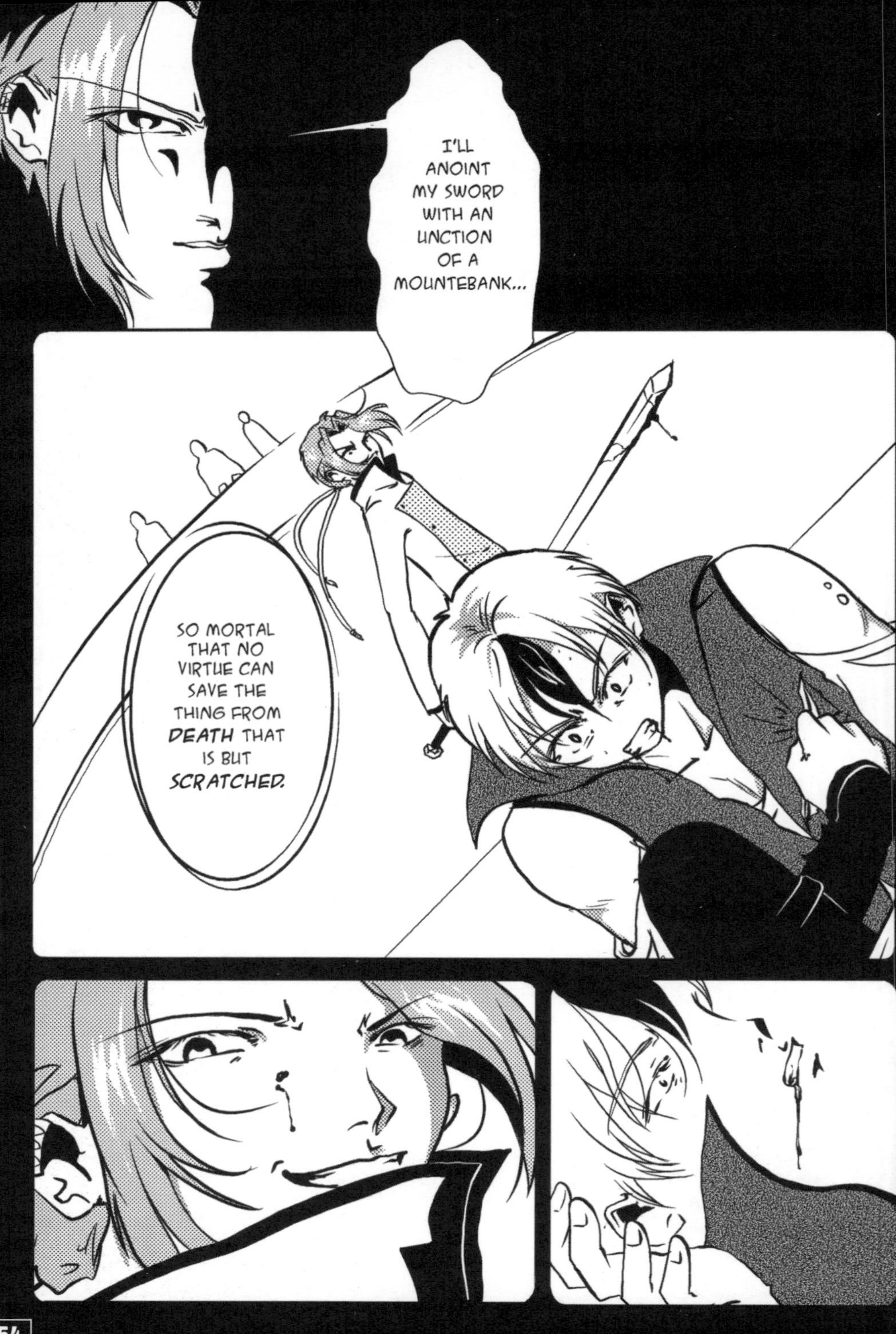
I'LL ANOINT MY SWORD WITH AN UNCTION OF A MOUNTEBANK...
SO MORTAL THAT NO VIRTUE CAN SAVE THE THING FROM DEATH THAT IS BUT SCRATCHED.

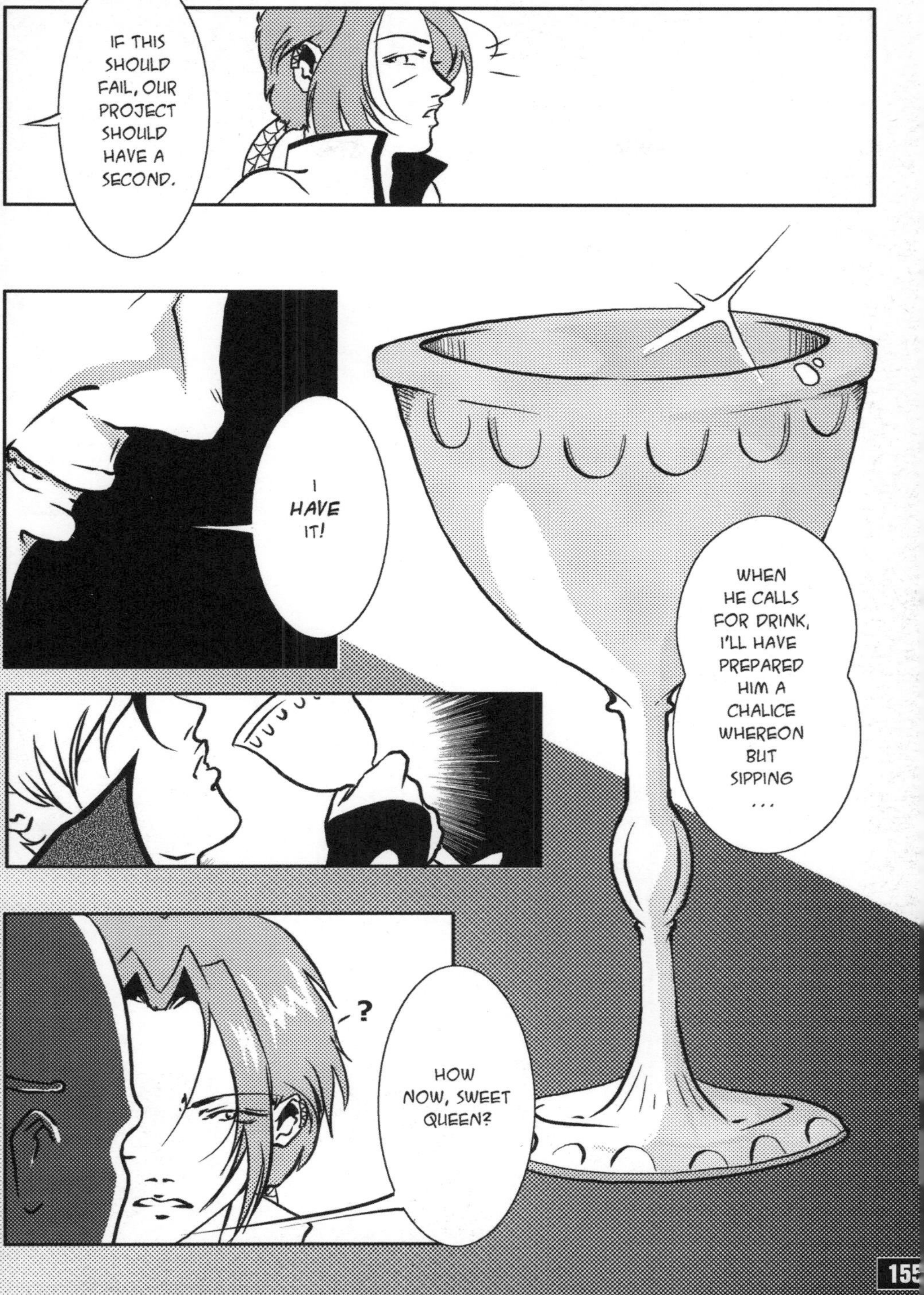
IF THIS SHOULD FAIL, OUR PROJECT SHOULD HAVE A SECOND.
I HAVE IT!
WHEN HE CALLS FOR DRINK, I'LL HAVE PREPARED HIM A CHALICE WHEREON BUT SIPPING ...
?
HOW NOW, SWEET QUEEN?

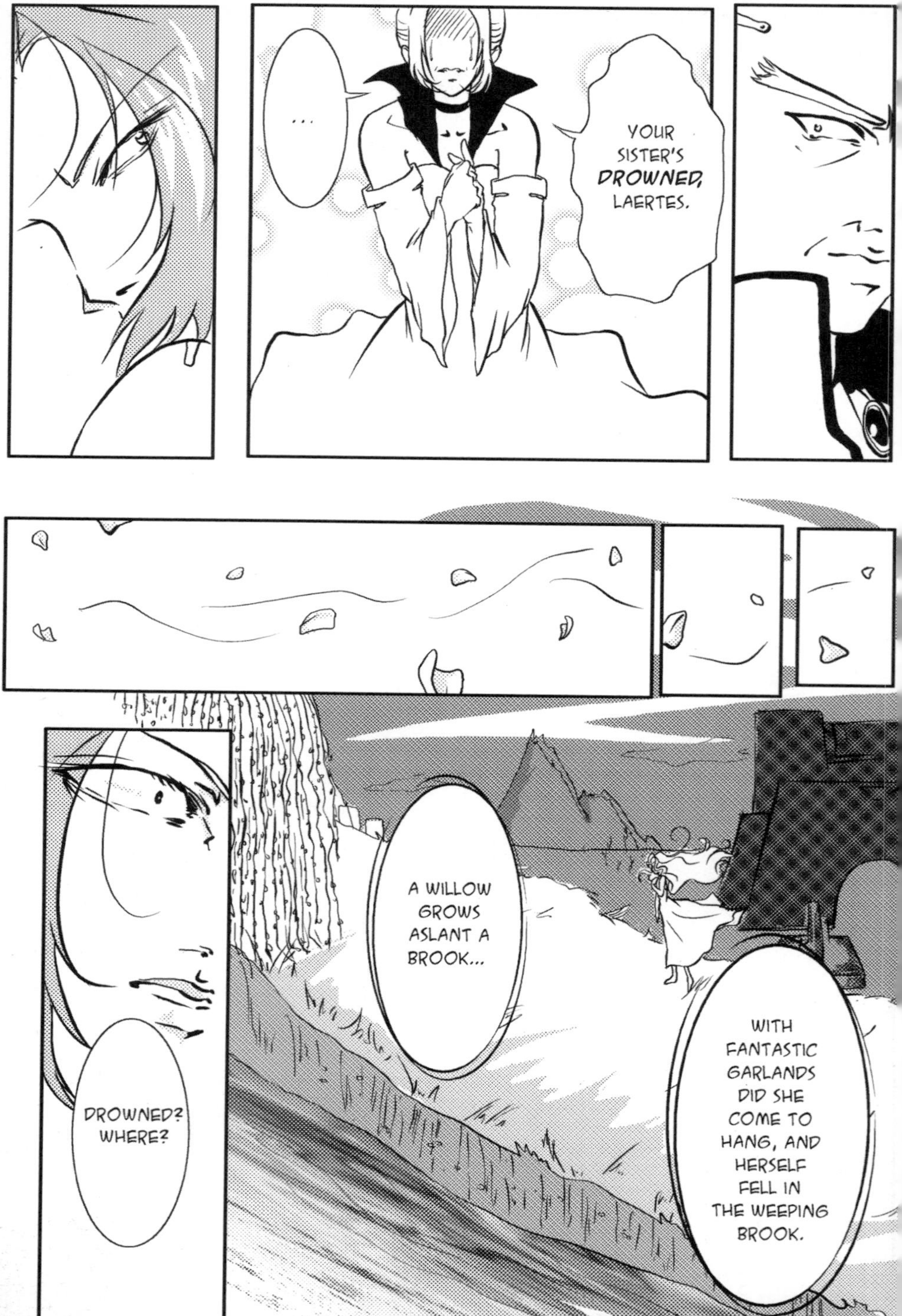
...
YOUR SISTER'S DROWNED, LAERTES.
DROWNED? WHERE?
A WILLOW GROWS ASLANT A BROOK...
WITH FANTASTIC GARLANDS DID SHE COME TO HANG, AND HERSELF FELL IN THE WEEPING BROOK.

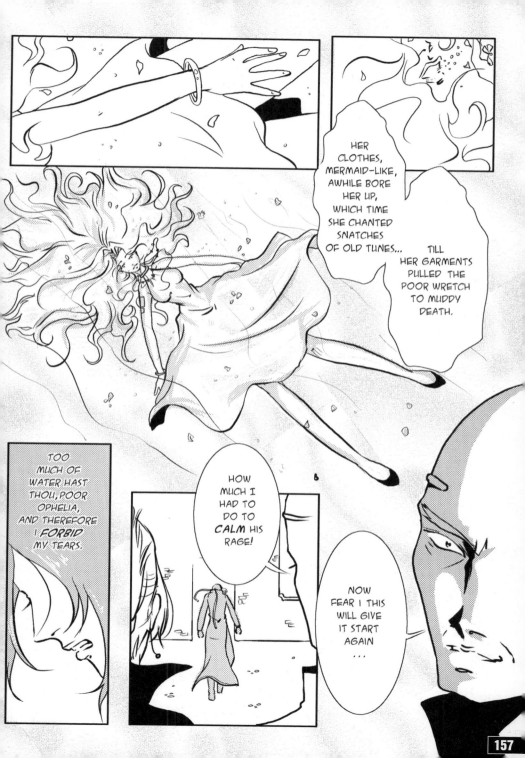

HER CLOTHES, MERMAID-LIKE, AWHILE BORE HER UP, WHICH TIME SHE CHANTED SNATCHES OF OLD TUNES...

TILL HER GARMENTS PULLED THE POOR WRETCH TO MUDDY DEATH.

TOO MUCH OF WATER HAST THOU, POOR OPHELIA, AND THEREFORE I *FORBID* MY TEARS.

HOW MUCH I HAD TO DO TO *CALM* HIS RAGE!

NOW FEAR I THIS WILL GIVE IT START AGAIN ...

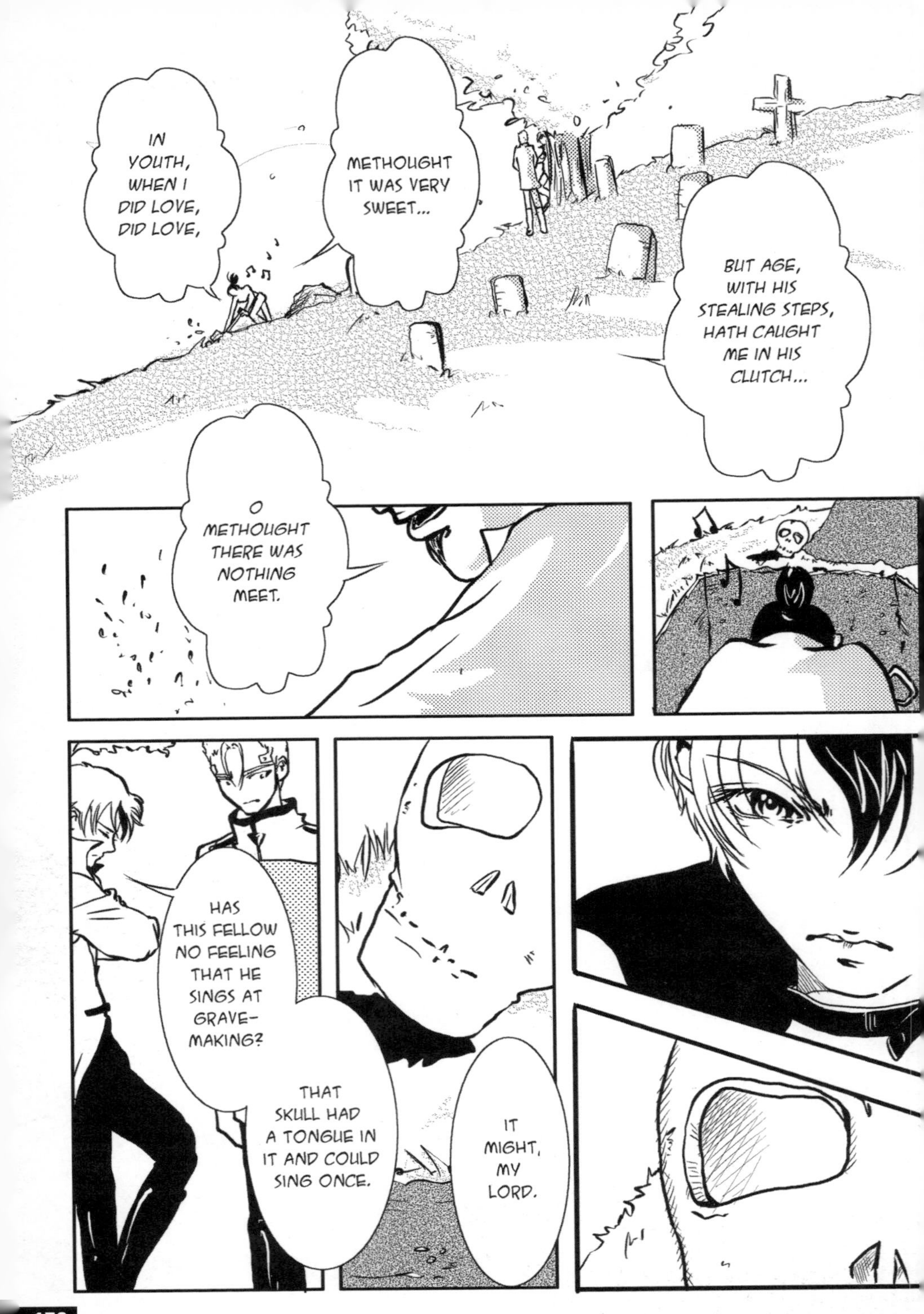
IN YOUTH, WHEN I DID LOVE, DID LOVE,
METHOUGHT IT WAS VERY SWEET...
BUT AGE, WITH HIS STEALING STEPS, HATH CAUGHT ME IN HIS CLUTCH...
O METHOUGHT THERE WAS NOTHING MEET.
HAS THIS FELLOW NO FEELING THAT HE SINGS AT GRAVE-MAKING?
THAT SKULL HAD A TONGUE IN IT AND COULD SING ONCE.
IT MIGHT, MY LORD.

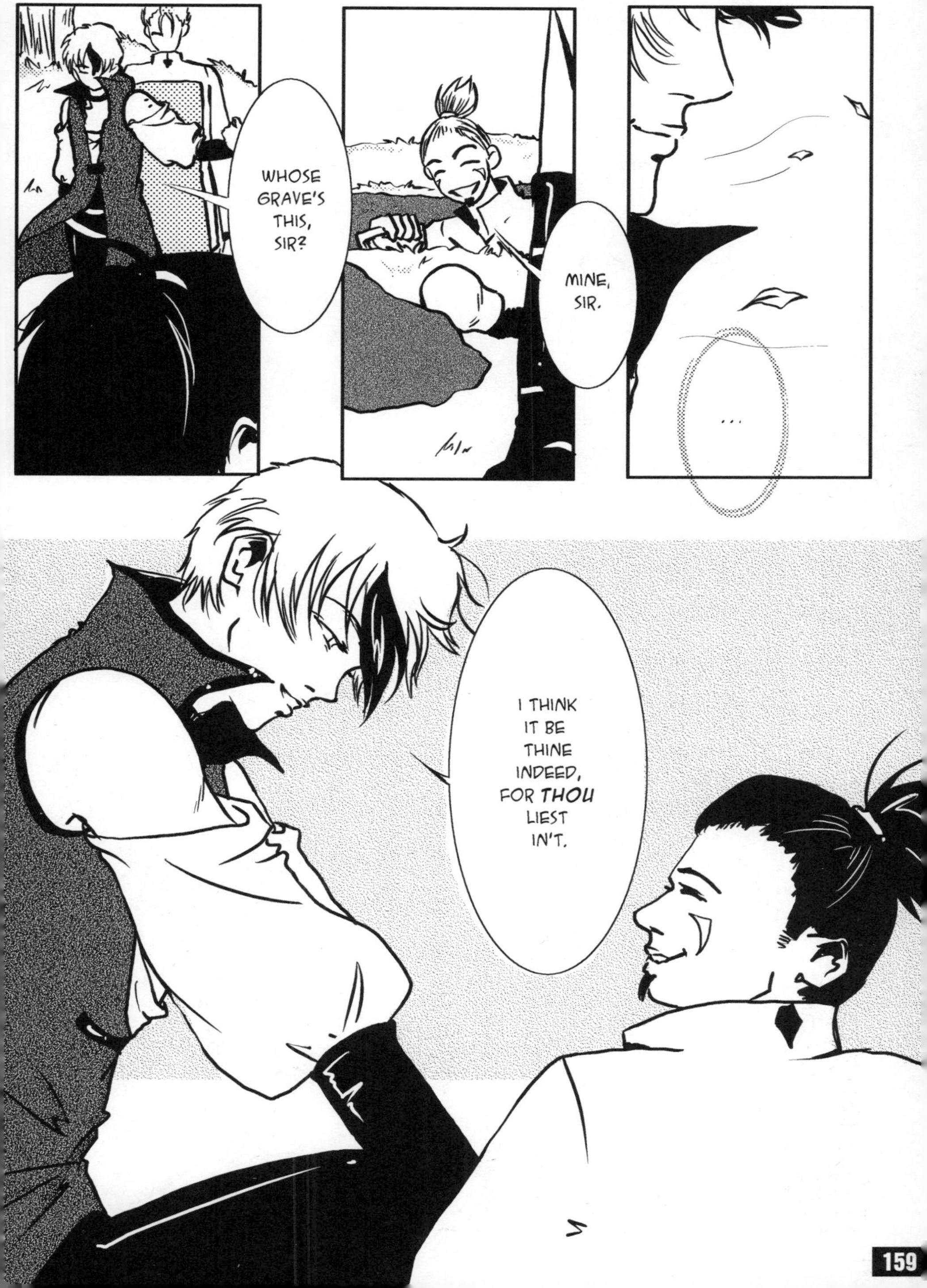
WHOSE GRAVE'S THIS, SIR?
MINE, SIR.
...
I THINK IT BE THINE INDEED, FOR THOU LIEST IN'T.

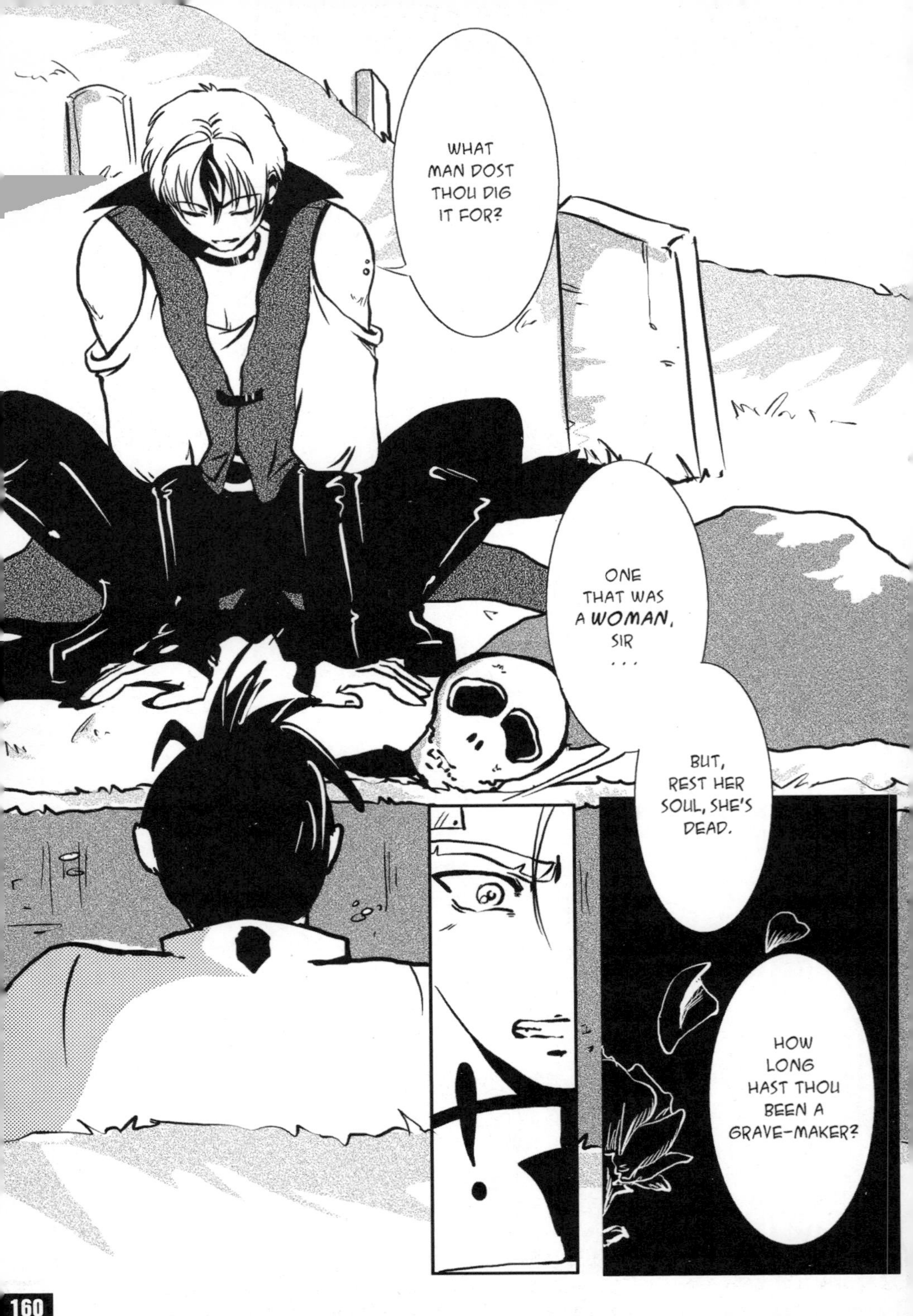
WHAT MAN DOST THOU DIG IT FOR?
ONE THAT WAS A WOMAN, SIR . . .
BUT, REST HER SOUL, SHE'S DEAD.
HOW LONG HAST THOU BEEN A GRAVE-MAKER?

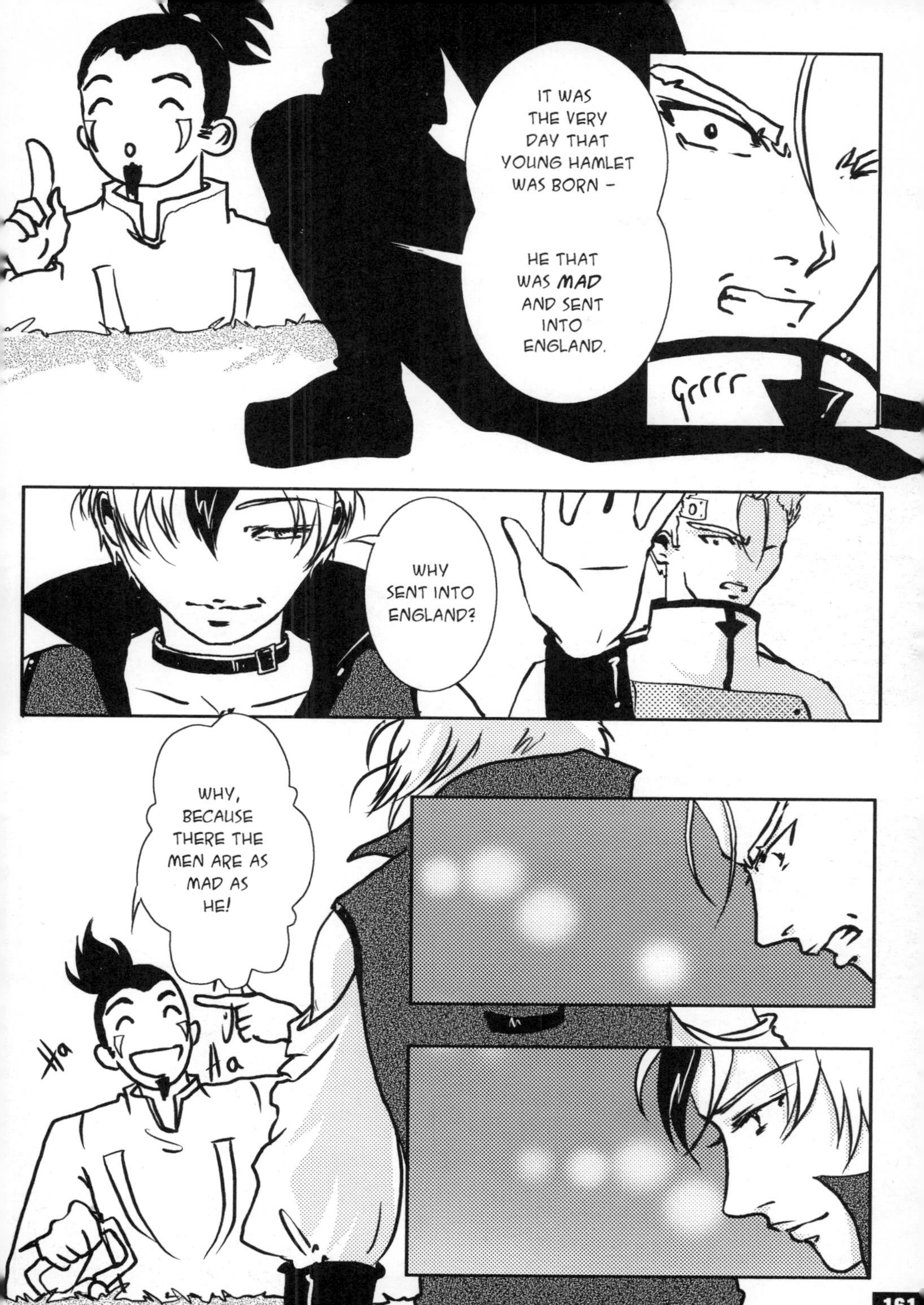
IT WAS THE VERY DAY THAT YOUNG HAMLET WAS BORN –
HE THAT WAS **MAD** AND SENT INTO ENGLAND.
Grrrr
WHY SENT INTO ENGLAND?
WHY, BECAUSE THERE THE MEN ARE AS MAD AS HE!
Ha Ha

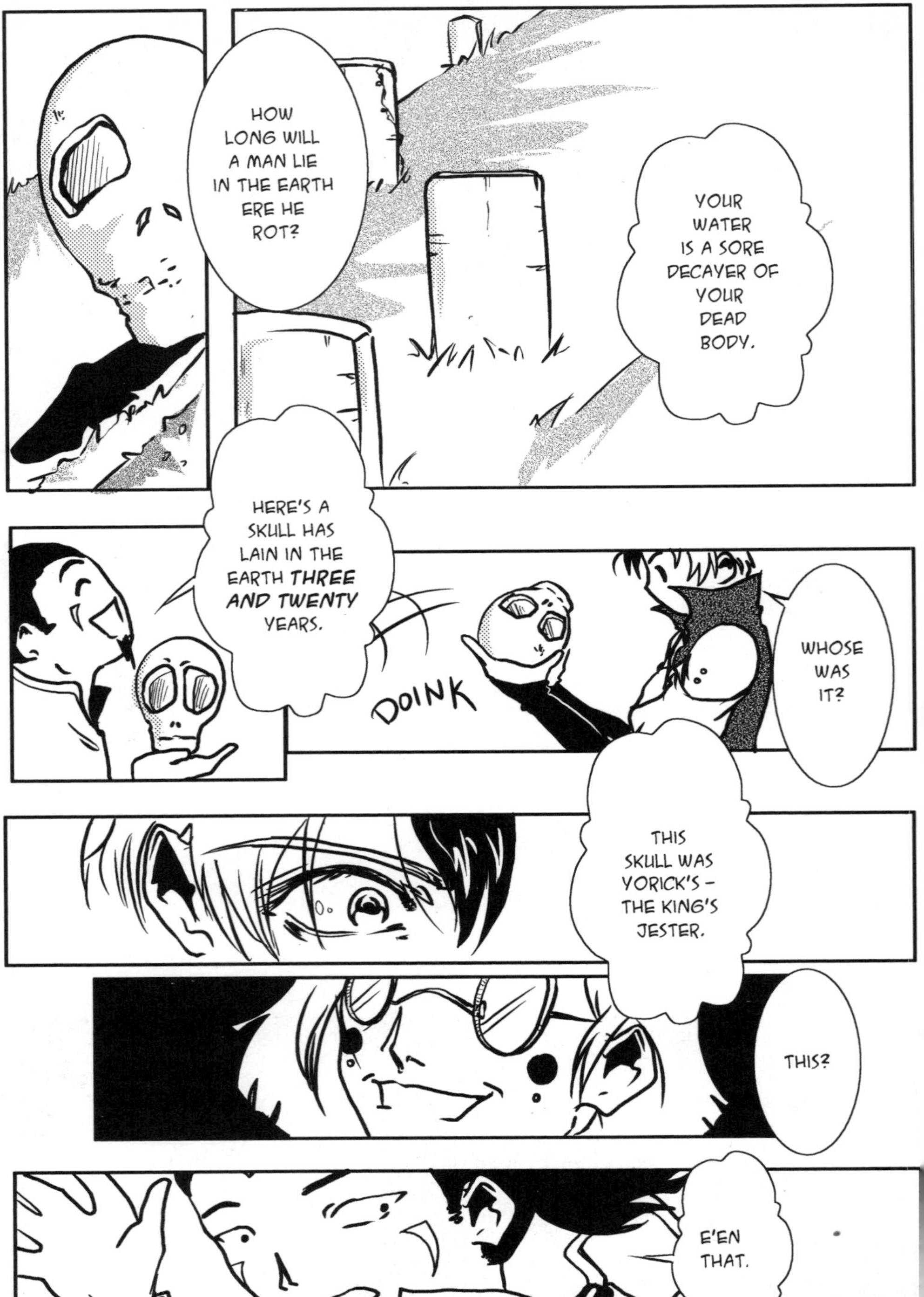
HOW LONG WILL A MAN LIE IN THE EARTH ERE HE ROT?
YOUR WATER IS A SORE DECAYER OF YOUR DEAD BODY.
HERE'S A SKULL HAS LAIN IN THE EARTH **THREE AND TWENTY** YEARS.
DOINK
WHOSE WAS IT?
THIS SKULL WAS YORICK'S – THE KING'S JESTER.
THIS?
E'EN THAT.

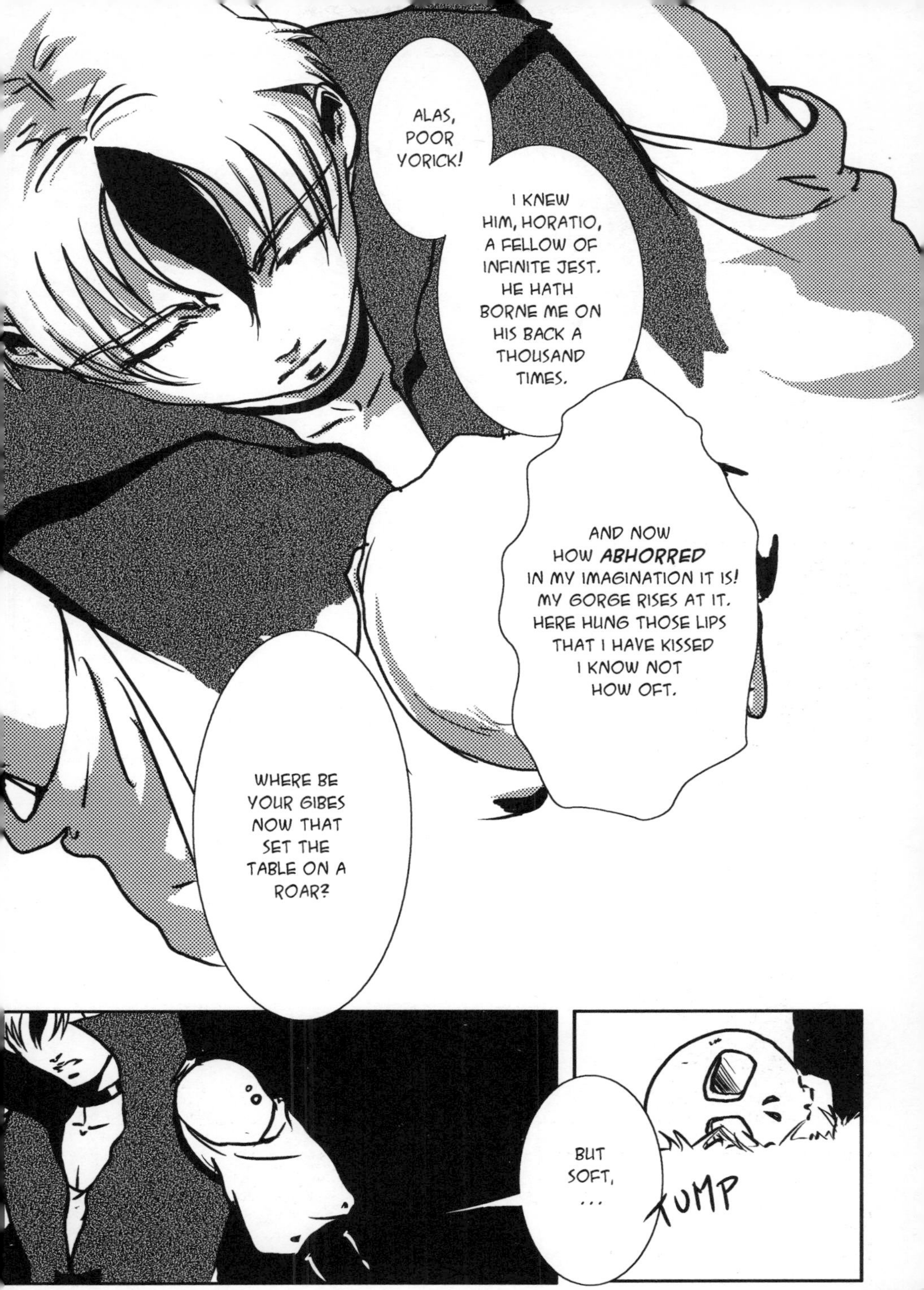
ALAS, POOR YORICK!
I KNEW HIM, HORATIO, A FELLOW OF INFINITE JEST. HE HATH BORNE ME ON HIS BACK A THOUSAND TIMES.
AND NOW HOW **ABHORRED** IN MY IMAGINATION IT IS! MY GORGE RISES AT IT. HERE HUNG THOSE LIPS THAT I HAVE KISSED I KNOW NOT HOW OFT.
WHERE BE YOUR GIBES NOW THAT SET THE TABLE ON A ROAR?
BUT SOFT, ...
TUMP

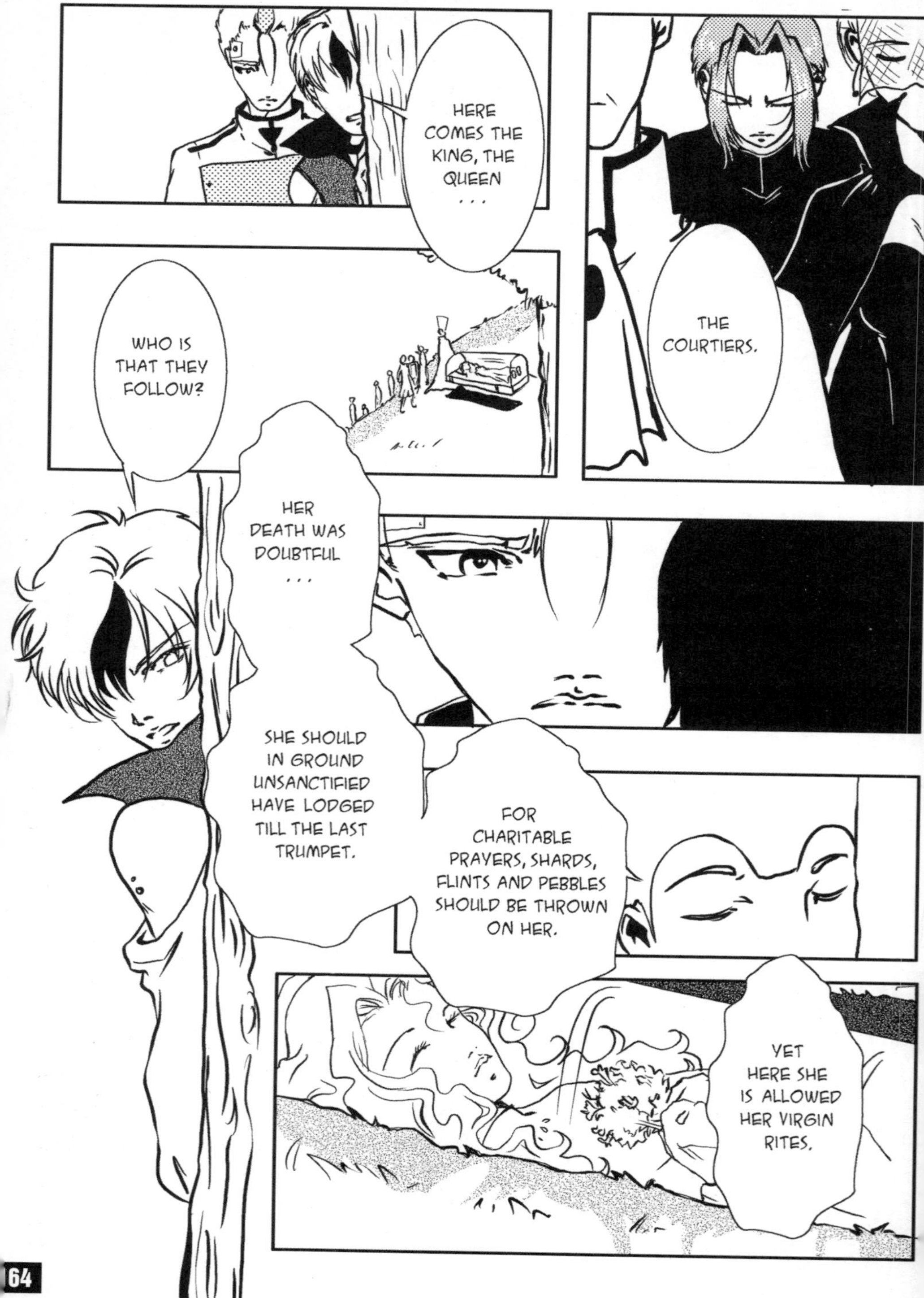
HERE COMES THE KING, THE QUEEN . . .
THE COURTIERS.
WHO IS THAT THEY FOLLOW?
HER DEATH WAS DOUBTFUL . . .
SHE SHOULD IN GROUND UNSANCTIFIED HAVE LODGED TILL THE LAST TRUMPET.
FOR CHARITABLE PRAYERS, SHARDS, FLINTS AND PEBBLES SHOULD BE THROWN ON HER.
YET HERE SHE IS ALLOWED HER VIRGIN RITES.

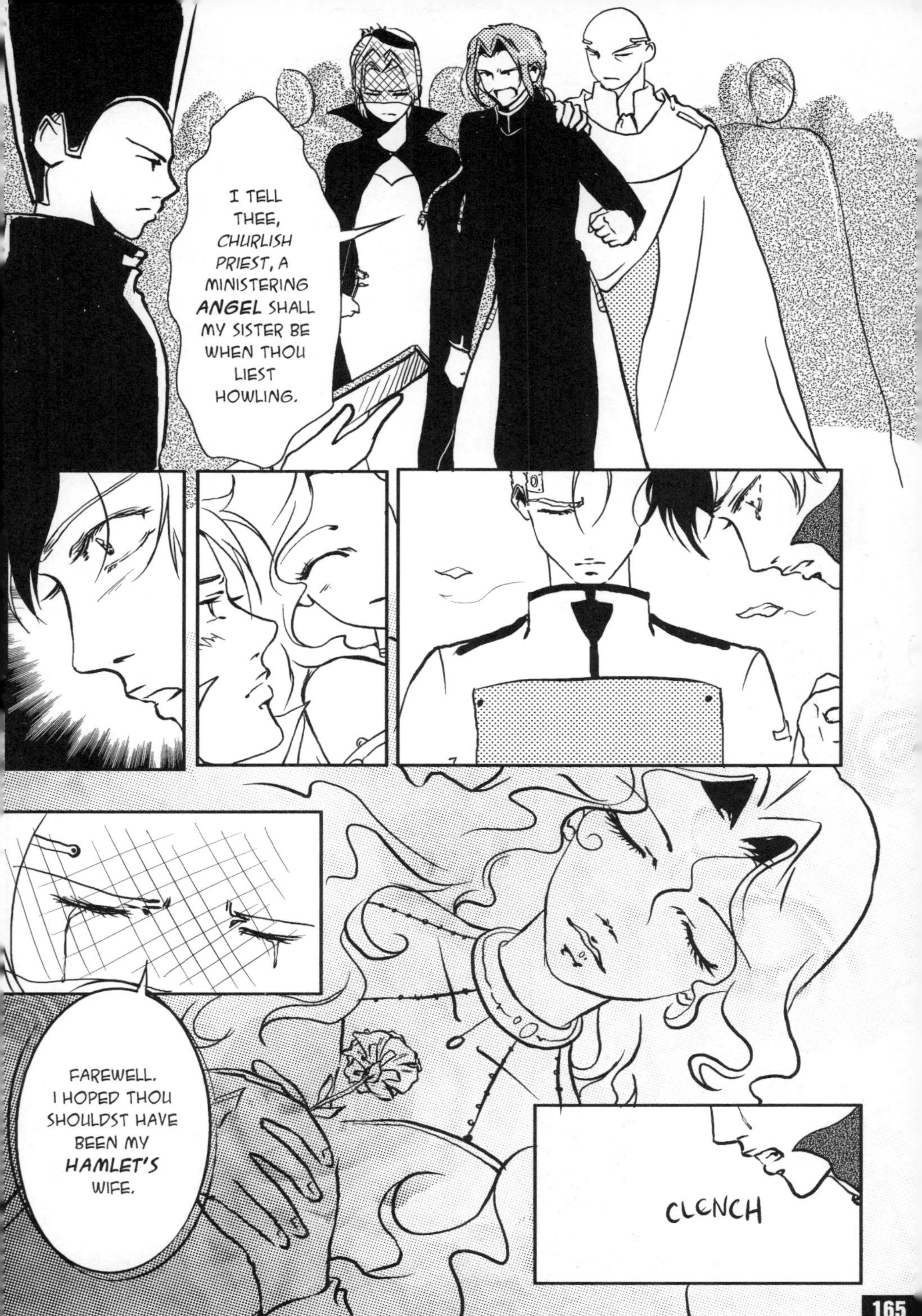

I TELL THEE, CHURLISH PRIEST, A MINISTERING **ANGEL** SHALL MY SISTER BE WHEN THOU LIEST HOWLING.
FAREWELL. I HOPED THOU SHOULDST HAVE BEEN MY **HAMLET'S** WIFE.
CLENCH

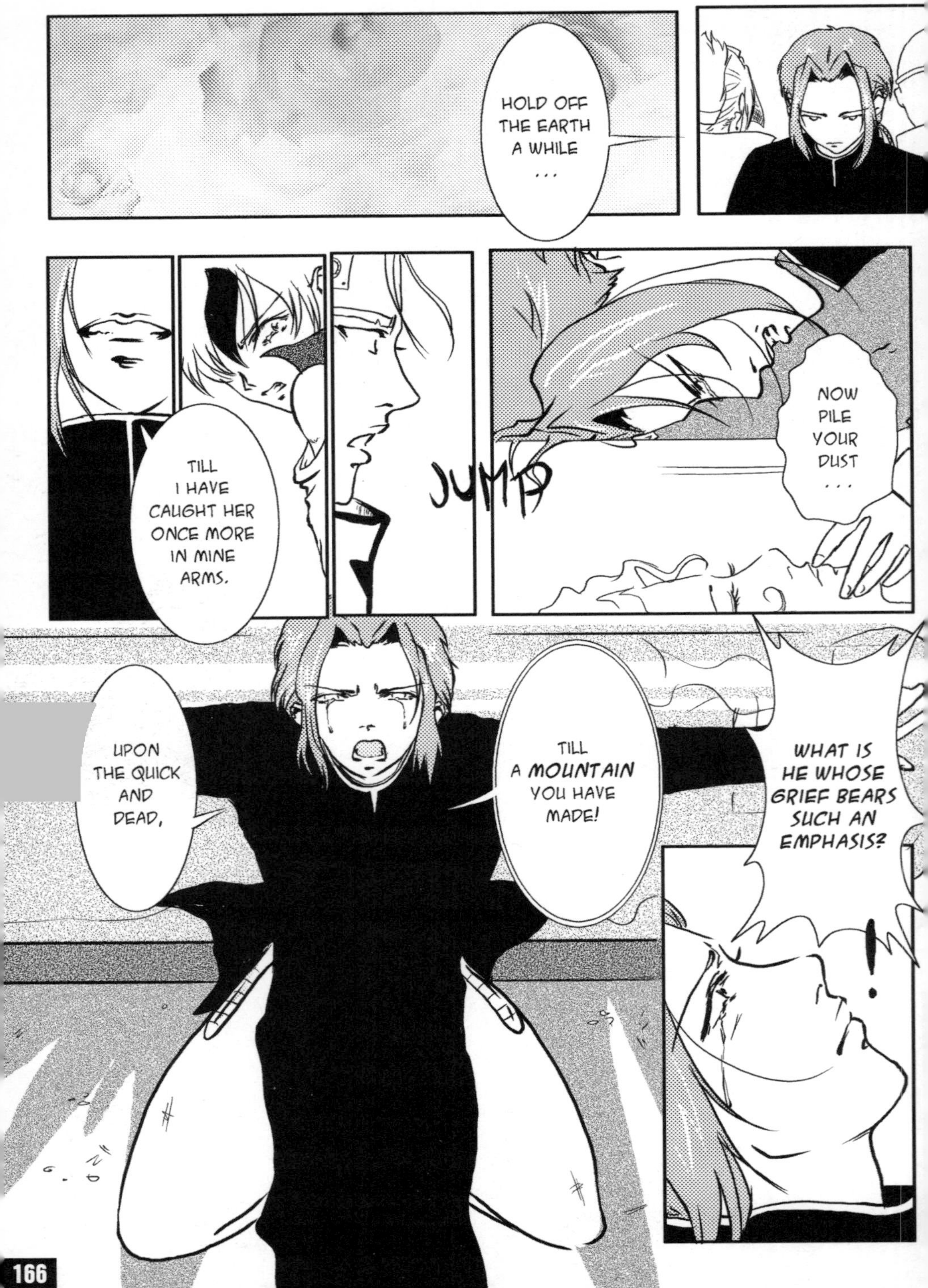
HOLD OFF THE EARTH A WHILE . . .
TILL I HAVE CAUGHT HER ONCE MORE IN MINE ARMS.
JUMP
NOW PILE YOUR DUST . . .
UPON THE QUICK AND DEAD,
TILL A MOUNTAIN YOU HAVE MADE!
WHAT IS HE WHOSE GRIEF BEARS SUCH AN EMPHASIS?

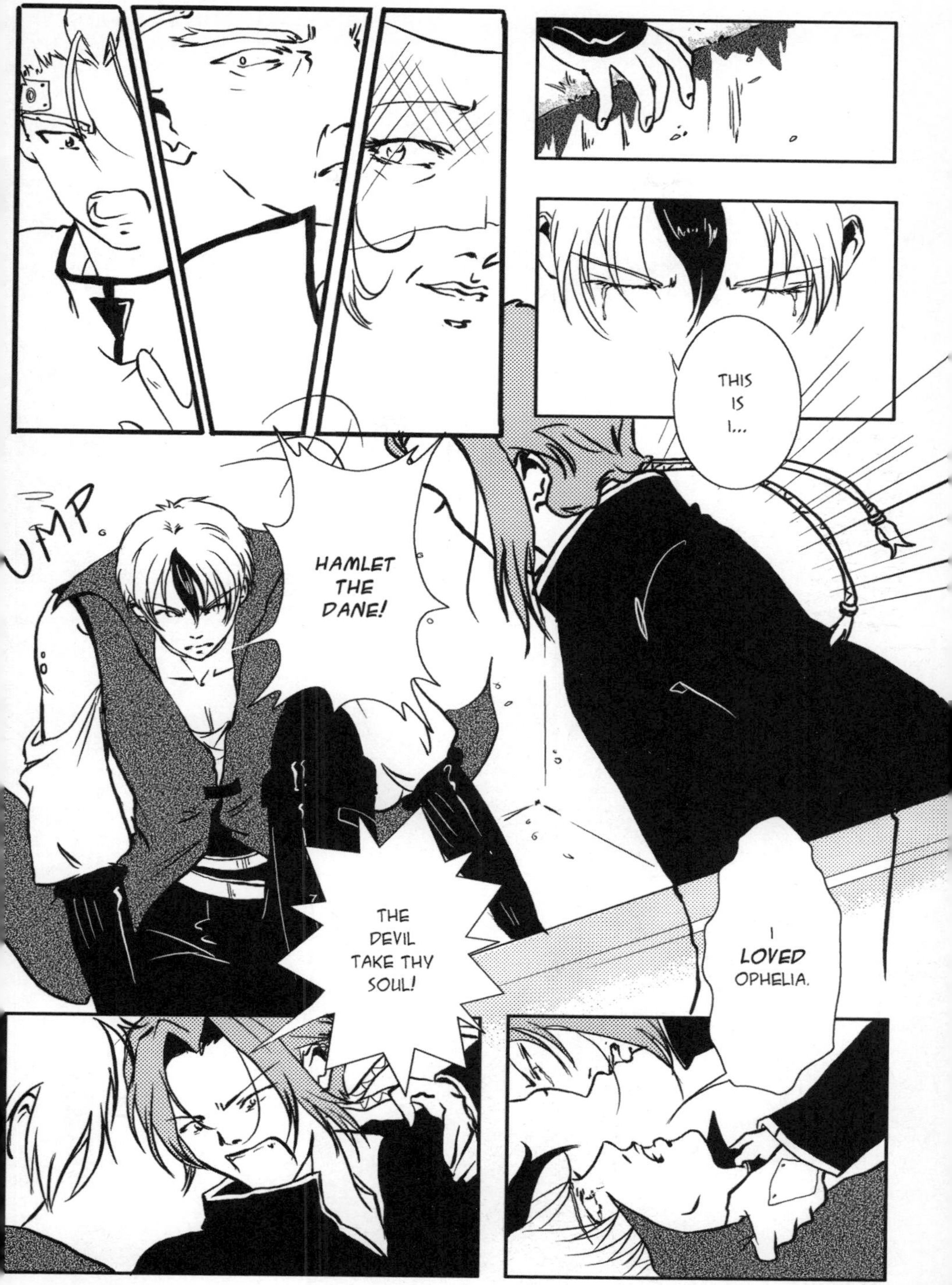
UMP.
THIS IS I...
HAMLET THE DANE!
I LOVED OPHELIA.
THE DEVIL TAKE THY SOUL!

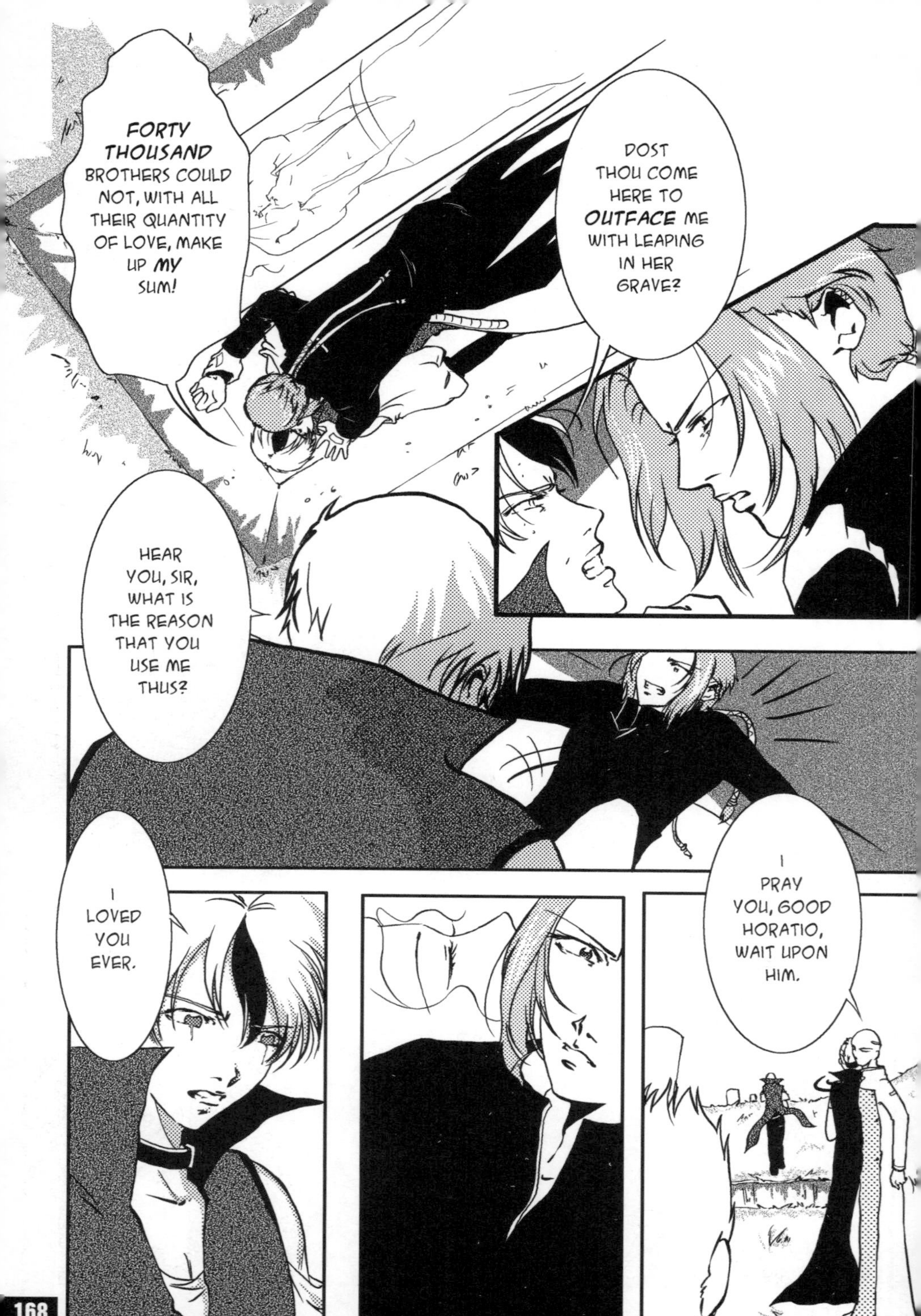
FORTY THOUSAND BROTHERS COULD NOT, WITH ALL THEIR QUANTITY OF LOVE, MAKE UP MY SUM!
DOST THOU COME HERE TO OUTFACE ME WITH LEAPING IN HER GRAVE?
HEAR YOU, SIR, WHAT IS THE REASON THAT YOU USE ME THUS?
I LOVED YOU EVER.
I PRAY YOU, GOOD HORATIO, WAIT UPON HIM.

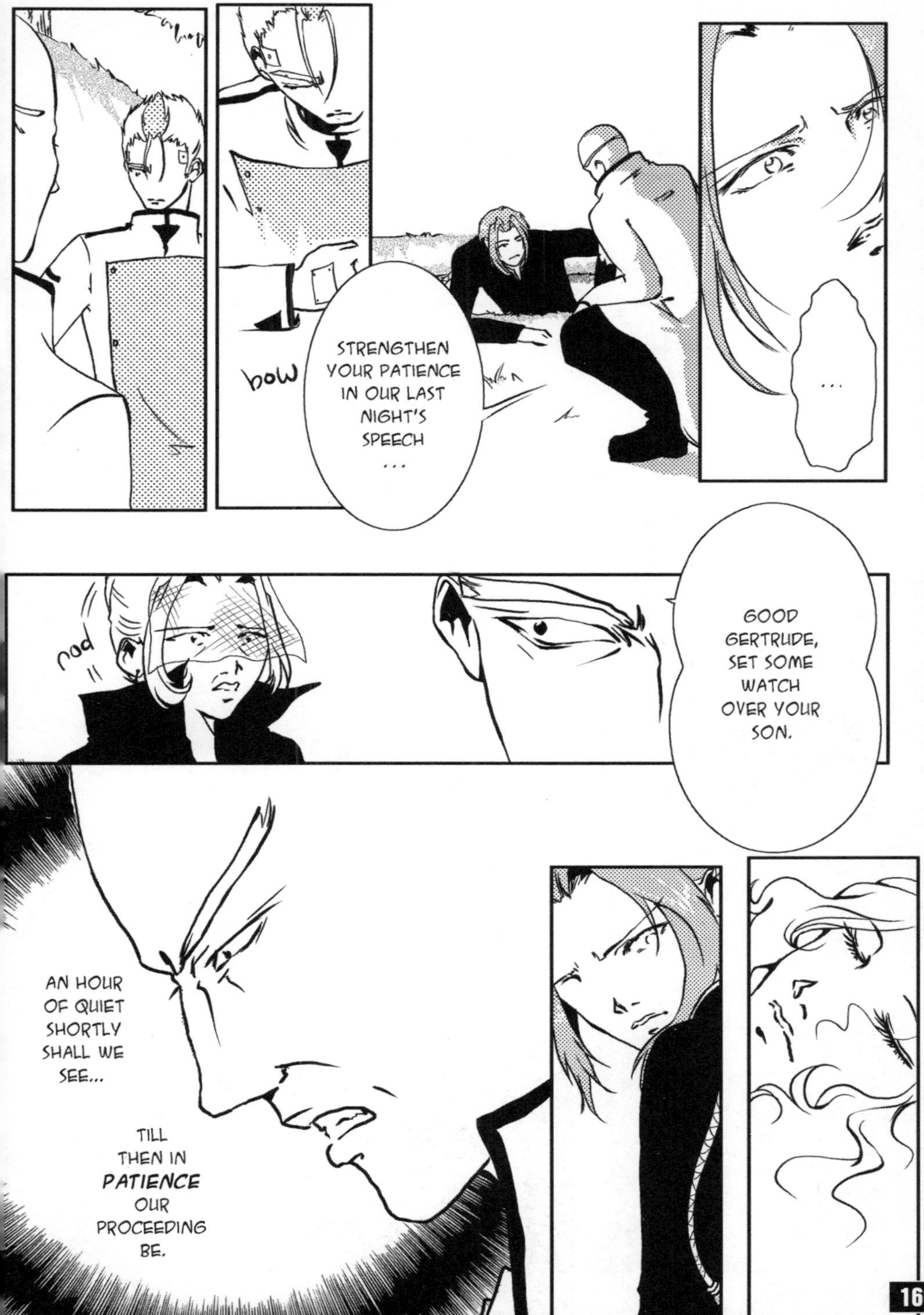
bow
STRENGTHEN YOUR PATIENCE IN OUR LAST NIGHT'S SPEECH ...
...
GOOD GERTRUDE, SET SOME WATCH OVER YOUR SON.
nod
AN HOUR OF QUIET SHORTLY SHALL WE SEE...
TILL THEN IN PATIENCE OUR PROCEEDING BE.

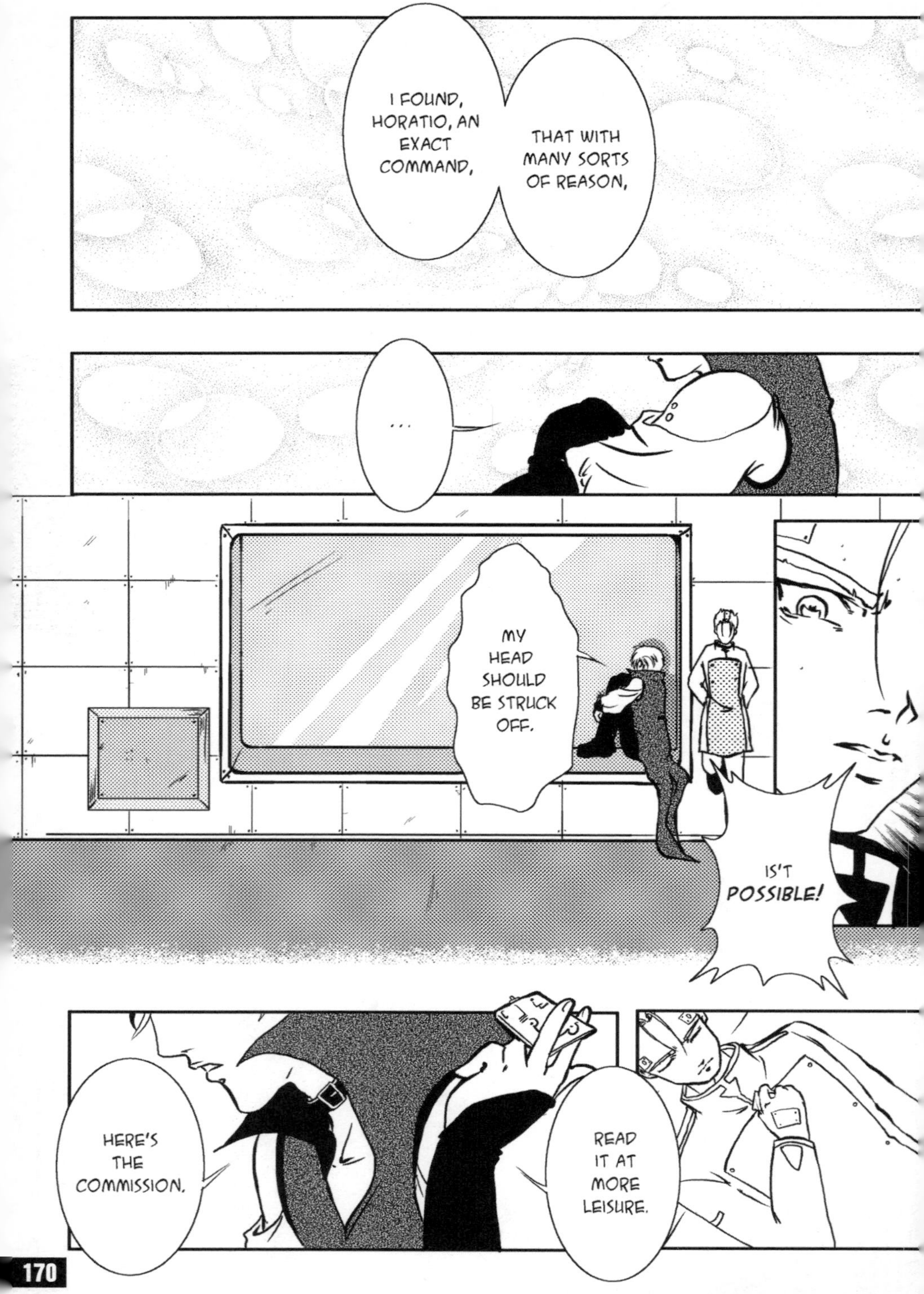
I FOUND, HORATIO, AN EXACT COMMAND,
THAT WITH MANY SORTS OF REASON,
...
MY HEAD SHOULD BE STRUCK OFF.
IS'T POSSIBLE!
HERE'S THE COMMISSION.
READ IT AT MORE LEISURE.

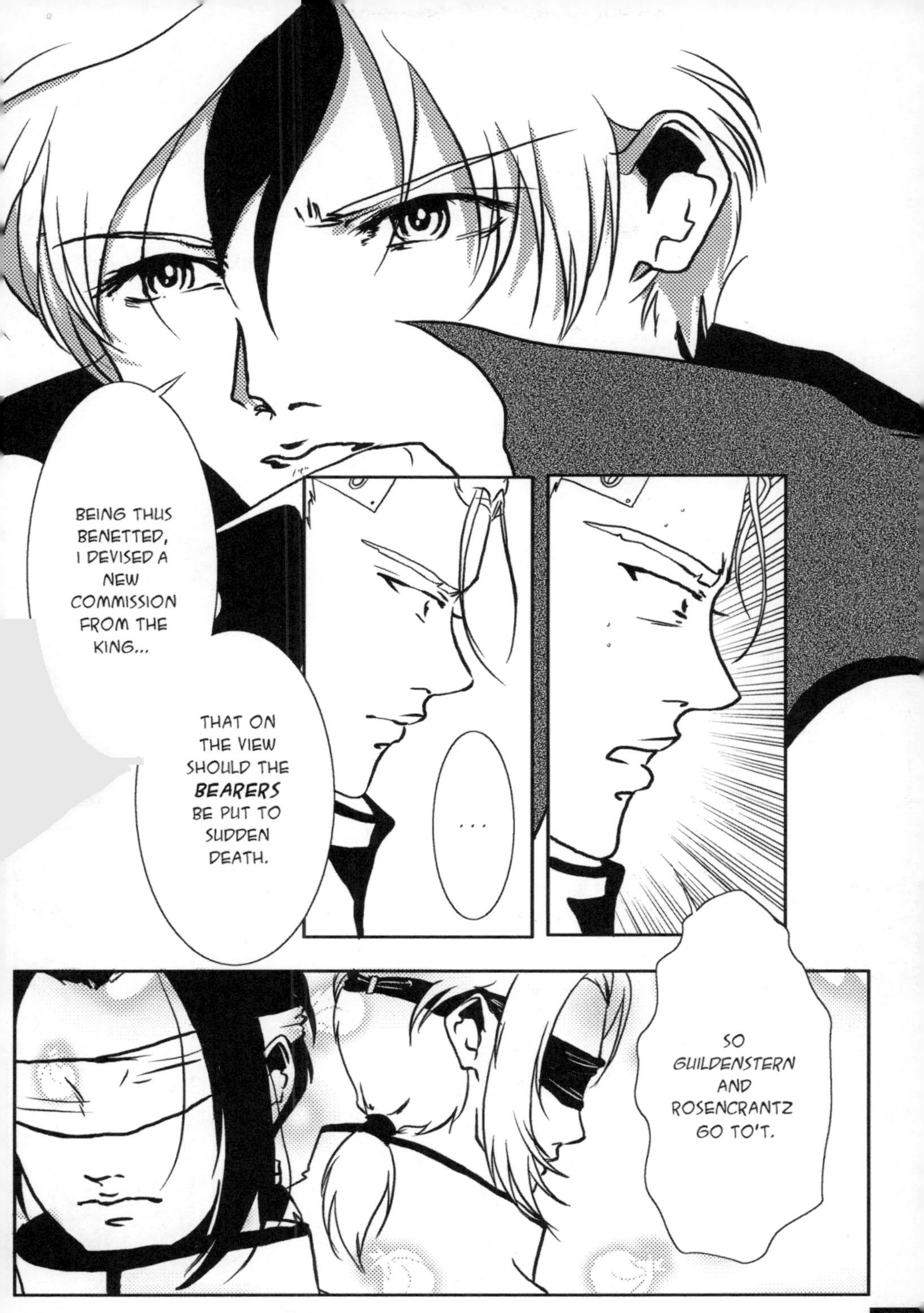
BEING THUS BENETTED, I DEVISED A NEW COMMISSION FROM THE KING...
THAT ON THE VIEW SHOULD THE **BEARERS** BE PUT TO SUDDEN DEATH.
...
SO GUILDENSTERN AND ROSENCRANTZ GO TO'T.

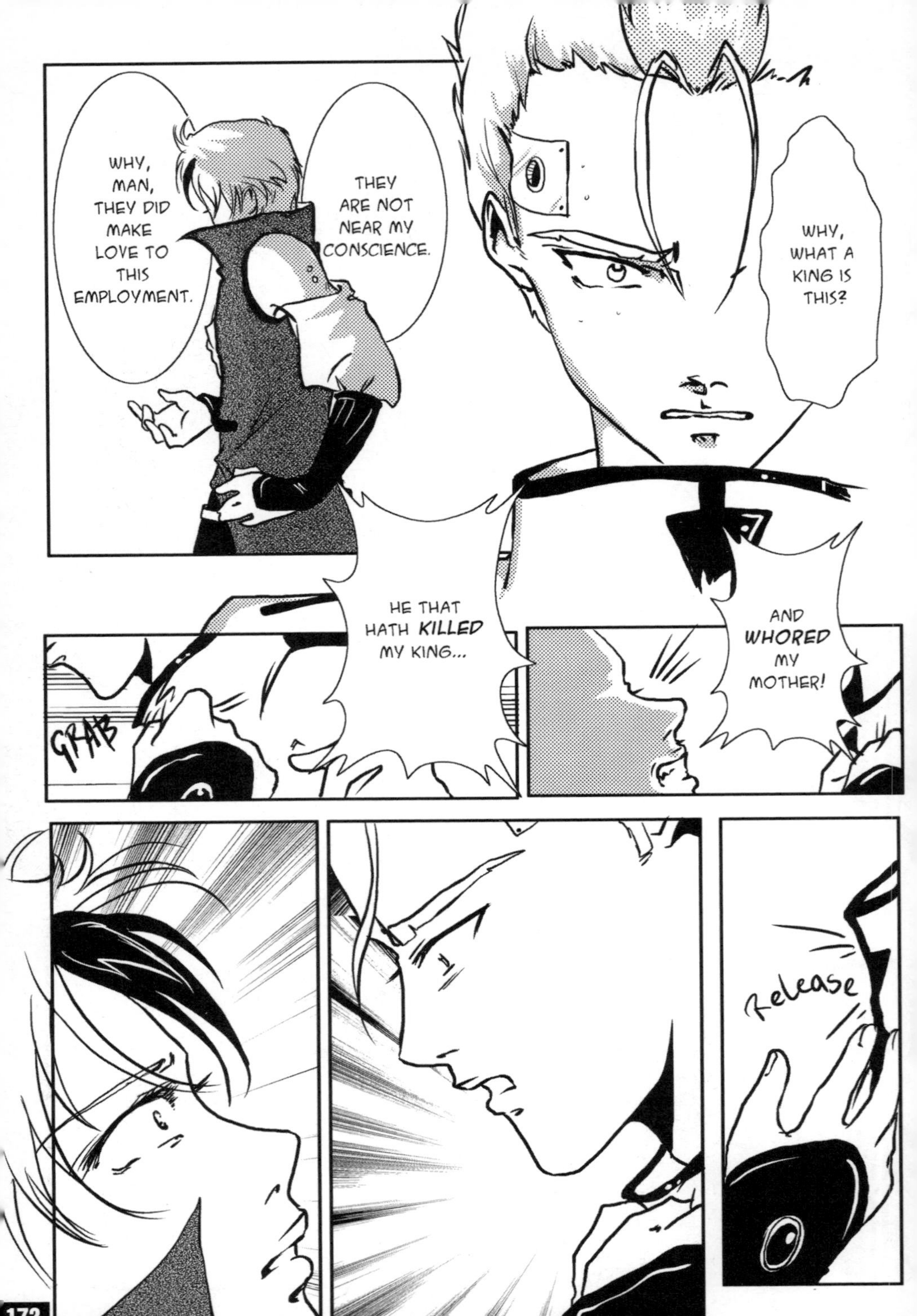
WHY, MAN, THEY DID MAKE LOVE TO THIS EMPLOYMENT.
THEY ARE NOT NEAR MY CONSCIENCE.
WHY, WHAT A KING IS THIS?
HE THAT HATH **KILLED** MY KING...
GRAB
AND **WHORED** MY MOTHER!
Release

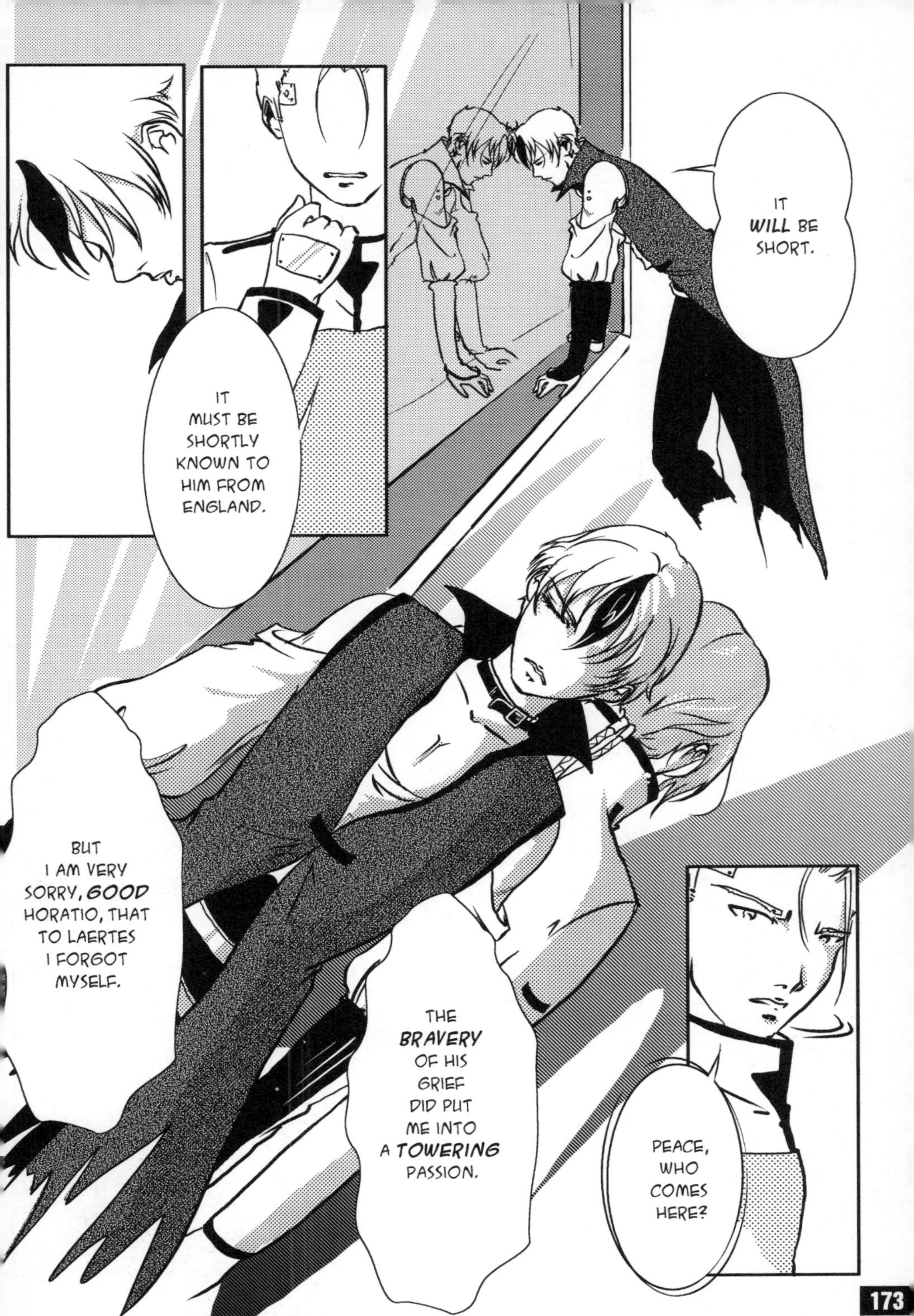
IT WILL BE SHORT.
IT MUST BE SHORTLY KNOWN TO HIM FROM ENGLAND.
BUT I AM VERY SORRY, GOOD HORATIO, THAT TO LAERTES I FORGOT MYSELF.
THE BRAVERY OF HIS GRIEF DID PUT ME INTO A TOWERING PASSION.
PEACE, WHO COMES HERE?

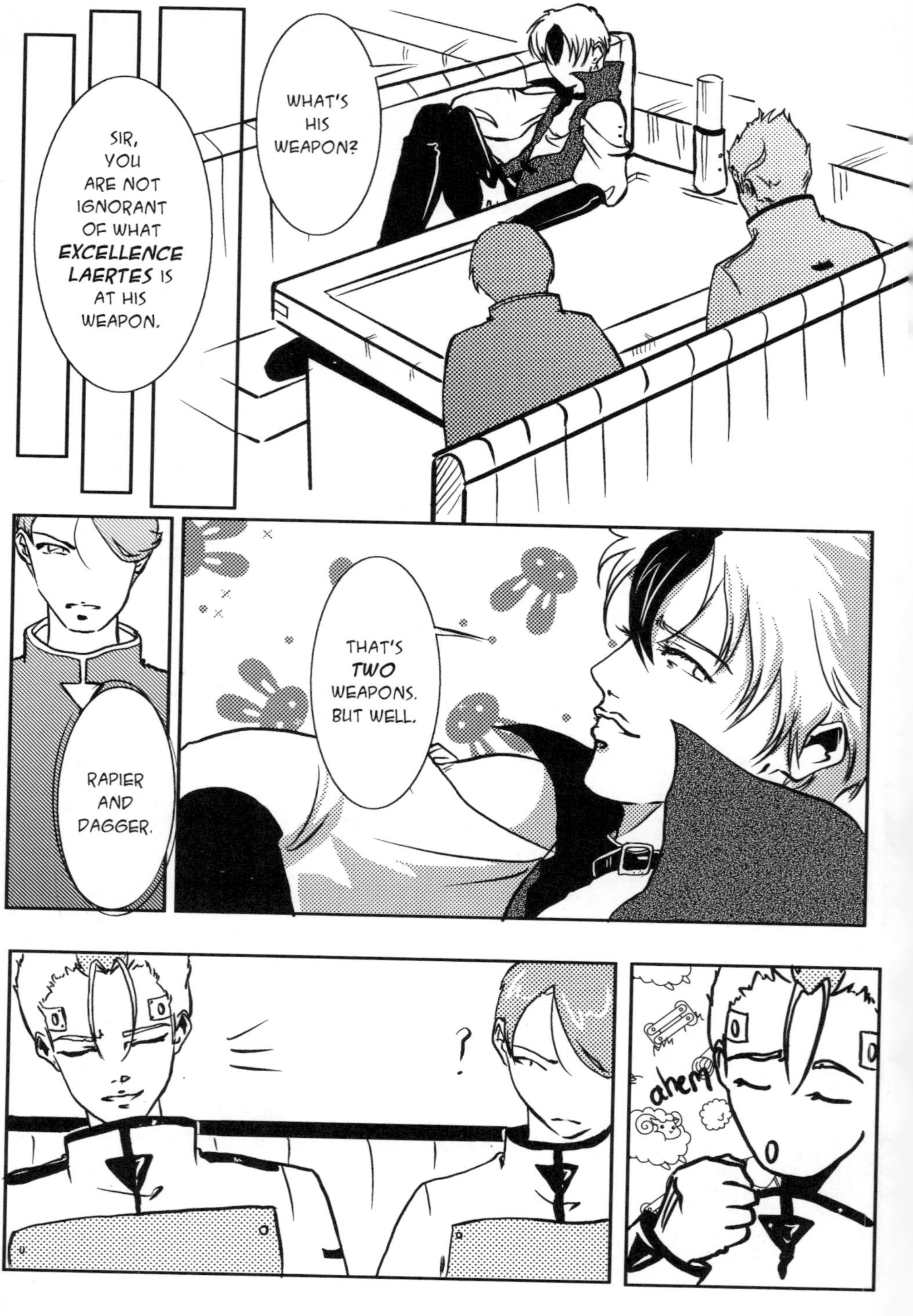

WHAT'S HIS WEAPON?
SIR, YOU ARE NOT IGNORANT OF WHAT EXCELLENCE LAERTES IS AT HIS WEAPON.
RAPIER AND DAGGER.
THAT'S TWO WEAPONS. BUT WELL.
?
ahem

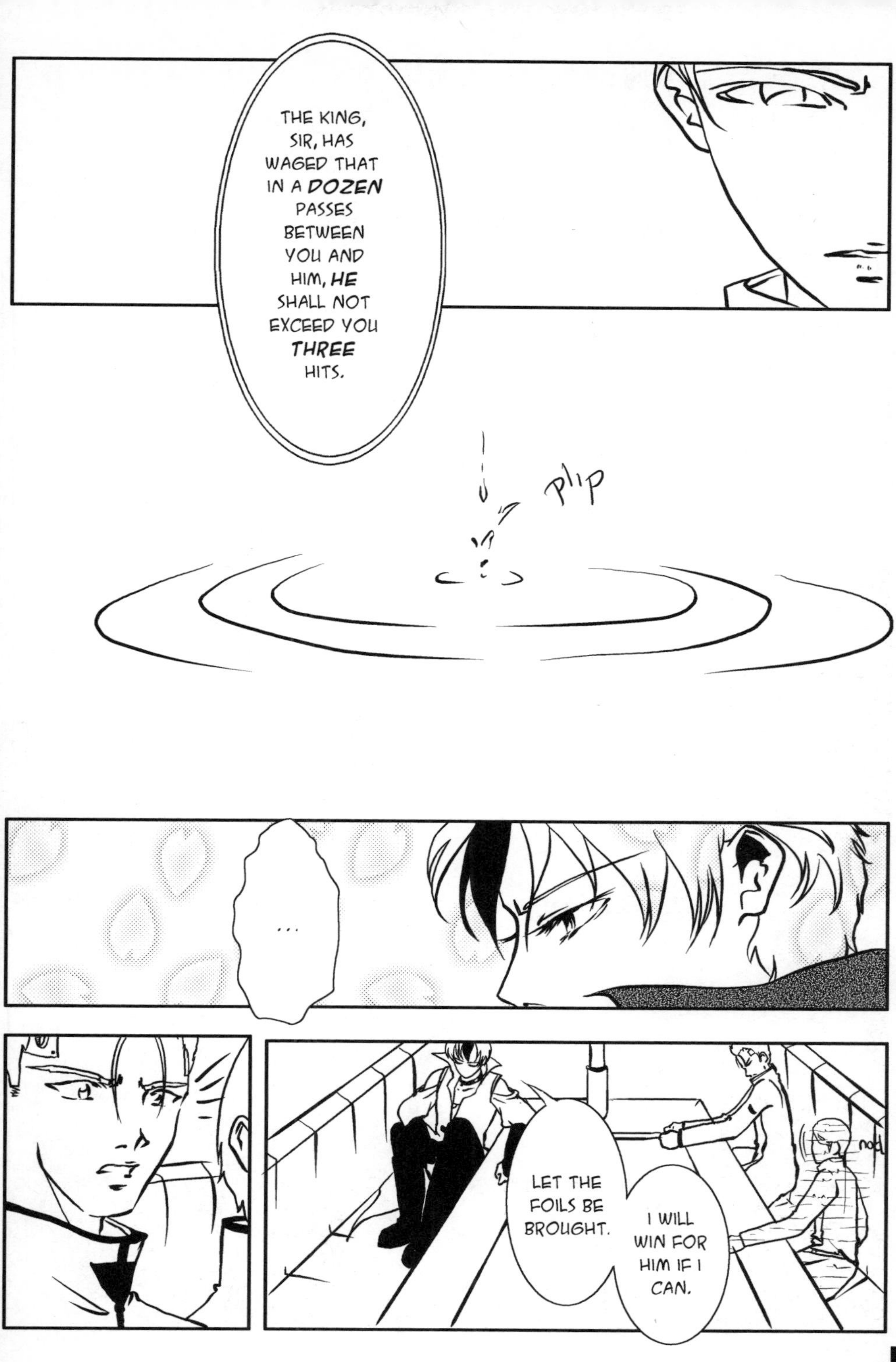
THE KING, SIR, HAS WAGED THAT IN A **DOZEN** PASSES BETWEEN YOU AND HIM, **HE** SHALL NOT EXCEED YOU **THREE** HITS.
plip
...
LET THE FOILS BE BROUGHT.
I WILL WIN FOR HIM IF I CAN.
nod

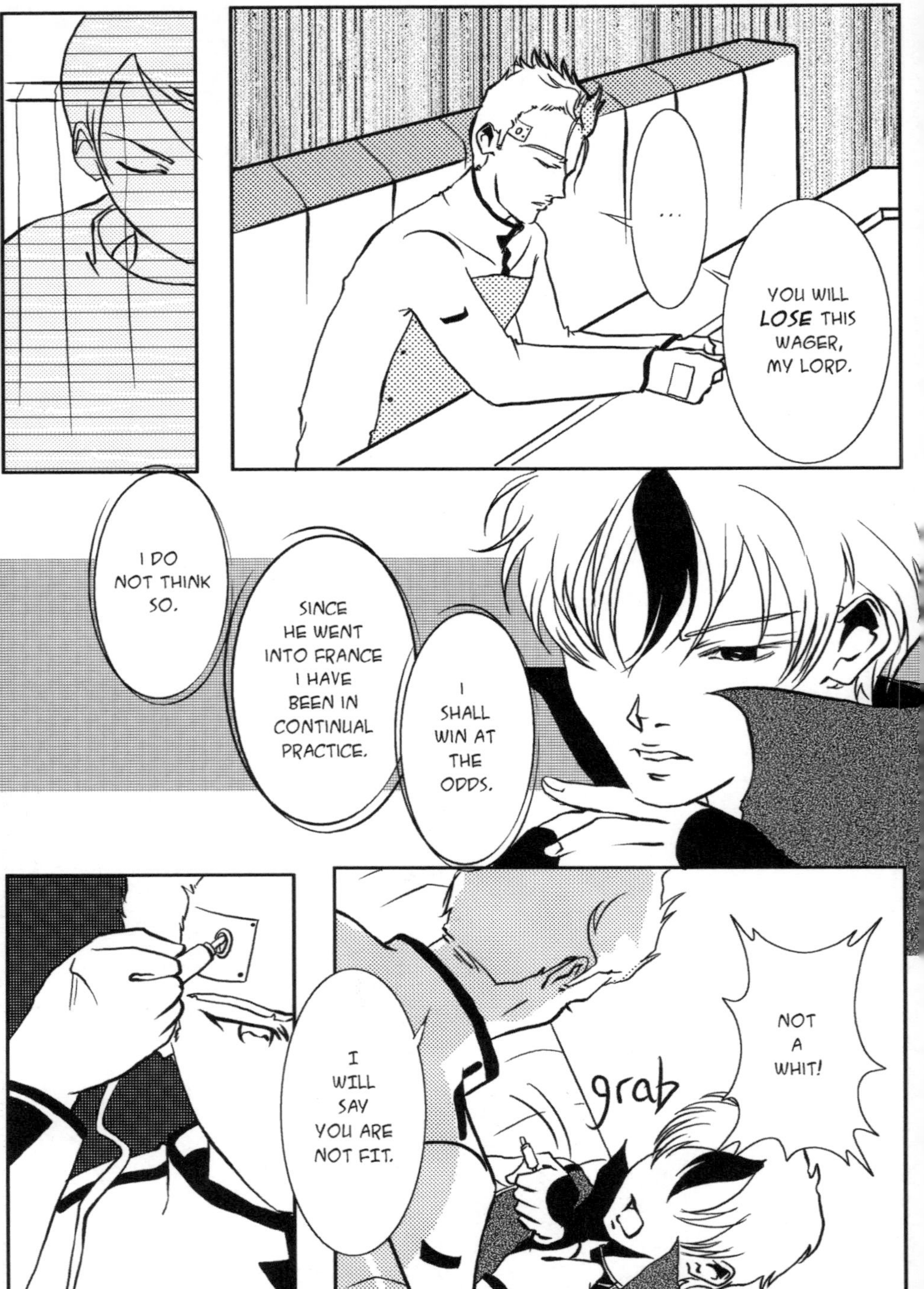
...
YOU WILL **LOSE** THIS WAGER, MY LORD.
I DO NOT THINK SO.
SINCE HE WENT INTO FRANCE I HAVE BEEN IN CONTINUAL PRACTICE.
I SHALL WIN AT THE ODDS.
I WILL SAY YOU ARE NOT FIT.
grab
NOT A WHIT!

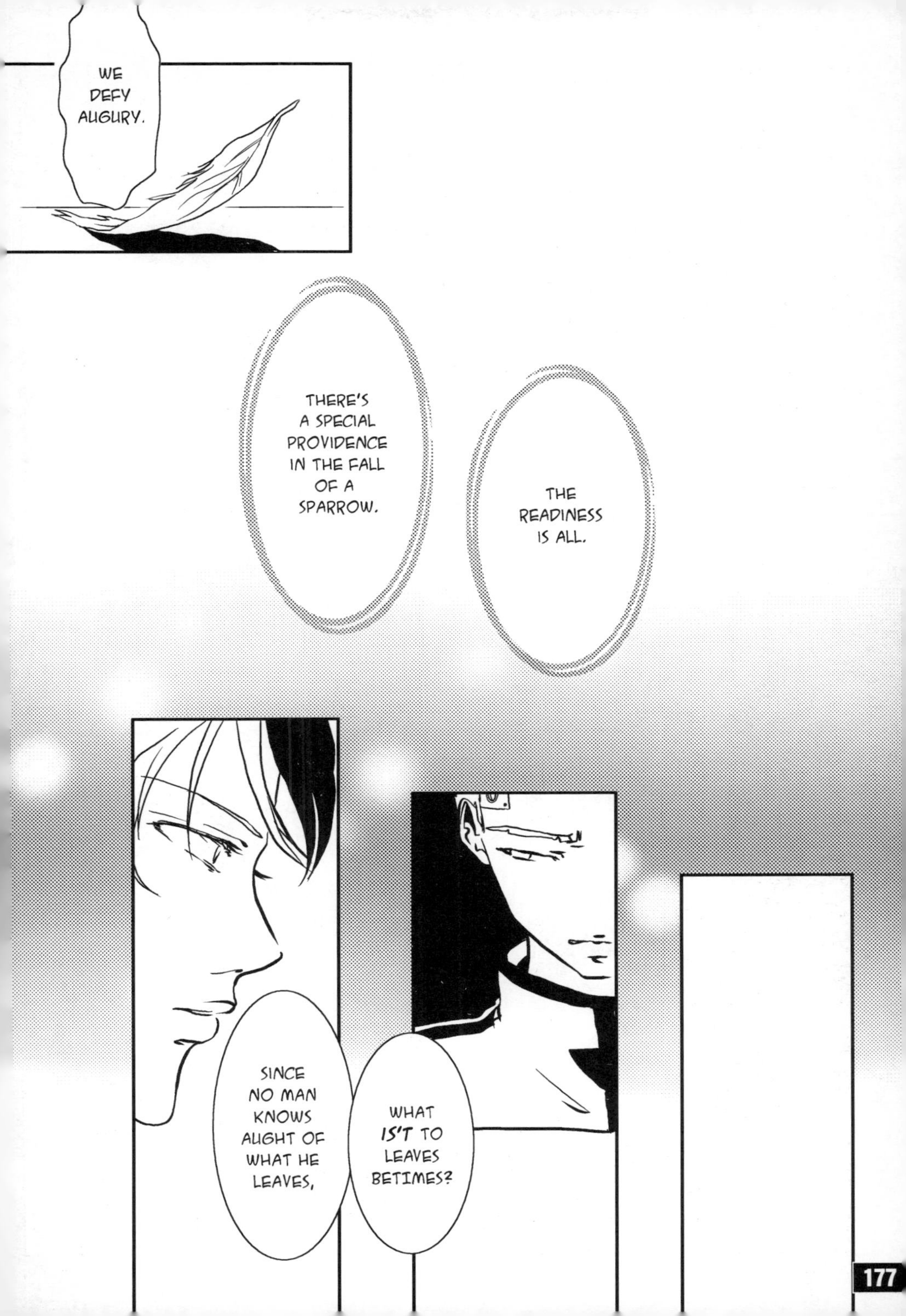
WE DEFY AUGURY.
THERE'S A SPECIAL PROVIDENCE IN THE FALL OF A SPARROW.
THE READINESS IS ALL.
SINCE NO MAN KNOWS AUGHT OF WHAT HE LEAVES,
WHAT *IS'T* TO LEAVES BETIMES?

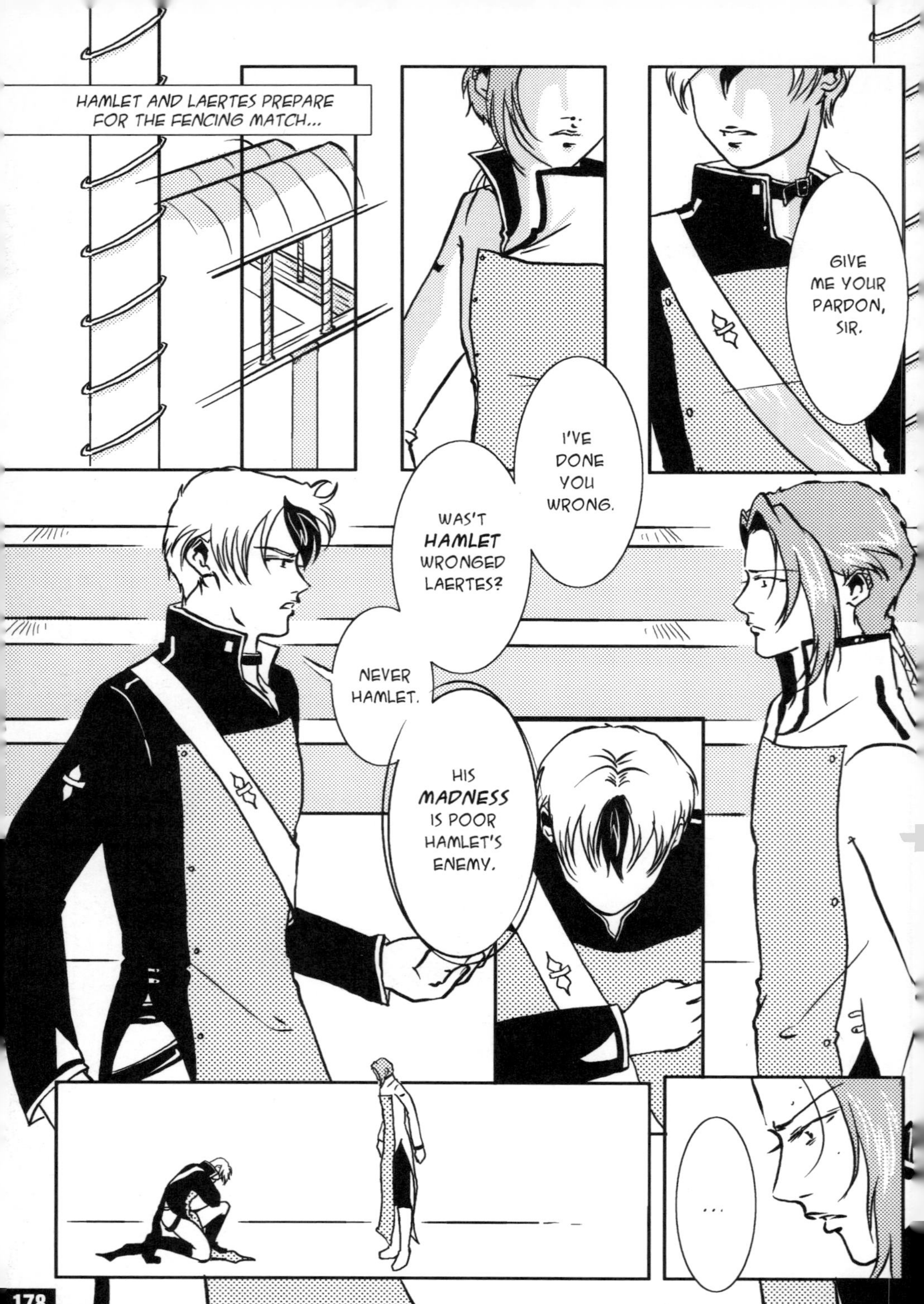
HAMLET AND LAERTES PREPARE FOR THE FENCING MATCH...
GIVE ME YOUR PARDON, SIR.
I'VE DONE YOU WRONG.
WAS'T HAMLET WRONGED LAERTES?
NEVER HAMLET.
HIS MADNESS IS POOR HAMLET'S ENEMY.
...

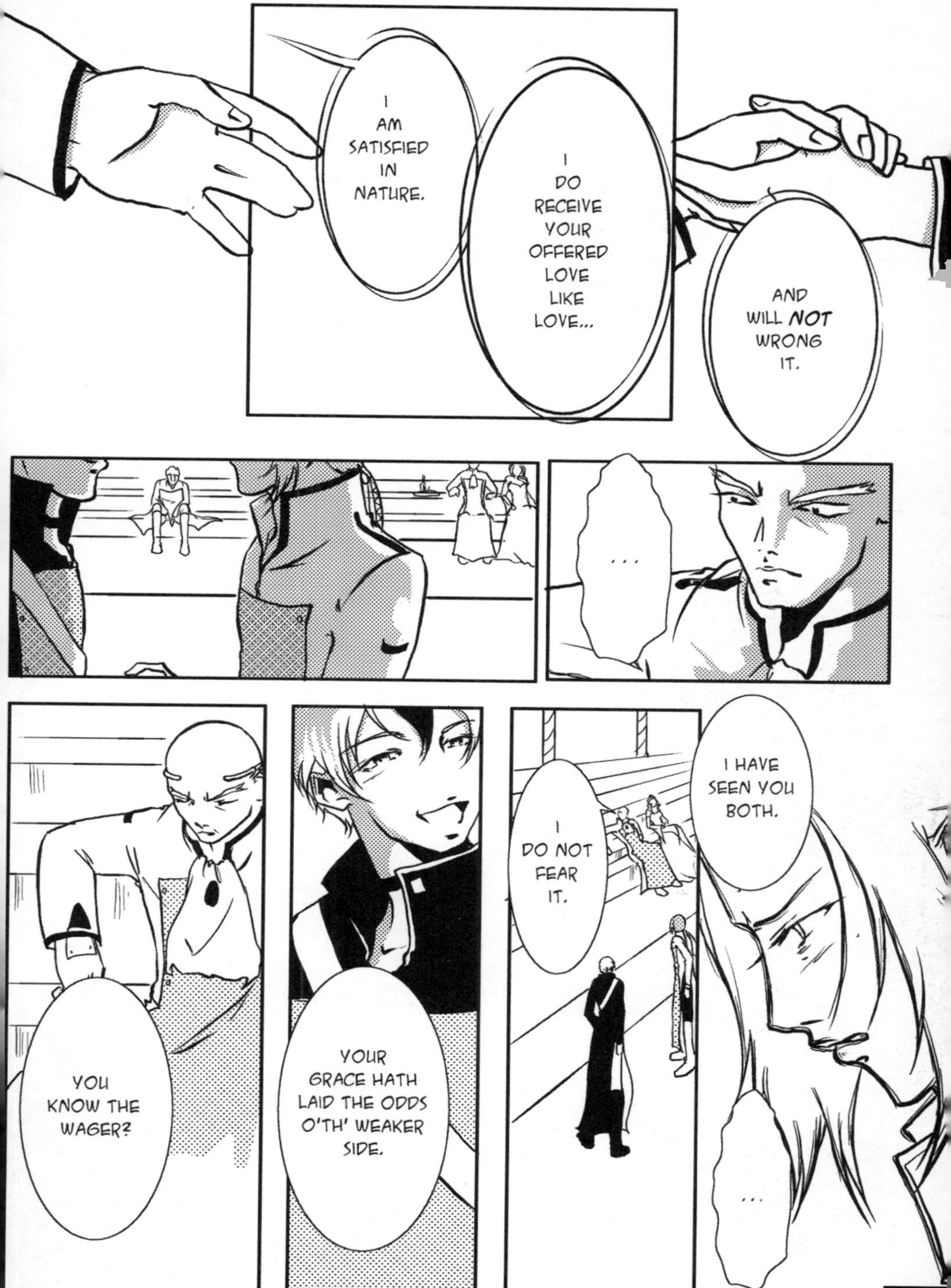
I AM SATISFIED IN NATURE.
I DO RECEIVE YOUR OFFERED LOVE LIKE LOVE...
AND WILL NOT WRONG IT.
...
YOU KNOW THE WAGER?
YOUR GRACE HATH LAID THE ODDS O'TH' WEAKER SIDE.
I DO NOT FEAR IT.
I HAVE SEEN YOU BOTH.
...

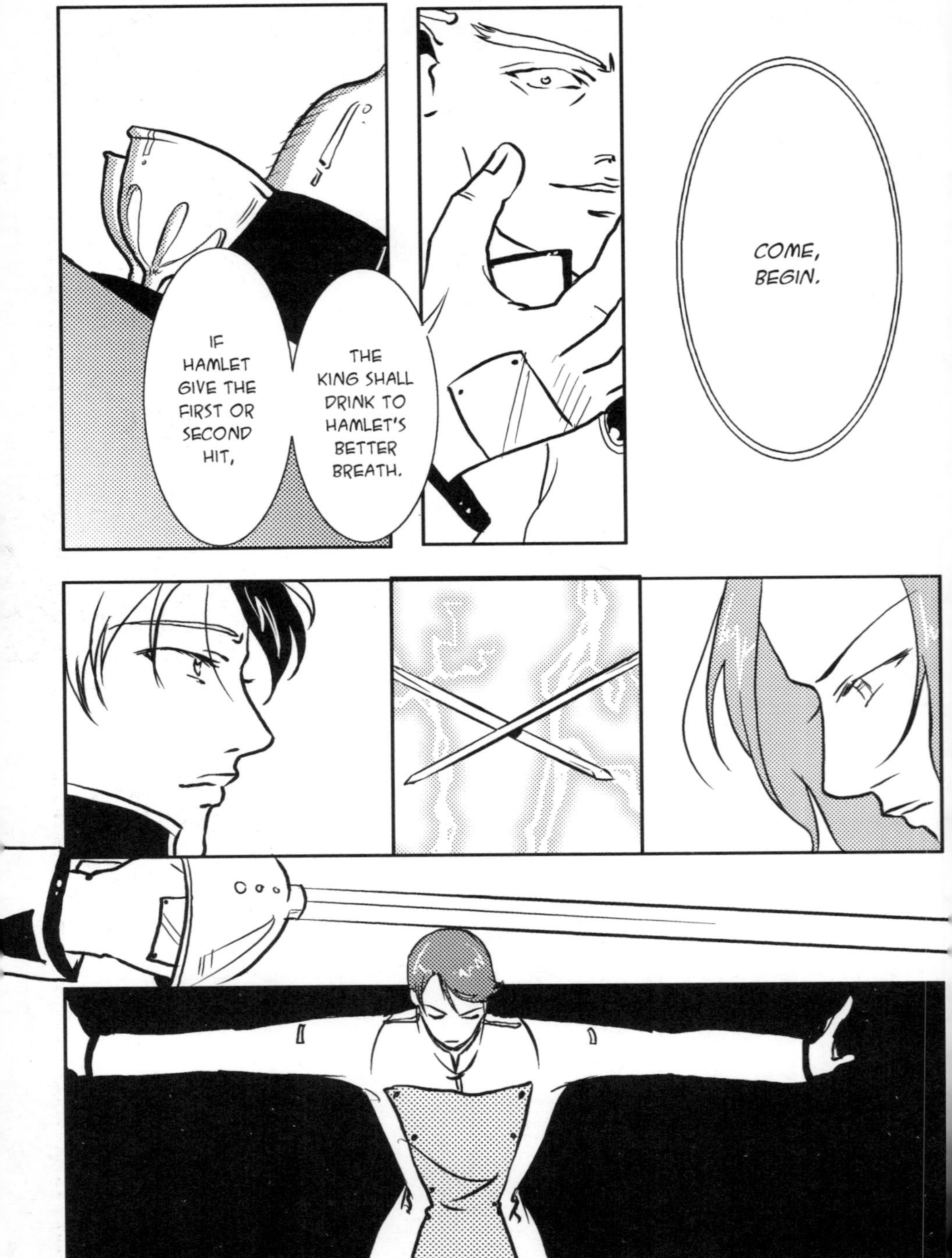
IF HAMLET GIVE THE FIRST OR SECOND HIT,
THE KING SHALL DRINK TO HAMLET'S BETTER BREATH.
COME, BEGIN.

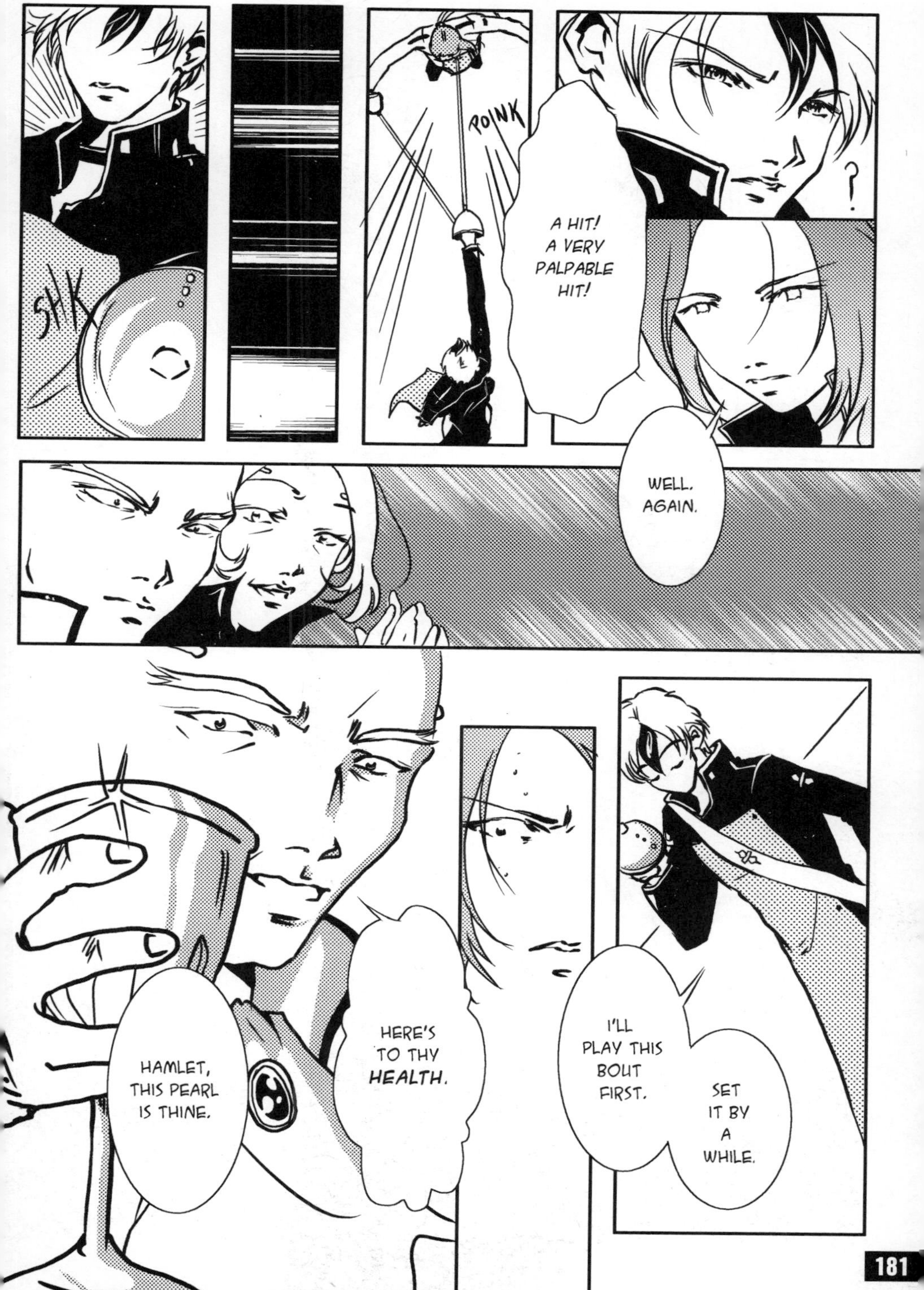
SHK
POINK
A HIT! A VERY PALPABLE HIT!
?
WELL. AGAIN.
HAMLET, THIS PEARL IS THINE.
HERE'S TO THY **HEALTH**.
I'LL PLAY THIS BOUT FIRST.
SET IT BY A WHILE.

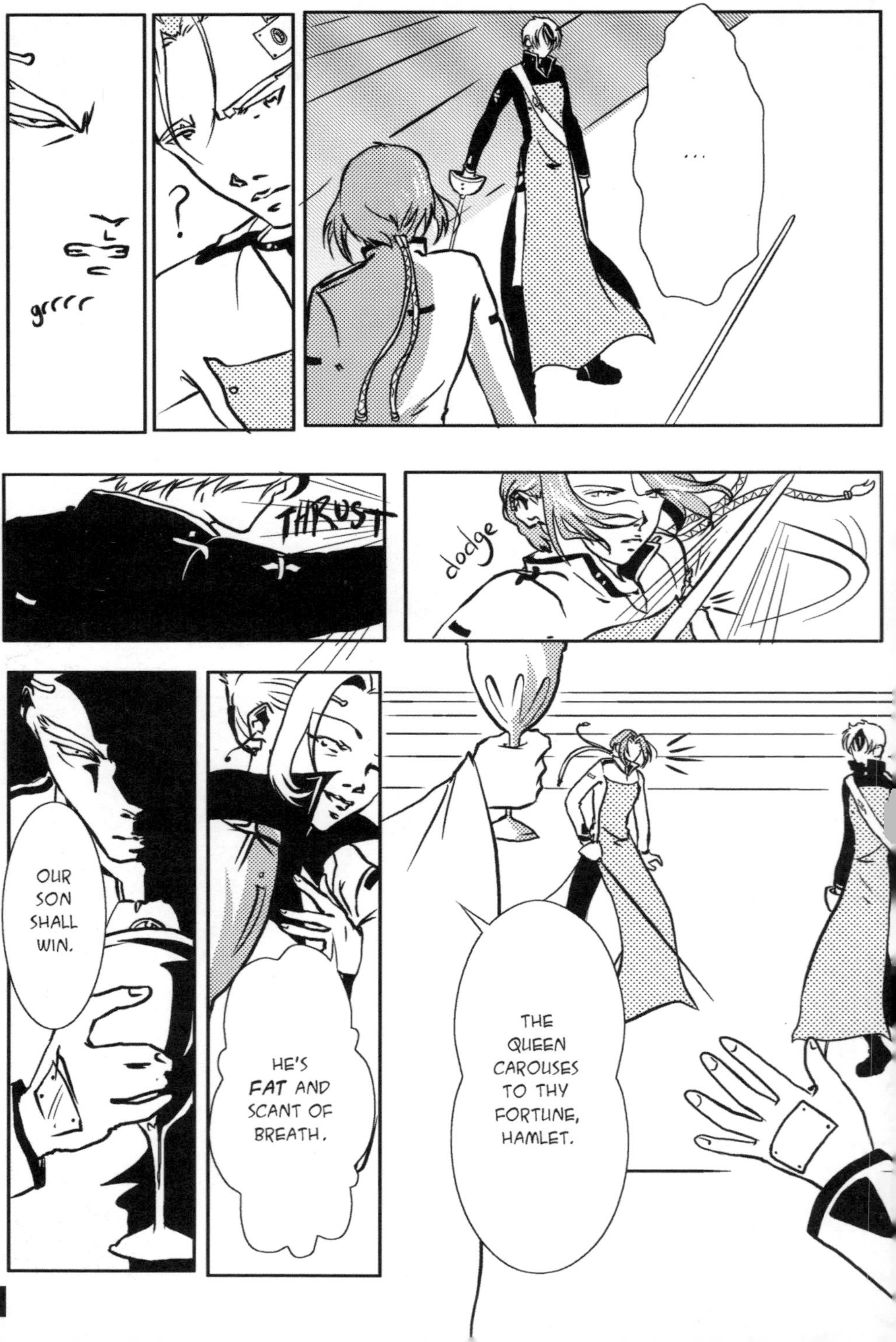
grrrr
?
...
THRUST
dodge
OUR SON SHALL WIN.
HE'S FAT AND SCANT OF BREATH.
THE QUEEN CAROUSES TO THY FORTUNE, HAMLET.

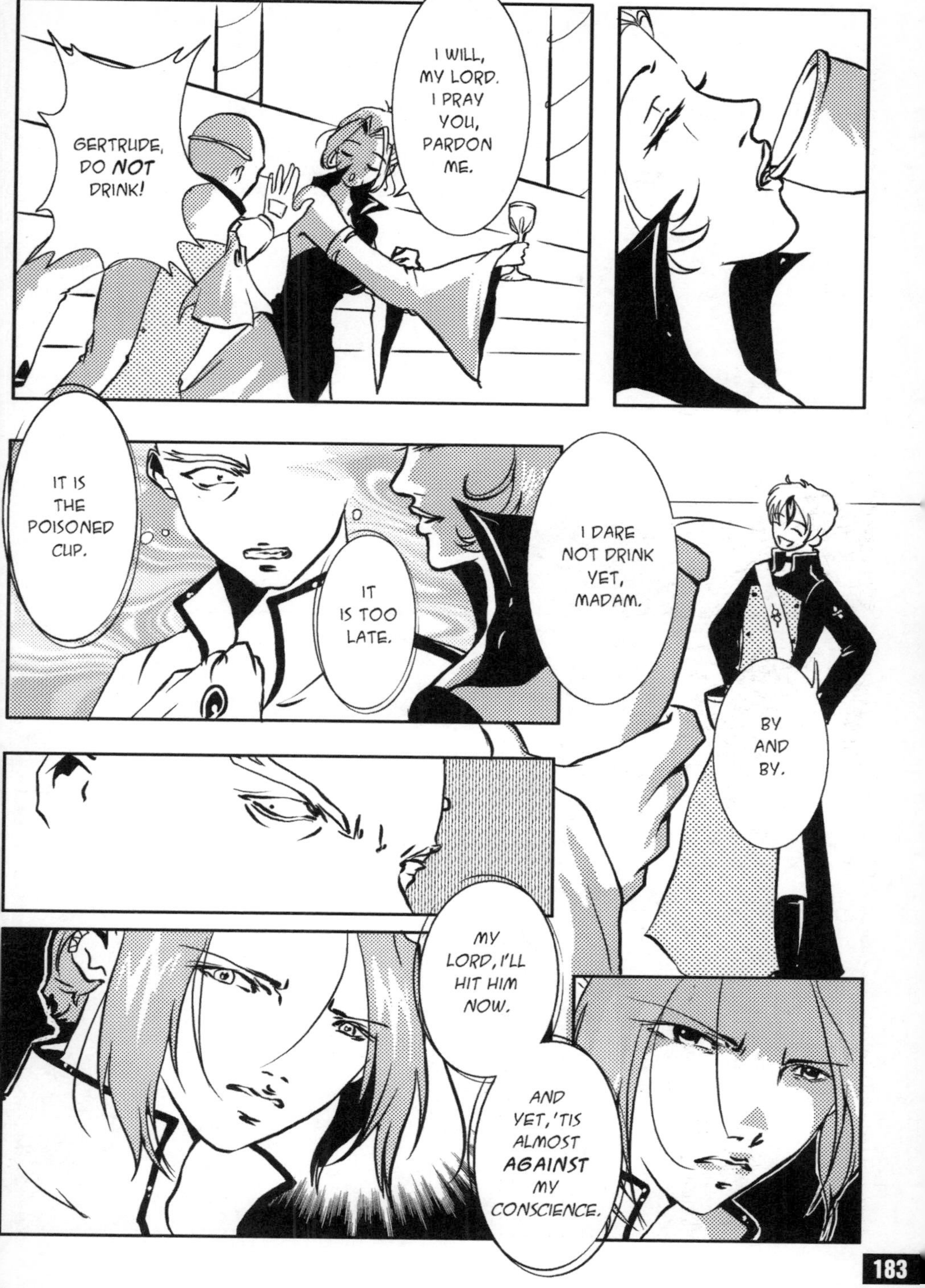
GERTRUDE, DO **NOT** DRINK!
I WILL, MY LORD. I PRAY YOU, PARDON ME.
IT IS THE POISONED CUP.
IT IS TOO LATE.
I DARE NOT DRINK YET, MADAM.
BY AND BY.
MY LORD, I'LL HIT HIM NOW.
AND YET, 'TIS ALMOST **AGAINST** MY CONSCIENCE.

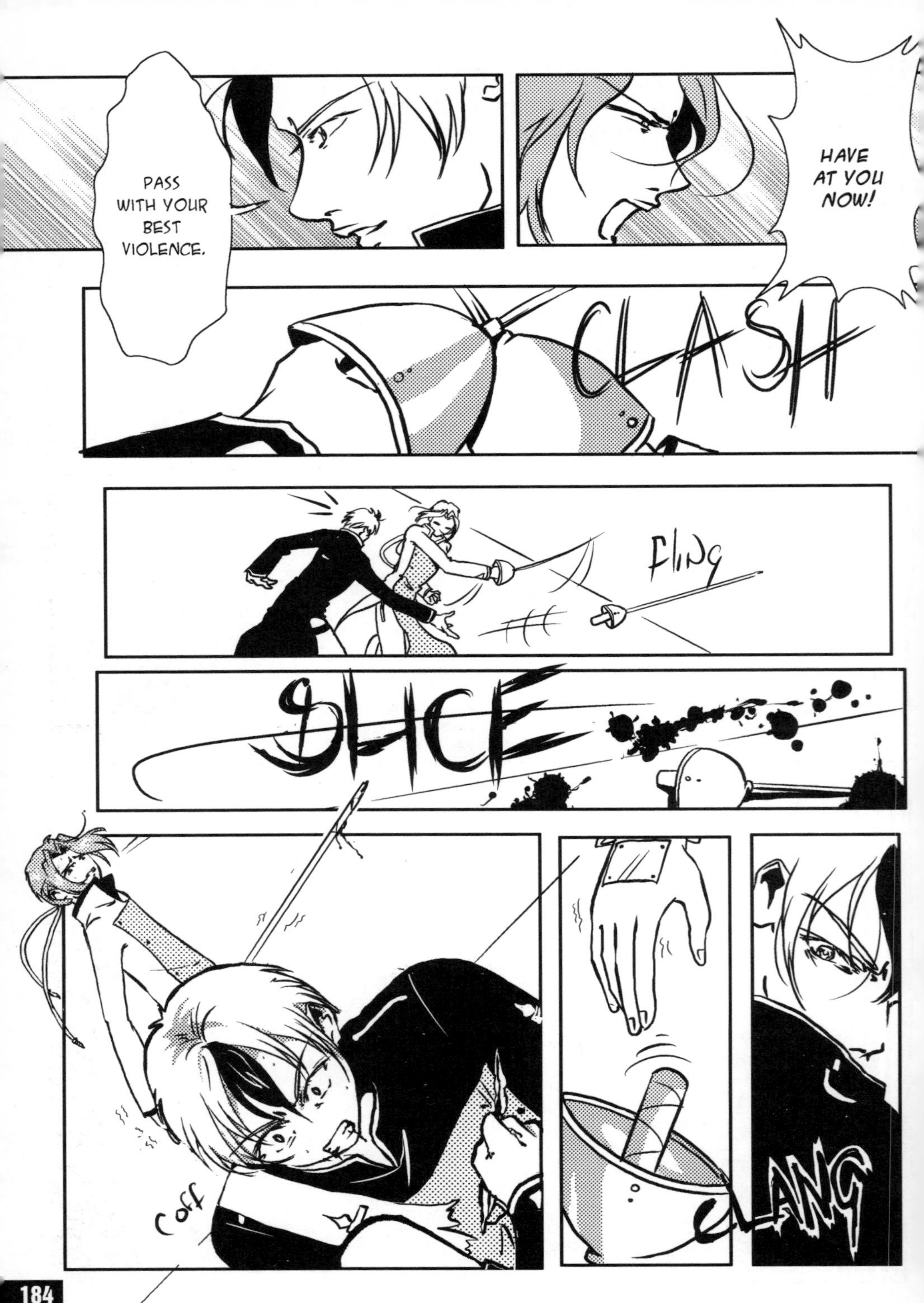
PASS WITH YOUR BEST VIOLENCE.
HAVE AT YOU NOW!
CLASH
Fling
SLICE
Coff
CLANG

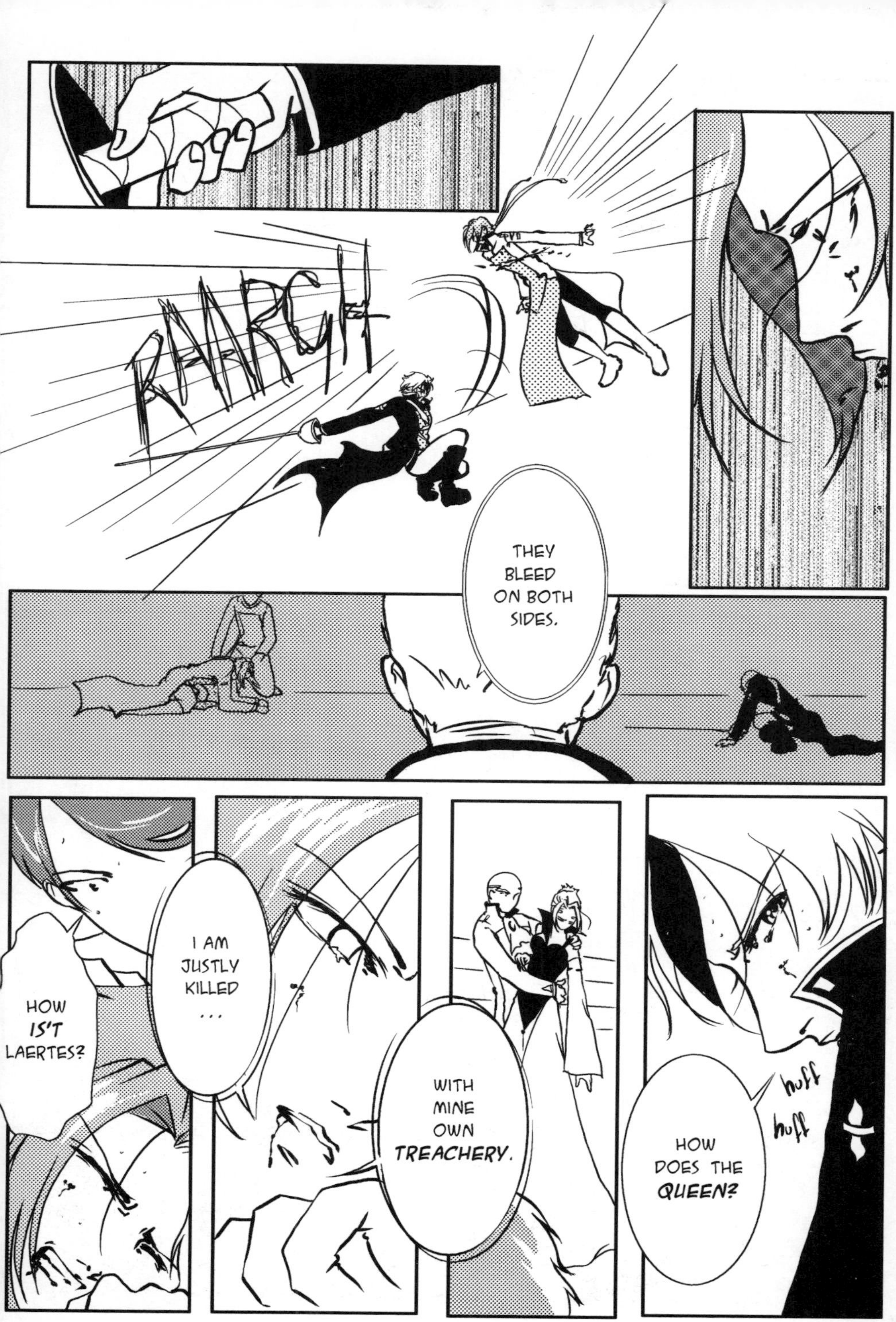
RAARGH
THEY BLEED ON BOTH SIDES.
HOW IS'T LAERTES?
I AM JUSTLY KILLED ...
WITH MINE OWN TREACHERY.
HOW DOES THE QUEEN?
huff
huff

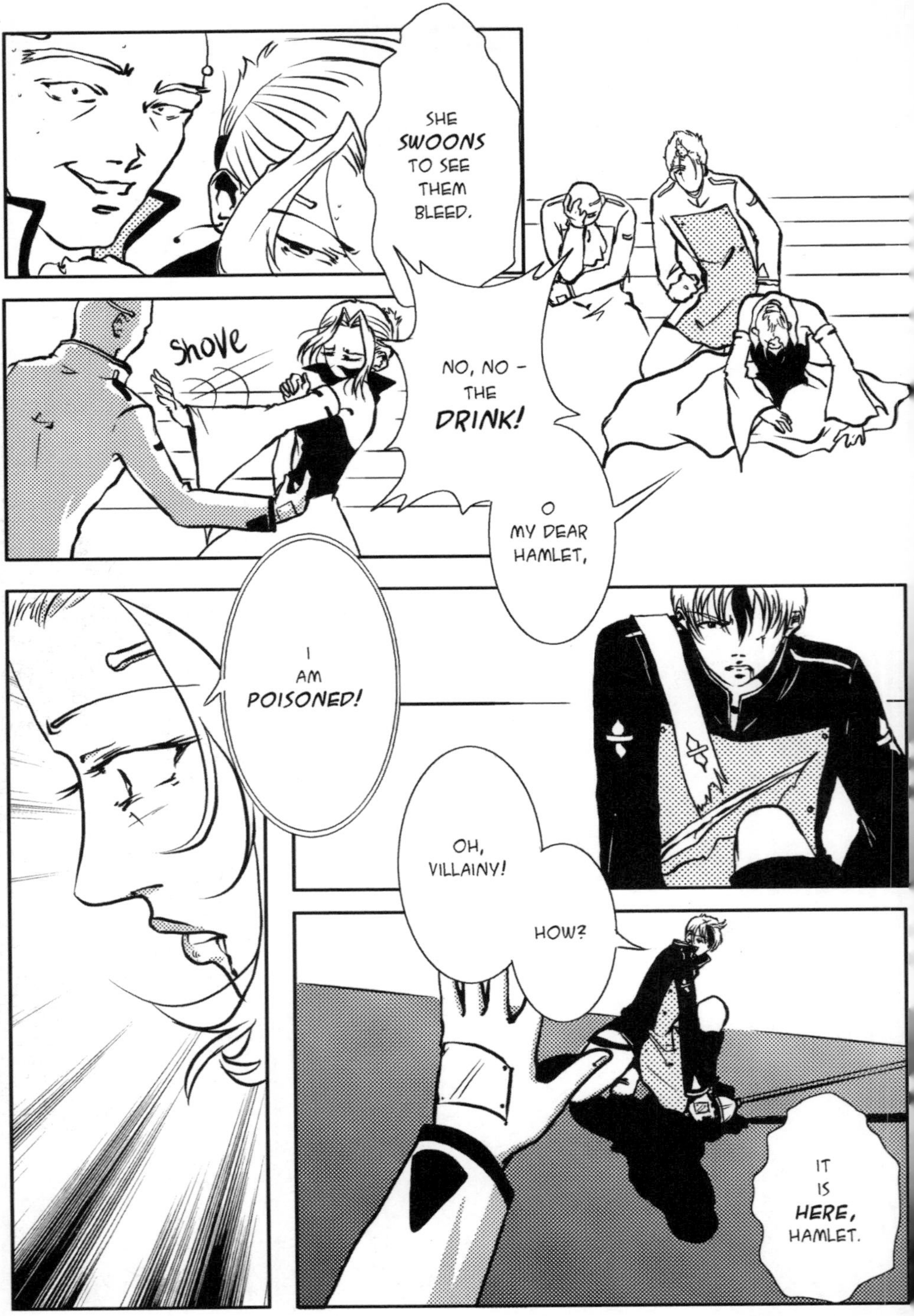
SHE SWOONS TO SEE THEM BLEED.
SHOVE
NO, NO - THE DRINK!
O MY DEAR HAMLET,
I AM POISONED!
OH, VILLAINY!
HOW?
IT IS HERE, HAMLET.

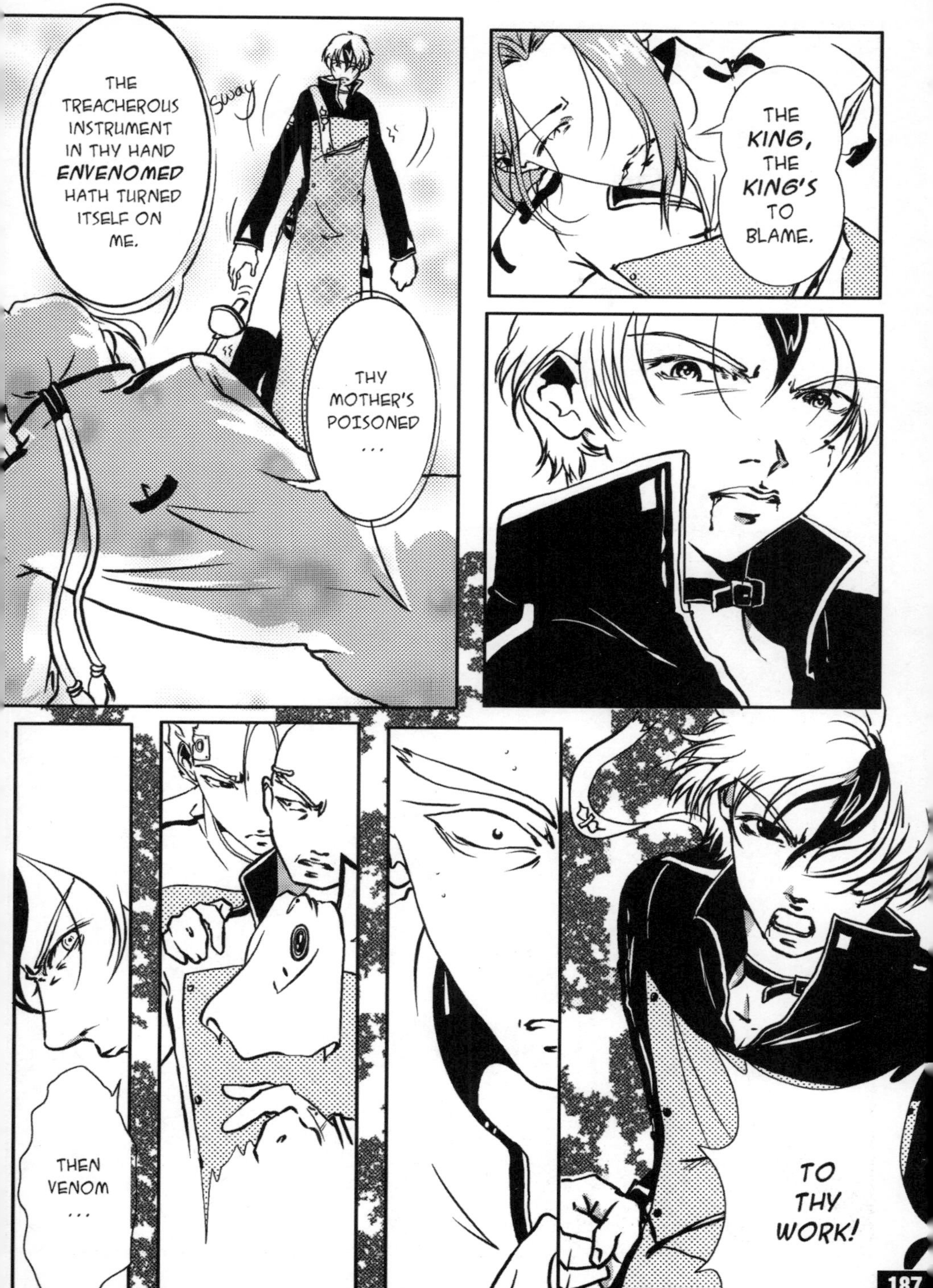
The treacherous instrument in thy hand envenomed hath turned itself on me.
Sway
Thy mother's poisoned ...
The King, the King's to blame.
Then venom ...
To thy work!

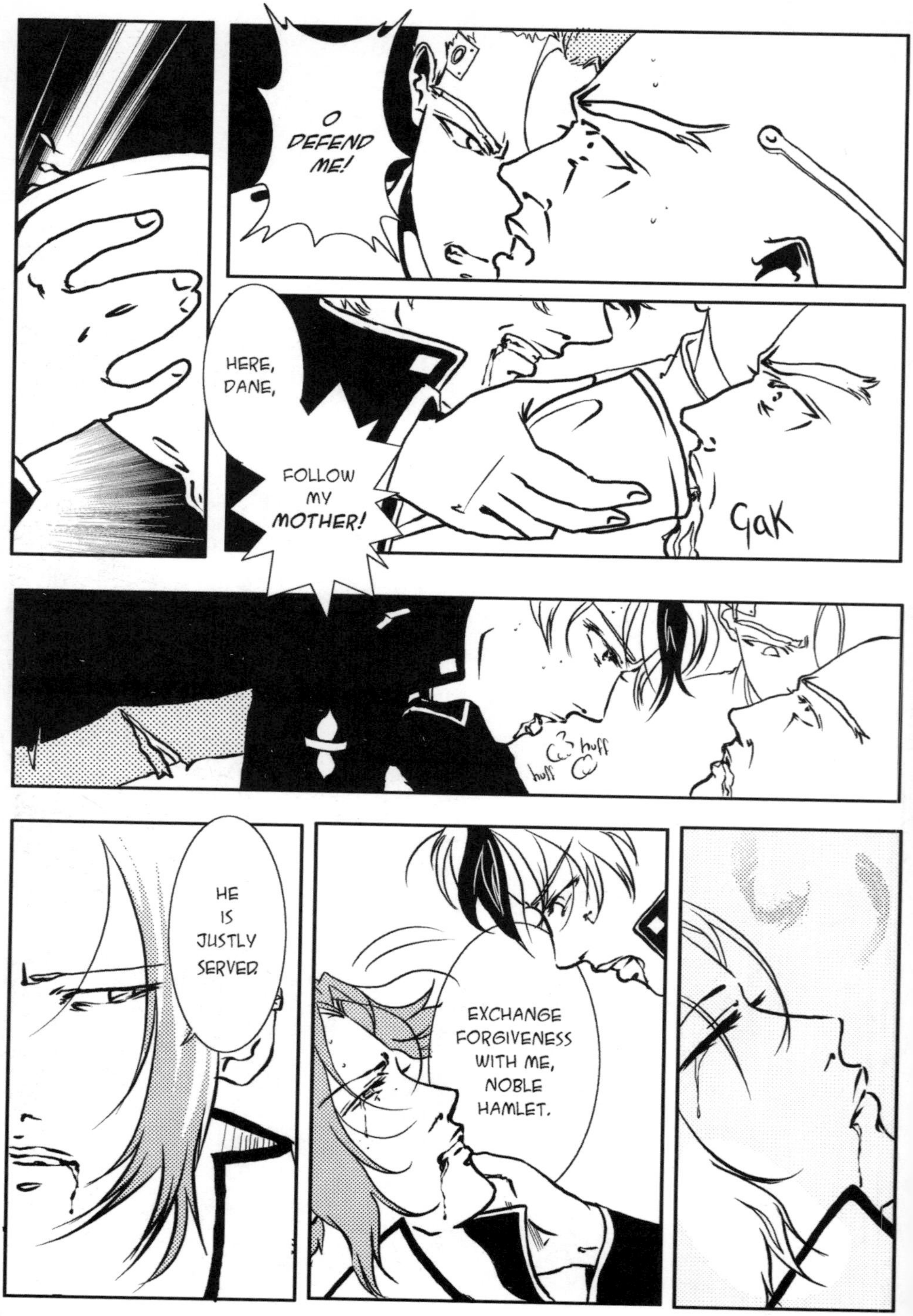

O DEFEND ME!
HERE, DANE,
FOLLOW MY MOTHER!
GAK
huff huff
huff
HE IS JUSTLY SERVED.
EXCHANGE FORGIVENESS WITH ME, NOBLE HAMLET.

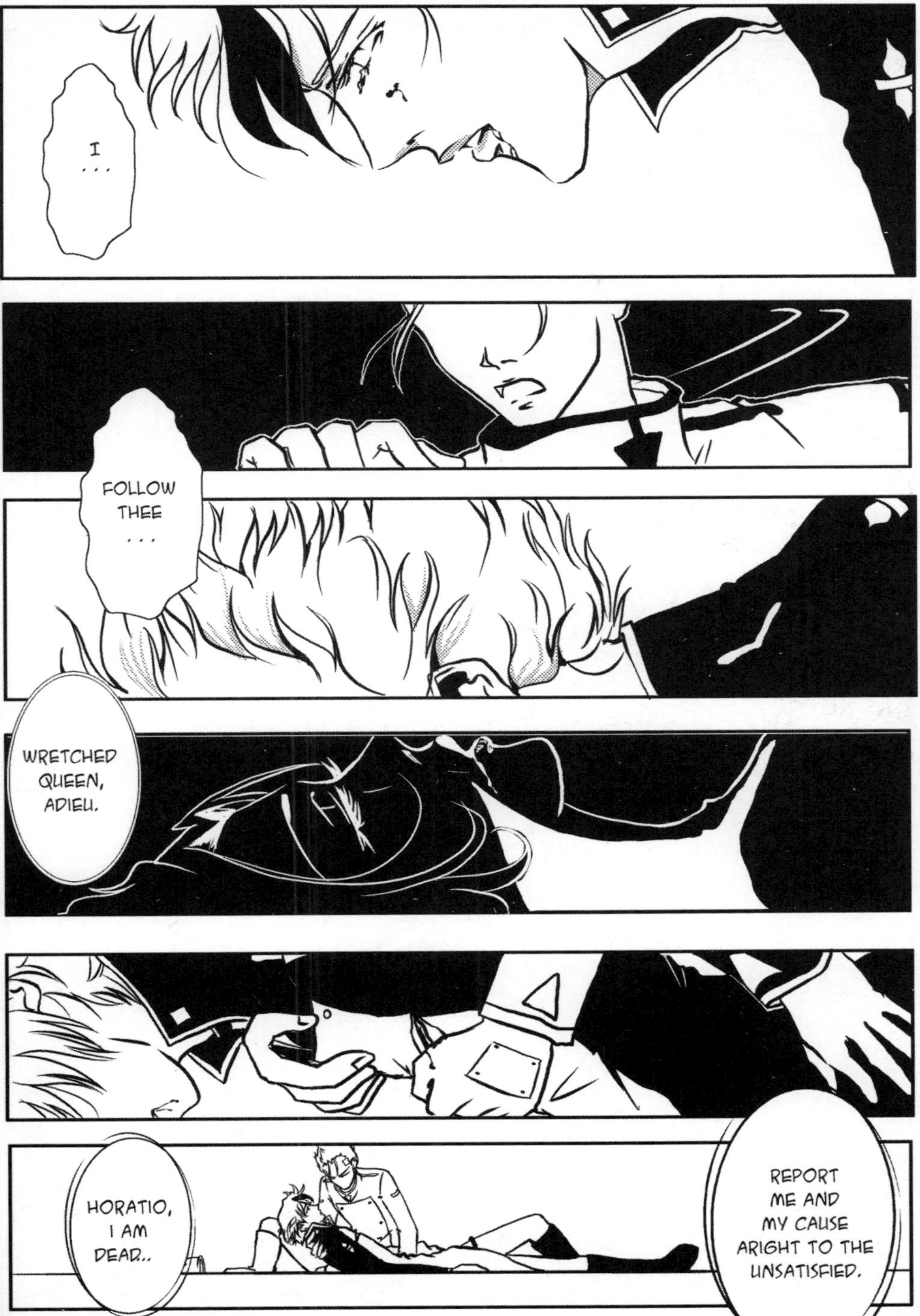
I . . .
FOLLOW THEE . . .
WRETCHED QUEEN, ADIEU.
HORATIO, I AM DEAD..
REPORT ME AND MY CAUSE ARIGHT TO THE UNSATISFIED.

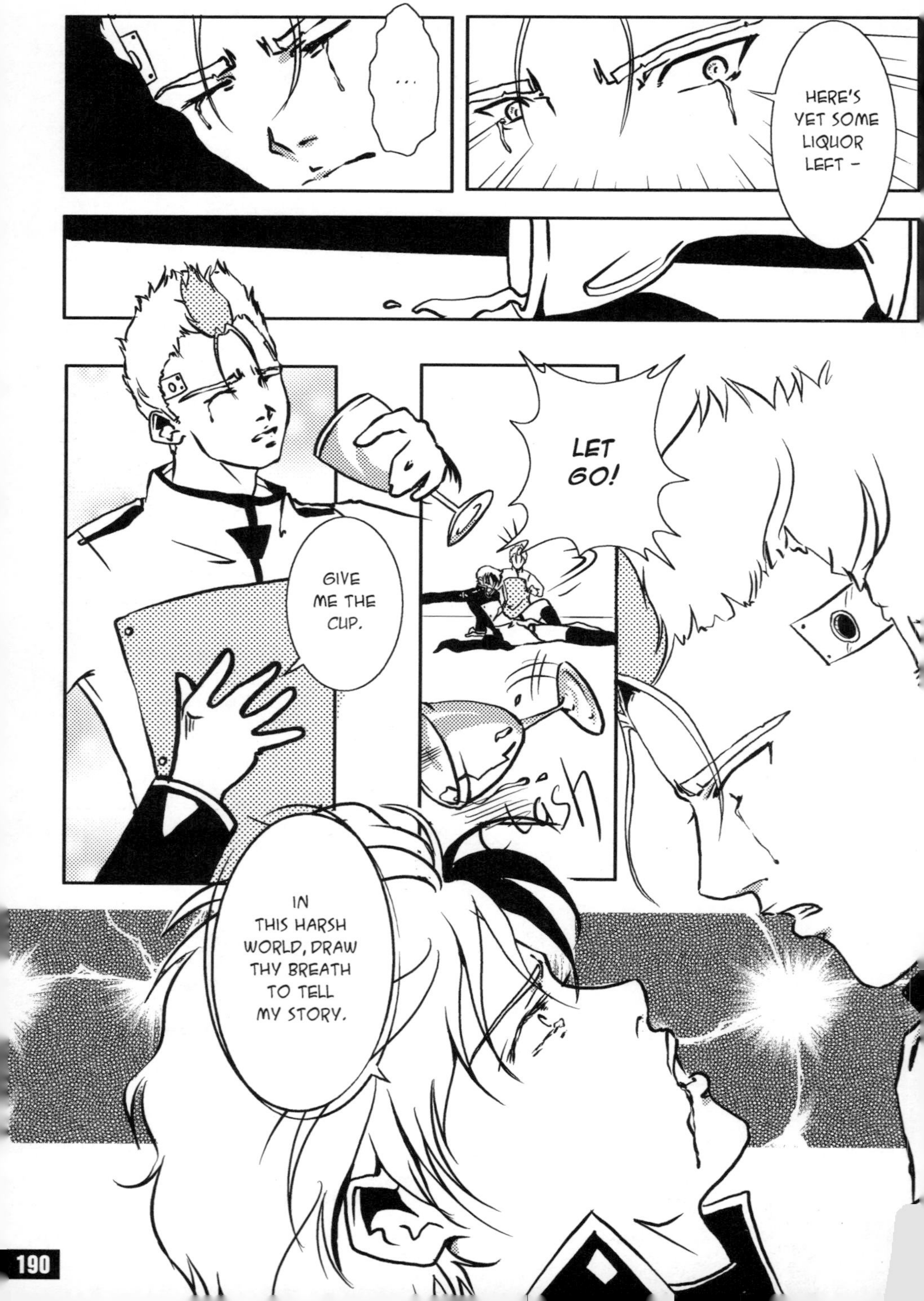
...
HERE'S YET SOME LIQUOR LEFT -
GIVE ME THE CUP.
LET GO!
IN THIS HARSH WORLD, DRAW THY BREATH TO TELL MY STORY.

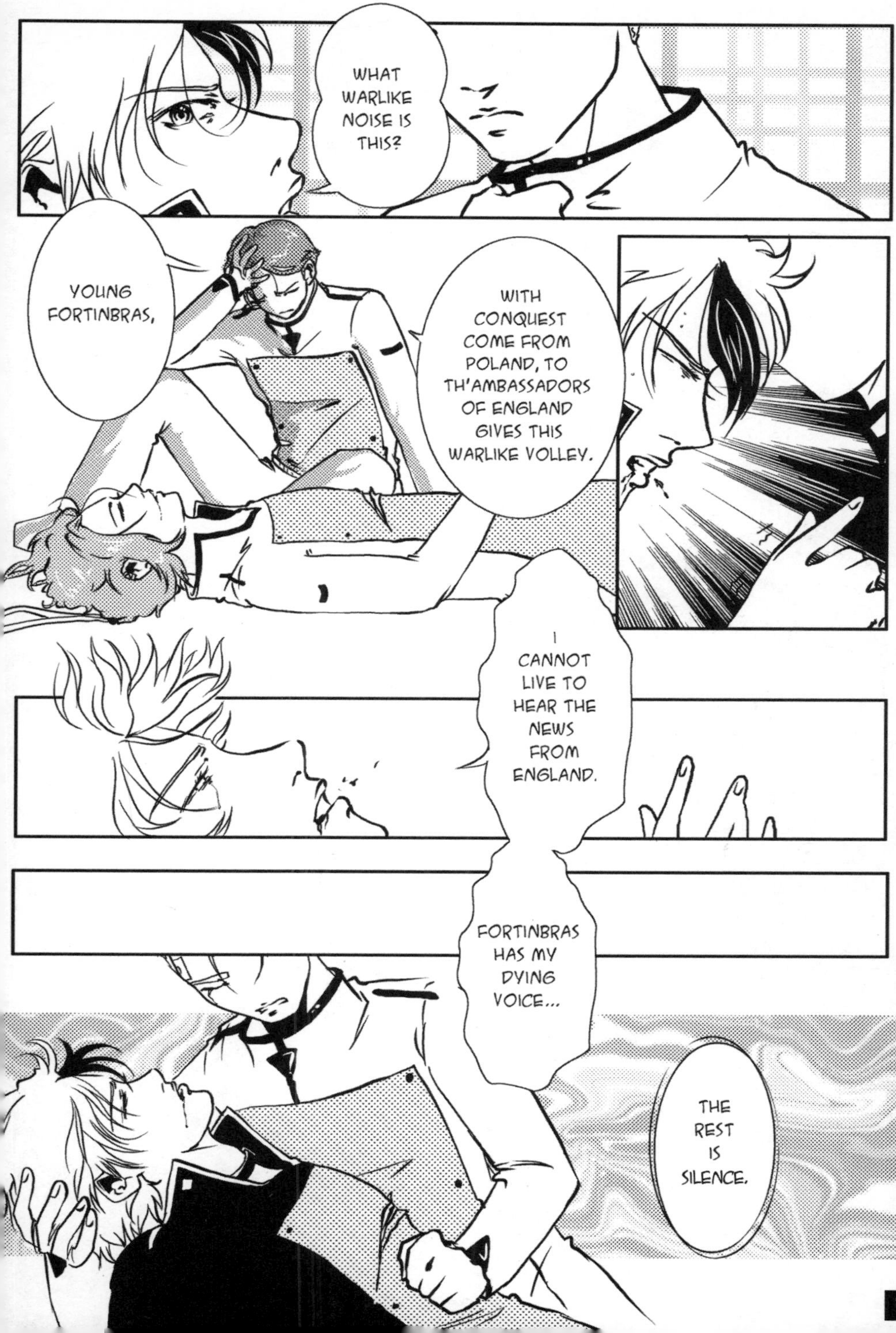
WHAT WARLIKE NOISE IS THIS?
YOUNG FORTINBRAS,
WITH CONQUEST COME FROM POLAND, TO TH'AMBASSADORS OF ENGLAND GIVES THIS WARLIKE VOLLEY.
I CANNOT LIVE TO HEAR THE NEWS FROM ENGLAND.
FORTINBRAS HAS MY DYING VOICE...
THE REST IS SILENCE.

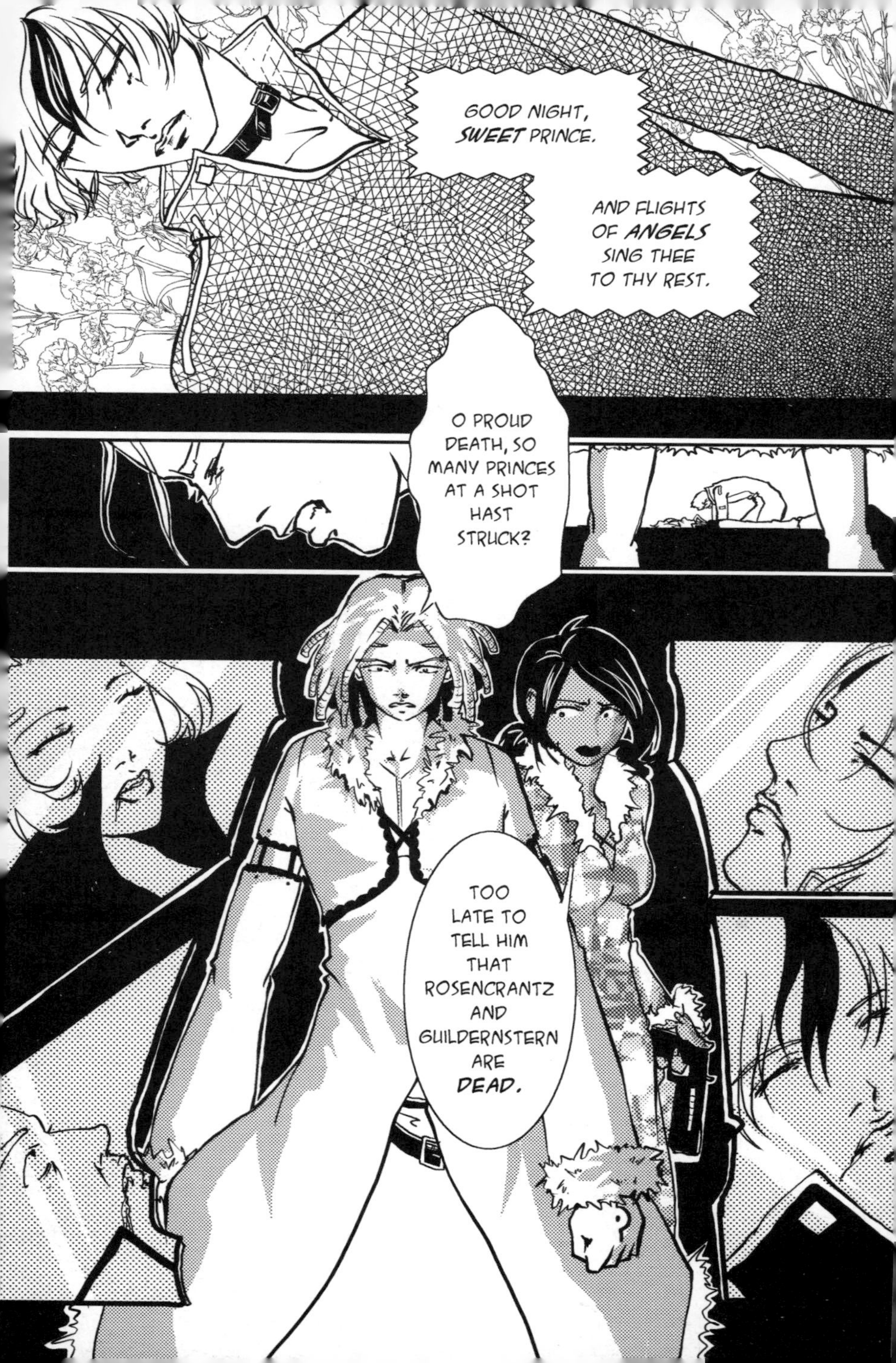
GOOD NIGHT, SWEET PRINCE.
AND FLIGHTS OF ANGELS SING THEE TO THY REST.
O PROUD DEATH, SO MANY PRINCES AT A SHOT HAST STRUCK?
TOO LATE TO TELL HIM THAT ROSENCRANTZ AND GUILDERNSTERN ARE DEAD.

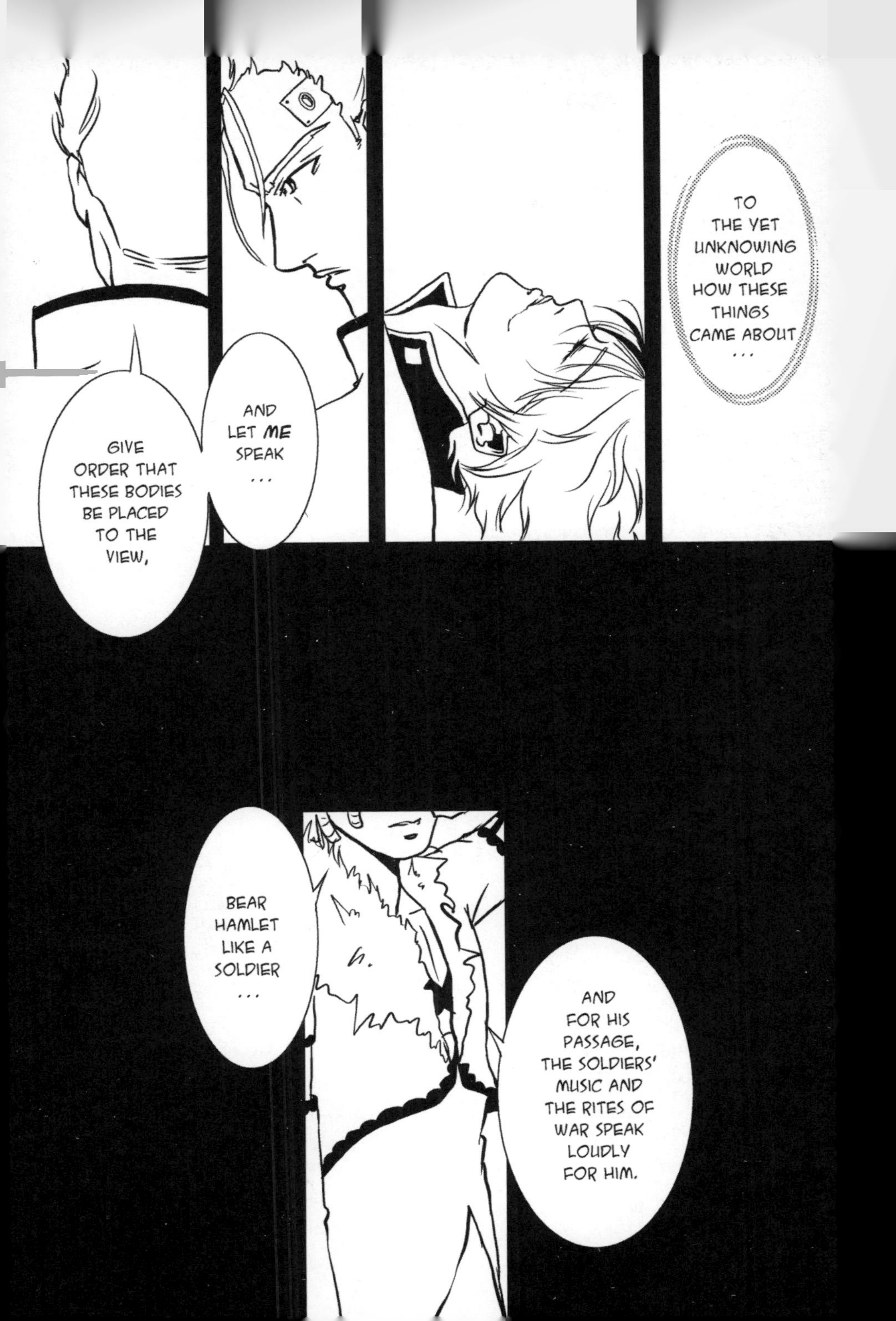
GIVE ORDER THAT THESE BODIES BE PLACED TO THE VIEW,
AND LET ME SPEAK . . .
TO THE YET UNKNOWING WORLD HOW THESE THINGS CAME ABOUT . . .
BEAR HAMLET LIKE A SOLDIER . . .
AND FOR HIS PASSAGE, THE SOLDIERS' MUSIC AND THE RITES OF WAR SPEAK LOUDLY FOR HIM.

PLOT SUMMARY OF HAMLET

The ghost of Prince Hamlet's father appears to the guards of Elsinore Castle. Hamlet's trusted friend, Horatio, reports it to Hamlet.

Laertes, son of Polonius, is leaving for Paris. He warns his sister Ophelia against Hamlet's attentions. Polonius, the Court Chamberlain, also commands Ophelia to avoid contact with Hamlet.

Hamlet speaks to the ghost of his father. The dead king reveals that his brother Claudius murdered him to get the throne and marry Queen Gertrude, Hamlet's mother. Hamlet vows to avenge his father's murder. Hamlet pretends madness to disguise his plans from everyone loyal to King Claudius.

Claudius and Gertrude recruit two of Hamlet's friends, Rosencrantz and Guildenstern, to keep watch on his strange behaviour. Polonius believes that Hamlet is mad for love of Ophelia, and proposes that Claudius and he watch in hiding as Ophelia meets Hamlet.

A band of travelling actors arrive at Elsinore. Hamlet plans to use their staging of a play to expose the king's guilty conscience.

Claudius and Polonius spy on Ophelia's encounter with Hamlet. Claudius remains unconvinced that Hamlet has lost his reason over Ophelia. Hamlet presents his *Mousetrap* play, which includes a mimed performance of a king being poisoned. Claudius recognizes his murder of Hamlet's father and flees in dread.

Hamlet visits his mother's chamber. Polonius, spying behind a curtain, is stabbed to death by Hamlet. Gertrude now believes Hamlet is truly insane.

Claudius orders Hamlet's departure for England. Rosencrantz and Guildenstern bear the king's secret command for Hamlet's immediate execution upon arrival.

Meanwhile, Hamlet's murder of Ophelia's father has driven her into real madness, as Laertes discovers when he returns from France seeking revenge for his father's death. Hamlet sends Horatio a message that his voyage has been intercepted by pirates, and that he is returning to Elsinore with them. Claudius now devises a plot with Laertes to kill Hamlet in a fencing match. Gertrude enters with news of Ophelia's death by drowning. Hamlet confronts Laertes at Ophelia's burial. Hamlet protests his true love for Ophelia.

Hamlet explains to Horatio that he rewrote the king's order so that Rosencrantz and Guildenstern will suffer the execution meant for him in England.

Hamlet accepts the king's wager of a fencing match with Laertes. Laertes fences with a poisoned sword and Claudius has a poisoned drink ready for Hamlet. During the match swords are exchanged and both Laertes and Hamlet are fatally wounded. Gertrude drinks from the poisoned cup and dies. Laertes reveals the king's treachery and Hamlet kills Claudius before dying himself.

Prince Fortinbras of Norway enters and claims his right to the Danish throne.

A BRIEF LIFE OF WILLIAM SHAKESPEARE

Shakespeare's birthday is traditionally said to be the 23rd of April — St George's Day, patron saint of England. A good start for England's greatest writer. But that date and even his name are uncertain. He signed his own name in different ways. "Shakespeare" is now the accepted one out of dozens of different versions.

He was born at Stratford-upon-Avon in 1564, and baptized on 26th April. His mother, Mary Arden, was the daughter of a prosperous farmer. His father John Shakespeare, a glove-maker, was a respected civic figure — and probably also a Catholic. In 1570, just as Will began school, his father was accused of illegal dealings. The family fell into debt and disrepute.

Will attended a local school for eight years. He did not go to university. The next ten years are a blank filled by suppositions. Was he briefly a Latin teacher, a soldier, a sea-faring explorer? Was he prosecuted and whipped for poaching deer?

We do know that in 1582 he married Anne Hathaway, eight years his senior, and three months pregnant. Two more children — twins — were born three years later but, by around 1590, Will had left Stratford to pursue a theatre career in London. Shakespeare's apprenticeship began as an actor and "pen for hire".

He learned his craft the hard way. He soon won fame as a playwright with often-staged popular hits.

He and his colleagues formed a stage company, the Lord Chamberlain's Men, which built the famous Globe Theatre. It opened in 1599 but was destroyed by fire in 1613 during a performance of *Henry VIII* which used gunpowder special effects. It was rebuilt in brick the following year.

Shakespeare was a financially successful writer who invested his money wisely in property. In 1597, he bought an enormous house in Stratford, and in 1608 became a shareholder in London's Blackfriars Theatre. He also redeemed the family's honour by acquiring a personal coat of arms.

Shakespeare wrote over 40 works, including poems, "lost" plays and collaborations, in a career spanning nearly 25 years. He retired to Stratford in 1613, where he died on 23rd April 1616, aged 52, apparently of a fever after a "merry meeting" of drinks with friends. Shakespeare did in fact die on St George's Day! He was buried "full 17 foot deep" in Holy Trinity Church, Stratford, and left an epitaph cursing anyone who dared disturb his bones.

There have been preposterous theories disputing Shakespeare's authorship. Some claim that Sir Francis Bacon (1561–1626), philosopher and Lord Chancellor, was the real author of Shakespeare's plays. Others propose Edward de Vere, Earl of Oxford (1550–1604), or, even more weirdly, Queen Elizabeth I. The implication is that the "real" Shakespeare had to be a university graduate or an aristocrat. Nothing less would do for the world's greatest writer.

Shakespeare is mysteriously hidden behind his work. His life will not tell us what inspired his genius.

MANGA SHAKESPEARE ®

EDITORIAL

Richard Appignanesi: Series Editor

Richard Appignanesi was a founder and co-director of the Writers & Readers Publishing Cooperative and Icon Books where he originated the internationally acclaimed Introducing series. His own best-selling titles written for the series include *Freud*, *Postmodernism* and *Existentialism*. He is also the author of the fiction trilogy *Italia Perversa* and the novel *Yukio Mishima's Report to the Emperor*. He is currently associate editor of the art and culture journal *Third Text* and reviews editor of the journal *Futures*. His latest book *What do Existentialists Believe?* was released in 2006.

Nick de Somogyi: Textual Consultant

Nick de Somogyi works as a freelance writer and researcher, as a genealogist at the College of Arms, and as a contributing editor to *New Theatre Quarterly*. He is the founding editor of the Globe Quartos series, and was the visiting curator at Shakespeare's Globe, 2003–6. His publications include *Shakespeare's Theatre of War* (1998), *Jokermen and Thieves: Bob Dylan and the Ballad Tradition* (1986), and, as editor, *The Little Book of War Poems* (1999), and (from 2001) the *Shakespeare Folios* series for Nick Hern Books. His other work has included contributions to the Open University (1995) and Carlton Television (2000), BBC Radio 3 and Radio 4, and the National Portrait Gallery (2006).

ARTIST

Emma Vieceli

Emma Vieceli is a freelance illustrator and manga artist. She is a key member of the UK's leading manga collective, Sweatdrop Studios. Her professional experience ranges from 'How to draw manga' books through corporate character designs to artwork for tabletop RPG card games. Her work has appeared in several publications as well as being exhibited at a number of large events and venues, including the Japanese Embassy and London County Hall. She was one of the winners of the first Tokyopop Rising Stars of Manga UK and Ireland competition as well as the 2006 *Neo* magazine manga competition. She is a keen promoter of the UK manga and anime scene.

PUBLISHER

SelfMadeHero is a UK-based manga and graphic novel imprint, reinventing some of the most important works of European and world literature.

ALSO IN THE SERIES

RICHARD III
THE TEMPEST
ROMEO AND JULIET
MACBETH
JULIUS CAESAR
A MIDSUMMER NIGHT'S DREAM

SELF MADE HERO